HALL OF MIRRORS

A BOOK

IN THE SERIES

LATIN AMERICA OTHERWISE:

LANGUAGES, EMPIRES,

NATIONS

*Series editors:*

*Walter D. Mignolo,*

*Duke University*

*Irene Silverblatt,*

*Duke University*

*Sonia Saldívar-Hull,*

*University of California*

*at Los Angeles*

# HALL
# OF MIRRORS

*Power, Witchcraft, and Caste in Colonial Mexico*

LAURA A. LEWIS

DUKE UNIVERSITY PRESS  DURHAM & LONDON  2003

3rd printing, 2006

© 2003 Duke University Press

All rights reserved.

Printed in the United States of

America on acid-free paper ∞

Designed by C. H. Westmoreland

Typeset in Carter & Cone Galliard

by Keystone Typesetting, Inc.

Library of Congress Cataloging-in-

Publication Data appear on the

last printed page of this book.

# About the Series

*Latin America Otherwise: Languages, Empires, Nations* is a critical series. It aims to explore the emergence and consequences of concepts used to define "Latin America" while at the same time exploring the broad interplay of political, economic, and cultural practices that have shaped Latin American worlds. Latin America, at the crossroads of competing imperial designs and local responses, has been construed as a geo-cultural and geopolitical entity since the nineteenth century. This series provides a starting point to redefine Latin America as a configuration of political, linguistic, cultural, and economic intersections that demands a continuous reappraisal of the role of the Americas in history, and of the ongoing process of globalization and the relocation of people and cultures that have characterized Latin America's experience. *Latin America Otherwise: Languages, Empires, Nations* is a forum that confronts established geocultural constructions, that rethinks area studies and disciplinary boundaries, that assesses convictions of the academy and of public policy, and that, correspondingly, demands that the practices through which we produce knowledge and understanding about and from Latin America be subject to rigorous and critical scrutiny.

Until the 1980s, colonial studies of the Viceroyalties of New Spain and of Peru focused mainly on the writings and deeds of Spanish men of letters, soldiers, notaries, royal authorities, and missionaries. Since then, attention has switched to the writings of indigenous intellectuals and the activities of the indigenous elite confronting the new social order brought about by Spanish colonization. Laura A. Lewis's *Hall of*

*Mirrors: Power, Witchcraft, and Caste in Colonial Mexico* is a landmark because it brings colonialism's most invisible peoples—women and men of African origins—to the forefront of colonial studies.

Furthermore, Lewis's book is making a signal contribution to our understanding of the history of racism. The prevalent understanding of racialization in the modern/colonial world has been written from the perspective of Northern European history (the French and British colonization of the world), ignoring the sixteenth century caste-framed foundation of the racial system in which we are still immersed. Lewis's detailed historical account and theoretical insight could be read as a provocation to revisit canonical views of the history of racism in the modern/colonial world, as well as the intricate relationships between gender, caste, race, and class.

FOR LUKAS

# Contents

ACKNOWLEDGMENTS  xi

NOTE ON SOURCES  xiii

Introduction  1

1. Forging a Colonial Landscape: Caste in Context  15

2. The Roads Are Harsh: Spaniards and Indians in the
   Sanctioned Domain  46

3. *La Mala Yerba*: Putting Difference to Work  67

4. From Animosities to Alliances: A Segue into the World
   of Witchcraft  95

5. Authority Reversed: Indians Ascending  103

6. Mapping Unsanctioned Power  132

7. Hall of Mirrors  167

NOTES  185

WORKS CITED  235

INDEX  255

# Acknowledgments

Many people have been generous with their advice and insights during the all too many years that this book has been in the making. While all errors of interpretation are, of course, my own, I benefited greatly from conversations with Solange Alberro, Linda Arnold, Ruth Behar, Fernando Cervantes, John Chance, Michael Ducey, David Marley, Colin Palmer, William B. Taylor, and Richard Warren. In addition, personnel at the Mexican National Archives, especially Roberto Beristáin and the staff of Gallery 4, were unfailingly helpful and kind, as were those who read portions of the manuscript over the years, including Lisa Botshon, Andrew Bush, Nahum Chandler, Jennifer Coffman, Rebecca Fielding, Audrey Fisch, Kathleen Hall, David Koester, Claudio Lomnitz, Howard Lubert, Diane Mines, Guillermo de la Peña, Patricia Spyer, Richard Thompson, and Brad Weiss. I am most grateful to Jonathan Amith and Peter Guardino for commenting extensively on early drafts, and to the anonymous reviewers for Duke University Press, one of whom in particular should be commended for his/her extraordinary patience and sensitivity. Finally, Duke's editor-in-chief, Ken Wissoker, was a friend when this project was first envisioned, and he has remained a steady source of support throughout the review and editorial process.

This book is based on my dissertation (Lewis 1993), which was supervised by Raymond T. Smith, Jean Comaroff, Paul Friedrich, and Friedrich Katz. These scholars made me especially aware of a number of issues. In particular, Jean Comaroff inspired me to "go with the contradictions," Paul Friedrich to attend more consciously to the context of textual production, Friedrich Katz to meld the "official" and the "popular," and Raymond T. Smith to argue more effectively for the tension between hierarchy and entanglement. I can only hope that I have adequately met their challenges.

Funding for research in Mexico was initially provided by the Center for Latin American Studies at the University of Chicago through a Tinker Foundation Travel Grant and then by the Organization of American States and the Wenner-Gren Foundation for Anthropological Research. I was extremely fortunate to be awarded a two-year dissertation write-up grant in Law and Social Science by the American Bar Foundation, and to be given the opportunity to develop my ideas beyond the dissertation at the Center for the Humanities at Wesleyan University, in a semester colloquium organized around "Race and Culture."

Part of the introduction appeared as "'Blackness,' 'Femaleness' and Self-Representation: Constructing Persons in a Colonial Mexican Court" in *PoLAR: Political and Legal Anthropology Review* 18 (2), November 1995:1–9. Portions of chapters 2 and 5 appeared as "The 'Weakness' of Women and the Feminization of the Indian in Colonial Mexico" in *Colonial Latin American Review* 5 (1), 1996; and portions of chapters 3 and 6 appeared as "Colonialism and its Contradictions: Indians, Blacks and Social Power in Sixteenth and Seventeenth Century Mexico," *Journal of Historical Sociology* 9 (4), December 1996.

# Note on Sources

Archival materials are drawn from a number of record sets held in the Archivo General de la Nación (AGN, Mexican National Archives) in Mexico City. The most significant of these sets are Inquisición (cited as Inq), Indios (Indios), Criminal (Criminal), Civil (Civil), and Bienes Nacionales (BN). Inquisición holds proceedings of the Holy Office of the Inquisition, which functioned to suppress heresy in Mexico throughout the colonial period. Indios contains texts relating to Indian matters that were heard before the viceroy and the General Indian Court. Criminal holds texts pertaining to penal matters heard and decided by the *audiencia* (royal high court), while Civil contains texts relating to what were deemed civil disputes, also heard by the audiencia. Bienes Nacionales consists of ecclesiastical records.

Additional information from the AGN was drawn from the following record sets: Ordenanzas (Ord), Historia (Historia), Reales Cédulas Duplicadas (RCD), Reales Cédulas Originales (RCO), General de Parte (GP), Mercedes (Mercedes), and Tierras (Tierras). Ordenanzas covers various official regulations concerning social conduct. Reales Cédulas Duplicadas and Originales hold royal orders directed to colonial authorities. General de Parte contains requests, complaints, and demands presented in writing to the viceroy or to the audiencia relating to viceregal decisions and orders. Historia is a series of manuscripts originally collected by the viceroy's office in the late eighteenth century in order to prepare a general history of the Indies. Mercedes is the registry for viceregal dispatches, mostly regarding royal land grants.

Tierras principally contains documentation regarding land and water disputes.

In addition to the AGN, I consulted microfilms of correspondence between viceroys and the crown from the Archivo General de Indias in Seville, Spain, which are held in the Museo Nacional de Antropología (National Anthropology Museum) in Mexico City, and several manuscripts from the Biblioteca Nacional de Antropología e Historia (National Anthropology and History Library), also in Mexico City. These are cited as AGI and BNAH respectively.

Of the approximately one thousand sixteenth- and seventeenth-century court cases, mandates, letters, and reports that I read, a representative sample of about three hundred is used in this book and cited in the following manner: Archive repository and record set, volume number, *expediente* (file), and/or *foja* (page) number, and date. A typical entry thus reads: AGN, Inq vol. 355, exp. 27, 1625. Additional abbreviations are v. for the verso or the left side of a page, r. for the recto or the right side of a page, and bis. for a duplicated expediente number. *Legajo* (leg.) refers to an unbound volume. In the text itself, place name spellings, which can vary in the documentation, follow Peter Gerhard's *Guide to the Historical Geography of New Spain* (1972).

HALL OF MIRRORS

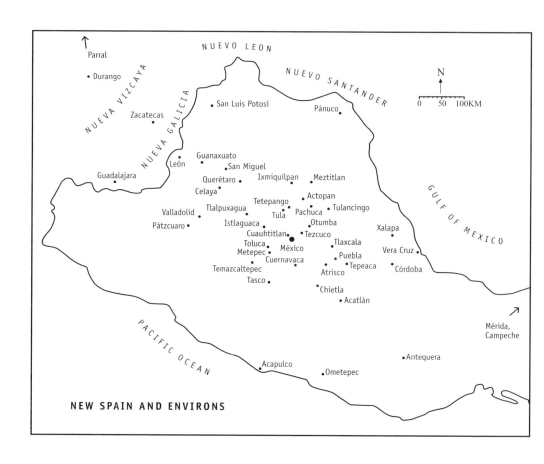

NEW SPAIN AND ENVIRONS

# Introduction

ADRIANA RUÍZ DE CABRERA AND
THE MEXICAN INQUISITION IN 1655

In 1655, at the midpoint of New Spain's three-hundred year colonial period, a woman named Adriana Ruíz de Cabrera was accused of witchcraft (*hechicería*) in the eastern port city of Vera Cruz.[1] She was carted off to Mexico City, the colony's capital, where she was condemned to a dungeon run by the Holy Office of the Inquisition. The records of her trial identify her as belonging to the black *casta* (caste), but while the majority of blacks in colonial Mexico were likely enslaved during this era, Adriana, as it happens, was not.[2]

The trial opened with the inquisitors' accusation that Adriana had used herbs, "superstitions," and "tricks" to uncover thefts and "take revenge" on people. The immediate complaint indicated that she had offered her services as a witch to ascertain who had robbed a boarder in the rooming house she owned. To do this, she had allegedly gathered together for a washtub-water divination a group of women who "know about and use the things" of witchcraft. In conformance to the caste classifications conventional in the colony, one of these women was identified as Spanish, one as mulatto, one as Indian, and one, like Adriana, as black.

Adriana claimed to be a confirmed and baptized Christian who knew "nothing of witchcraft." The washtub, she said, held only herbs to make a scented mixture for the religious sisterhood of which she was an elder. Moreover, she had grown up in the "unblemished" house of a Spanish lieutenant and his wife. Had she been raised by a "suspicious" woman, she added, she would more likely have blasphemed. While she might have succumbed in her youth to "women's weaknesses" (*flaquerías de mujer*), including sexual promiscuity in the form of incest with her brother, she had only once been called a witch, and that was in jest. From her point of view, the charges were therefore "tricks, lies, and false testimonies."

It was customary for the inquisitors to keep denunciants secret, which they did in this instance as well. But Adriana knew that her accuser was Ana María de la Concepción, another free black woman who had asked to rent a room at Adriana's boardinghouse and had then stolen items from one of Adriana's three black slaves. The plaintiff could not "be any other person than the black Ana María," Adriana insisted, for the woman was a "lying cheat" whose "evil" (*maldad*) had to be stopped. All of Ana María's accusations were lies, she added, "because [Ana María] is a black [woman] [*negra*]."

Tales like Adriana's illustrate the role caste played as a system of values, practices, and meanings in sixteenth- and seventeenth-century Mexico: the dispute ostensibly dealt with whether or not Adriana was a witch, but the textual narrative highlights how she, her defenders, and her accusers constructed their arguments in great part through claims about caste. In this vein, Adriana went on to defend herself with the help of two Spanish priests, who insisted that she had overcome her "natural" inclinations. She was once "rebellious and too much given to sensuality," said one, but had since come to control these "excesses" — she was respected, owned slaves, and had a well-appointed home. The other remarked that she behaved quietly and peacefully, prospered, and gave alms to the poor and to clergymen. Both told the inquisitors that Adriana regularly heard mass, confessed, took communion, and made sure that her family and slaves arrived punctually to church. Adriana's attorney then contrasted her with the "lying" Ana María: Adriana was "a *clean-living* black woman," he said.[3] She was devoted to the Virgin Mary and had dealings with the principal Spanish men and women of Vera Cruz. She was not idle, he insisted, and she gained a livelihood through her own hard work.

In support of Adriana, the attorney also discredited Ana María for what he claimed to be her instability as a woman and her baseness as a black. By law, he pointed out, "women are kept from testifying in criminal cases due to the fragility of their sex and their fickleness . . . They bring false testimony, and even civil law excludes them if, along with being women, they have an evil reputation." Ana María's "other vices," including the "vileness of her caste," also barred her from testifying. Adriana, he argued, was *not* a "similar case."

Ana María was not a native of New Spain, and a notary duly described her as a "foreign black." Born in Guatemala, she had apparently been stolen as a young girl and taken to Spain, where she was raised as a slave. She was eventually brought to Cartagena by the count who owned her. When he died, she fled with a slave girl she herself had abducted and kept by her side through various forms of subterfuge. After turning Ana María over to the authorities for stealing from one of her slaves, Adriana searched Ana María's clothing. There she found tucked into a pocket, a falsified deed of slavery for the girl. Because Adriana could not read, she gave the deed to a court clerk, who declared that Ana María should be "broken and burned."

For her part, Ana María testified that everyone was against her, for "people" said of her: *del monte sale que en el monte quema* (one who comes out of the backwoods burns in the backwoods). In the colonial imagination, the hills or backwoods (*monte*) marked the undomesticated spaces beyond civilized towns and cities. The backwoods were associated especially with runaway slaves and Indians who, having fled Spanish rule, were seen to have reverted to their former ways. By invoking this idiomatic phrase, Ana María must have been relating what others perceived to be her intractable wildness.

In her testimony, Ana María also insisted that Adriana and the Indian who had participated in the alleged washtub ritual were longstanding friends. This claim was loaded with a meaning that Ana María further pressed as she added that Adriana had once asked the Indian woman to divine for her and, in fact, had invited her to lead the divination in the washtub ritual, a request with which the Indian had complied. When all was said and done, then, Ana María might have been "of the monte," but Adriana was worse, for she had allegedly engaged an Indian witch right in the heart of town.

During her months-long trial, Adriana repeatedly claimed that she was innocent of the charges. In the end, she was indeed vindicated when Ana María finally conceded that she had lied. She never imagined that the Inquisition would act on her contentions, Ana María said, nor could she be held entirely responsible for her actions because the "devil had tricked her." She was fined a considerable sum, and Adriana was set free.

Court records such as the one that preserved moments of Adriana's life are the best sources available for gaining access to colonial people's quotidian experiences, for in them individuals testified about, censured, and defended their own and others' perspectives and day-to-day activities.[4] Although the records are ones of conflict, they more broadly tell us about the meanings and usages of caste in New Spain. As Adriana's dispute indicates, individuals drew on caste symbolism and caste practices to delineate social boundaries, values, and their own positions. Adriana thus verbally distanced herself from the "evils" of blackness, pointed out that she owned slaves, and tied her heritage to estimable Spaniards, while Ana María elaborated Adriana's bonds to an Indian "friend." Both of these women knew, as did the inquisitors who oversaw the proceedings, that proximity to Spanishness and Spaniards indicated conformity to proper colonial values. Conversely, proximity to Indians and Indianness marked a potent and nonconforming supernaturalism. It is more than suggestive that the discourse of the text draws connections between the black woman Adriana and both Spaniards and Indians, for colonial caste logic provided for a range of interstitial actors who took on qualities of power represented by Indians and qualities represented by Spaniards. In the end, the ambiguous question of Adriana's witchery turned on the ambiguities of caste itself. Was Adriana Spanish (and not a witch) in spite of her blackness? Was she really Indian (and definitely a witch) in spite of her Spanishness? Was she legally black according to the genealogies that the Inquisition typically policed? Or did her identity more complexly play off of the social and symbolic implications of her caste affiliations and practices?

The colonial politics of caste reflected a social world in which the divide between rulers and ruled was constantly criss-crossed and mediated by a multiplicity of subjects. In light of this, this book uses records that address inter-caste experiences and relationships involving people legally classified as "Spaniards" (*españoles*), as well as those classified as "Indians" (*indios*), "blacks" (*negros*), "mulattoes" (*mulatos*) (the offspring of a black and an Indian or a black and a Spaniard), and "mestizos" (*mestizos*) (the offspring of a Spaniard and an Indian).[5] Those records indicate that caste spoke to the distinct but interlocking kinds of power that each of these categories represented, while indexing a clever and multilayered process that pulled individuals into a colonial world while effectively allowing them to strategize within it.[6]

Colonial Mexicanists who write in English tend to translate casta as "race" and to base their analyses of the caste system (*sistema de castas*) prevalent in the colony on caste as a stratified set of sociolegal rankings. Yet while race was produced through taxonomies developed to exclude from power individuals western science construed as essentially different due to blood, ancestry, or color, caste constituted a more ambiguous and flexible set of qualities that combined social affiliations, kinship, and inherent differences as it worked to facilitate incorporation into systems of power.[7] Ultimately, caste was something of a capacity, elaborated through the genealogical, moral, and operational aspects of a person's place in relation to other persons. Such capacity was animated and transmitted through "dense webs" of social networks like those Michel Foucault identifies as key to the "thematics of power."[8] As he argues, such thematics do not rest on a "certain strength," an "elementary force," or an "essence." They are rather about the strategies deployed by persons who act on others, who in turn are potential actors in their own right.[9]

## THE SANCTIONED AND UNSANCTIONED DOMAINS

Especially because of its large populations of blacks and Indians, colonial Mexico raises interesting questions about the history of racial thinking and the enactment of power. In the documentation, one finds nothing so simple as a shared camaraderie or a mutual resentment between these two subordinated groups — the one initially imported as slave labor and the other enduring as conquered indigenes. Rather, every manuscript page reveals a complicated social sparring indicating that connections between blacks and Indians, and broader questions of domination and resistance, have to be contextualized in a world wider than one might initially suppose.[10] Indeed, analysis of what turns out to be a complex colonial politics of caste must include those classified as Spaniards, as well as the mulattoes and mestizos whose numbers grew rapidly after the initial conquest period.

As discussed here, the politics of caste involved two trajectories of power, which mirrored each other and were inextricably intertwined. The dispute around Adriana indicates that patterns of kinship (including figurative), friendship, and patronage tying people to Spaniards were meaningful, and so were ones tying people to Indians. The first set of patterns indexes colonizing processes that politically organized caste to privilege Spaniards and Spanishness while subordinating Indians and Indianness, and turning blacks, mulattoes, and mestizos into mediators who extended Spanish authority. In this book I call the social fields that constituted this domain *sanctioned* in order to convey a sense of routine caste behaviors and meanings that were implicitly — if not always legally—condoned by the colonial state and its agents. The second set of patterns indexes the world of witchcraft, a term which described state-censured sets of moral violations ranging from unorthodox religious behavior, including trysts and pacts with the devil, to popular forms of sorcery or "black magic." The social fields of this domain—which I call *unsanctioned*—reversed sanctioned patterns by organizing caste in ways that privileged Indians and Indianness, while subordinating Spaniards and Spanishness and reorienting blacks, mulattoes, and mestizos, who could now attach themselves to Indians in a bid to undermine Spaniards. Put simply, these domains were something of Spanish and Indian worlds bracketed by Spaniards and Indians, and integrated and brought together by the mediating groups. If the health of the sanctioned social body depended on the "vigor and proper functioning"[11] of its interrelated caste parts, so too, in the end, did its unsanctioned illness.

While the sanctioned and the unsanctioned referenced two possible trajectories of power, the unsanctioned also followed inevitably from the sanctioned ways in which the colonial state organized and gave meaning to caste. In particular, both trajectories spoke to a logic that converged around the Spanish attribution of weakness to Indians.[12] A feminized quality, weakness justified and made possible Indian subservience to Spanish governance in the sanctioned domain. But weakness also produced that domain's reversal, for in the unsanctioned domain the devil made victims of Indians, who came to wield authority over Spaniards through witchcraft. Colonial ideologies generated both domains, and colonial institutional and social policies drew into their spheres of influence a cross section of individuals from a range of caste categories.

In her study of contemporary Gawan (Papua New Guinea) society, Nancy Munn draws on the concept of hegemony and Foucauldian understandings of power as "the pressures embedded in social interaction"[13] to semantically situate Gawan witchcraft within the wider social field of Gawan conceptions of self and society, emphasizing negation in the form of witchcraft as an integral part of the social collective. Examining how the "world" of the witch and the "world" of the non-witch belong to the same cultural system, Munn concludes that neither world can be said to be prior;[14] instead, the witch personifies the "negative principles" that hold sway over everyday Gawan life.[15] Drawing on Munn's ideas, we can look at the colonial Mexican unsanctioned domain as, on the one hand, what Munn refers to as a "'world' of its own" with reference to Gawan witchcraft.[16] On the other hand, it was made operational in the context of a cultural system that included the sanctioned domain, which set the terms of the debate over values and with which the unsanctioned cohered through the idiom and implications of caste. In both domains, power filtered through the social affiliations people forged as the different castes were drawn into a unified system of meanings that shifted with the frame of reference: the same caste qualities made individuals less esteemed in one domain and more esteemed in the other. What remained consistent was the idea that prestige operated through the shaded distinctions to which caste spoke. Thus, while the sanctioned and the unsanctioned were in opposition, that opposition was itself constituted through the singular logic of a caste framework that delimited patterns of power, including the contrariness of witchcraft. Both the sanctioned and the unsanctioned produced spaces for elite *and* subaltern activity and passivity, and both provided viable paths to authority and its loss.

Raymond Williams's observation that "the dominant culture, so to say, at once produces and limits its own forms of counter-culture"[17] therefore bears keeping in mind. Colonial Mexican witchcraft, though at first glance seemingly counterhegemonic, derived from the hegemonic, which referred back to its own opposition in an endless loop. Witchcraft was not, then, an autonomous realm of resistance. It was instead a set of discourses and practices derived from the colonial implications of caste. The conflicts it embodied spoke to the struggles characteristic of hegemony, which William Roseberry describes as a "common material and meaningful framework for living through, talking about, and acting upon social orders characterized by domination."[18] That common material and meaningful framework generated in the present case by caste principles reveal fissures that both destabilized, through witchcraft, and reinforced, through not-witchcraft, the hold of colonialism on the populace.[19]

In his study of "wildness" and witchcraft in colonial and contemporary Colombia and Peru, Michael Taussig brings the above issues to bear on the Latin American case through an artful analysis of Indian *magia* (magic) as a hegemonic social force linked to Western ideas about race and the ongoing political economy of conquest.[20] As he explores the interpenetrating worlds of colonizers and colonized, Taussig calls social analysts to task for imposing order on the inherent disorder of social life.[21] In this book, I seek to explain aspects of that disorder by showing how Spanishness, Indianness, and other caste qualities constituted a deep logic in the colonial imagination and, consequently, in the lives and experiences of colonial peoples. In piecing together that logic, I turn to gender themes and, to a lesser extent, class themes in order to show how caste was organized by sets of meanings that seeped into these other configurations.[22] For instance, we have seen that the Indian witch brought to the fore in Adriana's case was a woman, as were the litigants themselves. Ana María described the Indian as the leader of a group of women gathered together for allegedly nefarious purposes, and certainly the problem that was femaleness otherwise runs through the narrative.[23] References to class do as well. Thus, for instance, Adriana's propertied status served to reinforce her honor by countering the fickleness assigned to Ana María, a thief and a vagabond.

In addition to extending the implications of power in the above ways, I maintain a focus on the forms of mediation and interstitiality represented by non-Indian, non-Spanish actors like Ana María and Adriana. This is because actors and qualities defined by blackness, mulattoness, and mestizoness straddled Spanish and Indian power and the Indian and Spanish worlds, while simultaneously reaffirming social hierarchy. In many ways, these actors best represent what Carolyn Dean, in her study of the Inca nobility, calls "the colonizer's quandry," which is "the paradoxical need to enculturate the colonized and encourage mimesis while, at the same time, upholding and maintaining the difference that legitimizes colonization."[24]

Finally, the significance of judicial punishment and restitution are crucial to our understandings of Spanishness and Indianness. The judicary's role as an institutional enforcer of caste difference made it central to colonization processes. But the judiciary also reveals a contradiction in those processes, for judicial authorities did not just punish. They offered restitution, especially to the Indians on whom Spaniards expended many of their ideological and material resources, and with whom they resolved most of their labor needs. Colonial justice therefore countered colonial exploitation, a point that takes on further significance and connections to caste politics because the dual character of Spanish authority was mirrored in the Indian kind. While Indians inflicted harm through witchcraft, they also had the ability to heal. Thus, in a profoundly colonial sense the judiciary acted as a kind of sanctioned magical force controlled by Spaniards (which echoes Taussig's consideration of the "magic of reason"), while witchcraft operated as a kind of unsanctioned system of justice controlled by Indians.

A number of anthropologists have studied the cultural consequences of "high" colonial formations in Africa, Asia, and elsewhere.[25] Their interests have included unpacking the mechanisms behind the creation and maintenance of social hierarchies; exploring tensions among classes of colonizers over colonial goals and practices; identifying confusions and contradictions in colonial ideologies; tracing the ways in which race, gender, class, and sexuality intertwined through material production; and examining the new social relations and cultural fields that brought colonizers and colonized together. Although institutional, disciplinary, and even area studies boundaries have in many ways conspired to keep anthropologists and historians unsympathetic to each other's strengths and struggles,[26] people trained in both disciplines share interests in understanding the perspectives of subordinated peoples in colonial situations, and in grappling with questions of representation.[27] Because of this, in recent decades historians and anthropologists have both been drawn to "subalterns" and to new ways of reading colonial documents. From this, the relatively new field of historical anthropology has emerged.

Studies of subalterns show that they are not a coherent group, and that their "popular" culture is not an autonomous domain.[28] Subalterns might act, but not necessarily in concert, and their culture cannot be disentangled from that of elites. One of the most important contributions historical anthropology has made to these questions has been a focus on what Brian Keith Axel describes as "the ways that supposed margins and metropoles, or peripheries and centers, fold into, constitute, or disrupt one another . . . constituting new centers of inquiry, just as it demonstrates the powerful positionality of the margins right at the center."[29] Central to this focus are the cultural worlds of European missionaries and colonizers, whose perspectives are rightly deemed as worthy of study as those of natives. Indeed, it is only by bringing the two sides together, and therefore destabilizing the divide, that the importance of the disruptions at the center of historical anthropological studies can be fully realized. By the same token, calls to move beyond "essentialist taxonomies of the subaltern"[30]—which typically fail to address the heterogeneity of subordinated persons and their experiences, and the consequent fluidity of relations of domination and subordination—recognize the difficulties of managing the tensions between simultaneously exposing power and acknowledging the agency of subordinated persons.[31]

Recent conversations among Latin Americanist historians over the "new cultural history" of Latin America, especially of Mexico, speak to the issues outlined above.[32] In particular, these historians have debated the failure to move beyond essentializing taxonomies, and the related tendency of some scholars to impute too much agency to subalterns.[33] Eric Van Young thus observes that in an effort to recover the perspectives and capacities of subordinated peoples, some new cultural historians have made of agency an "apotheosis" by imputing to colonized subjects what Alan Knight refers to as a near "rational-choice" instrumentality.[34] As Knight notes, this leads to the resulting "paradox that subalterns, who are defined precisely by their subordinate and disempowered status, are seen to be calling the shots."[35]

The problem, however, might not be so much whether subalterns have agency or how much they have, as it is the tendency to approach agency as if it had a universal and uniform character. Turning our attention to culture itself will perhaps help to resolve this problem. I understand culture not as one among many distinct realms of human life, nor as a set of mentalities or ideals, but as the symbols inscribed in words and things that reflect and shape unique qualities and logics in human thought and activity. Bringing culture to bear on creative human action, Sherry Ortner reminds us of the ways in which "every culture, every subculture, every historical moment, constructs its own forms of agency" as the "structure of domination" ascribes to both the superordinated and the subordinated values and traits making particular kinds of action possible and others inconceivable.[36]

Here I draw attention to how the Spanish colonial project in Mexico was itself implicated in the production of various kinds of effective actors whose practices generated various kinds of hierarchy. That project provided spaces for subalterns to act and to act subversively, but in ways that often conformed to the expectations of elites — expectations implemented by direct force but also through institutions like the judiciary, and through economic processes that inculcated networks of power. As I explore the cultural politics of caste in the colony's sanctioned and unsanctioned domains, then, I am therefore speaking simultaneously to the intersection of subaltern and elite spaces, domination and subordination, and power and culture.

In order to clarify the two patterns, the book treats the sanctioned domain first and for the most part separately from the unsanctioned one. In part, this organization follows colonial norms that juridically separated witchcraft from other kinds of conflicts; and in part it indicates how witchcraft was a world within the larger colonial world populated by individuals like Adriana and Ana María, and the Indians, Spaniards, and others with whom they were involved. Because witchcraft was part of and not apart from that larger world, it was as central to colonial reality as labor practices or civil controls. The sanctioned cannot therefore be fully understood without the unsanctioned, and vice versa. The reader will notice that at various points the one world creeps in as the other leaves off.

My methodological approach is interpretive. I therefore tease out from the documents thick cultural data, which I present through direct quotes from the records even as I weave together the various strands in order to systematize the meanings and social practices that caste shaped and that shaped caste. Interpretation does not eschew the laudable goal of objectivity. It rather recognizes the complexities of knowing, and of what one desires to know. Its point is to capture the noise that the statistician tends to find irksome in order to probe the deeper and messier meanings of human beliefs and behaviors, and to uncover what is inherently ambiguous and fragmented. Thus, I am reading texts that are already ambiguous and fragmented for their also ambiguous and fragmented content.

The materials are drawn mostly from colonial judicial records housed in the Mexican National Archives (AGN).[37] Although I do not define my work in what Knight describes as "simple time-place terms,"[38] most of the information pertains to Central Mexico and its vicinities. This was the most densely populated indigenous region both before and after the conquest. It had the highest concentration of colonial state institutions and activities and the largest numbers of blacks during the sixteenth and seventeenth centuries. The records date from 1537 to 1695, with three-quarters clustered between 1590 and 1675, a period Louisa Hoberman describes as the "heart of the middle colony."[39] I focus on the *longue durée* rather than on change over time, not because culture does not change but because the documentation suggests that caste patterns changed slowly, or only in their details rather than through substantive reconfigurations. Indeed, aspects of those patterns are still apparent in parts of Mexico today.[40]

The texts raise questions about documentation and construction that must be addressed, as I do in chapter 1, even if they cannot be fully answered. Chapter 1 also elaborates my understandings of what caste was, while providing an overview of political economy and judicial organization with respect to the ways that caste meanings informed– and in turn were informed by—both. Chapters 2 and 3 delineate the social fields characteristic of the sanctioned domain, first examining the Spanish/Indian relationship with particular attention to contradictions in Spanish colonial practices. The idea that these contradictions originated in Spanish perceptions of Indians as weak leads to an exploration of women/Indian analogies. Weakness favored certain kinds of colonial social affiliations and convinced elites that women and Indians could lose self-control, only to end up mired in the devilish witchcraft that gave to "passivity" a particular form of agency. Chapter 3 also investigates the ways in which blacks, mulattoes, and mestizos were put to work in the sanctioned domain, attending to how mixed-casteness itself became an idiom for arguing about rights, and to how Spaniards who facilitated the abuse Indians suffered then turned around to "heal" Indians through judicial and non-judicial interventions that punished the perpetrators.

Chapter 4 explores rebellions and alliances between Indians and the mediating blacks, mulattoes, and mestizos, focusing on the ways in which the intermingling "character" attributes of the different castes could pose challenges to Spanish authority. In chapters 5 and 6 I examine the caste hierarchies that characterized the unsanctioned domain, where Indians gained authority precisely because of their "weakness." Again, there are parallels between women and Indians, and also between Spanish and Indian power. Here, of course, Indians are the perpetrators of "abuse," while they also hold out the magical potential to cure. Chapter 6 addresses the entanglement of blacks, mulattoes, and mestizos in the world of witchcraft dominated by Indians. I attend to the amalgam of black/Indian witchcraft and to the surprising hybridity of the devil himself. Ultimately, I argue that the complete cycle of bewitching and healing included the Spaniards abused and cured by Indian witches, as well as the blacks, mulattoes, and mestizos to whom both Spaniards and Indians were connected.

Chapter 7 begins with a tale about a mulatto slave whose story of escaping with the magical help of an Indian brings her straight back to

Spanish justices. Using this tale to bring together the themes addressed in the book, I draw out the ways in which the objectives of witchcraft and the desires of witches were entwined with sanctioned social values. Witchcraft, I conclude, was not a revolutionary language of resistance as much as it was an affirmation of hegemony. In the end, it not only developed out of colonialism, it also upheld the allure of the wealth, mobility, and power controlled by elites.

# 1

# Forging a Colonial Landscape

Hernán Cortés landed on the coast of Vera Cruz in 1519. Over the next two centuries, Spanish influence on and control of the territory centered on New Spain came to extend from the mining zone of San Luis Potosí in the north, to the shores of the Pacific Ocean and the Gulf of Mexico, and to the present-day borders of Chiapas and Jalisco states to the southeast and northwest.[1] New Spain urbanized as Spaniards built cities and towns from San Luis Potosí to Antequera (Oaxaca) in the south, and the ports of Acapulco and Vera Cruz on the western and eastern coasts. Mexico City, built over the ruins of the Mexica (Aztec) center of Tenochtitlán, became the colony's administrative, political, and cultural center. Both the "belly" and the "hands" of the region, it was the principal point of convergence for consumption, production, and a trading network that extended the length and breadth of New Spain.[2]

Mexico City's symbolic and economic significance made it then, as now, the region's most populated and diverse city. An ordered space, the city transformed social values into physical reality. The outlying barrios of San Juan Tenochtitlán and the Indian town of Santiago Tlatelolco were separated from a Spanish core, from which the indigenous peoples Spaniards referred to as Indians (indios) were periodically banned.[3] The surrounding valleys produced wheat and vegetables, textiles made in workshops (obrajes), and other goods such as tools and furniture for consumption in Mexico City and in Puebla, the viceroyalty's second largest city. Trade routes traversed by muleteers (har-

*rieros*) also came together in Mexico City, bringing sugar, rice, cotton, tobacco, cacao, cochineal, indigo, and livestock principally from southern regions, and livestock, silver, and wheat principally from northern and central ones. Some goods were consumed domestically. Others, such as silver, dyes, and cacao were exported from Mexico City to Europe and points east through Vera Cruz, and to Manila and points west through Acapulco. Trade was also vigorous with southern regions of Spain's New World empire.[4]

The period from the late sixteenth to the late seventeenth century marks the height of New Spain's involvement in the Atlantic slave trade.[5] It also covers the demographic collapse of the Indian population, as well as that population's revitalization.[6] During this period, elite landholdings consolidated while rural Indian populations were displaced and regrouped, and Spanish ideas and values spread formally and informally. Legal institutions matured as caste rights and obligations were written (though not systematically) into laws that maintained distinctions between Spaniards and non-Spaniards, and among non-Spaniards themselves.

### INDIAN LABOR AND ITS CONTRADICTIONS

As in other Latin American colonies, New Spain's economy during this era was heterogeneous.[7] It included traditional forms of production, property ownership, and labor organization (such as state work drafts, tribute, slavery, and the domestic confinement of women) derived from both European and indigenous systems. Over time, however, notions of property rights and legitimate ownership came to be dominated by Spanish ideas,[8] as capitalist relations of production came to characterize important sectors of the colonial economy in manufacturing, agriculture, trade, and mining. In some economic enclaves, laborers were increasingly free and paid with wages even as they were constrained by legislation, debt-peonage, and force.[9]

Spaniards claimed rights to Indian tribute in the form of goods and labor through *encomienda,* the earliest economic institution. Encomienda had originated in the Caribbean, where the crown lacked a clear policy toward Indians.[10] Here, rapacious settlers, engaged in what many claimed was just war against heathens who resisted Spanish attempts to civilize and convert them, virtually enslaved Indians through encomienda and other extractive measures. As is well known, within decades of Spanish arrival, the native populations of the largest Spanish settlement on Hispaniola and of the smaller islands had been destroyed by disease, overwork, and violence. During this early period, clergy and crown debated Spanish obligations to Indians, the feasibility of converting them to Christianity, and whether and how Spanish authority was to be legitimately imposed on converted peoples.

The crown identified closely with the Catholic Church, its ally against Islam during the late-fifteenth-century reconquest of the Iberian peninsula from the Moors, and the source through papal decree of Spanish rights to New World territories. State decisions were therefore deeply informed by theological concerns which, while not uniform, did converge around the need to preserve Indian lives in the interests of evangelical projects. As settlers fought for a consistent labor supply, Dominican friars defended Indians, and called into question "the very legality of the Spanish New World enterprise."[11] Believing that the principal role of Spaniards was to evangelize, they soon refused to hear confession from, or give communion to, *encomenderos*.[12]

The crown had an interest in upholding the moral authority of the church and defending Indians from the excesses of settlers. It also had to pacify those settlers, however, and both the crown and the church wanted to reserve Indian labor for themselves. Indians therefore had to be protected, but they also had to be made to work. Early mandates of Spanish and Indian rights and responsibilities spoke to the conflicts inherent in a vision of authority divinely sanctioned and driven by self-interest. For instance, in 1502, the crown gave Indians freedom from enslavement once they became Christians. At the same time, it imposed an annual crown tribute on them, and authorized the governor of Hispaniola to compel them to gather and mine gold, to produce food for Spanish settlers, and to work on the construction of public buildings. In 1510, Spanish jurists again mandated improved treatment through the Laws of Burgos, which also gave priority to Indian conversion to the religious and sociopolitical norms of Christianity and Spanishness. But provisions for involuntary Indian labor continued under these laws, as the crown authorized the use of Indians for mining, agriculture, and public works projects, and permitted force to be used if Indians resisted Spanish governance.[13]

The manner in which Indians were to be utilized was still an open question in the first decade after the conquest, when Cortés proposed that New Spain's Indians provide labor to Spanish settlers. The crown objected that such service had killed most Caribbean Indians. Therefore, Cortés limited his proposal to tribute in foodstuffs and cotton to be produced by Indians on their own lands, the construction of dwellings for Spaniards, and the raising of Spanish-owned cattle. He also stipulated that Indians not be used in the particularly arduous environment of mining. But he insisted that settlers needed Indian tribute for their own sustenance, and that encomienda would ultimately benefit the crown without interfering with its interests. Moreover, as one duty of encomenderos was to facilitate the conversion of Indians, religious indoctrination could proceed apace.

The crown soon acquiesced, and encomienda continued to develop in New Spain, as the debate shifted from whether it should exist to how it should be administered.[14] Royal law called for the rotation of encomiendas granted only for a limited time. Nevertheless, as Peggy Liss observes, "a military mentality bent on living off the spoils of conquest predominated."[15] Many Indians became de facto slaves as the first generations of Spanish settlers attempted to retain their encomiendas in perpetuity. They also used Indians in a number of economic enterprises, including mining.

Over the decades, the crown became increasingly nervous about the increasing wealth and autonomy of settlers, as well as about the fate of New Spain's Indians, who were following their Caribbean counterparts into precipitous decline. In a bid to reassert its seignorial authority and to acknowledge the plight of Indians, the crown issued the New Laws of 1542. These were prompted by the priest and Dominican monk Bartolomé de Las Casas, who began a vigorous defense of all New World Indians in 1515, and would later become Bishop of Chiapas. The New Laws stipulated that encomiendas would be remanded to the crown upon the deaths of their owners, and that labor would be eliminated as a tribute obligation of Indians.[16] The laws also explicitly declared Indian enslavement illegal.[17] Although their full impact was short-lived—because encomenderos in Mexico, as well as those in Peru, resisted retraction of their rights—over the course of the sixteenth century, encomienda weakened in New Spain.[18]

In accordance with the moral and juridical tenets of the medieval Spanish legal code known as the Siete Partidas, the crown was a paternalistic, benevolent, and sacred institution.[19] The monarch was considered God's earthly representative whose rule was willed by divine mandate.[20] His duty was to preserve the law of the land and the integrity of the social body. In the New World, crown authority widened due to what was perceived as a "jurisdictional vacuum" and to the overt intervention of the crown in social matters.[21] There, the king's Old World obligation to see to the needs of "widows, orphans and the wretched of the earth" extended to Indians who, as the most "miserable"[22] people, were special wards of the crown.[23]

During the sixteenth century, the crown shifted toward free Indian labor compensated with wages. While this was a step toward constituting Indians as royal subjects equal to Spaniards, various forms of legal and extra-legal coercion also obliged Indians to work on Spanish-owned properties such as agricultural estates (*haciendas*) and ranches (*estancias*). These properties were expanding as the Indian population decreased, and as land — which, under Spanish law, could not be confiscated from subject populations — was subsequently freed up and acquired by Spaniards in often fraudulent ways. In some regions labor coercion was accompanied by debt-peonage, perhaps the most serious threat to free movement,[24] and decrees against vagabondage helped channel both Indian and non-Indian laborers to specific work-sites.[25]

Spanish organization of rural Indian populations to meet the needs of propertied Spaniards emptied outlying communities. Their inhabitants, along with isolated families, were moved to head towns (*cabaceras*) or to satellites of these towns.[26] This process of concentrating the population (*congregación* or *concentración*) freed up land for Spanish use, while Indians were given new plots for their own subsistence in areas more convenient to Spaniards. These were typically located near the monastery complexes whose friars were entrusted with religious conversion.

The Indian population began to rebound in the middle of the seventeenth century. Litigation over land rights then increased as Spaniards continued to take over vast amounts of land illegally as well as through legal grants (*mercedes*), consolidation, expansion, and purchase.[27] Conflicts also arose over Spanish needs for converts and labor: Spanish enterprises needed Indian workers, but religious indoctrination — at first by the regular and then by the secular clergy — required Indians to be present in their villages. So too did the crown labor draft known as *repartimiento*, which conscripted Indians for public works projects and specific industries — such as silver mining — important to crown interests.[28] Demands on Indians also came from remaining encomenderos, and more and more from the royal tribute mechanism of *corregimiento*, which was run directly by the crown's administrative officers and their deputies (*corregidores* or *alcaldes mayores*, *mayordomos*, and *alguaciles*). Some Indian communities came to owe tribute to settlers and to the crown.[29]

### SLAVERY AND FREEDOM

Spanish colonials in the Caribbean had turned to African slaves as early as 1501.[30] The use of such slaves accelerated there as Indians, "weak and of little strength," in the king's opinion, died out.[31] Until 1518, the crown only allowed slaves Hispanicized in Spain to be brought to the New World. Pressure from settlers, however, soon compelled slave importations directly from Africa.[32]

As its Indian population waned over the course of the sixteenth and early seventeenth centuries, New Spain came to have one of the largest concentrations of African slaves in the Americas.[33] Indeed, during its first two centuries New Spain received on average two-thirds of all African slaves brought to Spanish America legally, as well as many brought illegally.[34] Although the peoples Spaniards referred to collectively as "blacks" (negros) were only a small part of the colony's overall population, in 1619 Philip III declared there were so many in the colonies that in "a short while the Indies would become theirs."[35]

Most African slaves brought to Mexico were men.[36] Those Hispanicized elsewhere were Spanish-speaking (*ladinos*) and already skilled in Iberian modes of production.[37] Due in part to their relative scarcity, African slaves were expensive. Spaniards also considered them, and blacks in general, to be hardier than Indians. Brought through the port of Vera Cruz, slaves were sold and then sent to do hard physical work in the northern silver mining regions, on ranches to the north and west of Mexico City, and on the sugar plantations, ranches, and mines that followed the southwestern belt running from the city of Puebla to the Pacific coast.[38] They were also taken to major urban centers such as Mexico City, Puebla, Guadalajara, and Vera Cruz. Here they toiled in Spanish households, in obrajes, in craft guilds, and as day laborers whose masters took most of their wages in a practice known as *jornal*. Although slaveholders were generally Spanish, slave ownership extended to some high-ranking Indians and even to aspiring free blacks, such as Adriana Ruíz de Cabrera, whom we have already met.

The crown mandated that all African slaves be baptized before they reached the New World. Baptism, therefore, took place on board slave ships or immediately on reaching port. Slaveholders were obliged to feed and clothe their slaves. They were also required to see to their slaves' ongoing religious training. That is why, as part of her defense, Adriana made sure the inquisitors knew that she regularly took her own slaves to mass.

The Siete Partidas outlined several routes to manumission, including slaves' rights to freedom if they married free persons, a provision nullified in the 1520s by the crown and local officials. Still in effect, however, were provisions for slaveholders to free their slaves, third parties to purchase and free them, or slaves to purchase themselves for an agreed-upon price (which they sometimes paid in installments with their share of jornal wages).[39] In addition, according to the Siete Partidas the status of children followed their mother. The offspring of female slaves who, willingly or not, had Spanish partners automatically became slaves if they were not freed by their fathers. The offspring of male slaves who partnered with Indian or other free women, which was often the case, were then free.[40] Interestingly, and perhaps ironically, this might have meant that mulattoes of Indian/black ancestry were more likely than their Spanish/black counterparts to have been free.

The right of slaves to marry was provided by the Siete Partidas and encouraged by the church.[41] Yet colonists controlled slaves by forcing convenient marriages slaves did not desire, thwarting ones that they did, or forbidding marriage altogether. The tension between law and colonial practice is clear from a conversation the Spaniard Francesca de Aguilar had with her friends in 1572, while they sat around the table at her home in Pachuca. Over a meal the group was discussing how the service of slaves deteriorated after they married, when Francesca interjected that her experiences with her own slaves had taught her that married blacks did not make good servants because they did not "settle down." She then squabbled in front of her friends with one of her female slaves, telling the woman that "with these dogs one does not have to do what God orders." With her conscience weighing heavily, Francesca turned herself in to the Inquisition for blasphemy.[42] As Francesca's confession indicates, although slaveholders knew that their resistance to slave marriages contradicted official morals, they found affective kinship incompatible with servitude, because in becoming "people" by forming their own families, slaves' ties would be redirected away from their masters.

Many slaveholders thwarted not only their slaves' wishes to marry but also the possibilities for slaves to gain freedom legally. The judiciary tended to favor the interests of slaveholders in this respect,[43] but by the middle of the seventeenth century perhaps 15 percent of blacks and mulattoes were nevertheless classified as free. Many were women and children, which might have reflected Spaniards' favorable treatment of their mistresses and the offspring they had with them, but many of the mulattoes might have been the offspring of Indians, free because of their mother's status.[44] Legally barred from certain occupations, free blacks and mulattoes—like most of the urban lower classes—found work as laborers and servants.[45] Beginning in the 1580s, they were required to pay crown tribute alongside Indians. They also had to petition to carry weapons, live under Spanish supervision, and conform to dress codes that distinguished them from Spaniards.[46] Finally, legislation controlled their spatial and temporal movements, for all blacks and mulattoes were forbidden from holding dances "in the plazas and streets," gathering in groups of "more than three," and going out at night.[47]

Although provisions for freedom existed for individual black and mulatto slaves, the protracted debates over Indians' rights to freedom that took place in the sixteenth century were never at any time fully extended to blacks and mulattoes as a class. From our perspective, this might be one of the most difficult issues to understand, particularly because both Indians and slaves were subject to processes of religious conversion. Nevertheless, Indians were freed from enslavement in part because of this conversion while, until Independence in the early nineteenth century, blacks (and mulattoes with slave mothers) could be legally enslaved in spite of conversion.

CASTE AND RACE: THE QUALITIES OF BLOOD

As was the case throughout colonial Latin America, individuals in New Spain were legally and socially classified according to *casta*. The etiology of the term is unclear, but it originated in Iberia, where it indicated breed, kind, or lineage.[48] Iberians brought the concept to different parts of the world inhabited by different peoples. Caste therefore came to have several meanings. In Latin America it did not refer to the endogamous and ascribed socioreligious groups the Portuguese understood as characterizing Hindu India. Instead, it was more akin to modern notions of race, insofar as it referred to descent and to putative distinctions carried in blood, ancestry, and color. But caste was not exactly race, at least in the sense that the latter has come to be understood — above all in the Anglo West — as the unambiguous separation of the world's peoples according to alleged biological differences.[49]

The term *race (raza)* coexisted with caste during the period under question here, but the two words did not refer to the same thing. Consider, for instance, a Spanish woman suspected of witchcraft, who was asked by the Mexican inquisitors in the late sixteenth century whether her blood was "clean" (*limpia*).[50] She replied that she did not know if there was any "evil (*mala*) raza" in her "casta." What did she, in fact, mean?

Raza is the more modern of the two terms, and its first documented use in 1438 was in the phrase "good race."[51] In fifteenth- and sixteenth-century Spain, however, a national identity began to build around Catholicism and the Castile region of Spain. Indeed, the Spanish Inquisition was established in 1478, specifically to target converted Jews (*conversos*), who were widely thought to be heretics hiding their religion under a thin veneer of Christianity. Through genealogical proof before the Inquisition, "Spaniards" distinguished themselves from such conversos, as well as from converted and equally secretive Moors (*moriscos*). As the social community (*república*) came to be defined more and more around Spanish-speaking Christians, status-seeking individuals became obsessively concerned with their blood purity (*limpieza de sangre*), and Spanish writers began to link raza explicitly to genealogy and blood.[52] Following the final stages of the 1492 Reconquest, raza was on its way to losing positive associations as it came to refer to Jews and then to Moors, both of whom posed challenges to Christian dominance. By the early seventeenth century, raza must have fully taken on a negative sense, for in his definition of the term, the Spanish lexicographer Sebastián de Covarrubias indicated that it meant "possessing the raza of a Moor or a Jew."[53] By this time as well, the Spanish state had forced conversions and expulsions of both converted and unconverted Jews and Moors, while forbidding these groups from settling in its colonies.[54] Indeed, as Deborah Root writes with reference to Moors, "orthodoxy, heresy, dissimulation [were] all collapsed into the physical body, into the ethnicity that could not be changed by any action or belief."[55]

As raza became associated with Jewish and Moorish "blood" — an immutable and undesirable substance — it thus came to also signify the religions that challenged Spanish Christianity. When the Mexican inquisitors asked the Spanish woman about her mala raza, then, they clearly wanted to know if she had any Jewish or Moorish blood. She could not answer their question. But clearly, like other colonial subjects, she had a caste that could be "contaminated" by such blood. What, then, was caste?

Covarrubias defined caste as both a "noble and pure-blooded lineage; one who is of good line and descent" and, in the vernacular, as referring to people as of "good" or "bad" caste.[56] At first glance, it seems not very different from raza, as both linked social qualities to blood or ancestry. But according to the Spanish etymologists Joan Corominas and José Pascual, while raza embodied the idea of purity, casta had a "neutral sense that did not affirm or negate the purity of the kind [of thing]."[57] Caste, then, seems to have been a less charged quality that applied to any kind of (non-Jewish or Moorish) ancestry. Yet such ancestry could still be desirable or undesirable, and each caste had a set of associations. In this respect, Covarrubias offers another clue about the meaning of caste, for he locates the *naturaleza* (nature or disposition) of a person in his or her caste.[58] This might be oversimplifying the issue, but his discussion does seem to correspond to the dispositions that in the colonial context made Spaniards attribute reason to themselves, weakness to Indians, and aggressiveness to blacks. These qualities became central to the politics of caste, and they were generated by, even as they maintained, processes of colonization.

During the period under discussion here, the Spanish state was expelling persons with mala raza and forbidding their entry to the New World, while the colonial state was simultaneously inculcating a system of castas. Claudio Lomnitz intermingles converted Indians, Jews, Moors, and Africans in his discussion of the colonial "racial hierarchy," and Irene Silverblatt argues compellingly for connections between New Christians and Indians in colonial Peruvian discourse.[59] Yet, it is important to keep in mind that while none of the non-Spanish groups — Jews, Moors, Indians, blacks, mulattoes, and mestizos — could claim legitimacy as Old Christians or Spaniards, they were also not entirely interchangeable in the colonial imagination. For example, as Silverblatt also documents, at least some theologians believed that Indian resistance to Christianity did not run as deeply as that of the Jews.[60]

At base, the castes included Spaniards, as we have already seen from the case of our Spanish witch. Additionally, Indians — as well as blacks, mulattoes, and mestizos — were essential to Spanish prosperity in the New World, while Jews and Moors threatened it in the Old. As a result, the colonial state initiated a system of inclusion through similarities while the budding Old World nation-state tried to rid itself of the contamination of difference. Jews and Moors thus retained a kind of ineradicable otherness that conversion could not erase, but officials in the colony went to great lengths — with varying degrees of optimism and success — to make Christians of all the non-Spanish castes, including African slaves and Indians. Some came to be more Christian than others — indeed the evidence suggests that blacks, mulattoes, and mestizos were on the whole more Christianized than Indians[61] — but by stressing the possibilities of conversion and concurrently generating an inclusive system based on distinctions, colonialist ideologies put difference to work while national ones attempted to expel it.

CASTE AND LINEAGE

The concept of lineage is a useful way to think through the meaning of caste because of the semantic links between the two terms, the importance of descent in Iberian culture, and the genealogical and more broadly social implications of the concept. Even if we confine caste to the idea of blood connections, people who belonged to different castes were concurrently linked genealogically to one another. In its simplest sense this meant, for instance, that a mulatto would have a Spanish parent and a black parent, or a black parent and an Indian parent. And as genealogical branches proliferated in the New World, so did caste terms, at least in the works of colonial writers. The blood of casta was therefore more easily blended than the blood of raza, and the genealogical implications of caste convey a sense of kinship constituted by potentially infinitely traceable connections.

Because caste was transmutable, caste taxonomies had a complex segmentary effect through which operated a principle of achievement culminating in Spanishness. Lomnitz argues that because of this, almost everyone was "redeemable" over the course of several generations.[62] He excepts blacks from his scheme,[63] but if the idea of caste is expanded to include kinship claimed symbolically through the kinds of pseudo-genealogical ties that Adriana proposed for herself, even blacks could argue that they were "Spanish." While the connections that established caste identities thus included parents, they might also have included symbolic genitors.

The concept of caste can be yet further extended to embrace a more abstract sense of social connectedness people developed with other persons that they did not necessarily claim as kin. Thus, Adriana was associated not just with the Spaniards who raised her but also with the entire Spanish community of Vera Cruz, including the priests who defended her. She was also accused of consorting with the Indian witch said to be her friend and confidant. Hence, this black woman could conceivably take on both Spanishness and Indianness through the various kinds of ties I have proposed as being central to caste. In the end, while understanding caste requires attention to the importance placed by the state on blood connections, it is also important to trace how people could assimilate the attributes of another caste through the various sets of symbolic and social affiliations that were equally a part of caste's cultural terrain.

## INDIOS

Lineage was central not only to the construction and enactment of caste. It also provides a clue to Spanish evaluations of what we might call "personhood" and, consequently, to colonial social dynamics. Lomnitz notes that slavery was "predicated on destroying group identities" while Indian collectivities were recognized.[64] With this as a starting point, we can begin to evaluate the different ways that Indians and blacks were drawn into colonial processes and therefore into relation with one another.

For Spaniards, cities were the realm of the civilized, and lineages and families the foundations of civil life.[65] Spaniards had encountered peoples without cities in the Caribbean. But upon their arrival to the mainland they found that the central region of what would become New Spain was dominated by the urban space of Tenochtitlán, a city remarkable even to the conquistadors who methodically destroyed it while building their own paeans to civilization over the wreckage.[66] Spaniards recognized the familial ties of New Spain's sedentary Indian inhabitants, and they gave all Indians a communal status as a "people." This is evident in caste terminologies. Spaniards designated as indios groups who, before the conquest, had disparate cultural and linguistic traditions and names for themselves.[67] "Indio" did not maintain these distinctions; indeed, it homogenized dissimilar groups. It was also a misnomer insofar as it rested on Columbus's erroneous assumption that he had reached Asia. Yet indio nevertheless conveys the idea that Indians belonged to a geographical place (the Indies), and were thus members of a juridico-political entity in much the way that Spaniards (*españoles*) were natives of Spain, which was also an organized juridico-political entity.

The indigenous polities Spaniards came upon were highly stratified. They distinguished commoners from nobles, and Spaniards recognized such hierarchical distinctions, which they translated into their own categories and used to further their own interests. Indian town government continued to be led by the nobility long after the conquest.[68] Nobles gained special privileges, such as permission to ride horses and wear Spanish clothing, and exemption from tribute requirements and labor services to Spaniards as long as their lineages survived.[69] Spaniards also married noble Indian women, and used indigenous ranking systems to extend Spanish authority over Indian commoners.

In many respects, the Indian nobility was given a legal status similar to people classified as mestizos. Indeed, one royal decree noted that wearing Spanish clothing "inspired arrogance in [Indian commoners]" and caused them to be easily confused with mestizos and Indian nobles.[70] In a bid to distinguish himself sartorially from commoners, one Indian noble figuratively cloaked himself in Spanishness as he petitioned in late-seventeenth-century Mexico City to wear Spanish clothing. It was argued that he was "fluent in Spanish" and—like the black woman Adriana several decades earlier—that he was brought up by Spaniards. Even more pointedly political claims were made on his behalf: "Ever since it was announced [that Indians could not wear cloaks] there is a great deal of outrageous disorder and common Indians have no respect for noble ones, because all are considered equal . . . among all types of nations persons are distinguished and separated by the quality of the decoration of their clothing or by knowledge of their ancestors; all is ordered not only by divine providence but also by natural and practical law."[71] The phrase "knowing one's ancestors" spoke directly to the importance of lineage in Spanish idea systems, and probably in Indian ones as well. The noble's references to order stemming from divine judgment, as well as from "natural" and "practical" law, also indicate the ways in which Spanish views could be taken up to serve the interests of non-Spanish subjects.

Spanish distinctions between noble and commoner Indians benefitted the nobility. Yet Spaniards also recognized rights of commoners. All Indians were special wards of the crown, and it is important to recognize that although early extirpation campaigns sometimes entailed the removal of children—including that of the nobility—from their parents, Indian families were generally not broken up by the state, even when later concentraciones forced whole villages to relocate. Thus, Indian collectivities were recognized at the familial, community, and political levels.

Sedentary Indians engaged in what to Spanish eyes were recognizable—if seriously misguided—religious rites. Although at first Spanish settlers set out to destroy Indian religious life outright, the official position soon moved to coaxing Indians toward a transformation in beliefs, for at least initially many missionaries viewed them as either "pure" and "true" Christians, as was the Dominican view, or as pre-Christian "meek innocents," as was the Franciscan view.[72] Catechism redirected Indian spirituality, as did the plays that taught Indians to act (often as Spaniards) in dramas with Spanish themes by transforming their outer selves with the help of costumes and makeup. By conveying political, cultural, and religious messages in a highly controlled setting through these plays, missionaries hoped to shape Indians into "reasonable people" who would welcome the triumph of Spanish honor and the Christian tradition.[73]

Sedentary Central Mexican Indians set themselves apart from the nomadic northern Chichimecs, and Spaniards followed suit.[74] In missionary theater, Chichimecs came to stand for Spanish fears and therefore everything the sedentary Central Mexican tribes should reject.[75] Indeed, if sedentary Indians were marginally civilized to the colonizers, then Chichimecs were savages, for they appeared to live in "unstructured groups with no means of exchange, no communication (*conversación*) with other groups, no identifiable social organization and no material culture."[76] Chichimecs threatened Spanish expansion at New Spain's northern frontier. Said to "infest" the roads surrounding Spanish towns and to attack "with inhuman stealth," they moved about "invisibly, like elves (*duendes*),"[77] assaulting churches and priests, Spanish settlers, and the "domestic" Indians and blacks who accompanied them to the region.[78] Colonial officials rendered Chichimecs as "barbarous" Indians (*indios bárbaros*) and cancerous sores on the body politic.[79] Settlers felt free to enslave Chichimecs long after Indian emancipation. In fact, as late as 1672, the king was still issuing special orders demanding freedom for Chichimec slaves.[80]

Anthony Pagden argues that because Africans were not vassals of Spain, the Catholic monarchs took no responsibility for them and did not debate their status.[81] But this position begs the question of why, as David Brion Davis puts it, "certain peoples were always considered more expendable than others."[82] In fact, while the use of Indian slaves was contested almost immediately, even theologians initially took for granted that blacks should take their place. Las Casas himself obtained a license to import black slaves in 1544 while criticizing the taking of Indian slaves "as if [the Indies] were African lands."[83] He appears to have later rejected the notion that blacks deserved enslavement any more than Indians, a position taken as well by his contemporary, the archbishop of Mexico, Alonso de Montúfar.[84] But crown officials never fully addressed the issue.

Religion had helped to abrogate enslavement for Indians, but it actually helped to justify it for blacks. In European thought, blackness was associated with cursed descent from the biblical Canaanites, which "condemned blacks to perpetual bondage."[85] Religious discourse also turned slavery into a kind of penance for blacks' former "savagery." As the Portuguese Jesuit Antonio Vieira informed slaves newly arrived in early-seventeenth-century Brazil, "Jesus himself . . . washed the apostles' feet, [was] sold like a slave by Judas, tied up and flogged like a slave, forced to carry a cross through the streets like a slave, and crucified like a slave."[86] Slaves should "thank God for having removed them 'from the country where [they] and [their] ancestors lived like savages,'" he said, and while their African brethren would "burn in Hell," Brazil's slaves "would go to heaven instead."[87] The religious discourse that made "innocents" out of Indians, thus simultaneously made blacks "guilty." This contrast indicates that the romantic vision of Indians that had already developed in the sixteenth century did not in any way extend to blacks, whom Spaniards as a rule considered unfit for freedom.[88]

Spanish caste terms again offer clues. While Indians were given a sociopolitical designation, Africans were labeled with a color term, *negro*. Covarrubias wrote that "black" was an "unlucky and sad" color, while citing in his definition the proverb "although we are black, we are people."[89] Spaniards thus saw indios as something like themselves, but about blacks they were more ambivalent. As proper nouns, both *español* and *indio* would be capitalized in English, while the noun/adjective *negro* would not. It is for this reason that I do not capitalize black and do capitalize Indian and Spaniard here. To do otherwise would be an anachronistic attempt to equalize what were clearly distinct orders of being in the Spanish imagination.

The nomenclature invented for the "mixed" offspring of Indians, Spaniards, and blacks adds to the impression that blacks were distinct from both Indians and Spaniards. For instance, the word *mestizo*, derived from the Spanish word *mezcla* (mixture), implied that although they were clearly separate, Indians and Spaniards were nevertheless blendable and might successfully mate to create new persons. In contrast, *mulato*,[90] which derives from the word *mulo* (mule), a sterile cross between a donkey and a horse, advances the notion that blacks were of a different kind insofar as the offspring they had with Spaniards or Indians were seen to produce nothing replicable; that is, no lineages.[91]

One reference to a woman as belonging to "the Angolan caste" suggests that African-born blacks, like Indians, were identified with a place.[92] Indeed, slaveholders sometimes attributed their slaves' personal qualities to their geographical origins, as did one who linked his slave's defects (*tachas*) as a "thief," a "runaway," and a "traitor" to the slave's Tierra de Cape birthplace.[93] But, like Mexican-born slaves, "socialized into the racial slavery of the Americas from birth,"[94] African-born ones would have eventually joined the homogeneous ranks of "blacks," whom Spaniards typically stereotyped as naturally belligerent. According to what one Dominican friar told the Lima Inquisition in 1575, in addition to their skin color, an emblem of genealogical sin, blacks were "untameable and bellicose and would disturb themselves and others if they were free."[95]

The notion that free blacks "disturbed" themselves is also apparent from a letter a priest sent to the Mexican Inquisition in 1609.[96] The priest had been sent to evangelize the Gulf Coast runaway slave (*cimarrón*) community, where he found practices he thought were contemptuous of Spanish norms.[97] For instance, although "fish, corn, squashes and fruit" were available, the cimarrones defiantly ate meat on Fridays, Saturdays, and holy days. And although the priest offered to sanction one of their "rebellious" marriages, which he saw as an illicit cohabitation (*amancebamiento*), the cimarrones roundly rejected his gesture. When an emissary from the cimmarón head town came to the village to assess the situation, he became enraged that the villagers had received the priest at all. For his part, the priest tried to soothe the emissary by telling him to "hear mass so that the Lord opens the eyes of your soul."

But the man scornfully replied that he did not want the priest's mass, for the priest was nothing but an "imposter."

Although a very few cimarrón communities were able to survive, generally by accommodating themselves to the demands of the colonial state, cimarrones generally endured in the monte, at the margins of Spanish-controlled territory. Some records of cimarrón activity echo descriptions of Chichimecs. For instance, colonial officials wrote that cimarrones "disturbed" not only themselves, but robbed, assaulted, and murdered "travelers" and Indians alike.[98] They were reported to enter Spanish houses to abduct mulatto and black slaves, whom they presumably carried to freedom.[99] One account states that a group of cimarrones on the southern Pacific Coast lived "as if actually in Guinea," and "threatened" a nearby Indian community.[100] The implication, of course, is that liberated blacks would inevitably revert to their former "savage" state, becoming a danger not only to themselves but also to the social spaces and norms of Spaniards, as well as to the pliant Indians and even to the "domestic blacks" (*negros domésticos*) that Spaniards included in their plans.

Cimarrones were routinely hunted down, often by groups of Spaniards and Indians. Domestic blacks were sometimes made to help, as documented in materials from the Pacific and Gulf coasts, and by the aforementioned priest, who had in fact used his own "domestic" slaves to spy on the cimarrones.[101] Captured runaways and rebellious slaves merited equal punishment, such as mutilations like castration.[102] This procedure was meant to tame as well as to castigate, and of course it confirmed that blacks had no rights to family.

As they instilled the idea that blacks were uncivilized, Spaniards therefore thwarted blacks' claims to group identities. We have already seen that the Spanish woman Francesca blurted out what many Spaniards must have believed about the marriages of their individual slaves. But the slave trade itself broke both community and family bonds, leaving blacks "socially dead" to Spaniards in ways that Indians—however much their internal social differences were erased—were not.[103] Enslavement replaced African kin groups with the authority of Spaniards, who forced Christianity on slaves, claimed them as property and pseudo-kin, and sometimes branded their own names on their slaves' bodies.[104]

The denial to blacks of what Lomnitz calls a "world of their own"[105] gave them and their mulatto offspring particularly liminal positions. This is evident in court proceedings, where all litigants were identified by caste. The inquisitors went a step further than other authorities because they routinely requested genealogical information from litigants. But they explicitly excluded blacks and mulattoes from such inquiries. Sometimes we find notary comments like those regarding the slave Juana Maria de Chaide, who was not asked about her family "for having declared herself a black born in Guinea."[106] When slaves born in the New World were asked their genealogies, they could sometimes trace them to their parents, but not beyond. For instance, María de los Angeles, a mulatto slave woman born and raised in Spain, identified her parents as Don Francisco Esteban de Zuñita de Xerez, "her master and father," and Esperanza, his black Angolan slave, who died when Juana was three. She did not know her paternal grandparents; her "mother's side were blacks from Guinea and she does not know anything of her lineage there," wrote a notary. For their part, the inquisitors "did not ask about her maternal grandparents because she said that her mother was a black Angolan, nor about the rest of her relatives in this line."[107] Free blacks and mulattoes also had a lineage disadvantage. The inquisitors thus deliberately omitted Adriana Ruiz de Cabrera's genealogy from their inquiries into her activities as a witch because, as the notary's record of the proceedings flatly stated, "she is black."

In disregarding her kinship ties, the inquisitors were excluding Adriana from membership in a proper community of persons, a denial that extended to all blacks, regardless of legal status. Yet Adriana still spoke of her mulatto son, and the Spaniard Francesca would not have had to confess had she not had experience with married black slaves.[108] This serves as a reminder that people who often appeared "alone in the world," as Solange Alberro has put it, were not.[109] At the same time, the fact that Spanish officials denied kinship to blacks and mulattoes highlights the importance of lineage in colonial discourse and practice.

Because it was Spanish lineage that elevated one's status, and because lineage could be negotiated through connections other than strict kinship, even blacks might claim a kind of Spanishness. Adriana, as we have seen, symbolically tied her genealogy to the Spanish couple that raised her. More subtly still, she extended her definition of family to include her three slaves, as well as her mulatto son. This perhaps captures the ironies of being a colonial Mexican black slaveholding woman with a genealogy irrelevant because of the infamy of slavery associated with blackness: Adriana makes herself "Spanish" in part by claiming her slaves as "family." She even takes everyone to church! Her claims repudiate the denial of lineage to blacks. But that those claims tied her to

Spaniards and to Spanish moral codes also shows that non-Spaniards had to and could appeal to Spanishness to establish their sanctioned status.

Importantly, the colonial state actually wrote the benefits of connections to Spaniards into law. As an example, black and mulatto women who were married to Spanish men were permitted to wear shawls, although "not luxurious ones."[110] In another instance, the mulatto Joseph Gómez creatively juggled legal norms and lineage when he petitioned for the privilege of carrying weapons because he had a Spanish wife and therefore, according to him, Spanish children.[111]

### THE COLONIAL PYRAMID

Colonial Mexicanists have tended to approach caste as a set of stratified legal rankings resting on pseudo-biological distinctions.[112] Yet attempts to derive social status from such rankings do not accord with the historical evidence.[113] How, for instance, is one to explain why blacks consistently had contact with and power over Indians, even though as a class the latter had a protected status and a higher rank than the former, including freedom from enslavement?[114] Lomnitz reasons that blacks and Indians cannot be organized in a single model of stratification because Indians were legally set apart from non-Indians, while blacks were at the bottom rung of a hierarchy headed by Spaniards.[115] To some extent, the distinction holds, for blacks were in many respects Hispanicized and attached to the Spanish world in ways that most Indians were not, and Indians retained an autonomy that blacks did not enjoy. Yet blacks and Indians also had extensive and systematic contact, and the nature of that contact has to be explained. If the autonomy, freedom, and "difference" of Indians were problems that Spanish settlers were compelled to overcome, and caste was an integrated system of relations and dispositions rather than a series of distinct stations, then we might want to understand colonial society as something of a fluid pyramid, with Spanishness most associated with the Spanish elite at the top, Indianness most associated with the masses of Indian commoners at the bottom, and interstitial spaces most fully inhabited by blacks, mulattoes, and mestizos at various points in between.

We can begin at the bottom by noting that, although legislation might have protected Indians from the most labor-intensive industries, including mining and textile and sugar production, such legislation was only sporadically enforced because labor needs coupled with the expense of black slaves made Indians indispensable. Indians therefore came to perform most unskilled tasks in those industries as well as on haciendas and other Spanish properties.[116] They were often joined by newly enslaved Africans (*bozales*)[117] who, for pragmatic reasons (for instance, lack of Spanish language skills), were also initially incorporated into colonial political economy as unskilled workers.[118]

At the other end of the extreme, the Spanish elite owned virtually all of the estates, plantations, and mines, held all high-level offices, and ran the legal system. Spaniards also owned most of the slaves and employed free blacks, as well as mestizos and mulattoes, many of whom had family ties to Spaniards. Together, these groups acted as specialized workers or supervisors, as majordomos and deputies of Spanish officials, and as assistants and servants of Spaniards. In these capacities, they were pushed into sustained contact with the Indians on whom Spaniards depended for their own prosperity. Sometimes the intermediaries oversaw Indian workers and other unskilled laborers directly.[119] At other times they guarded and benefitted from Spanish political and economic interests, and in even more indirect ways they worked to draw "weak" Indians into spheres of Spanish influence.[120]

Yet, while Spaniards held power, they were also vastly outnumbered. There were probably three times as many blacks, mulattoes, and mestizos as there were Spaniards by the middle of the seventeenth century, and ten times as many Indians.[121] As a result, the colonial pyramid consisted of successive and interpenetrating layers, with the order of each layer inversely related to its volume. Prestige and authority flowed from the relatively small Spanish top to the vast Indian base, wending its way through the middle layers of mestizos, mulattoes, and blacks. As one seventeenth-century Indian noble lamented, "From the priests and corregidores to the vilest negro and mestizo [everyone] beats [the Indians] and mistreats them."[122]

The political philosopher Hannah Arendt proposed a pyramid model for the Christian type of authoritarian rule that developed during the Middle Ages. As she writes, "the seat of power is filtered down to the base in such a way that each successive layer possesses some authority, but less than the one above it, and . . . precisely because of this careful filtering process, all layers from top to bottom are not only firmly integrated into the whole but are interrelated like converging rays whose common focal point is the top of the pyramid."[123] Arendt perhaps overemphasizes consensus and conformity. And of course she does not attend to the pyramid's inversion in the Mexican case, as Indians became the producers of the witchcraft that undermined Spanish power. But Arendt's important focus on filtering and the circulation of authority does emphasize the way hierarchy works to "incorporate inequality and distinction as its all-permeating principles."[124] In her model, then, inequality, distinction, and integration together characterize the formation of power, which is diffused and consolidated at the same time. Hierarchy is therefore not so much about separation and isolation as it is about the relational nature of its layers.

Arendt notes that the source of authority for her model actually lay outside of it.[125] That source was the Christian God, who also commanded the pyramid in Mexico, where crown legitimacy had sacred foundations and where all of the castes, including Indians, were theoretically part of the Christian world. However, because religion, like caste itself, joined non-Spaniards to Spaniards without making them equal to them, it served as another way for Spaniards to maintain the pyramid as a "natural" hierarchy of "superior, middle and inferior ranks."[126]

## THE COLONIAL STATE, LEGAL ORGANIZATION, AND SOCIAL REALITIES

As in other early modern colonial centers, New Spain's legal environment was at first characterized by "legal pluralism," defined by Lauren Benton as the coexistence between, and overlapping jurisdictions of, colonial and indigenous, or metropolitan and local, legal institutions and customs.[127] But, as Susan Kellogg has shown, by the end of the sixteenth century pluralism and respect for Indian custom in such areas as property and inheritance had already given way to Spanish rhetoric and procedures.[128]

Legal institutions that emerged in Spain prior to the sixteenth century were closely tied to the centralizing state and to a Spanish national identity given definition through the Inquisition that simultaneously constructed and condemned Jewish and Muslim "deviance."[129] Similar processes characterized English state formation and the making of English citizens, especially during the crucial late-sixteenth-century Elizabethan consolidation.[130] A national identity was not yet at issue in New Spain, and some of the cultural processes Phillip Corrigan and Derek Sayer identify as central to English state formation might be more fully applicable to later periods of Mexican history.[131] Nevertheless, colonial state law became hegemonic in New Spain as judicial institutions produced and regulated subjects through overlapping moral and civil codes. These codes must be read for their symbolic content, as well as for their overt protection of elite interests.[132]

Theoretically, the colonial Mexican judiciary was to apply what Peggy Liss calls Spain's "mania for order."[133] At base, it policed the caste system integral to colonial political economy by maintaining distinctions that reflected what colonial texts refer to as "the differences between people" and "respect for Spaniards."[134] Although, as Cope points out, much of this caste legislation was ineffective or "activated (for brief periods of time) in moments of crisis,"[135] it nevertheless organized, classified, and quantified populations through registries and produced endless statutes stating peoples' rights and obligations.[136] Laws dictated who could ride a horse, who could carry a weapon, where people could live, and who was to participate in work drafts, as well as how those drafts would be organized. Laws also produced "outlaws" by defining and persecuting vagabondage and idleness (which English Elizabethans considered "the mother of all vices").[137] They determined how populations would be shifted to benefit Spanish enterprises; what constituted sobriety (sometimes coupled with religious purity) as *peyote* was banned and *pulque* regulated;[138] and which sexual acts and marital patterns were transgressive, such as sodomy, bigamy, and common-law unions. Finally, the legal system included prisons to hold those who violated social norms.

Because of their special legal status, Indians were separated juridically from non-Indians through the tribunals of the General Indian Court.[139] Although many Indian legal cases never went beyond provincial courts, the General Indian Court was a court of the first instance in the capital and surrounding areas, and an appeals court for cases outside of that jurisdiction.[140] It heard Indian complaints against local magistrates, appeals of their decisions, and suits brought by Indians against Indian defendants. Its findings and decisions were signed by the viceroy, New Spain's highest judicial and administrative authority.[141] The viceroy also directly handled Indian cases considered administrative (such as land petitions and grievances against officials), along with criminal and civil suits initiated by Indians but involving non-Indian defendants.[142] In addition, the viceroy was president of the *audiencia* (Royal High Court). Its civil and criminal chambers[143] heard non-Indian complaints and criminal cases against Indians.[144] (These were rare because, as Viceroy Velasco wrote to Philip II, Indians were usually victims rather than defendants in cases involving non-Indians.[145]) An ecclesiastical court, also subject to viceregal authority, heard matters regarding church doctrine, family law, and clergy.[146]

The Inquisition was the only legal body officially outside of viceregal control, although inquisitors could not openly challenge the viceroy.[147] Inquisition tribunals had spread with Spaniards to every part of the New World, and New Spain's reached the height of its activity in the mid-seventeenth century.[148] Indians had been released from its jurisdiction when the formal tribunal was established toward the end of the sixteenth century, in part because they were newly converted, "weak, and of little substance," as one priest wrote.[149] But even newly converted blacks, along with Hispanicized ones, were — together with mulattoes, mestizos, and Spaniards themselves — vulnerable.[150]

As was the case in seventeenth-century England and in Spain itself, colonial Mexican church and state identities and goals "echoed back" on each other.[151] The Inquisition was especially enmeshed in upholding moral order and its civil implications, and it is the institution that perhaps best speaks to church/state interpenetrations. Like its Spanish counterpart, the Mexican Inquisition was to guard royal and aristocratic privilege from the encroachment of newly wealthy elites, and the Catholic faith against heresy and blasphemy. It policed lineages and behaviors that challenged state and church authority, punishing idolatry, Protestantism, Judaizing, and "unnatural" practices like bigamy, polygamy, same-sex acts, prostitution, cohabitation, pacts with the devil, witchcraft, fortune-telling, astrology, and superstition, which, though milder, fell under the same category as witchcraft.[152]

The Spanish Inquisition developed an overtly political function in tandem with the centralizing state, shifting its attention from the witchcraft closely associated with women to the religious heterodoxy of conversos, moriscos, and, later, Protestants. In New Spain, however, Protestants and Judaizers were less of a threat, and the Inquisition there maintained a focus on witchcraft which, as in England, was considered to be an affront to the "godly state."[153] Mexican witches were tried consistently during the sixteenth and seventeenth centuries, and the relatively few suspected Judaizers only during the last decades of the sixteenth century and briefly during the middle of the seventeenth.[154] As in Spain, witchcraft in Mexico was a shortcoming usually attributed to women. But as Spaniards consolidated their control in New Spain, witchcraft was also associated with the non-Spanish castes, and practitioners were often male.[155]

Despite its central role in regulating morality, the Mexican Inquisition was constantly on the verge of bankruptcy. It had few personnel for the vast territory it covered.[156] It often failed to investigate the denunciations and testimonies that poured in, and inquisitors neglected their duty to exhort confessions and offer consolation to prisoners like Adriana, who languished in damp and noxious dungeons.[157] Indeed, the colonial Spanish position on witchcraft was ambivalent in other ways. During most of the colonial period Indians were not under the Inquisition's jurisdiction, and a high proportion of witchcraft accusations were never even brought to trial, particularly when defendants were women. This was especially true in later periods when the witchcraft of women came to be more consistently seen as superstition born from ignorance and a lack of good sense.[158] In the final analysis, then, although women and Indians were the classes most consistently associated with supernaturalism and therefore with threats to the sanctioned order, they also had to be excused from the consequences of their own ignorance because of their imputed weakness.

The contradictions in colonial perspectives and policies highlight methodological problems, especially with respect to Indians, who almost never appear as defendants or plaintiffs in Inquisition litigation and are not on the descriptive covers of Inquisition manuscripts. This has probably contributed to the erroneous belief that there are no Indians in Inquisition cases,[159] for their presence cannot be gleaned from a glance at the index housed in the AGN. But even if Indians were not persecuted directly, Inquisition transcripts are nevertheless full of Indian witches, healers, diviners, and devil's advocates.[160] The consistent presence of Indians in Inquisition cases is due to several factors. First, while bishops no longer acted as inquisitors after 1571, they did continue to rely on the Inquisition to investigate Indian idolatry.[161] Church authority over Indians was therefore confused as Inquisition investigations of Indians continued throughout the colonial period.[162]

Second, and more importantly, Indians were at the center of the social forces that developed around witchcraft, and were continuously implicated in the witchcraft of non-Indians. In fact, the documentation often registers second order acts of witchcraft, that is, the witchcraft of those who both directly and indirectly had received powders, herbs, instructions, and cures from Indians who charged money for their services. These Indians were not chimerical. They were often named and placed, their relationships to plaintiffs and defendants were described, and although they were not punished, they were sometimes called before the inquisitors to testify about their actions and the contours of their moral universe. All of this might be surprising if we take the Inquisition's lack of authority over Indians to mean that the Inquisition had no contact with them. But it is less surprising if we realize that the point was not for the Inquisition to punish Indians; it was rather for the Inquisition to "correct" others who made use of witchcraft, a process which inevitably involved Indians.

All told, the people who came before the courts were often entangled outside of the courtroom in ways that did not necessarily accord with bureaucratic structures. Because individuals of different castes, who might have been subject to different forms of justice, were so entangled, attempts to separate persons juridically were bound to meet with failure. In reality, then, judicial activities and the documents they produced speak as much to the disorder of social life as they do to the regiment of rule.

The functional separation of judicial units itself also defied the Spanish mania for order.[163] First, the responsibilities of the colonial courts sometimes overlapped. For example, Indian administrative business had technically been removed from the audiencia's jurisdiction and made the responsibility of the viceroy by the mid-sixteenth century, but conflicts over jurisdiction prevailed for decades after.[164] As another example, secular, ecclesiastical, and Inquisition authorities all ostensibly oversaw slaveholders' treatment of their slaves.[165] Because of such overlaps, proceedings sometimes focused on jurisdiction rather than on the merits of a case.[166] Second, texts could include aspects of both sanctioned and unsanctioned "crimes" because such crimes were mutually invoking and provoking — that is, witchcraft occurred in tandem with secular violence. And because witchcraft challenged not only church morality but also ate at the activities and identities sanctioned by the state/church, it fell under the Inquisition's jurisdiction while seeping also into the secular courts.[167] Third, confusion occasionally arose over how an incident should be legally defined. This happened, for instance, when the Indian Domingo de la Cruz of Tulancingo was beaten nearly to death by two mulattoes who accused him of refusing to cure an Indian woman they alleged he had bewitched. When Domingo complained of the beating to the local alcalde mayor, the Inquisition had to inquire into his activities as a witch before the gravity of the mulattoes' crime could be determined.[168]

As he sought justice in the early morning hours following the beating, Domingo appealed to the authorities by referring to himself as a "vassal of the king" who was owed protection. His words and actions expose another crucial set of issues: as legal forums became widespread and accessible during the sixteenth and seventeenth centuries, New Spain saw a range of people develop the quite astonishing "habit" of litigation as they negotiated state controls, their rights, and the state's definition of who they were while narrating the social strategies that took place both inside and outside of the courtroom.[169] This is not to deny that Spanish men controlled the courts and therefore the contexts in which social relations were represented in them, nor that courts favored certain classes of people over others. Agents patrolled the streets looking for malefactors, and individuals often came to the Inquisition to confess after hearing an Edict of Grace, or were victims of serious charges of heresy.[170] But many people caught up in everyday and not-so-everyday problems saw judicial forums as a way of putting their consciences to rest, of negotiating their rights, and of settling interpersonal disputes.[171]

As in other regions of the colonial world, in New Spain the shift from legal pluralism to state-run judiciaries was in fact in part precipitated not by the "top down" imposition of the state on subject peoples but rather from the actions of litigants themselves, who strengthened state control through "forum shopping," and appeals to the "highest representatives of imperial authority."[172] As litigants appealed to such representatives, the state gained more influence and the monopoly on determining the "truth" that came with that influence.[173] In the process, state courts became potent sources of hegemony, for in confirming the importance of caste, that each caste had rights and that such rights were negotiable, they probably deflected more radical attacks on the system.[174]

Indians were especially notable litigators.[175] But, as we have already seen, free blacks threatened each other with the Inquisition; together with mulattoes and mestizos they also argued for the right to carry weapons and other privileges. Slaves petitioned for their freedom and complained of ill-treatment by their masters. They also sometimes tried to punish those masters by reporting them to the authorities as heretical Judaizers veiled as "Portuguese."[176] Slaves also denounced each other for blasphemy and witchcraft.[177] Although most women, Spanish or not, were prohibited from litigating on their own, they often voluntarily confessed to witchcraft and found ways to air grievances against other parties, as we saw Ana María do. Sometimes women directly approached the justices. More commonly, they testified through priests, officials, or male relatives, thus establishing their sanctioned legitimacy by affiliating themselves with Spanish men.

Although we have no way of knowing what percentage of the population actually made use of the courts at any given time, and cannot specify the exact relationship between the textual narratives and lives lived outside of court, the fact that even Indians, slaves, and women litigated, shows that a legal consciousness had permeated the pyramid as people used courts for the expression and negotiation of power and identity through the language and enactment of caste.[178] Not everyone was equal. But the appearance of justice encouraged a variety of people to believe they had a stake in the system.


COURT PROCEEDINGS

The available documentation ranges from regulations, petitions, and summaries of oral proceedings to initial inquiries and full-scale reports with testimony, counter-testimony, arguments by counsel, ratifications, and sometimes sentencing. Full-scale proceedings produced the richest and most complex testimonies, but initial inquiries and criminal and civil complaints, as well as Inquisition confessions / denunciations that were never pursued, are also good sources because they constitute succinct statements of issues more fully elaborated in trial proceedings.[179]

The Inquisition and secular courts used similar personnel, but Inquisition judges were also prosecutors. In addition, while secular judges focused on the facts of a case and on punishment, inquisitors were more concerned with moral instruction.[180] Trials typically began with complaints. But Inquisition hearings could be prompted by confessions, in which case no trial was necessary. If an investigation was undertaken and a case built (the standard formula being three witnesses for the prosecution), the accused was arrested. The Inquisition confiscated its defendants' money and belongings, which were used to cover court costs and to support the defendant while he or she was in jail. Inventories of these goods were recorded, and they were often part of trial records, as they were of Adriana's.[181] Justice was relatively swift in criminal and civil trials, and for Indian complaints.[182] Inquisition defendants like Adriana, however, could languish for months in dungeons as testimony was repeatedly entered by plaintiffs and defendants. Special attorneys and advocates aided the poor, Indians, and slaves,[183] and defendants could answer the testimony of plaintiffs and witnesses. But the inquisitors shrouded everything in secrecy by withholding from the accused the names of witnesses and plaintiffs until after sentencing. Yet, while secrecy might have instilled fear, defendants often had a good idea of who their accuser might be, as Adriana did.

Defendants were immediately told the charges in civil and criminal suits, but in Inquisition ones they were not. Inquisitors first asked defendants to "search [their] conscience."[184] They then moved to open-ended questions regarding a person's knowledge of crimes she had committed against the faith. If the defendant said she did not know, the inquisitors admonished that "the Holy Office did not arrest people unless it had sufficient information." If the accused still did not answer, they read the denunciation and solicited her response to specific points.

Because the inquisitors did not initially reveal the charges, people often confessed to failings that had nothing to do with the original complaint, as when Adriana admitted to incest in her youth. Witnesses, including character ones, also added information, much of it only tangentially related to the charge. The most effective witnesses in all kinds of venues were Spanish men, such as the priests who defended Adriana's reputation. But many different kinds of people testified, even, at times, slaves. In the end a variety of factors, including physical evidence recorded by notaries, influenced the outcome of a trial.[185]

Torture to extract confessions was uncommon in the New World, and it was never used against witches.[186] Although confession without torture could be the last resort for an accused witch who had suffered a stay in an Inquisition jail and was willing to exchange punishment for freedom, people like Adriana might also uphold their innocence in the face of extreme discomfort and coercion. Moreover, authorities did not always believe confessions, and they sometimes reexamined defendants. Sentences handed down by the different tribunals included forced labor, fines, and lashes. But the secular courts often resorted to incarceration in jails or obrajes, and punishments meted out by the Inquisition for witchcraft offenses ranged widely.[187] The institution's "instruction" could and did include death.[188] Yet in contrast to witches in early modern France and Germany, New Spain's witches never suffered such a fate, and neither did Spanish ones after the early sixteenth century. In Spain, witches were often "rehabilitated" by forced removal to villages where their "unsavory reputation was not known."[189] In New Spain, punishment included the occasional whipping, but more often fines, public confessions and humiliation, temporary exile, and confinement to the feminized spaces of home, church, and hospital.[190]

## READING THE TEXTS

Secular judges were more interested in what a defendant might have done, while inquisitors were more concerned with the defendant's moral world and motivations.[191] Because of the inquisitors' broader concerns, Inquisition texts as a class are longer and more detailed than their secular counterparts.[192] Historians of Europe have long used stories from a range of inquisition tribunals to reconstruct popular belief systems.[193] Many emphasize the forums inquisitors provided for giving voice to the voiceless and the accuracy with which Inquisition notaries recorded testimony.[194] Emmanuel Le Roy Ladurie, for instance, draws attention to the "direct testimony" of French peasants meticulously recorded by the inquisitors.[195] Such approaches can be criticized for ignoring the context of power in which the texts were produced,[196] but many Inquisition scholars have nevertheless approached the texts in measured ways, emphasizing neither their verity nor their falsity, but rather their multilayered representations.[197]

Those representations evolved in contested situations bounded by the very categories they reveal. Thus, in colonial Mexico, people negotiated meanings and strategies around caste as they acted out their participation in a hierarchical community of subjects in front of Spanish justices. Through the tensions between authority and its questioning we learn something about Spanishness as well as about the other caste identities and qualities that developed against and around it. Thus, it is because of, rather than in spite of, the context in which they were produced, that the records offer insight into caste. Moreover, while trials did not take place on neutral ground and the cultural meanings they generated were not uniform, the records nevertheless contain a necessarily shared language because people of all backgrounds had to communicate with each other in court. The texts therefore indicate what people were capable of and interested in expressing in a particular context, how they responded to one another, and what terms and meanings were central to the debate. The trick in studying them is to manage the tension between the texts as "constructed" and as historiographic "windows" on peoples' lives.[198]

Translation is a major interpretive difficulty, in no small part because most of New Spain's Indian subjects did not speak Spanish.[199] Officials met this and other linguistic challenges by providing interpreters.[200] An early royal decree also tried to ensure fair hearings for Indians by allowing them to bring "Christian" (Spanish-speaking) friends to court. The best-intentioned translations are inherently problematic, however, because often there is no primary equivalency in meaning between words, which both reflect and map social worlds. The use of interpreters might also have encouraged the tendency to summarize portions of reports rather than to record what was said verbatim, and summaries were standard procedure for Indian cases heard by the viceroy.[201] When testimony was in a language other than Spanish, it was virtually always recorded in Spanish in the material under question here. We therefore have no way of comparing, for instance, material in Nahuatl with its Spanish equivalent. Indian "friends" who spoke Spanish were also not always faithful to Indian plaintiffs and defendants, and Spanish-language statements given by Indians often suffered from the imposition by clerks of Spanish stylistic conventions, which reshaped those statements by making the wording conform to that of native Spanish speakers.[202]

Nevertheless, attempts to capture and affirm what people said indicate Spanish attention to accuracy, as well as the desire to ensure fairness by gathering and transcribing all of the available evidence.[203] The elaborate appeals process might have also been meant to promote what Spaniards considered just for all. Moreover, court personnel routinely read back what notaries had written as they solicited ratifications from defendants and witnesses. Even the notary foibles and personalities attested to in the documentation by misspellings and written asides in the margins add authenticity by suggesting that notaries were not producing records according to a singular standard.

In the end, of course, we cannot gauge how freely ratifications were given nor how accurately the texts we have in hand reflect what was said in court. Non-Spanish speakers could not challenge a scribe's accuracy. And even those who spoke Spanish but, like Adriana, were not literate, might affirm what the Inquisition notary *read*, but could not corroborate that with the written account. In short, because no one wrote their own words, unmediated written testimony—especially by nonliterate peoples, Spanish-speaking or not—did not exist, even in the secular court documentation that routinely goes unquestioned by scholars.

But the presence of mediation in these texts does not mean that they were fabricated by court personnel,[204] or that Spanish-language texts cannot teach us about non-Spanish speakers. Serge Gruzinski offers us the important reminder that although no colonial voice can be "dissociated from European modes of expression" neither can it be from "the colonial situation," which was shaped by the world views of both colonizers and colonized.[205] In this respect, the documentation speaks to what William Hanks calls, with reference to colonial Mayan texts, "hybrid discourses" created out of conquest.[206] As a measure of colonialism itself, hybridity is key to reading Spanish-language texts and even indigenous-language ones, many of which follow Spanish legal and writing conventions but are nevertheless privileged by some ethnohistorians for what is considered their more direct reflection of Indian beliefs.[207]

The problem of translation is thus really the problem of colonialism itself, and it goes beyond the practical to embrace broader problems of interpretation—mine as well as that of colonial interpreters and notaries. I try to remain faithful to the original texts, and to privilege the voices of my "informants" as they are recorded in those texts.[208] From my perspective, one cannot examine the events and beliefs described in the records without considering the context of the courtroom, and the justices with whom litigants interacted, as well as the structures and conventions of the world beyond the courtroom. In this sense, the texts perhaps best capture what Derek Sayer calls individuals' "performances" of "the lie that is 'the state.'" As he writes, "[Individuals'] beliefs are neither here nor there," but "believers or not, participants are by their very actions affirming the power of what is sanctioned."[209] The fabric of the state, of Spanishness, and its determination of authority were, one might then say, insinuated in the very "truth" of court performances. Whatever those performances reveal about consciousness, authenticity, and beliefs, they surely speak profoundly to that ambivalent social reality Taussig refers to as the "sweaty warm space between the arse of him who rides and the back of him who carries."[210]

# 2

# The Roads Are Harsh

## SPANIARDS AND INDIANS IN

## THE SANCTIONED DOMAIN

Let us now turn to the story told by Ursula de Castañeda, a Spanish woman who, in 1643, was living in Xochimilco, a village just south of Mexico City. Ursula approached the criminal court on her own to report about an altercation she had with a mulatto named Juan de Agilera, his Indian mother, Juana Bautista, and another Indian woman named Angelina.[1] The courage it took to do this must have stemmed from her faith that the justices would believe her version of what had happened, for she might have been a woman but she was also a Spaniard like them. The justices did respond swiftly, first arresting and then fining the mulatto Juan. But they also they left Juan's Indian mother free and even allowed her to speak in her son's defense. The narrative that unfolds in court documents has much to say about the nature of Spanish authority, as well as sanctioned caste performances and meanings.

Ursula told the justices that she had been in her house the previous day, quietly nursing one of her children, when the defendants arrived at her door. According to Ursula, they demanded to know if she had accused them of stealing, and then selling, a hen belonging to her sister, Magdalena. When Ursula affirmed that she had done so, the defendants beat her badly, giving her, in her own words, "many slaps about my body and face, leaving me all black and blue." If her sister and her father had not come to her aid, she continued, "[the mulatto and the Indians] would have killed me out of hatred and anger."

Most of Ursula's indignation seems to have derived from the social rather than from the physical wounds she claimed to have suffered. As she explained, "they injured me with dishonorable words . . . they committed grave crimes worthy of punishment because I am a married woman and a noble and honorable one. They are mulattoes [*sic*] and Indian people, vile and low." According to one Spanish witness, Juan had even declared to Ursula that he and the Indians were "better" than she. Ursula's husband had not been at the scene of the crime, but he testified anyway. His wife was "Spanish," he pointed out, and a "noble person," defiled and degraded in particular by the "vile" and "lowly" mulatto, who had dared to mistreat a woman of such "quality" as his.

Under questioning, the mulatto Juan denied that he had attacked Ursula, although he did admit that he knew her. When the justices summoned his Indian mother, she defended her son by insisting that his imprisonment reflected "favoritism" toward the Spaniards. The accusations had scant basis, she contended, because all of the witnesses—many of whom were not even present at the scene—were Ursula's "intimate friends," including Hernán Pérez, her father and accomplice. Other Indian witnesses corroborated Juana's testimony, adding that Ursula had tried to bribe them into testifying on her behalf. A priest then came to the mulatto's defense. He contended that the suit should be dismissed because Ursula did not have her husband's permission to bring it.

The defense countered Ursula's story by insisting that Juana had gone to Ursula's house in search of bread and candles to buy, and that the Spaniards had attacked her for an unstated cause. In this version, Juan ran to his mother's aid, as did a Spanish woman named Leonor de Abiego who had been visiting Juana's home when Juana left for Ursula's. Leonor was Juana's co-mother (*comadre*).[2] This was a fictive kin relationship marked by mutual obligation as well as lineage symbolism. It is unclear whether Leonor was Juan's godmother (*madrina*) or even whether the comadre relationship between Leonor and Juana was formalized, but Leonor and Juana were obviously close. Indeed, shortly after Juana had departed for Ursula's house, a young Indian girl had come straight to Leonor, shouting "Ma'am Leonor de Abiego, go to Ursula de Castañeda's house, for she is beating and mistreating your comadre." When she arrived at Ursula's, Leonor found that Juan was tied up and that Ursula and Hernán were beating Juana. Leonor positioned herself between the Spaniards and the Indian. As she did so, she advised the Spaniards that "it looked bad to be mistreating natives."

They ignored her, however, and continued to flog Juana. At one point, they called her "an old whore witch" (*una puta vieja hechisera* [*sic*]), thus associating the Indian with a feminized sexual and religious immorality.

The different phases and facets of this dispute expose the broader politics of sanctioned gender and caste principles. Ursula, a Spaniard, was the principal plaintiff, but her gender subordination was highlighted by the priest's objection to the suit she had initiated without her husband's permission and by the fact that her husband spoke on her behalf. Similarly, the Indian Juana's caste subordination was signified by the Spanish woman Leonor speaking on her behalf, as well as by the beating she endured. From one angle, then, Ursula and Juana occupied analogous structural positions, for both were women with "weak" voices and both had to appeal to their kin or fictive kin of a higher status: Ursula-the-Spanish-woman therefore linked herself to her Spanish husband, who spoke to her "value"; Juana-the-Indian-woman's most vocal advocate was her Spanish comadre Leonor, who spoke to her innocence, and therefore to her credibility. As in Adriana's case, a Spanish priest also came to the defendant's aid. Yet Ursula might have won had two witnesses to her bribery not come forward.

Leonor defended Juana in part by speaking for Spanishness in general when she admonished that "it looked bad to be mistreating natives." Her reprimand did not rest on her personal relationship to Juana; she did not, for instance, say "stop beating *this* woman because she is *my* comadre." Instead, she made Juana stand for all "natives," while she, Ursula, and Ursula's relatives, stood for all "Spaniards." Her statement seems a bit extraordinary if, as Nicholas Dirks observes, colonialism is a "trope for domination and violation."[3] What do we learn from Leonor's words about what colonialism was like in Mexico? To whom did it look bad to be mistreating the natives? Why did it look bad? Why would a Spanish woman admonish other Spaniards? Why would she defend an Indian?

At base, Leonor's comment reflected inherent contradictions of Spanish rule. That rule was characterized by the ongoing abuse typified by Ursula and her family, but it also spoke paternalistically to Indian defenselessness and to Spaniards' roles as providers of justice in both its narrow and broader senses, the position Leonor and the justices who left Juana free upheld. Philosophical and theological dimensions of this contradiction have been explored by others.[4] My purpose here, however, is to situate the paradox in the day-to-day life of the colony by explaining the logic of violence and connecting it to the logic of Spanish protection, both of which rested on colonial understandings that Indians were weak. That weakness was linked in the Spanish mind to Indian indolence, which produced a range of "bad" behaviors from laziness to witchcraft introduced by a devil who provoked breaches in rules of sanctioned comportment and undermined "proper" production. The acts and comments of Ursula and her cohorts—who beat the Indian but also conflated her sexual and supernatural faults with derogatory claims that she was an "old whore witch"—speak with violence to this consequence of Indian frailty.

## THE WEAKNESS OF INDIANS: THE CREATION OF SEPARATE REPUBLICS

The missionaries who accompanied Spanish conquistadors to New Spain set out to evangelize their new charges with firm conviction grounded in teleology and prophetic history.[5] Some missionary writings—such as those of Diego Durán and Bernardino de Sahagún—"prefigured an ethnographic process" as they described Indian customs and history in order to facilitate conversion.[6] The writings are still of ethnographic interest[7] even though (or perhaps because) they blended the exotic Indian both chronologically and ideologically with the European past and the colonial present, as they assimilated Indian customs to cultural and historical traditions familiar to Spaniards trying to make sense of their own presence and purpose in the New World.[8]

Sahagún hoped to replace European Christianity and the "Spanish way of life" with a new church peopled by the "good savages" of the New World living in their "golden state."[9] For him and for other Franciscans, Indians were "innocents," and the wholesale destruction of Indians and things Indian that came with conquest therefore called for a policy of indirect crown rule that would bypass the vices of the colonists to reach Indians through their own elites.[10] The Franciscan Gerónimo de Mendieta, who was one of the most vocal proponents for the separation of Indians and Spaniards in the colony, wrote in the same vein. For he believed that "the Indian with respect to the Spaniard is like a small dog in front of a mighty lion. The Spaniards have all the evil desire and the strength to destroy all the Indians of New Spain, if they were ever given the chance . . . The Indian is so phlegmatic and meek that he would not hurt a fly. Consequently, one must always assume in case of doubt that the Spaniard is the offender and the Indian is the victim."[11] Mendieta then called for "two republics, two nations—the Spanish and the Indian" that would "never live together."[12] Many missionaries favored such a division in the hope that it would protect Indian autonomy and facilitate the conversion process. These two issues were connected insofar as, in the view of some missionaries, common Spaniards not only thoughtlessly exploited Indians. They also morally corrupted them.[13]

Crown and church interests in New Spain initially coincided in the issue of Indian separation from Spaniards. Through the New Laws, the crown had reined in the excessive demands of settlers. Through the nominal creation of two republics, subject to different regulations and expectations, it established its authority over Indians. The two republics were not strictly geographical entities, yet the Indian Republic (*república de los indios*) roughly corresponded to Indian rural villages and the Spanish Republic (*república de los españoles*) to Spanish urban areas. Angel Rama's contention that New World cities were the physical incarnation of social ideas can thus be expanded to include the countryside.[14] Beyond their spatial significance, however, the two republics also symbolized what for Spaniards seemed different ways of life: the barbaric and the civilized; the irresponsible and the responsible; the pagan and the Christian; that of *gente sin razón* (people without reason) and that of *gente de razón* (people of reason).[15]

In practice, the notion of two republics defended Indian political structures and autonomy as long as Spanish interests continued to be served and legislation was developed to protect Indian communities from outsiders. For a time, many of those communities continued to be self-contained and self-governing, with their own strategies for resisting incursions of outsiders or even for incorporating them into their internal politics.[16] Yet, in legislating Indian protection, the state also imposed uniformity by creating "Indians" out of what had been separate polities, and by homogenizing disparate native legal traditions so that Indians could not independently resist infringement by settlers or profoundly influence colonial policy on their own terms.[17]

The idea of two republics also brought to a head essential contradictions between material and philosophical ideals: while protection of Indians through separation from Spaniards was in theory the objective, especially for the early friars, in practice it was impossible to achieve. Indians were the principal labor and tribute source that Spaniards, including the crown, depended on for their own fortune. The state thus came to acknowledge limited indigenous autonomy while keeping Indian communities in "a condition most amenable to official control."[18]

Peter Wade notes that "indians were often treated extremely badly" despite the fact that they had a special relationship to colonial officialdom and bureaucracy.[19] In part this was because Indian autonomy and rights came continuously under attack. As they did, the ideal of the two republics broke down, and Indians effectively became an estate within colonial society.[20] As such, they were subject not only to Castilian laws and institutions but also to the "barbarous" practices of such Spaniards as Ursula, Magdalena, and Hernán. It might indeed have "looked bad" that these Spaniards were beating Indians, as Leonor pointed out, but such behavior can also be read as perfectly logical given the conflicting aims of crown policy and the interests of colonizers. Leonor's intervention was equally logical, however, because it embodied the protective side of sanctioned Spanish authority. Such protection rested on charitable crown and church policies meant to defend Indians, including the establishment of the General Indian Court and the release of Indians from the Inquisition; the emancipation of Indian slaves in the middle of the sixteenth century; and Indians' general status as the king's most "miserable" of vassals, which in theory excluded them from the more arduous work situations.

## "IT LOOKS BAD TO BE MISTREATING NATIVES"

By the middle of the seventeenth century, Spaniards were settled densely next to Indians in New Spain's cities and in many parts of the Central Valley countryside.[21] Judicial records from this period include hundreds of directives outlining the boundaries meant to be enforced between the Indian Republic and the Spanish one as Indian autonomy and rights eroded.[22] These directives forbade persons such as muleteers (*harrieros*) with business in Indian villages from staying for more than three days at a time; and Spaniards, as well as their black, mulatto, and mestizo slaves, servants, overseers, deputies, and majordomos, from residing in or holding office in Indian villages. Indians protested often and loudly about their encounters with Spaniards. Whether or not these encounters represented the norms of daily life, they were consistently pernicious to Indians, as contemporary observers and modern historians alike have noted.

Although the overall patterns of Indian complaints are well known, they hold to several consistent themes that can be highlighted here: Spaniards stole from Indians; they forced Indians to work against their will without pay; they kept them in debt and destroyed their land; and they caused whole villages to empty as the inhabitants fled into the hills. Indian grievances were widespread, both geographically and chronologically. We can begin in 1590, when an Indian official from the Tututepec region, which was to the northeast of Tulancingo, lamented that his village was "dying" from agents of the Spanish onslaught:

> The governor, *alcaldes* and community of Cayuca have told me how a Spaniard named Ju(an) Martin has a ranch outside the village. On his own authority and against the will of the natives he enters their houses and takes them to serve him each week and he pays them for eight days two *tomines* [a unit of currency] and others he does not pay at all. He mistreats them and beats them. There are few of them and they are poor. They could not tolerate him and they had no legal support nor anyone to favor them. This was the reason that the village was dying.[23]

In the same year, the Spanish alcalde mayor of the mining town of Tasco, in what is now northern Guerrero, was ordered to expel two Spaniards residing illegally in the Indian village of Tetipac. The Spaniards customarily "annoyed" and mistreated the Indians, "taking their hens and other things by force and beating them and entering their houses and loading things up by errand boys and making them give them hay and other things as their horses and mules eat and destroy [the Indians'] fields."[24]

Three years later, several Spaniards, along with "the people" residing within the boundaries of their farms and estates, attempted to persuade the Indians of Zinacantepec, located just west of Toluca, to take money in advance, thus landing them in debt and perpetual bondage to the Spaniards. "They take them from their quietude and treat them like slaves and take them to the haciendas," read the complaint.[25] That same year, Indians from the Ometepec region of what is today southeastern Guerrero reported that cattle ranchers from Mexico City had let loose on their land 100,000 head of cattle (surely an exaggeration), destroying their crops and causing several small villages to empty out. The authorities sent a delegation to determine the extent of the damages.[26]

In 1620, Indians from several north-central Oaxacan villages recounted how two Spaniards had "entered the villages at night, stirring them up and taking an Indian man and an Indian woman . . . to the mines, because of which [the Indians] have left their villages and houses and moved to the mountains."[27] From the city of Cholula, a mid-seventeenth-century account declares that "in this city and its surroundings, many Spaniards on farms and cattle ranches . . . customarily take Indians from the city against their will, using them and doing other annoying things to them." Appealing to crown authority by reminding the justices of the king's obligation to his most "miserable" vassals, the Indian plaintiffs pointed out that "all of this is against what his majesty has ordered."[28]

Royal obligation showed itself again as the crown responded to Indian complaints against its own officials and those of the church. Sympathizers like Viceroy Martín Enríquez would document the grounds for such complaints noting, for example, that "the Indians, as miserable people who have no resistance" were being mistreated even by friars, corregidores, and their agents.[29] In response, Philip II directed his viceroys to gather information pertaining to the "excesses of the corregidores and other officials . . . the harm and annoyances [they] cause . . . especially to the Indians."[30] Later crown decrees regularly named almost every type of Spanish official, including alcaldes mayores, priests, deputies (*tenientes*), prelates (*prelados*), and attorneys (*letrados*).[31] Rather than helping the Indians, the king repeatedly protested, those who were responsible for their well-being had become their "worst enemies." A typical decree reads as follows: "The attorneys that the Indians of these provinces and especially those of the city and province of Tlaxcala have appointed to defend them at trial, instead of protecting them and favoring them are their enemies and spies . . . *it cannot be believed that people named by my viceroys could act like that;* that instead of protecting and defending the Indians from the annoyances, offenses and vexations that they ordinarily receive from every type of person . . . *they are their enemies.*"[32]

Such statements expose the paradoxes of Spanish colonialism as the crown strove to protect Indian lives against its own settlers and agents, who made those lives miserable. That the crown so often issued decrees favoring Indians suggests that the abusive practices documented in the texts were common. When crown agents sanctioned these practices, in defiance of crown decrees, it was not because they were legal, but because they were the customary and logical outcome of Spanish colonial interests. In part, this situation arose from the fact that not just settlers but the crown itself extracted wealth from Indians. Indeed, the king's own welfare could be used as a pretext for Indian exploitation. In seventeenth-century Metepec, to the northeast of the mining center of Temazcaltepec, Indian officials protested the labor conditions villagers were forced to endure. Every week eleven Indians were to present themselves in the mines for repartimiento.[33] When they were finished, another eleven were supposed to take their places. But the miners would typically keep the Indians against their will for two, three, or four weeks, forcing them to work day and night "without letting them go to mass." They would fail to feed them, and they habitually locked them up and mistreated them. If the Indians were paid, it was in "shoes, ribbons and other things from the store that they do not need, and not in money." Over a six-year period, thirteen Indians died "because of the bad treatment they received." And when those who survived escaped or were let go, many returned home to find their kin — including their women and children — dead and their belongings gone.[34]

While Indians appealed to crown authority for protection, miners also appealed to it in order to justify their treatment of Indians. As one foreman insisted while overseeing a brutal beating of Metepec's Indian laborers, "work you dogs, [so] that the king is served."[35] The responsibility of these "dogs" was therefore to serve under duress the very king who shielded them.

### BENEFICIADOS ARE SERVED FOR FREE

In the sixteenth century, the church had shifted away from the large monastery complexes organized around Indian territorial (*altepetl*) units, and toward small parish churches with secular clergy.[36] The friars' initial mission to convert Indians was then replaced with a priestly one to preach to the already converted and to administer the sacraments in Indian communities. Friars and priests feuded among themselves over control of Indian parishes throughout the late sixteenth and seventeenth centuries.[37] Friars allied themselves closely with the viceregal administration and the king's officers — composed for the most part of native-born Spaniards (*peninsulares*) — and fought Mexican-born Spaniards (*criollos*) under the pretext of protecting the sorely demoralized Indians (but also probably in support of the labor needs of their own haciendas). In contrast, the secular clergy had closer links to the criollo lay population, which consisted of their "cousins and friends."[38]

The crown claimed that the "complete mission" of friars and priests was to be "found in the Indian."[39] Nevertheless, the British friar

Thomas Gage noted that the Spanish American clergy loved money and "vainglory" more than God.[40] One of his first observations when he entered Mexico in 1625 was "the power of the priests and friars over the poor Indians, and their subjection and obedience unto them."[41] While his words should probably be read more as a political commentary than as a faithful rendition of colonial Mexican social conditions, royal decrees also suggest that Indians fared little better under the religious than they did under settlers and crown agents. The king might have insisted to his viceroy that friars and priests were to "lighten the Indians' burden," but he was also forced to acknowledge that certain clergy had made personal slaves of the "miserable natives," who were not slaves, he had to remind the viceroy, but rather the king's own free vassals, "worthy of his protection," as Indians themselves were aware.[42]

Because the "Indian problem" can in part be couched as reflecting conflicts in crown and settler interests, it is perhaps not surprising that the documentation indicates Indians saw priests as enemies more often than they did friars. This might have been because for Indians, priests represented the exploitative side of Spanish authority as embodied in the criollo settler population with whom priests were closely allied, rather than the protective side as embodied in the friars, the king, and the Spanish-born elite of the church and royal administrations.

The secular clergy had long been forbidden from taking extreme measures against native religious practices, which were generally understood as "idolatry," because such clergy tended to abuse their power and because the prerogative to discipline Indians was royal.[43] Both the courts and the crown directly admonished priests who defied the orders. The Inquisition called one priest to task in 1625 for taking matters into his own hands in Chiautla (to the south of Chietla) by punishing an Indian who had taken *ololiuque*.[44] The Inquisition's wrath might have also been stoked by the fact that the priest had proclaimed himself a commissioner of the Holy Office as he brought the Indian to church, naked from the waist up, read him a sentence, and ordered him given fifty lashes.[45]

Some years later, Philip IV informed his viceroy that he had heard the Indians of the far eastern territory and Yucatán were suffering from priests who demanded alms. He reminded the viceroy that Indians should be protected and treated with "complete charity and love."[46] Toward the end of the century another priest, with, in fact, "little love [or] charity," had apparently whipped an Indian in a village near Mexico City, cut off his long hair (*melenas*), and verbally abused him because he missed a mass.[47] "It was too much punishment" for such a minor transgression, the plaintiff argued in ecclesiastical court.[48]

One series of incidents involving a priest elucidates the cultural themes of Indian weakness. The priest's behavior was reported to the ecclesiastical authorities in the late seventeenth century by the Indians of Acapetlaguaya, a village to the southwest of Tasco.[49] The priest, Francisco de Zarate y Molina, could not ride by himself on horseback but instead had to be "very gently" led by an Indian. If the Indian was careless and went too quickly, Zarate whipped him right there in the road before continuing on to his destination. He insisted that every village have a "gentle" horse waiting for him as he made his rounds, and if the villagers failed to comply he cursed them, had them whipped, and forced them to carry him in a litter. This was "impossible," said one Indian in a comment striking for its evocation of Indian fragility, "for the roads are harsh and the natives are not made of similar things." The villagers were "disconsolate," they told the justices, because although they wanted to give their priest a good horse, there were no Spaniards to provide one.

During the first day of a four-day stay in the village, Zarate "upon rising from bed . . . went to the kitchen and broke all of the cooking jars and made the women kneel and whipped them." The day he was to leave, he requested a mule belonging to a municipal council member. But the mule was hiding from torrential rains, and the angry Zarate again whipped and beat the Indians. He then ordered the black slaves who accompanied him to drive the Indians into the church. One slave wielded a machete, with which he ran the Indians about, going after in particular a church constable named Marcos, who escaped. Zarate searched Marcos's house but found only his wife, who had just given birth. He kicked the woman, in the process knocking her to the floor and ripping her shirt. Zarate then took the woman to his house and would have sent her to jail but for the intervention of an Indian official. She subsequently became gravely ill.

During his stay in the village, Zarate had apparently also beaten two young girls for failing to wash his clothes as quickly as he would have liked; he had flogged a young boy "for no reason"; and he had repeatedly hit an Indian in the head. One Indian fell ill and could not go to Mexico City at Zarate's request, thus angering him. Zarate thrashed yet another Indian who asked him for candles, and he beat the alcalde who requested that Zarate pay for the Indian messengers and mules he wanted the community to send to Mexico City. Zarate then announced to the Indians that "because he is *beneficiado* (clergy) they have to serve him for free."

Zarate's seemingly frenzied actions emerge as a complex statement about the politics of caste. On the one hand, "Indianness" was characterized by servility while "Spanishness" was equated with the honor of literally being carried by Indians. On the other hand, Spaniards found it highly aggravating and inefficient to depend on Indians. In this respect, many of Zarate's excesses appear to have been reactions to what he perceived as defects in the Indian character: that Indians were physically weak was indicated both by their propensity to illness and by their admission that they were incapable of traveling the "harsh" roads while carrying Zarate on their backs; that they were morally infirm was signified by their idleness and by the failure of the two young girls to wash the priest's clothing rapidly enough. The priest attempted to "correct" the Indians with the aid of his black slaves, who chased the Indians into the church — the holy site of redemption.

### THE FEMINIZATION OF THE INDIAN: REASON AND ITS IMPLICATIONS

The contradictory treatment of Indians, both exploitative and protective, can in part be attributed to Spanish beliefs about the Indian capacity for reason. This matter was central to Spanish theological and political concerns, for reason entailed not only full knowledge of God but also a strict adherence to Spanish norms of conduct.[50] It was something Spaniards — especially high-born ones — came by naturally because it was carried in their blood. Mendicants like Las Casas believed Indians could be transformed into reasonable beings who would receive Christianity voluntarily and recognize the kings of Castile as "overlords and emperors."[51] But others saw Indians as "perpetual children" and "weak-willed."[52] Many of the first friars advocated the separation of Indian children from their idolatrous and irresolute parents.[53] They also turned those children into one of the principal vehicles for the "inner reconstruction" of all Indians: as sedentary Indians were made into good Christians in missionary theater, and as Chichimecs represented evil, Indian children played angels and Christians against Indian adults who acted as "devils, infidels or enemies."[54] These plays thus made sedentary Indians "good" in relation to Chichimecs, and Indian children metaphors for these "childlike" Indian peoples.

Childishness implied a certain purity and virtue, but it also spoke to Indian defectiveness, which the royal chaplain and philosopher Juan Gínes de Sepúlveda emphasized when he insisted on the Spanish right to rule Indians. Advocating a position that found wide support among Spanish settlers, Sepúlveda entered into a well-known debate with Las Casas.[55] The debate brings out the ways certain colonialist logics worked not just to infantilize but also to feminize Indians.

Shortly after the New Laws were implemented, only to be resisted by settlers, Sepúlveda wrote an impassioned treatise justifying the wars waged by Spaniards against Indians. The treatise blended Christian and Aristotelian notions of humanity, the doctrine of natural law, and the divine origins of Spanish social norms to prove the inferiority of Indians, their unwillingness to accept Christianity, and the right of Spaniards to rule them by force. In Sepúlveda's view, Indians were "barbarians," or Aristotle's natural slaves.[56] He then leapt "metaphysically," as John Leddy Phelan puts it, into arguing that Indians were best governed by Spaniards, who were Christians and followed proper (Spanish) norms of conduct.[57]

Sepúlveda wavered on Indian defectiveness, noting in one passage, for instance, that Indians did not completely lack reason and were not exactly "bears" or "monkeys."[58] Yet the overall thrust of his argument placed Indians outside of civil life because for him they were cruel and extreme, practiced cannibalism and human sacrifice, and were sexually indiscriminate — committing, in his view, both sodomy and bestiality. He also cited their "primitive" technology.[59] Indians might therefore have approximated civilized beings, but all told they lacked in their material and spiritual lives a certain quality, the Christian "humanitas" of Spain, which would have made them fully human.[60] Moreover, for Sepúlveda the imperfections of these "inhuman people" (*gente inhumana*) were located not in individuals, for any individual could sin, but in the entire people, who failed to recognize the natural law of God in its "customs and public institutions."[61]

Some modern scholars deem Sepúlveda an extremist.[62] But others argue that he articulated a pervasive view of the nature and status of the Indian in Christian and European intellectual thought.[63] Certainly his contention that Indians needed to be forced to comply with "things Spanish" quickly found favor with settlers,[64] who most fully represented the exploitative side of Spanish authority.

Las Casas rejected Sepúlveda's position because it negated Las Casas's own belief that Indians, like all people, could achieve Christian reason.

For Las Casas, "all the 'races' of the world [are] men," as he wrote in one famous passage, while for Sepúlveda Christianity was an essence with which some people were naturally endowed. Las Casas considered Sepúlveda's Aristotle to be "a gentile philosopher burning in hell."[65] In his view, Indians were not the barbarians. Rather, Spaniards "with their cruel and abominable acts" had "devastated the land and exterminated the *rational* people who fully inhabited it."[66]

Las Casas published those lines in 1552 in his defiant and remarkable work, *The Devastation of the Indies*, which reverses the conventional imagery of "civilized" Spaniards and Indian "barbarians" while conflating the qualities of Indians with those of meek mendicants.[67] The publication was Las Casas's angry response to the slow implementation of reforms by the crown, which had passed the New Laws at his prompting and whose jurists favored his position over Sepúlveda's. The debate between Sepúlveda and Las Casas over who Indians were in relation to Spaniards resonates with a pervasive conflict between two competing views of the world and humankind. But these two positions were not just in ideological tension; they were woven into the social fabric of the colony. Hence, Indians were "dogs," but they were equally innocents owed protection.

Like other Spanish theologians, Sepúlveda wrote paternalistically of Indians through analogies with children. Aristotle compared natural slaves to children, whom he also associated with women when he argued that neither could truly master their passions.[68] To Sepúlveda, women and children were also imperfect, but he went a step further in employing a child/woman analogy to argue against Indian autonomy.[69] "In prudence, talent, virtue and humanity," he wrote, "[Indians] are as inferior to Spaniards as children are to adults and women to men."[70] In Sepúlveda's imagination, then, women, children, and Indians were essentially "incomplete men."[71] Elsewhere in his treatise he narrowed these analogies by focusing on what he saw as the feminine qualities of Indians, such as their second-rate minds and their cowardice.[72] As evidence he claimed that during the conquest of Mexico "thousands and thousands of [Indians] fled like women from very few Spaniards," while Moctezuma, "cowering like a woman," reluctantly received Cortés.[73]

Although Indians and women were often compared independently to children, Sepúlveda's explicit linking of women to Indians was rather unconventional. Philip II had passed laws making two Indian or three women witnesses "worth one Spanish man" (an equation that considers one Spanish man a complete human being and women and Indians only partial ones), but woman/Indian analogies were not elaborated by other commentators.[74] Sepúlveda himself abandoned this feminine imagery when he later re-presented the Mexica as a "more dignified" and "heroic" warrior-like foe of the victorious Spaniards, but it is nevertheless worth pausing to consider his initial logic.[75]

Nancy Stepan has convincingly shown how nineteenth-century scientists used gender analogies to confirm their notions about race. She also notes that the history of such analogies has yet to be explored.[76] Anthropologists of Latin America have examined the Indianization of women and the feminization of Indians in several contemporary contexts.[77] Other scholars have pointed out the presence of feminizing imageries in Spanish colonial discourse, noting that beginning with Columbus's letters and diaries such imageries were central to many Spanish accounts of the natives of the New World.[78] Spanish women, in turn, were themselves Indianized and "primitivized" in the conduct manuals written for them in the sixteenth century.[79] The judicial texts examined here describe women and Indians in similar ways: both were ignorant (*de poco saber*), weak (*flaca*), and sinful (*pecadora*). The texts thus speak to the parallel and overlapping cultural and juridical basis for the subordination of women and Indians; to the historical development of interdependent gender and caste ideologies and hierarchies; and, ultimately, to the core logic of the caste system as it played out in colonial people's day-to-day lives.

### CONTAINING WOMEN AND INDIANS

Under Spanish law, women in general and children under the age of twenty-five were legally prohibited from litigating on their own behalf. Instead, they were to be represented by "male guardians, tutors, husbands, parents and relatives."[80] Until women reached adulthood, they were legally controlled by their fathers. Once married, they were controlled by their husbands, who managed most property in the marriage and whose permission was needed for legal transactions. Independent decisions were reserved for grown women without male superiors, notably widows, who acquired control over their own dowries when their husbands died, and could continue to run their husbands' businesses. These women could receive loans, as well as bequeath their own property.[81]

We have seen both the unmarried black woman Ana María de la Concepción and the married Spanish woman Ursula de Castañeda bring legal suits on their own. Moreover, we know that the black woman Adriana, also unmarried, possessed quite some property, including three slaves. These few examples indicate that the law was not a "dead letter": women did buy and sell property, own slaves and free them, borrow money, and initiate suits. Moreover, patriarchy was especially limited with respect to choice of marriage partner.[82]

But gender ideologies could also be invoked to thwart women's independent action. We might recall in this respect that the legal prohibition against women litigating, as well as the "fickleness" of women in general, was cited by Adriana's lawyer as he discredited Ana María's testimony. The legal prohibition was also invoked by the priest who defended the mulatto Juan from Ursula's accusations. Susan Kellogg has demonstrated the vigor of such prohibitions by showing that, although Indian women initially enjoyed much greater autonomy than Spanish ones, by the seventeenth century Indian women too had become legal minors, placed under the protection of their husbands.[83]

The notion that women possessed inferior reason can be found in widespread western cultural codes linking passion to femaleness and reason to maleness. Yet it is important to recognize that male as well as female qualities are always situated in particular social and historical contexts. In this respect, Spanish culture was characterized by an ethos of self-control emphasizing lineage and the maintenance of family honor.[84] Honor referred both to social status (characterized by wealth and blood) and to the preservation of virtue in the form of virginity, which signified a morally pure life and respect for the church. Virginity also guaranteed the character of future lineages in societies highly stratified by wealth, color, and religion. In theory, sexuality was a site of social control for both men and women.[85] But because women were regarded as more carnal than men, they required closer supervision. Supervision protected them from their own weaknesses, but more generally it protected Spanishness itself by preserving male salvation and honor, which were vulnerable to corruption by women, who could weaken men's minds with lust and their bodies with venereal diseases.[86]

Rates of illegitimacy were extraordinarily high for Spanish women as well as for Spanish men in colonial Mexico, where all kinds of non-Spaniards posed lineage threats. Unlike men, however, women could not legally decide who their legitimate children were.[87] Female sexual freedom in this regard was therefore also more dangerous than male, and maintaining Spanish purity in the New World became the particular onus of Spanish women. Protection was accomplished in part through the enclosure conventions that ideally kept all women—but especially Spanish ones—at home, where they were charged with performing or overseeing domestic chores like spinning, weaving, and, most importantly, food preparation.[88]

Women carried their domesticity with them outside of their homes. They were expected to do charitable work for hospitals and focus their energies on church activities, such as mass and religious sisterhoods, where they could also be supervised by men. The state of enclosure was complete for nuns.[89] Prostitutes were enclosed as well, required to reside in brothels or "public houses" where, in the words of a sixteenth-century Spanish clergyman, "the filth and ugliness of the flesh are gathered like the garbage and dung of the city."[90] Gatherings of women outside the control of men could have potentially nefarious intents and therefore raised suspicions. We might recall in this respect how Adriana deftly transformed a suspected water divination with a group of women friends into work for her religious sisterhood in order to establish her sanctioned social place.

Although domestic confinement was the ideal, many women had no other means of subsistence than "the power or skill of their hands."[91] Women compelled by economic circumstances to be on the outside were mostly non-Spanish or poor Spanish women (of which there were few, since there were few Spanish women altogether). They labored at domestic tasks such as dressmaking and cooking both outside and inside the home, worked in mines and sweatshops, and ran small commercial enterprises. Unable to comply with enclosure etiquette due to their class and their caste status, these women inevitably lost honor and value.[92] Adriana tempered this potential loss by running a boarding house, thereby earning a livelihood that melded the domestic and extra-domestic spheres. She also had three slaves who performed household chores for her. Free women who had to work outside their homes did such chores for pay, and were often called into other homes to help elite women or single men manage their own domestic tasks.

Like women, Indians had their "appropriate" place in the moral economy, and when they were not engaged in outside labor under Spanish supervision they were also subject to forms of enclosure. In an echo of women's domestic spaces, they were expected to remain in the villages of the Indian Republic. Just as husbands, fathers, and priests were supposed to teach women right from wrong, so too were Spaniards supposed to teach Indians. Enclosed Indians could be protected from the dissolute. They could also be organized for efficient prayer and production by the priests who morally guided them, and by the Spanish district officials who supervised them and made them available for tribute and labor drafts.

We might highlight here the fact that while domestic labor for the benefit of men was performed mostly by women (of all castes), public labor for Spaniards was performed mostly by Indians (including some Indian women). While not all women were removed from public life, and while not all (and of course not only) Indians labored for Spaniards, it could be argued that ideals of honor made men "Spanish" by distancing them from manual production both inside and outside the home as colonial labor became the domain of women and Indian producers.[93] Because the producer/consumer relation between women and men parallels the one between Indian and Spaniards, the caste/gender analogies under consideration here can be extended to include the idea that Indians were "feminized" and women were "Indianized" through the dishonor of production.

## LAZINESS AND ESCAPE:
## THE PERILS OF PRODUCTION

Enclosure was meant to increase productive capacities and cultivate moral qualities. But both women and Indians had to be coerced into focusing their energies on their appropriate tasks, and both were constantly on the verge of moral escape. Indians were "such loafers," Archbishop Montúfar wrote in 1554, that they did not even want to "work for themselves."[94] And as a viceroy wrote to the king some fifty years later, "experience has shown the Indians are enemies of work, and they cannot be persuaded in any way nor are they inclined [to do] what is so opposite their nature."[95] Indian idleness and unwillingness to work were seen as vices that could and should be cured by benevolence.[96] Yet church and state demands could not long be ignored while Indians were gently coaxed into performing their duties. Just as straying wives were physically disciplined "within reason" by their husbands,[97] Indian "laziness" was met with force, as we saw with the priest Zarate and the Metepec foremen who called Indians "dogs" as they beat them.

Indians responded to such force by fleeing and hiding, thereby eluding the control that Spaniards tried to impose.[98] As they left their dying villages, they dodged labor obligations and escaped abusive neighbors while avoiding the surveillance of Spanish priests and friars, who lamented that escaped Indians were living without catechism and mass. Colonial discourse linked this lack of religious instruction to general social disorder. In the words of one priest, who was referring to the Coyoacán region just south of Mexico City, "[Indians abandon] established villages, and have gone up, and continue to go up, to live in the hills and mountains [where] they make their fields, leaving much good land and the comforts of their villages." They "lack religious instruction," he continued. "If it is not stopped . . . it will do general and irreparable harm to the republics."[99]

The "hills and mountains" to which Indians fled were extra-domestic wilderness spaces where they lived without appropriate supervision—like cimarrones, Chichimecs, and women who escaped their homes. And it is no coincidence that in the wilderness witchcraft and devils flourished; it was there that Indians readied the herbs and powders used for witchcraft. These spaces thus symbolized the intertwined themes of sacrilege and moral flaccidity, an entwinement made more explicit by Archbishop Montúfar: "Not with little labor," he observed while connecting work, discipline, and prayer, "do the religious find themselves having to undo the tangle of . . . indolence" once Indian runaways were redirected to their care. In a somewhat convoluted way, then, witchcraft might be seen as a consequence of the Indian unwillingness to do sanctioned work and therefore as both a challenge to and a confirmation of the state's organization of Indian labor. For Indians sold their witchcraft to a wide clientele, and thus did join the market economy—they just produced something other than what the state desired.

Female slothfulness was also a sign of witchcraft. Food preparation, in particular, was a double-edged sword, for women could nourish with food or use it to ensorcel. Ensorcelling often entailed feeding with adulterated victuals, but withholding food altogether could also be a sign that a woman was a witch, for it too spoke to her transgression of the gendered rules of production, which included not just making good food but furnishing food at all. In support of this point, we can take a brief look at what happened to the mulatto Francesca Cerdan, who was knocked to the ground at her home in Vera Cruz by a Spaniard named Francisco when she failed to produce his midday meal. She claimed to be ill and unable to do so, and went on to describe an altercation that illuminates gender roles and qualities: she explained to the inquisitors that she had resisted when the Spaniard physically assaulted her, and protested when he tore a religious print from her wall (an act that of course equated women's laziness with their lack of Christian principles). But the Spaniard dismissed her objections. "What do you know?" he allegedly asked her. And then he said that "he knew more because he was a man."[100]

This gendered representation of links between knowledge and power was bolstered by another of the Spaniard's contentions: that the woman had been seduced by the devil, who turned her into a witch. She, in turn, had allegedly "tied" (*ligar*) the Spaniard so that he was unable to have intercourse with any woman but her.[101] His loss of control over her productivity (the fact that she failed to nourish him with a meal) thus led to the loss of his own (he was unable to have sexual relations with any woman he desired). These losses were further linked in his mind to the mulatto woman's perversions of the closely intertwined themes of legitimate sexuality, religious orthodoxy, and gender power. In the end, then, the Spaniard's maleness depended on the mulatto woman carrying out her proper female role, but through her own laziness, which was so attractive to the devil, she undermined the sanctioned order that surrendered women's material production and moral guidance to the control of men.

We might be inclined to believe that women and Indians were regarded as evil with their disobedience interpreted as resistance. Yet disobedience was deeply enmeshed in issues of power, and therefore in the imputed qualities that rendered women and Indians subordinate in the first place. Again, one way to understand this subordination is to draw on the metaphor of the child, which was invoked with reference to both women and Indians as capricious, ignorant, and weak, and apt to get into trouble when they escaped the control of their superiors. When Indians fled spaces governed by Spaniards, including their own villages, they essentially left "civilization" and returned to their old ways in hills populated by witchcraft and the devil. And women who literally or figuratively fled the confines of domesticity were also returning themselves to a "pre-social" state by unwittingly hurling themselves into a world full of "corruption and dishonor," a world that, as we shall see, was also full of witches and devils.[102] In some profound sense, Spaniards and men saw themselves battling the forces of nature, doing so in part by socializing and civilizing "immature" Indians and women. Thus, the religious and colonial officials tried to keep Indians in their villages in order to teach them Christian ideals of work and prayer, while the Inquisition punished women by, for instance, confining them to their homes, which they were to leave only to attend mass.

Enclosure as a cognitive metaphor for the state of women and Indians persisted, as did the image of the outside as a source of corruption. But it was also inevitable that the borders between domestic and public, control and disorder, would be breached. The most serious threats came from "darkness": non-Spaniards, especially, were among the "dangerous guardians of the erotic arts," and dark women were doubly afflicted with "superstitious" tendencies.[103] Spanish women routinely had contact with non-Spaniards, including the female slaves and servants they brought into their homes and the ones they mingled with outside. These women then became important conduits for nefarious forces brought directly into Spanish homes, and so often inflicted on Spanish men. The devil himself was typically a dark-skinned man, and he at times invaded women's beds.

Inter-caste contact also provided occasions for the social boundaries between Indians and Spaniards to blur and for the social order to reverse, in part through the alliances blacks, mulattoes, and mestizos forged with Indians beyond watchful Spanish eyes. Ironically, these intermediaries facilitated Indian productivity for Spaniards, and were therefore vital to colonization processes that depended on the inter-penetration rather than on the separation of the Spanish and Indian worlds. In many ways blacks, mulattoes, and mestizos figured in the Spanish domination of Indians and their communities. The exploitation Spaniards inflicted on Indians through these intermediaries inevitably led to Spanish intervention not only because, as the Indian Juana's Spanish comadre Leonor put it, "it look[ed] bad to be mistreating natives," but also because Spaniards feared affiliations among the lower orders.

3

*La Mala Yerba*

PUTTING DIFFERENCE TO WORK

In the early seventeenth century Viceroy Velasco sent a letter to Philip III scornful of the "many free blacks, mulattoes and mestizos" in New Spain. He also wrote of his fear that these people would multiply in the colony like weeds, because "weeds always increase" (*la mala yerva siempre crece*).[1] The viceroy's attitude both masks and illuminates the pivotal positions of intermediaries who were scorned by an elite that simultaneously put them to work as its sanctioned agents and collaborators. These intermediaries have not gone unnoticed by other scholars, but their significance to colonization processes and to the caste meanings and enactments that entwined with those processes has not been systematically examined.[2] This is most likely because colonial society and its state apparatuses were dichotomized into Indian and Spanish sectors.[3] Yet the intermediaries carried a deep social and symbolic importance, and as Spaniards encouraged their extensive contact with Indians, an ironic, if entirely logical, twist to the colonizers' intentions developed: the intermediaries could become formidable antagonists to their Spanish bosses if they allied with Indians instead of assailing them. For in closing the social spaces between rulers and ruled with what Foucault would term the "thugs" carved out of the social body,[4] the colonizers engendered threats to their own positions as blacks, mulattoes, and mestizos were pushed closer to Indian terrain. Caught up in the spheres of both Spanish and Indian influence, blacks, mulattoes, and mestizos thus came to be like Spaniards in some respects and like Indians in others.

Many civil and criminal complaints Indians brought before the courts point only to black, mulatto, or mestizo malefactors. But the ensuing tales generally unmask the important roles Spaniards played in facilitating the chains of command. With respect to this issue, an interesting phrase repeatedly turns up as Spaniards are described as "powerful hands" (*manos poderosas*) backing blacks, mulattoes, and mestizos in their dealings with Indians. Frequently, however, it was not Spaniards who found themselves before the justices, but the intermediaries. This situation was mirrored in the judicial handling of the unsanctioned domain. Untouchable Indians mostly escaped punishment for the witchcraft that originated with them, while blacks and especially mulattoes were routinely brought before the Inquisition. The intermediaries — blacks, mulattoes, and mestizos — were not entirely interchangeable in either domain. Here I highlight the most prominent practices of each group in the sanctioned domain.

### TAKING ACCOUNT OF BLACKS

In the 1560s, while he was living in Guatemala, the Spanish chronicler and conquistador Bernal Díaz del Castillo wrote his memoirs of the conquest of Mexico. One arresting passage describes an epidemic in 1520, the first to hit Indians particularly hard. Díaz identifies the source of the epidemic as a black man who arrived "covered with smallpox." He then declared the matter to be a "very black affair . . . for it was owing to [the black] that the whole country was stricken and filled with [the pox] . . . [and] a great number of [Indians] died." He concluded, "[Black] was the death of so many persons who were not Christians."[5]

Given that Spaniards linked blacks to Indian suffering and to other calamities of conquest, this passage might be read as a symbolic commentary on Spanish perceptions of black/Indian relations fed by black venom and Indian vulnerability. Colonial officials consistently portrayed blacks and, to a lesser extent, mulattoes, as "bellicose," "pugnacious," and "vicious," and as threats to "miserable" Indians.[6] Toward the end of the sixteenth century, for instance, Viceroy Enríquez wrote to Philip II that "one has to take special account of blacks in this land. Although arms are prohibited to them, they carry hidden knives, and whatever the offense they cause many deaths." Cruelest of all, he continued, blacks mistreated "wretched" Indians, who had no "resistance."[7] Decades later another viceroy called Philip III's attention to blacks, noting that "laborers and blacks . . . are more powerful [than Indians and] will do anything they want to the maceguales of the villages . . . they will oppress them."[8] Still later in the seventeenth century a high court judge asserted that blacks "treat Indians as their slaves, while they themselves enjoy more leisure and comfort than anyone else."[9]

Indian complaints against blacks began to surface in the courts not long after the initial conquest period. In 1544, for instance, a group of Indians in the Toluca region spoke of a slave who had gone to an estate owned by a Spaniard and, "without cause or reason," hit and whipped both Indian men and women. "Not content with this," the charges continued, "he slashed the face of an Indian woman."[10] In the middle of the same century, another Indian from the same region complained of a black man who had stolen his sheep.[11] Thirty years later, an Indian noble from a town in the Tlaxcala region recounted how a black slave he had inherited from his father and brother went about "freely in this village and others nearby . . . armed with a knife, a firearm, bows and arrows, forcing and aggravating the Indians and bothering the married Indian women, taking them from their husbands, who are not powerful enough to defend them."[12] The plaintiff might have had legal control of the slave, then, but he did not have physical control, for Indians had no sanctioned authority over blacks. Indeed, the slave exerted his own authority over the Indian. It was rare for Indians to own black slaves, and the paradigmatic caste hierarchies of the sanctioned domain make it perhaps unsurprising that a single black slave of an Indian noble would be able to subdue his master and even entire Indian communities.

When Indians brought their grievances against blacks to the authorities, the Spanish judiciary carried out its protective role by holding inquiries and punishing some of the perpetrators. Yet as the judiciary busied itself protecting Indians from blacks, Spanish settlers, officials, and clergy were using blacks to extend Spanish control over Indians. The affiliations blacks developed with Spaniards arose from enslavement and Spanish command of the blacks they owned. But such affiliations also developed as free blacks and mulattoes took on mediating roles in the political economy of conquest.

In early-seventeenth-century Mexico City, a Spanish baker used a rather inventive punishment to turn his wayward slave into a "Spaniard," and he answered to the ecclesiastical authorities for his ingenuity. He had to explain why he had dressed the slave up in a long garment like those used by monks who were, of course, celibate, and then paraded the slave around in the public plaza in front of the city's cathedral. But the baker had not only dressed the slave in a monk's habit (which had a gender twist insofar as he had made it out of some of his wife's old dresses); he had also shaved the man's head in the manner of a monk's tonsure and, perhaps most startlingly, he had whitened the man's face with flour. The authorities thought he was showing contempt for the clergy, but the baker explained that he was rather punishing and "shaming" the slave, whom he described as a "wicked" scoundrel who had tried to run away.[13]

In domesticating his bellicose slave, then, the baker symbolically erased his blackness. As he did so, he achieved a transformation of the "devil" into something "holy." The way he conjoined caste, religion, and even sexuality bears more than a passing resemblance to Adriana Ruíz de Cabrera's metamorphosis from a person who was "not quiet or calm, but rebellious and too much given to sensuality," into one who fraternized with the most important Spaniards of Vera Cruz.

As both of these examples suggest, colonial ideology presented blackness as something of an affront to Spanishness. Yet Spaniards gladly took on the bellicosity they assigned to blacks as they turned them into extensions of Spanish authority. The Mexico City baker might have forced the issue, but Spanishness did seep into blackness, especially where control of Indians was at stake.

The story of a black slave named Domingo, who belonged to one Captain Francisco de Córdoba and worked on his hacienda to the north of Mexico City, illustrates the vise that gripped blacks, especially enslaved ones. The Indian residents of Tultepec had brought Domingo to the attention of the justices of the criminal court.[14] Their village abutted the hacienda, and the captain probably considered its residents a legitimate and perpetual labor source. Apparently, the immediate problem was the slave who, while armed and mounted on a horse, had assaulted an Indian he encountered on the road with seven oxen belonging to the hacienda. "Dogs [*sic*]," he reportedly said, "where are you taking those oxen?"[15] The Indian explained to the court that he had been leading the animals to the village corral after they had trampled Indian corn fields, a situation that had become so serious that for two years running the corn crop had failed.[16] According to the plaintiffs, Domingo had been harrassing them for years: "Customarily Domingo enters Indian houses and takes the Indians out to work on the hacienda. If they try to defend themselves, as they are afraid of the poor treatment they receive there, he beats them up and says vicious words to them." Domingo also destabilized the community by routinely destroying houses. He dismantled the roofs, removed the doors, and took bricks from the foundations, and then carted the whole lot up to the hacienda. The record does not include a verdict or a punishment; nor does it directly accuse the Spanish captain. Yet the Spaniard was clearly essential to understanding the interaction between the slave and the Indians: the cattle destroying the Indian cornfields belonged to him, and his slave harassed the Indians with the goal of compelling them to work on the captain's hacienda. It was also to the hacienda that the slave moved pieces of the Indians' destroyed homes.

Don Juan Nicolás, the local Indian council head (*alcalde ordinario*) told the justices that the Indians feared Domingo so much that they had not dared speak out against him. The "said black," he declared in what must have been an appeal to Spaniards and their cultural notions, was "naturally unsettled, depraved and does not want to submit [to authority]." The Indian principal Don Miguel de San Luis repeated the charges using similar imagery when he added that Domingo was "arrogant," "haughty," and "extremely bold," and "never repaired the damage he caused."[17]

Many stories illustrate similar patterns of affiliation, and some of them explicitly name Spaniards as parties to suits. We have already seen how the priest Zarate ordered his slaves to help him subdue Indians by chasing them with machetes into the Acapetlaguaya church. Several decades before this tale, Indians from Western Puebla brought a suit against a priest and "his blacks":

[the priest] order[ed] his slaves [to annoy the Indians] . . . everyone flees . . . and if the Indian nobles [come] for us he beats them . . . [the priest] does not preach nor take confession before he calls another to do it, because he does not know our language;[18] [the priests] are occupied with their business of fish roe, tobacco and fish with much work from the natives who are whipped for not bringing the fish that they ask for and since the natives are occupied fishing they do not hear mass; [this priest] burdens them with seventy pies that they are to take to Sacapuastla, seven leagues away, and they return burdened with flour, salt and earthenware.[19]

A much earlier story from the same region has Indian officials complaining about the local Spanish corregidor, who forced them to labor without pay and sent his slaves to their houses with the pretense of searching for pulque but really to take Indians "prisoner."[20] Around the same time, a number of Indians approached the viceroy about slaves belonging to the Spanish alcalde mayor of the Tlalpuxagua mines of northeastern Michoacán, who "mistreat[ed] and aggravate[d]" them with the Spaniard's consent. The Spaniard was brought to task with the explicit order that he forbid his servants and slaves from abusing Indians "in deed or in word," for they "greatly aggravate them, taking from them whatever they have so that many, unable to tolerate it, go to live elsewhere."[21]

On other occasions, Indian nobles from south of Coyoacán reported that a Spanish deputy had ordered a black slave to beat them for collecting tributes in the wrong manner. Quite conscious of their rank — higher than that of the slave as well as that of commoner Indians — the two nobles stressed the "humiliation and gossip" they had suffered due to the beating.[22] A black slave once testified that he was often sent to guard Indians making trips to Mexico City to sell goods, with the profits going to the alcalde mayor who owned him.[23] In another instance, an Indian woman from the town of Ixmiquilpan reported that she had been assaulted and jailed by a black slave on the orders of the Spanish alcalde mayor, to whom she had gone asking for justice after her husband was murdered by the Spaniard's own manager.[24] And a group of Indians from a village near Atrisco complained that the owner of an obraje and "one of his blacks treat[ed] them badly in deed and word without paying them."[25] In mid-seventeenth-century southern Oaxaca, one mulatto slave intercepted on the road two Indian men whose village was disputing with his master. "Dogs," he remarked, "why do you go around . . . accusing my master?" He tied them up by their wrists and took twenty-five pesos along with their possessions. Drawing out a knife, he proceeded to cut off the right ear of one of the Indians.[26] Finally, he dragged both some distance to Antequera, where he deposited them in his master's house, claiming they had tried to rob him.[27]

Enslaved black and mulatto women were also potential Spanish weapons. One Spaniard from Mexico City sent his female slave and one of his Indian servants to assault another Indian that the Spaniard had accused of theft.[28] As the slave and the servant beat the Indian, they called him "*puto*" and other "infuriating words."[29] In another incident, the mother of the alcalde mayor of Tetepango sent her female slaves to catch "rebellious" Indians and take them to jail.[30] Finally, Indians from Cuajimalpa, in the Coyoacán jurisdiction south of Mexico City, complained of the Spaniard Don Luis de Ramón de Abengara, who stole firewood and mules from them, threatened them with a firearm, and beat them when they tried to retrieve their goods. He also took Indians forcibly from their homes and made them serve him on his ranch "as if [they] were his slaves." Don Luis's mulatto slave "companion" helped him by stealing from Indians. In the immediate complaint, she had incited her dogs to attack the Indian Diego Martín, who sustained severe injuries.[31]

These incidents suggest that if Indianness implied a kind of passivity that feminized Indian men and women, then blackness implied a kind of agency that masculinized black men and women. Black and mulatto women were therefore in an especially liminal position, for as women they were expected to maintain their domestic place, yet as mulatto or black they were also considered to have something of the assertiveness of their caste. In an interesting conflation of these two qualities, black women marketers were considered particularly adept swindlers who easily parted Indians from their own market goods.[32] Food shortages then resulted for everyone as prices rose and Indian sellers disappeared. As one Mexico City suit explained, "[black women] go out to the roads and walkways and take [the produce] from [the Indians] and pay a lesser price; for something that is worth one *peso,* after taking [the thing] they throw them one *real* . . . afterwards they turn around and resell it in the plaza and get two or three *pesos* for what they took." The attorney prosecuting the case on the Indians' behalf wrote, "I beg that these black women be punished . . . and that they be ordered to not do these things and that the corregidor proceed against all of those found to be selling and that their [selling] locations be taken from them and given to the Indian women gardeners and that they be protected and any black woman who lowers the price of the produce not be tolerated."[33] The text goes on to refer to the black women as expert "hagglers" (*regatones*), good at extracting produce from Indians (by force or otherwise) at less than acceptable prices.

The well-known *Cuadernos de Mestizaje* series of paintings, although from the later colonial period, are intriguing because they further suggest that in some ways the caste qualities assigned to blacks were gendered, just as were those assigned to "weak" and feminized Indians. The caste paintings display the various outcomes of caste "mixing" through stylized representations of a woman of one caste, her husband of another caste and their child, who is of yet a third.[34] In them difference and hierarchy are visually represented through clothing, food, occupation, etc. Several portray scenes of violence that reverse the traditional relationship of male dominance and female submission, and in all of them black women are tyrannizing Spanish or mestizo men as well as the offspring they have with those men. Thus, one eighteenth-century portrait from the Seville Series (*De Español y Negra, Mulata* [From a Spanish man and a black woman comes a mulatto girl child]), depicts a black woman beating a Spanish man with a kitchen tool while her little mulatto daughter tugs at her skirts. In another eighteenth-century portrait from the Mexico III Series, the same scene is repeated, with the details varying only slightly. In the eighteenth-century Madrid I Series portrait *De Español y Negra Sale Mulatto* [From a Spanish man and a black woman comes a mulatto boy child], a black woman threatens her child, who wipes tears away with a clenched fist and looks up at his mother fearfully, while his Spanish father comforts him. And in a nineteenth-century portrait from the Mexico I Series, a mulatto woman bashes her "coyote-mestizo"[35] husband over the head with a bowl while her young child (called an "*ahí te estás,*" or "there you have it") nearly falls out of his mother's shawl, which has come unsecured.[36]

## IN THE MIDDLE OF THE MIDDLE

The women in these portraits are depicted as volatile blacks, a characteristic lessened in their mixed offspring due to the "dissolving power of white blood."[37] The women therefore terrorize their more temperate children along with their non-black partners. Verena Martínez-Alier writes that in Cuba the social rule of hypodescent prevailed by the nineteenth century because the "racially inferior parent" determined the status of the child.[38] Clearly this was not yet the case during the period under question here, as we see from the portraits that the mixed offspring of black women were considered to be less black than their mothers. Martínez-Alier also argues that although kinship was reckoned bilaterally, "women were the true perpetrators of the lineage."[39] The caste paintings also contradict this, however, since the "civilizing" blood has not only come from fathers but seems to moderate whatever caste qualities a black or mulatto mother might have been thought to pass on to her offspring. This does not necessarily mean that descent was strictly patrilineal, but in unions between Spaniards and non-Spaniards the Spanish partner was usually male. Fathers thus became important sources of their mixed offspring's status. Taken together, the evidence tells us both that hypodescent was not (yet) the rule, and that, because of the ways in which caste pairings took place, mothers were not necessarily the "true perpetrators" of the lineage, although they could, of course, be such. What counted in arguments about status and character were the qualities imputed to caste, the context of the argument, and the needs of the person making the claims.

Sanctioned lineage discourses of sixteenth- and seventeenth-century Mexico had something of an "up" orientation: their logic was based on inclusion through Spanishness rather than on exclusion because of blackness. Arms petitions, which are ubiquitous in the archives but have never, to my knowledge, been closely examined, make this clear as they show that Spanish fathers had an important legitimizing function not so much because they were fathers but because they were Spanish.

The privilege of carrying a weapon in colonial Mexico was part of the honor complex associated with Spanishness and a light complexion. Beginning in the early colonial period blacks, mulattoes, and mestizos (but most consistently blacks and mulattoes) were legally prohibited from bearing arms. Punishments for infractions of the prohibition ranged in one ordinance from one hundred lashes, the loss of an ear, and a fine for any mestizo, black, or mulatto caught armed, to death for any who "takes out a weapon against a Spaniard."[40] It was not always clear, however, who was a mulatto or mestizo and who was not. In 1620, Thomas de Rizo, who was born in the Canary Islands and lived in Valladolid, discovered just how powerful a visual cue skin color could be when his dark complexion had him constantly mistaken for a non-Spaniard and therefore subject to judicial complaints for carrying a weapon. He petitioned for the right, arguing that his color was irrelevant to his status. "All Spaniards born in that land are dark," his attorney noted. "Coming to these lands and others they are not taken to be Spaniards because here they do not know the Canary Islands and their people. Furthermore, here there are so many mestizos, mulattoes, and other castes that the justices think Thomas Rizo is one of them and not a Spaniard at all. Therefore, they try to prevent him from carrying arms. He is, however, the son of Spaniards, both father and mother, and has presented information to that effect before the court."[41]

This passage indicates that skin color was clearly linked to caste in the colony, especially to the "mestizos, mulattoes, and other castes," as non-Spaniards were sometimes referred to collectively. But Rizo was a Spaniard by birth, and therefore his skin color in and of itself did not decide his status. Neither, however, did it stand in the way of Joseph Gómez, mentioned above, who was the son of a Spaniard and a woman "of dark color," and therefore probably legally classified as a mulatto. Gómez's own "dark color," like that of Rizo, initially barred him from carrying a weapon. But Gómez claimed Spanishness laterally by declaring that he was married to a Spanish woman and was therefore Spanish by affinity. He also claimed to have "Spanish children," which is interesting for several reasons.[42] First, probably few mulattoes would have had Spanish mothers. Therefore, we normally see mulattos linked to Spanishness through their fathers, as Gómez himself had the option to argue. More generally, however, to see Spanishness attributed to children through their mother, and Spanishness also claimed through marriage, further supports the idea that lineage claims were made on the basis of expediency rather than according to normative descent principles. In other words, the fact that the Spanishness of Gómez's children came from their mother says more about the Spanishness than it does about the mother. All told we would have to concede again that caste mattered more than the sex of the carrier, and that even strict genealogy supported a certain flexibility with respect to caste claims.

Due to prevailing gender and caste hierarchies, the vast majority of mulattoes had Spanish fathers and black mothers, as did Gómez himself, or black fathers and Indian mothers, as did Juan in the Ursula de Castañeda case. Both types are referred to as "mulattoes" in the texts under consideration here, but of course only "white" mulattoes could lay claim to Spanish blood. Many mulattoes mentioned their Spanish fathers when they petitioned to bear arms, which of course indicates that they were white mulattoes (and they are sometimes called *mulatos blancos*). Often these petitioners linked their lineage advantages with markers of superior comportment, claiming to be not only part Spanish but also "quiet and calm," "not noisy and virtuous," "well-liked and loved," and gainfully employed or married.[43] One mulatto claimed legitimacy by arguing that because he lived in a Chichimec region where he voluntarily "served the king," he needed a weapon to defend himself.[44] Qualities and practices beyond those associated with genealogy seemed to count, and they were often invoked by mulattoes who presumably had no Spanishness to claim. Indeed, as far as I can discern, no mulatto invoked black or Indian paternity or maternity in support of a petition, because Indianness and blackness did not improve one's sanctioned status.

Socially, if not legally, free white mulattoes seem to have had a higher status than Indian ones. This is not surprising, given the redemptive power of Spanish blood. And such blood was inherited patrilineally not because fathers necessarily carried the lineage but because it was usually the fathers who were Spanish. Like the caste portraits and Joseph Gómez's claims about his Spanish wife and children, the arms petitions that mention Spanishness (and, more subtly, the ones that do not) also support the position that caste was more important than the sex of the parent and that caste classifications had something of an "up" (hyper) orientation rather than a "down" (hypo) one.

The distinction between white mulattoes and Indian ones is obliquely alluded to in some sources, such as a letter written by Viceroy Enríquez in the late sixteenth century. In addition to considering blacks people of whom "special account" had to be taken, Enríquez deemed mulattoes "pugnacious . . . and not given to work." He wrote to Philip II, "The number of free mulattoes is growing. In order to avoid the great danger that there is with these mulattoes in this land, it should be ordered that all of the children that Indians and mulattoes have with blacks be enslaved, and that blacks be prohibited from marrying Indian or mulatto women . . . so that there are not so many mulattoes . . . the blacks marry Indian women because they know that their children will [then] be free."[45]

Enríquez explicitly targeted the offspring of blacks and Indians for enslavement, not those of blacks and Spaniards, whom he does not even mention. He might have omitted white mulattoes from consideration because many offspring of Spanish men and black women would have been enslaved if their mothers were slaves themselves. Yet much of the freed slave population probably did consist of the mulatto offspring of Spanish fathers, who go unmentioned in the viceroy's correspondence. Did the viceroy believe that the mulatto offspring of blacks and

Indians, or those of blacks and mulattoes (who technically were not mulattoes), lacked the advantages conferred by the "civilizing" influences of Spanish blood?

## VAGABONDAGE AND *GENTE SUELTA*: CASTE, CLASS, AND MARGINALITY

The importance of lineage for establishing status and for expanding our understandings of the ways in which the state inculcated ties to Spanishness and its qualities can be examined from another angle: through the discourse of vagabondage. Scholars have attempted to account for the way caste actually worked on the ground by presenting class as a competing status determinant that supported or countered race or racial classifications in defining a person's place in the social hierarchy. Some posit race as the more powerful determinant during the earlier colonial period, after which it declined as economic factors "undermine[d] the racial system."[46] Others maintain that class never replaced race or racial classifications, even as capitalism began to displace the colonial feudalistic tribute- and trade-based economy organized around sociracial divisions.[47] Despite their contrasting positions, both groups present class as an independent and later phenomenon while interchanging race and caste. The discourse on vagabondage suggests, however, that in some respects caste and class overlapped historically and ideologically. On the whole, sixteenth-century texts identify the vagabonds (*vagamundos* or *vagabundos*) who roamed the undomesticated spaces between Indian and Spanish settlements as black, mulatto, or mestizo. As a form of social deviance, vagabondage was first attributed to mestizos, whose Spanish fathers' relationships with Indian women were only rarely formalized. The earliest accounts identify vagabonds as the illegitimate mestizo offspring of Spaniards and Indians, and sometimes as blacks.[48] In the sixteenth century, Viceroy Enríquez also linked vagabondage to unsupervised mulattoes, who "do not serve or have to answer to anybody," as he wrote to the king in a letter several years earlier than the one cited above.[49]

Associations between skin color and vagrancy quickly developed, as did the belief that non-Spaniards in general had to be policed because they rejected the norms that kept everyone in their appropriate social and geographical place. Vagabonds were not only free in a physical sense; they were free in the sense that they did not have to answer to anyone, a condition that made them all the more dangerous and despicable as they refused to adhere to Spanish social norms. Like wild Indians and runaway blacks, vagabonds were too free. As if to emphasize their lack of restraint, the documentation typically describes them as "unattached" or "loose" people (*gente suelta*). Because they were unsupervised, their lives — like that of Adriana's nemesis Ana María — lacked lineage, order, and structure, "without . . . income or houses or their own land or goods or jobs or parents or relatives to feed them, or masters to serve" as one decree explained.[50]

Metaphors of infestation and pestilence inform narratives about vagabonds, just as they do those focused on Chichimecs, cimarrones, and black, mulatto, and mestizo "weeds." One decree, for example, describes vagabonds as "lost" and "indecent" people, who "infested the roads . . . in the bad country." Accordingly, as colonial officials constantly reiterated, the land was to be kept "clean" of them, for vagabonds committed acts "offensive to Our Lord and to the residents of the Republics."[51] The "Republics" were the Spanish and Indian cities and villages that bounded and civilized the spaces of New Spain. The texts contrast such Republics with "bad land," "residents" with "vagabonds," Indians and Spaniards with blacks, mulattoes, and mestizos, "cleanliness" with "infestation," and a place in the social hierarchy with freedom from restraint. In short, order came in the form of Spaniards in their cities and Indians in their villages, of people linked to places and to the families that made up those places; chaos came in the form of vagabonds, mulattoes, mestizos, blacks, cimarrones, and Chichimecs, all of whom were in varying ways without lineage and thus without a solid place in the Spanish imagination.

Although the first vagabonds were non-Spanish, by the late sixteenth century Spanish vagabonds were joining the ranks of blacks, mulattoes, and mestizos. Rather than forcing a dismantling of the "racial" discourse of vagabondage, however, that discourse simply expanded to include "unruly" Spaniards who, as Cope writes, also had to be "compelled to work for a living."[52] Caste and class ideologies thus merged through the idea that the civilized remained firmly ensconced within the hierarchized social body. In becoming vagabonds and breaking off from that social body, Spaniards themselves could join the ranks of the "weeds," the "indecent" people who had no place in either the Indian or Spanish Republics.

Linkages between class status and caste outsidedness through vagabondage are clarified in an ordinance from 1632 tying vagabonds to yet another group, the "homicidal, wicked, impudent and stupid" people, the "foremen and servants," who served hacendados. Such foremen and servants, who this ordinance implies were low-status Spaniards brought to the New World to work for the Spanish elite, were "bold" and possessed of "little intelligence"; they were prone to mistreat Indians, the ordinance went on to say, and they typically ran away to escape the ensuing punishment. The status of Spanish foremen and servants could thus easily shift from supervised and employed people to "'unattached' [ones] without obligation."[53]

Indians often complained of such foremen. Indeed, in the Metepec mining incident recounted in the previous chapter, Indians named their immediate aggressors as mine foremen. These foremen were responsible for beatings ("so that the king is served"), for withholding food, and for giving Indians useless goods rather than money in payment for their labor. In 1648, an Indian from Cuernavaca also mentioned a foreman with unspecified caste as he accused a Spaniard of habitually intercepting Indians on the road, stealing their goods and beating them. "Yesterday," he said, "I was coming from my village with some fruit and as I came upon his hacienda he came out on the road, as always, and as I resisted when he tried to take away a load of fruit that I carried, he beat me and left me for dead . . . He also took my cloak and hat and gave them to his foreman."[54] Taken together, the evidence suggests important categorical slippages between vagabonds and foremen, lower-class Spaniards and blacks, mulattoes and mestizos: all either lived chaotic lives or could easily slip into disorder and out of legitimate control. In another discursive and practical link, the dark-skinned lower classes also became mediating bodies, especially in the far northern cattle zones where vagabonds brokered relationships between "wild" Indians and Spanish ranchers.[55]

## CASTE CONTENTIONS AND CONTRADICTIONS: THE FREE INTERMEDIARY CLASSES

There are clear similarities between the free non-Spanish intermediary classes in New Spain and Taussig's Huitoto Indian *muchachos de confianza* (trusted boys) and Barbados blacks used by Putumayo rubber traders to manage Indian labor.[56] In New Spain, such intermediaries acted as work foremen, deputies, and servants of Spanish hacendados and officials. In 1623, Indians from Coyuca (in what is today Guerrero state) accused one mulatto deputy of taking by force "everything that they had in their houses" through "methods and tricks" and the "backing" of the Spanish alcalde mayor: "He mistreats them very badly in deed and in word, making them give him people for service without paying them anything. He also goes to the plaintiffs' house, steals their women from them and hides them. It appears he is taking advantage of them. Because of this, many natives have absented themselves . . . the mulatto has not been punished since he has been favored by the alcaldes mayores."[57]

Several years later, Indians from the Tlaxcala region brought a suit against Spaniards who lived near their village of Teticpac. Accompanied by their foremen and "other mulattoes and mestizos," the Spaniards removed the Indians from their houses by force, sometimes tying them to the tails of their horses. They would then force the Indians to work for them "night and day" on their haciendas, treating them, the Indians said, more cruelly than they treated their own slaves.[58] In another incident, a free mulatto woman from Zoyaltepec, to the northwest of Antequera, was said to be under the protection of the local Spanish teniente as well as the alcalde mayor. She made local Indians give her cotton and "Indian women to serve her," and then refused to pay them.[59]

Those legally classified as mulattoes and mestizos often anchored themselves to Indian communities as officials, where they also worked at the behest of Spaniards. Neither group had legal rights to office in either the Spanish or the Indian Republic because by law certain regional offices were legitimately held only by Spaniards (teniente, corregidor, and alcalde mayor, for example), and only Indians were permitted to hold office in their communities. Typically, mulatto and mestizo officeholders acted as employees of Spaniards and as village leaders. According to the texts, highly placed Spaniards usually backed with a "powerful hand" the appointment of mestizo or mulatto intermediaries to posts meant to be held by Indians, or backed these intermediaries in other ambiguous ways. The mestizos or mulattoes appointed then acted in the interests of their Spanish patrons rather than for the Indians they were meant to be serving. None of these texts mentions black officeholders, most likely because blacks could not directly claim Spanish or Indian genealogy, while both mulattoes and mestizos could slip in and out of a range of caste statuses.

Indians sometimes called into question the caste identities of these officeholders in their villages. Take, for example, the mulatto Hernández Munro, who was treasurer of an Indian village near Ixmiquilpan. Villagers complained that he was not allowed to hold this office, "by express edicts of the government that blacks, mulattoes and mestizos cannot be elected [in the Indian Republic]." The charges against Munro stated that "with little fear of God and less esteem for Royal Justice, and contrary to his majesty's decrees and edicts that urge the support, good treatment and liberty of the Indians," he routinely "aggravated and oppressed" them by approaching them in their homes, where he threatened and tricked them into carrying "messages" up to Spanish estates. The mulatto had a "powerful hand," said the Indians, in a reference to his Spanish support. If they refused to go, Munro would catch and beat them; but if they went, they were made to work for weeks on end, treated badly and not paid. In fact, claimed the Indians, Munro was paid by hacendados for the work done by Indians, "as if the Indians were his slaves."[60]

Scholars have noted that the Indian nobility used "mixed-race" persons to achieve its ends, as over time its interests came to coincide more with those of the elite and its agents, who included mulattoes and mestizos.[61] Thus did the Indian "Don" Diego Lorenzo de la Cruz, together with a "mulatto or mestizo" named Luis de Orozco, take Indians out of their village and "sell" them for one or two weeks as laborers in distant areas, far away from the local hacendado for whom they "voluntarily" worked for good pay and food, and from whose hacienda they could return home at night, to "sleep in their own houses."[62] Such a development makes sense in light of colonization processes and a colonial culture that generated myriad classes of go-betweens and obscured the differences between Indian nobles and mestizos. These processes tell us more, ironically, about the meaning of caste mixture through the discourse of class, as class antagonisms between Indian nobility and Indian commoners played into the ways caste was socially and politically constructed.

In order to grasp the thematics of power communicated by the texts, we need to attend to that construction, for taking mixed ancestry as a biological given does not fully address the malleability of caste classifications and the centrality of this malleability to the politics of caste in the colony. Lockhart argues from Nahuatl-language texts that Nahuas negatively stereotyped certain people as "mestizos," and used that stereotype to attack political enemies.[63] But Spanish-language texts also provide nuanced insights into the ways in which "mestizoness" and "mulattoness" were generated in the context of village disputes. These disputes are typically presented as class conflicts within Indian communities. Whether the mestizos and mulattoes referred to were actually "mixed-race" is of course both spurious and unknowable. The only tangible issue is how Indians with different statuses constructed "mixed-raceness" and lineage claims in order to win their disputes.

Juan Manuel, a man accused of selling maize at inflated prices to the Indian residents of Iguala in Guerrero, would buy all the corn at the height of the harvest season, when prices would be low, and then resell it in times of scarcity when the price was high.[64] When he was charged, questions arose about his caste and therefore about his relationship to the local community. He insisted that he was a native Indian and a noble (principal) of Iguala. But the other Indians claimed to be "the actual natives" and said that Juan Manuel was a "mulatto." Juan Manuel's identity clearly went beyond his reputed ancestry. In this respect, we might read the dispute over his caste as an indication of his marginal status in the Indian community, a status captured through the term *mulatto.*

Incidents involving non-Indian village officials help us to further debiologize caste and come to see it instead as a politicized contention about power, foreignness, and place coded as blood. A group of Indians from Zinacantepec, just west of Toluca, complained that their governor, Alonso Martín, was a mulatto and an outsider (*forastero*). Yet competing claims had Martín's father, an undisputed mulatto, married to an Indian woman from the village, which would have made Martín himself a "native" of the place. Martín's defense attorney used Martín's phenotype to support his client's claims to "Indianness," an identity seconded by other witnesses who said that Martín was the son and grandson of local Indian nobility.

Like Hernández Munro, Martín was a village official entrusted with governing Indians in a beneficial manner. But he allegedly stole local women and made them "serve him in his house," and he forced the men to work naked. Again like Munro, Martín sold Indians to Spanish farmers, who then mistreated them. The contradictory claims that Martín was of the village but also not of the village, and that Martín was mulatto but also not mulatto, were tangled up with internal Indian class antagonisms. Unlike in Munro's case, Martín's genealogy became central, and the debate about his blood proffers more information about class divisions expressed through caste discourses. The witnesses who claimed Martín was a mulatto, and thus wished to see him ejected from the village, were uniformly Indian commoners (*maceguales*). In contrast, his backers were Indian nobles or officeholders who without exception emphasized his Indianness. The elite Indians characterized the maceguales in terms commonly used to describe blacks, mulattoes, mestizos, and vagabonds, for such commoners were "persons whose lives, reputations and customs were evil," as they set out to "destroy the governors by making the other natives rebel." The principal plaintiff, the nobles insisted, was "an Indian *macegual* . . . rebellious . . . an instigator of riots throughout the republic," "vile and low."[65]

Here we again see the manipulation of caste and genealogy in the context of political disputes linked to class interests and to wider conceptions of legitimacy and illegitimacy as Indian commoners and nobles jockeyed for position through caste and class appeals to colonial authority. From the perspective of noble Indians, "good" Indians were noble ones while "bad" Indians were commoners; yet from the perspective of commoner Indians, "good" Indians were Indians while "bad" Indians were actually mestizos.

### MESTIZOS AND INDIANS: DECLARED MORTAL ENEMIES

Indians seem to have reserved much of their antipathy for mestizos, at least in these texts.[66] Scholars have debated the status of mestizos during the period under review here.[67] In part, the debate derives from the fact that colonial directives sometimes classified mestizos with blacks and mulattoes as "castas," and sometimes not. Mestizos were also the first mixed population to be labeled as such and, as noted above, they were first to be identified as "vagabonds."[68] Indeed, during the sixteenth century, "mestizo and illegitimate became almost interchangeable words"[69] as mestizos were relegated to the fringes of the Spanish Republic along with the growing numbers of blacks and mulattoes.

Yet it is also the case that, beginning in 1580, free blacks and mulattoes were ordered to pay tribute alongside Indians while mestizos, like Indian nobles, were exempted. In the 1580s, mestizos were allowed to enter the priesthood while mulattoes and blacks continued to be barred. And although craft guilds to a certain extent restricted all blacks, mulattoes, and mestizos, in some of them mestizos were accorded a status clearly superior to other non-Spaniards. In addition, whether they were free or enslaved, blacks and mulattoes were usually more harshly punished for routine infractions of the law than were mestizos.

And although not all mestizos were members of the elite (neither, for that matter, were all Spaniards), a largely mestizo elite also emerged from the intermediate groups during the second half of the sixteenth century.[70] Finally, I state the obvious but often overlooked point that throughout the colonial period slaves came from the ranks of blacks and mulattoes, never from those of mestizos. Therefore, even as mestizos as a class were developing closer ties to Spaniards, all blacks and mulattoes, enslaved or free, had the infamous distinction of slave descent and thus of broken lineages.

Laws determining the right to carry a weapon again help delineate the particularities of mestizoness. As we have seen, the definition of which citizens were "responsible" enough to bear arms certainly bent enough to accommodate many mulattoes, and even some blacks, depending on the extent to which such persons could lay claim to Spanish lineage or good behavior. But blacks and mulattoes were always legally forbidden from carrying weapons whereas the laws regarding mestizo rights seem to have shifted back and forth over the course of the sixteenth and seventeenth centuries. In the process, the laws appear to have confused the colonial officials supposed to enforce them. In 1606, for instance, the mestizos Miguel Hernández and Miguel Fránquez were given permission to bear arms because "it is not prohibited that mestizos use [arms]."[71] During a Mexico City criminal trial in 1634, which involved a Spaniard injured in the nose by a knife-wielding free mulatto "friend," the justices asked the defendant whether it was true that he carried a knife in defiance of the ban against "all mulattoes and blacks" carrying arms. They made no mention of mestizos.[72] Yet five years later, when officials granted a mestizo permission to carry a sword and a dagger, they also mentioned "the order that prohibits it."[73] Eleven years later, another mestizo was given permission to carry a weapon "in virtue of the fact that he is not included in the proclamation that prohibits it."[74] Four years later, however, a royal cedula again forbade "slaves, mulattoes and mestizos" from carrying weapons.[75]

The petitions tell a slightly different story than the laws: in the early colonial period mestizos often entered such petitions along with blacks and mulattoes. But mestizo petitions seem to drop off as the seventeenth century progressed, which suggests that mestizos were no longer banned, in practice if not in theory, from bearing arms, and therefore no longer had to petition for the privilege.[76] It might be that while colonial officials displayed some confusion about the legal status of mestizos, social and historical processes were linking mestizoness more and more closely to Spanishness, thus removing people classified as mestizos in a de facto if not a de jure sense from arms bans.

Unlike mulattoes, and of course blacks, every mestizo could lay claim to Spanishness—the vast majority through the father. One Spanish nobleman even commented that mestizos "aspired" to more than blacks and mulattoes because of the "Spanish" blood and the "responsibilities" they carried. They were "no less presumptuous than the [blacks and mulattoes]," he wrote, "but in a somewhat more elevated manner . . . their presumption is better controlled and more subject to reason."[77] A Spanish settler also offhandedly remarked on the differences when he described a man named Francisco as a "mestizo or *castizo* [who] does not get involved with blacks."[78]

It is likely that by the seventeenth century mestizos had achieved a sanctioned status higher than that of other non-Spaniards. From the Spanish perspective, mestizos were superior to mulattoes with their black ancestry, and of course to blacks themselves. And it was mestizos rather than mulattoes who would much later become the ideological symbol of the Mexican nation—a new Indian/white raza that I see as an amalgamation of the caste system/values of the Spanish colony and later European racializing discourses.

## INDIAN OR MESTIZO?

The fact that people said to be mestizo were an early thorn in the sides of Indians also lends credence to the idea that mestizos were considered to be more Spanish than were mulattoes. Such mestizos were particularly adept at infiltrating Indian villages, and this was probably because Spaniards wanted those villages controlled by people who, as the Nahua annalist "Chimalpahin" wrote, "imagine themselves fully Spaniards and mistreat [Indians] and deceive [Indians] in the same way some Spaniards do."[79] It must have been ironic from the Indian perspective that such mestizos could also claim genealogical links to Indians, which complicated their "outsider" status in Indian villages.

This situation is highlighted in a late-seventeenth-century civil dispute that indicates the ways power coursed through social affiliations while off-handedly acknowledging the habitual nature of Indian/mestizo antagonism.[80] The incident documents longstanding tensions between an Indian family and one of mestizos in a village near Mexico City. These tensions culminated in charges of idolatry by the local priest, who bypassed the authority of the alcalde mayor as he confiscated money and goods from the Indians, whom he then tied up and carted off to jail. Declaring them "dogs" (*perros*) and "drunks" (*borrachos*), the priest also accused the Indians of missing mass for many days.

Some time back, the Indians had tried to expel the mestizo family from the village for allowing cattle to graze on Indian land, which grazing typically destroyed Indian crops before they could be harvested. The mestizos, the Indians pointed out, were "enemies of all the Indians and want[ed Indians] to suffer." The Indians themselves, in contrast, were "good Indians, peaceful, fearful of God," said one Indian witness, who went on to describe the priest as a close friend of the mestizos. As it turns out, the mestizos initially "discovered" the Indians' alleged idolatry, and it was they who reported it to the priest. When the priest carted the Indians off to jail, the Indians' attempts to eject the mestizos from the village were aborted.

The mestizos were not intruders into the village; nor were they even newcomers. In fact, the head of the family, Lorenzo de Rosas, had thirty years previously married a local Indian woman who he claimed was a noble and had left him her land when she died. He had always paid crown tribute, as Indian commoners but not mestizos (or Indian nobles) were supposed to do, and he was a longtime resident of the village, where one presumes his children had been raised. Yet for all of their "Indianness," when it was convenient the de Rosas family still shifted to being "mestizo," a move that might have been enhanced by the Indian mother's status as a noble, and a move that enabled the family to affiliate with a Spanish priest and distance itself from the Indian plaintiffs by invoking the Indians' religious heterodoxy.

That it "looked bad to be mistreating the natives," as Leonor de Abiega had commented, was confirmed by the Spanish district attorney in this case, who commented that the priest must have had a reason other than idolatry to "afflict [the Indians] with such an unusual and uncustomary annoyance." To appease the mestizos, the district attorney then pointed out, the priest had defied every decree dating back to 1577 forbidding priests from investigating idolatry and confiscating goods from Indians. "They cannot take gold and silver from the Indians, even if they are in the figure of idols," he reminded the court. And while the dispute was in part over access to land, the district attorney went on to insist that the real reason the Indians wanted the mestizos to leave the village was simply that "they were mestizos."

Antipathy toward mestizoness was made even more explicit by the Indian commoner Lucas Martín, who was from a village to the west of Cuernavaca. Indian village officials accused Martín of naming himself governor, of leading a band of Indians that constantly disturbed the village's "peace and calm," and of generally causing such dissent and confusion that villagers were unable to live up to their labor and religious obligations.

For his part, Martín adamantly denied that he was a nuisance. "On the contrary," he defiantly declared, "all the Indians of the village love and esteem [me] for the good works that [I] have done for them." His exasperation exploded in an outburst unusual for these texts, as he asserted with a great deal of "rage and anger" that the governor, the alcaldes, and all the officials of the republic were "his declared mortal enemies." Equating those officials with Indian oppression, he insisted that they did not look after the people properly because "they are mestizos and not Indians." Whether the officials were "actually" or even legally mestizo is (and probably was) beside the point. Looking after Indians was not in the interest of "mestizos." Therefore, officials who did not look after Indians as was their duty were for all intents and purposes mestizos.[81] Here we see that even fairly early on "Indian" and "mestizo" have to be understood as cultural classifications rather than as biological ones. We also again see the melding of caste and class discourses as, this time, mestizos, Indian nobility, and colonial officials shade into one another, and the sanctioned Spanish Republic makes incursions into the Indian one.

### MESTIZO GOVERNORS IN INDIAN VILLAGES

At the time of the conquest, dependent Indian commoners had paid tribute to local nobility (*pipiltin* and *tlatoque*) of dynastic office- and landholding lineages, while ordinary commoners and the nobility both paid tribute to the indigenous sociopolitical altepetl.[82] As Spaniards exempted the Indian nobility from tribute, they also made them instrumental as tribute collectors in Spanish governance of Indian commoners, who had initially paid tribute to Spaniards through encomienda and to Indian nobility through indigenous institutions. By the middle of the sixteenth century, however, the Indian nobility had been displaced as commoners came to pay tribute exclusively to Spaniards.[83] At this time, mestizos were already identified as enemies of Indians who were unable to "seize" them when they invaded their villages.[84]

In order to gain control over the tribute collection process, Spaniards introduced the office of governor, which was to be held by elected or appointed Indian village officials. But during the seventeenth century, the Indian officeholding class became largely Indian / mestizo in composition, creating another link in the hierarchy connecting Spaniards to Indians.[85] By this time, mestizo governors were a ubiquitous presence in Indian villages and in Indian complaints.

Governors (*gobernadores*) served as important switch points between the colonial state and its labor force, for they tied the Indian Republic to the Spanish one as they transformed Indian value into Spanish value by organizing labor drafts and collecting from Indians tribute destined for the state. Failure to collect such tribute could mean jail for these officials,[86] who were often backed by Spaniards. In this way, then, as in the others that I have reviewed, Spaniards used a "powerful hand" to control the Indian masses. Typical is a case from mid-seventeenth-century Yanhuitlan, to the northwest of Antequera: "Although the Indian principales of the village come to ask justice against the violence of the [mestizo] governor, he had such favor and care that he ended up with the office. With it he has greatly aggravated the principales because they try to impede his election since he is incapable of holding the office. Now he threatens them by saying that he is favored by the encomendero and the alcalde mayor to be elected again, or that they will elect whomever he wants."[87]

A few years later in central Puebla, Don Francisco de Escobar, a mestizo and the son-in-law of a Spaniard, "had the hand of some powerful people and [their] agents, in order to be made governor of the village, as he now is."[88] In 1644, the mestizo Pedro del Castillo was elected governor of Azcapotzalco, just northwest of Mexico City, "from which has resulted much aggravation and vexation to the natives."[89] Several years later another mestizo, who formerly had been a governor and then a mayordomo of the alcalde mayor, was accused of inflicting great damage on the Indian community of Ixmiquilpan, both directly and through his own mayordomo.[90] Shortly after that, a mestizo with Spanish backing tried to have himself elected governor of a Puebla community.[91] Finally, the mestizo Bartolomé de Guzmán, described by Indians from the Metepec region west of Mexico City as a "foreigner," an "outsider," and an "upstart," was said to have taken on the post of governor in their village for several years running, during which time he collected excessive tribute, jailed Indians without cause, and sent them to work on haciendas without pay.[92]

A mestizo governor of Xochimilco was accused of extorting money and goods from Indian villagers over a number of years, and also of forcing them to labor on nearby haciendas, where they were neither fed nor paid and often made to work naked. The Indians complained that the governor was "favored by powerful people" and city constables. As in other incidents, the hacendados were paying the governor rather than the Indians for the use of Indian labor. And the governor had threatened to sell Indians to obrajes while he used them to collect illegal tributes (*derramas*) from children and other Indians who wanted to sell their goods on market days. Five years later, having continued to commit similar offenses, the governor, Diego Juárez, was cited in a royal cédula.[93]

In his declaration to the criminal court in 1640, Juárez pointed out that he was required by repartimiento law to send thirty Indians to work on the building of the local cathedral every fifteen days, and eight to work in a gunpowder factory. According to his attorney, "none of the witnesses [against the governor] should be given faith or credit because besides being vile and lowly Indians, they ordinarily get drunk on pulque and on other drinks until they fall to the ground." Of course they were the governor's enemies, the attorney continued, "because he makes them go do [personal service] and keeps them from getting drunk, cohabiting and [committing] other public sins." The governor himself invoked Spanish conventions of Indian laziness and immorality when he argued that his Indian subjects were drunk half the time and rioting the other half. The caste issue has more than its usual ambiguity here, yet it echoes the way caste plays out in other contexts as the Indian plaintiffs claimed that the governor was "mestizo" while the governor, in his own defense, called himself an "Indian." The implication, of course, is that mestizos were commonly known to be "declared mortal enemies" of Indians, while Indians would never do harm to their own.

This story invites other ways of elaborating the thematics of power. By virtue of his official post as an intermediary between the Spanish and Indian Republics, Juárez had sent several of the most uncontrollable Indians to jail, where he ordered the mulatto warden to beat them, practically killing one old man, an Indian witness claimed.[94] We have already seen how Spaniards used black and mulatto slaves to keep Indians organized and under control. That the mestizo Juárez engaged a mulatto for this purpose suggests another way in which people aspiring to power took on some of the caste attributes of Spanishness.

The multiple themes of this chapter and the previous one converge around several points. First, like Spaniards themselves, blacks, mulattoes, and mestizos wielded sanctioned power over Indians. Second, this power emanated from Spaniards, who backed intermediaries with "a powerful hand." Third, such backing, whether immediate or not, was constitutive of sanctioned authority, which flowed through caste affiliations and categorical slippages from the apex to the base of the pyramid. Hence, implicitly or explicitly, intermediary classes gained their power over Indians from their social affiliations with Spaniards, to whom they were structurally linked.

At this juncture, however, we might want to return more pointedly to another and equally important issue by recalling that, during the altercation between the Spaniard Ursula and the Indian Juana, the actions and words of Juana's Spanish comadre Leonor exposed a central contradiction in Spanish authority: while Spaniards exploited Indians, they also leapt to their defense. The political economic processes of incorporation facilitated by blacks, mulattoes, and mestizos brought Indians to the margins of the sanctioned domain controlled by Spaniards, to whom blacks, mulattoes, and mestizos were anchored as henchmen. The ensuing assaults on Indians and their communities that defied colonial laws designed to protect them then compelled the Spanish judiciary to step in to ameliorate what was essentially Spanish rapaciousness. In this sense we might speak of the judicial system as offering something of a "cure" for the ills routinely inflicted on Indians.

At times, both the benevolent and exploitative sides of Spanish-sanctioned authority were alluded to at once, one hand slapping the other, as it were. For instance, a decree regarding mestizo governors has colonial officials exercising their own protective role while simultaneously emphasizing that mestizos acted against Indian interests with Spanish backing. The decree notes that mestizos, in particular, should not hold office in Indian communities because "experience has shown that they take the Indians' land, take money from them and make them work on the haciendas for [the mestizos'] own benefit." The text goes on to emphasize the support these mestizos received from Spaniards, who were apt to "order that only mestizos be elected" to offices. Disputes and dissension among Indians would then result, and Indians would lose all respect for legal authority.[95]

We might want to understand access to Spanish courts in general as serving a hegemonic function. But it also behooves us to seek a more specifically cultural explanation for the protective side of colonial authority, which might help to explain why Indians were so quick to appeal to it. We cannot really know how effective such appeals were: the numbers of Indian complaints could have reflected either the inability of colonial authorities to control Spanish settlers and their lackeys or the success of those authorities, which encouraged Indians to continue to use the system and even to manipulate Spanish sympathy to their advantage. But in the broader configuration of colonial power, Spanish justice might be fruitfully understood not simply as a tool used by Spaniards to control the masses, or as an instrumental means-end solution to violence and exploitation for Indians. Rather, it was a counterpoint to other kinds of Spanish authority. That is to say, because such authority was clearly the source of so much Indian misery, it might have made cultural sense from the Indian point of view that only a Spanish cure could counter Spanish abuse.

Spanishness in the sanctioned domain, which oppressed Indians and dispensed justice to them, was therefore dualistic. Discerning how its two aspects worked together perhaps opens the way for a cultural rather than a purely utilitarian explanation for Indian litigiousness. Such an explanation partly resides in the ways in which caste was given meaning: Indians did not simply go to Spanish justices because those justices were capable of ameliorating through the courts the abuse Indians suffered; they went because those justices were Spanish and in this domain "magical" power was recognized to be in Spanish hands. Although Taussig does not write about the role of the judiciary, in many ways it seems to be at the core of what he terms a colonial culture that "bound Indian understandings of white understandings of Indians to white understandings of Indian understandings of whites."[96] An interesting parallel was effected in the unsanctioned domain, where power was broadly recognized as Indian. Here Indians inflicted the greatest harm but were also the most effective healers. This power also bound Indian and "white" understandings.

As the highest sanctioned authority and the head of the legal system, the king himself embodied charity. While his welfare could be used as a pretext for Indian exploitation, his role in meting out justice did not go unnoticed by Indians. We saw in chapter 2 how Indian plaintiffs appealed to crown authority by reminding the justices of the king's obligation to them, and by pointing out that "all of this is against what his majesty has ordered."[97] We also saw in chapter 1 that when the Indian Domingo de la Cruz was attacked by two mulattoes who accused him of witchcraft, he invoked the explicit role of the king in protecting his Indian "vassals and tributaries."[98] With respect to this incident, it is perhaps ironic to find judicial authorities instrumental in protecting Indians from popular vengeance stemming from general witchcraft anxieties, but this was an aspect of the magic wielded by Spaniards, and it was probably preferred more often than we know.

Spanish power came from all corners, not just from the high-level colonial officials who operated through the courts and who represented the king's authority and role as protector of his most miserable vassals. It also came from the ordinary Spaniards who intervened when Indians were unable to control blacks or mulattoes, or when they needed protection, even from other Spaniards, as we saw with Leonor de Abiego, who shielded her Indian comadre explicitly from a beating and implicitly from the accusation that she was a witch. Not long after the conquest, a group of Mexico City Indians showed just how helpless they were with respect to blacks when they caught a slave who they alleged had robbed them. On their way to jail with the slave, they were quickly waylaid by a dozen other blacks who assaulted the Indians and freed the captive. It took the slave's Spanish master to catch him, and the slave was then sent off to jail in the company of a Spanish constable.[99] A much later incident also indicates that Indians were no match for blacks, and sometimes found themselves embroiled in situations from which they were extricated by the Spaniards whose peers had put them in those situations in the first place. Here a Spanish corregidor in Otumba caught two escaped slaves and sent an Indian municipal council member (alcalde) to guard them. When one of the slaves escaped the Indian's control, the angry corregidor took the Indian prisoner for eight days, and even tried to sell him for the price he would have received for turning in the slave. The Indian had to appeal to a local Spanish priest for protection.[100]

Later in the seventeenth century two mulattoes attacked and attempted to rob an Indian couple in Pachuca. The couple immediately sought out a Spanish rancher, who aided the Indian town officer in tying up the mulattoes and taking them to jail.[101] In an act of what could only have been symbolic emasculation, the mulattoes removed the trousers of the male Indian. A deficit of "maleness" might also be imputed to the Indians mentioned in the earlier reference to the Indian noble's marauding slave, who were said to be unable to protect their own women, to the Indian miners who returned home from their forced labor to find their women dead or gone, and to the Indian men punished by black and mulatto women at the bidding of Spanish masters. That Indian men were depicted as unable to fight women and for their own women reinforces the theme of Indian feminization that runs throughout this discussion and is crucial to understanding reversals through witchcraft of the sanctioned social order. That theme might also offer clues as to why the mulattoes who accused the Indian Domingo de la Cruz of being a witch focused their outrage on his testicles, which they ripped at and tore as they beat him half to death.

# 4

## From Animosities to Alliances

### A SEGUE INTO THE WORLD OF WITCHCRAFT

As Spaniards dominated Indians through black, mulatto, and mestizo intermediaries, they concomitantly created possibilities for affiliations between the intermediaries and Indians. Blacks, mulattoes, and mestizos, after all, were never fully integrated into the Spanish Republic. Instead, they were contradictory actors who bridged what Bonfíl Batalla calls the two "fundamental universes" of Spaniard and Indian.[1] By forcing contact between these groups and Indians in order to extend their own dominion, Spaniards undermined the delicate balance necessary to serving their own ends. As a result, while the aggression and unruliness Spaniards assigned especially to blacks and mulattoes came to serve the colonial project well, valuations in systems of colonial social control of some as leaders and others as led also had the potential to sabotage that project. This is perhaps another way of understanding the far-reaching judicial system: in protecting Indians, whose numbers were larger than any other group, from abuse and corruption, Spaniards were surely also protecting themselves from alliances between Indians and the very intermediary groups used to aggrieve them.

Colonial Mexico experienced no sustained insurrection over its three-hundred-year history. But slave revolts did occur with some frequency during the sixteenth and seventeenth centuries. These were sometimes planned under the cover of church-sponsored religious brotherhoods or confraternities (*cofradías*).[2] Colin Palmer describes one such revolt, planned only sixteen years after the conquest but betrayed by an informer before it could be fully realized. Palmer also writes about the most famous of these revolts, which broke out in 1611 following the death of a female slave, allegedly at the hands of her master. On the day of the funeral, 1,500 confraternity blacks, both slave and free, took the corpse and marched through Mexico City to confront the dead woman's master at his home. When that rebellion was quashed, another quickly developed. But before the second was fully realized, the leader died.[3] Military battalions en route to the Philippines also stopped for several weeks in Mexico City, further postponing the revolt. The plotters replanned it for Holy Week of 1612, with the directive that "all Spanish males were to be killed, but the women would be spared to serve their former slaves."[4] The rebellion aborted for a second time, however, when two Portuguese slave traders who knew "Angolan" overheard a black woman discussing it. These leaders were jailed, and eventually thirty-five black conspirators, including seven women, were executed.[5]

Slave rebellions took place not only in Mexico City. A letter from a viceroy to Charles II relates an incident that happened in 1671 as several Spanish merchants and their Spanish servants were leading inland a group of three hundred slaves, who had just entered the port of Vera Cruz. According to the viceroy, the slaves rioted right there on the road, "calling one of their own their 'king' whom they had to obey." Grabbing the Spaniards' own weapons, the slaves turned on their captors, overwhelming them while cheering, "Kill, kill." Several Spaniards managed to flee, but the merchants and many of their servants nevertheless died from "stabbings and blows."[6] In addition to punishing participants in such incidents, Spaniards responded with orders proscribing gatherings of blacks and mulattos and directives that free persons live under the aegis of Spanish "guardians."[7]

While some black slaves clearly plotted collectively to overthrow their tormentors, the mostly Indian countryside saw little organized unrest. Instead, Indians typically engaged in spontaneous outbursts aimed at correcting limited wrongs.[8] Frequent targets of attack included local Spanish officials, parish priests who raised clerical fees, and hacendados demanding labor.[9] These attacks ended when the specific goal was achieved, usually within a day's time. Otherwise, Indian rebellions were confined to the margins of colonial expansion where state institutions were weak: the northern Chichimec regions and the southern fringes of Spanish-held territory where, in Tehuantepec for instance, an Indian noble was named king in 1665 after a group of Indians killed the alcalde mayor and other Spaniards of the province.[10] Despite the long drawn-out resistance to Spanish domination in southern Mexico, Nancy Farriss comments that even with the Mayan "Great Revolt" of 1547, on the whole, "colonial Yucatán was . . . a tranquil place."[11]

It is difficult to gauge to what extent Spaniards feared slave and/or Indian revolts, and also to what extent more subdued slave/Indian interactions undermined the tension between distinction and inclusion that Spaniards were trying to maintain. Although I shall show that slaves and Indians were caught up — sometimes together — in witchcraft directed against Spaniards, there is scant evidence that groups of Indians and blacks — either slave or free — otherwise formed lasting alliances that seriously threatened overall Spanish control. Thus, while David Davidson writes that cimarrones from the Guanaxuato mining region joined with unpacified Chichimec Indians "in a brutal war with the settlers," a claim repeated by Cope,[12] in my opinion, the primary sources do not substantiate this scenario. The manuscript Davidson cites is part of a series of reports to the king on runaway blacks in the north. He interprets the phrase *andan asi a las chichimecas* to mean that blacks were roaming about *with* Chichimecs. Yet in my reading "the Chichimecas" seems to refer not to the Indians called "Chichimecs" but to the part of the territory called "the Chichimecas," which would have been the area around Zacatecas, where runaway blacks would flee from the brutal conditions of the silver mines. The document in question instructs "Juan Sánchez de Alanis [the local judge of the Chichimecas] together with some Spaniards who reside in the Chichimecas and one hundred and fifty Indians" to capture the runaways.[13] There is no mention of Chichimec Indians, only of runaway black slaves. None of the other reports in the series specifies that Chichimec Indians developed alliances with such slaves, and it is therefore doubtful that if such alliances occurred, they happened with any regularity. Moreover, Spaniards often used bands of Indians to aid them in spotting and catching runaway slaves.

But it is also the case that colonial officials raided Indian villages, and even houses, looking for hidden black slaves. This suggests an empathy between blacks and the Indians who might shelter them.[14] Caste mixing and poverty were also endemic to seventeenth-century Mexico City, which was the site of several large-scale multicaste riots. The first of these was provoked by a food shortage in 1624. It involved Indians, mulattoes, mestizos, and blacks, as well as some poor Spaniards.[15] A riot in 1692 was also prompted by famine and inflation, this time brought on by flooding. Charles Gibson believes that Indians planned the revolt over three months, selecting an Indian king as their leader and intending to "burn the city and slaughter the Spaniards as they fled from their houses." Cope, in contrast, sees the riot as a spontaneous unplanned affair involving "plebeians" of all backgrounds. Either way, Spaniards must have been fully aware of the potential for revolt in affiliations between Indians and other castes. While the 1692 uprising was unsuccessful, it apparently left colonial authorities "shocked and stunned" by alliances of Indians, mulattoes, and mestizos, and by the realization that Indians, who were the vast majority of the population, could rise up at any moment. The state reacted forcefully, putting to death eleven Indian leaders (several of whom died in jail before they could be publicly executed) along with two mestizos, one mulatto, and a Spaniard.[16] Following the riot, the early post-conquest policy of banning Indians from the city center was renewed.

### A DOUBLE-EDGED THREAT

Policies implemented by Spaniards in the cities were aimed at keeping Spaniards safe. On the face of it, those implemented in the countryside were aimed at protecting the integrity of Indian communities by barring from them black, mulatto, and mestizo interlopers.[17] A typical order to this effect, issued in 1578, declared that blacks, mulattoes, and mestizos "treat [Indians] badly and make them serve them." Yet crown decrees also suggest that beyond protecting Indians, Spaniards were again shielding themselves, for they were worried about the consequences if "simple," "clean," and "ignorant" Indians were goaded to disobedience by blacks, mulattoes, and mestizos. In fact, the decree just cited — which records Spanish officials' dismay with the violence "blacks, mulattoes and mestizos" perpetrated against Indian communities — hints at such worries, for it continues by noting that such people taught Indians "their bad customs and viciousness and some errors and [ways of] life that can spoil or hinder the fruit desired for the Indians' salvation, as well as their cleanliness, because from similar company nothing can take hold that improves [the Indians], as mulattoes, blacks and mestizos are *universally inclined to evil*."[18] As this section of the decree suggests, Spaniards were as worried about the ways in which caste proximity could undermine Spanish efforts to "improve" Indians as they were about the integrity and autonomy of Indian communities themselves.

Colonial authorities had to contend not only with the fact that blacks, mulattoes, and mestizos acted as extensions of Spanish authority, but with the sentimental and kinship ties many of them had to Indians. Although the state discouraged intercaste marriages, as well as less formal liaisons, for the church, marriage took precedence over caste separation. Thus, many blacks, mulattoes, and mestizos, as well as Spaniards themselves, married or otherwise partnered with Indians, with the result that the mothers of many people identified as mulattoes, and of virtually all of those identified as mestizos, were themselves Indian. Some mulatto and mestizo offspring were brought up in Indian villages. While we have seen from the case of the de Rosas family that such people could self-identify as mestizos and manipulate lineage claims to curry favor with Spaniards, it could work the other way as well. As a result, it might have been the case that while the non-Indian offspring of Indian nobles were apt to identify as mestizo, the non-Indian offspring of Indian commoners were more likely to have identified as Indian. A friar spoke directly to this issue in a 1625 letter to the inquisitors from the western province of Michoacán in which he defended the rights of mulattoes and mestizos residing in one Indian village. The mulattoes and mestizos in question had confessed to eating meat on days prohibited by the church, but the friar did not want them punished for religious offenses because they were born to, and had been brought up by, Indian women in Indian villages. They spoke and dressed like Indians, he wrote, and because they were "in all ways like [Indians]" he believed they should be treated as such: Indians would not have been prosecuted for such violations of religious law, and neither should their sons and daughters be even if, in a strictly genealogical sense, they were not Indians themselves. The friar further warned that if these mestizos and mulattoes were prosecuted, there would be trouble in "each of the villages," a clear indication of the sentimental bonds that could exist between Indians and non-Indians.[19]

The friar de-emphasized legal status in favor of shared cultural practices and social and kin affiliations. But his position conflicted with that of the state, which could appeal to legal classifications to insist on the boundaries it marked between people. We have seen such classifications contested as people claimed rights for themselves and denied them to others. And the Spanish elite both could and did do the same in an effort to further its own interests by keeping mulattoes and mestizos linked to the Spanish Republic rather than losing them to the Indian one.

A dispute between a mulatto woman of Indian/black ancestry and a

Spanish hacendado over where she should reside featured genealogical sparring. The woman had been jailed by the authorities of Temazcaltepec after the hacendado accused her of witchcraft and "tricking Indians and other simple people." One Spanish witness described the situation as follows: "[The mulatto] has a public tavern where natives, mulattoes and mestizos get drunk, which results in many scandalous brawls and grave sins . . . she lives in and owns this tavern in an Indian village where she cannot live, because it would be against the law; she has also committed a crime worthy of punishment having told the viceroy that she was born and brought up in [the village]."[20]

In her own defense, the woman testified that her mother was an Indian from the village, that the Indians "supported her" and that she lived among them "quietly and peacefully," even contributing money to their celebrations. Her father, however, had apparently been a slave on the hacienda, and the hacendado claimed that the mulatto woman had been born and raised on his property rather than in the Indian village. In coupling the woman spatially and (pseudo) genealogically to Spaniards through her black slave father, the Spaniard was essentially claiming that the mulatto was something like a runaway slave who had found shelter (and perhaps witchcraft) among Indians but did not belong with them. Legally, of course, the mulatto woman was free because her mother was Indian, but she claimed that the hacendado had pressured her after she was jailed, by telling her that if she wanted to serve him he would see that she was released.

This incident raises two important points. First, as we have already seen, genealogical and social affiliations were in play and in constant tension, with both wielded to serve different interests. Second, Indians were not merely physically imperiled by blacks, mulattoes, and mestizos; they were morally imperiled, at least in the view of Spaniards who wanted to believe that Indians were "simple people."

### BELLIGERENCE AND IGNORANCE: THE PROBLEM OF PERSUASION

I have suggested that Spaniards considered mestizos somewhat more "reasonable" than blacks and mulattoes; and that mestizos, in turn, seem to have had closer affiliations to Spaniards and Spanishness. Blacks and mulattoes, in contrast, were often identified by officials and others as baser sorts, as we have also seen. Spaniards gave them roles as henchmen because of this, while also believing they had a more per-nicious moral influence on Indians. One priest told the inquisitors that blacks and mulattoes had convinced the Indians of the Pánuco region that there was no "life," "pain," or "glory" after death, that only what the priest termed "the bestial life" was important. He complained that the royal justices "do not keep an eye on the continuous communica-tion that there is between blacks, mulattoes and Indians, nor on their living among Indians, which is prohibited by his majesty. Hence, there is great harm."[21] In an earlier letter to the crown, Viceroy Enríquez had also singled out blacks (as he seemed to have a tendency to do) when he reported that he had to disband a Mexico City religious confrater-nity because its members were fomenting rebellion, spreading rumors that Indians were "determined to revolt," undermining the job of con-verting the Indians, and hindering their Hispanization through the use of such "vile language" that the Indians came to believe they were "part of nothing."[22]

Attorneys also based legal arguments on the ideas about Indian gull-ibility and black shrewdness that fed the colonial imagination. When the Indian accomplice of a black slave who had robbed a group of Indians near Cuernavaca was brought before the criminal courts, his counsel argued that the man, Juan Agustín, was "Indian and ignorant" and acted out of "fear," while "the said black" (who went unnamed) "advised" him and was "the aggressor of all of it." Juan Agustín was a "domestic" Indian, the attorney continued, and "of little knowledge and understanding . . . [whereas] the black insisted."[23] While the slave eluded capture (which further manifested his shrewdness), the Indian was harshly punished with "two hundred lashes" and ordered paraded around naked on a horse.

The defense attorney's account of the black aggressor and the placid Indian spoke to colonial and, hence, to judicial understandings of In-dians as weak and blacks as bellicose. When we take into consideration the harsh punishment meted out to the Indian for consorting with the black slave, and the number of Indians put to death after the intercaste riots of 1692, the overall account indicates general tensions over po-tential alliances between "cunning" blacks and "ignorant" Indians. Thus, a mulatto (black/Indian) taverness could be accused of tricking "simple" Indians; an official could argue that an insistent black led a naive Indian to commit criminal acts; and Viceroy Enríquez could con-tend that blacks were spreading rumors of Indian revolt and otherwise undermining Spanish attempts to draw Indians into the Spanish sphere of influence. Taken together, the evidence suggests that attempts to isolate Indians were motivated in part by efforts to remove them from blacks' subversive influence, as well as from their abuse.

In the minds of Spaniards the social order could be disrupted through the moral corruption of Indians by blacks, just as in the minds of men disruption might occur through women's contacts with "darkness." Yet we cannot fully understand the consequences of either kind of contact unless we also understand that in the colonial imagination the "passive" agent was just as threatening as the "active" one. That is, it was precisely the feminizing weakness of Indians that opened them up to "darkness" in all of its guises. As blacks, mulattoes, and mestizos threatened to lead Indians astray in the sanctioned domain, the politics of caste took an interesting turn: Indians came to have a special relationship to the devil precisely because of their gullibility. The devil, often depicted as a "dark-skinned" man, is a figure that in many ways consolidates the colonial politics and symbolism of caste. He worked by means of Indians to threaten Spaniards and to aid blacks, mulattoes, and, it seems, mestizos. At the same time, "weak" women made use of the devil, with whom they were said to have intercourse. The weakness of Indians and women thus posed a threat to the Spaniards and men charged with protecting them.

In the Indianized and feminized unsanctioned domain of witchcraft, Indian contact with blacks, mulattoes, and mestizos led to a kind of dispersed rebellion, an "open secret," as legislation separating Indians from others failed in its goals. Women also benefitted from the circulation of Indian knowledge as domestic enclosure produced its own failures. In addition, the witchcraft idiom took on class dimensions, as the lower orders used it to ameliorate the disadvantages of their social position. It is in this sense that Behar reminds us of the metaphorical connection between the witchcraft of women and slaves.[24] But, as we will see, this connection was more than just a metaphorical one.

# 5

# Authority Reversed

## INDIANS ASCENDING

### FICKLE INDIAN "DOGS"

Like the sanctioned lie that was the state, the unsanctioned domain worked according to caste principles. Here, however, authority derived from Indian rather than from Spanish affiliations. Awareness of this fact entered into peoples' day-to-day interactions with and perceptions of their neighbors, friends, and family. Consider, in this regard, Juana Isabel, whose neighbors and acquaintances from Querétaro were perplexed about her caste and therefore about her social location.[1] In this case, skin color, genealogy, and social affiliation were contradictory, as Juana Isabel's neighbors tried to reconcile her light skin with her Indian dress and her apparent talent for transforming herself into an animal and walking through walls.

Evidence of Juana Isabel's "Indianness" included one witness's contention that Juana "had scared her on two occasions because she saw her in her Indian dress and then she transformed herself into a dog and went out on the street through the door without opening it." Yet, it confused this witness that Juana Isabel was also "tall" and had a "reasonable countenance." For how could these physical characteristics be reconciled with the fact that Juana Isabel dressed in Indian clothing and had "black hair"? Or that she had been "heard to speak in church with others in the Mexican language [Nahuatl]"? Juana Isabel looked like a mestizo and went to mass, but comported herself like an Indian witch and spoke "Mexican" with Indians. In short, as another witness declared, it was hard to believe that "a Christian would turn into a dog." Given that Juana Isabel's occupation was to "serve Spaniards," with whom she therefore had intimate contact, finding a resolution to this problem would have been particularly urgent.

Indians did not fall under the Inquisition's jurisdiction. Therefore, the inquisitors who heard the case in 1621 had to figure out whether Juana Isabel was a "Christian" or a "dog."[2] While her neighbors focused on her appearance and her social networks, the inquisitors focused on her genealogy, which was relevant because she was not black or mulatto and therefore had one.[3] Knowing that being Indian would nullify the Inquisition's authority over her, Juana Isabel was understandably eager to establish her Indianness. This, however, was no simple task. In an interesting commentary on Indian attitudes toward skin color, she noted that both she and her sister—who was even "whiter" than she was—had been ostracized from their own family because of their light skin, a feature especially troubling to her father, who she insisted was governor of Mexico City's Indian barrio of Santiago Tlatelolco. Apart from their skin color, Juana Isabel insisted, she and her sister looked like him and therefore were not the *pepenadores* (foundlings) two maternal aunts claimed them to be.

The inquisitors closed their inquiry by requesting that Juana Isabel's claims be further investigated. Their failure to successfully determine her caste—whether she was an Indian (and a dog who walked through walls) or a mestizo (and a Christian who went to church)—underscores the colonial riddle of social location. The resolution of this riddle rested on lineage discourses that moved from the company one kept in the abstract to genealogy in the concrete. Paradoxically, in establishing her Indianness to escape the Inquisition's jurisdiction, Juana Isabel also excused her sacrilege in some veiled way, for Indians by nature were considered "dogs."

Sometimes Indians literally dogged Spaniards, as the Indian market woman Mariana was perceived to do. Known as the "one who sells cheaply" (*la bende barata*), one day she took the form of a large dog and repeatedly entered the house of Doña Isabel de Tovar. Doña Isabel warned her Spanish neighbor not to harm the animal because "it was [Mariana] and if she were to be mistreated she could do something bad." But the dog was an annoyance and Doña Isabel's daughter soon gave it a swift kick. As her foot, leg, and even face swelled up, Doña Isabel's belief that the dog was Mariana-the-witch in disguise was confirmed.[4]

Juana Isabel and Mariana embodied the contradictions at the heart of colonial social dynamics: Indians were "miserable" people serving the Spaniards who paternalistically protected them, but in the colonial imagination they were also and equally dogs who were beaten down and walked through walls. To her neighbors, it was only logical that if Juana Isabel was Indian she would be able to take the shape of a dog and walk through walls; and Doña Isabel Tovar seemed not at all surprised that the Indian Mariana could also metamorphose into a dog. How did the supernatural side of Indianness insinuate itself into the experiences of colonial Mexicans?

We can turn first to a late-seventeenth-century denunciation made by a Spanish woman against a Spanish man named Juan Ortíz de Toro, for what the Inquisition described as engaging in "superstition" and a "pact with the devil." As women were apt to do, instead of going directly to the Inquisition, this one first made her accusations to a male intermediary — a priest — who then approached the Inquisition on her behalf. Ortíz owned a *pulquería* in a Mexico City barrio. According to the denunciant, the vessels he used to mix the pulque contained marks that appeared to be parts of a "painted hand." Indians had allegedly given Ortíz a nickname, *semomache,* which meant "your hand" in "their language."[5] If he thought he was selling too little pulque, he would insert his own hand into the vessels to swish the pulque around. Sales of the beverage would then multiply, soon exceeding those of nearby pulquerias and often reaching "more than forty pesos worth in a day." The interesting Indian hand imagery is reminiscent of the "powerful hands" of Spaniards. In both instances authority courses from those who possess such hands to those embraced by them. This chapter explores the hold Indian hands had on Spaniards.

The Spanish woman strengthened her story by recounting to the inquisitors what others had said about Ortíz. First, his commercial success led everyone to believe that he was doing something "unnatural." Astonishingly, Ortíz had once suggested with "daring and arrogance" to a wealthy Spaniard that the man marry Ortíz's daughter, which he subsequently did. This breach of class boundaries struck observers as an accomplishment that could only have been realized with some extra(ordinary) help. The second sign that something untoward was happening in the pulquería was that the place was always the scene of a great deal of disorder and dishonesty, "unnatural, vile acts" and homicides. Most startling of all, the Spanish woman told the priest, she had been told by an Indian woman that the evils that went on there were so many that "*even the Indians themselves* were astonished."[6]

The classic story of modernity as a bargain struck with the supernatural has been examined in interesting ways by others.[7] Indians were at the center of such bargains in colonial Mexico, and they were also implicated in more general impulses to achieve at the expense of social decorum. Indians helped fulfill a range of desires in sometimes convoluted ways. I use the word *convoluted* because while at certain points the stories present Indians as awed by the supernaturalism of non-Indians, it turns out that Indians were rarely beaten at their own game.

Let us turn for an example to the Spanish corregidor Francisco del Castillo Maldonado, denounced for witchcraft in Atrisco[8] after he asked the Indian Juan Ximénez to lend him some oxen to collect lumber from the surrounding hills. When Ximénez refused the loan of his oxen, Castillo allegedly predicted that the Indian's animals would die within three days, and indeed they did. Castillo was said to have regularly imbibed "Indian" remedies such as peyote and *ololiuqui*, and had once shown a woman a piece of *puyomate*, claiming that when it mixed with sweat from his palm he could have any woman he desired just by touching her clothes.[9] One witness claimed to have overheard Indians describing Castillo as "a witch that they feared," a claim that echoes the "astonishment" of Indians over the sordid goings-on in Ortíz's pulquería. It also echoes what people said about a Spanish woman from Mérida named Doña Leonor de Medina, who had "witchcraft papers and enchantments," and had "communicated" with an Indian woman named Ixcach, herself a "famous witch" once jailed for superstition. According to the denunciants, Ixcach maintained that Doña Leonor "knew more than she did," and she herself did not recognize the herbs the Spanish woman possessed.[10]

These three tales have certain points in common: they pertain to Spanish witches who are compared to Indians, but the Indians are then "duped" by the Spaniards. It is important to note, however, that all three of the preternaturally powerful Spaniards in fact infused their supernaturalism with what we might call "Indianisms"—that is, Indian solutions to their magical games. We saw, for instance, that Indians gave Ortíz an Indian nickname as he used their imagery and rituals to carry out his witchery. Denunciants of the Spaniard Castillo reported that he had learned indigenous magical remedies from an Indian, with whom he "studied" for five months. Castillo himself admitted to one of these denunciants that the Indian had taken him to a small round mud hut (*quescomate*) "where the Indians store their vegetables," and had taught him the uses of various herbs.[11] And when the Indian Ixcach asked Doña Leonor who had taught her what she knew of witchcraft, the Spaniard allegedly "read her the names of some Indians who had been her teachers."

These witchcraft tales indicate that if sanctioned power originated with Spaniards, who transferred that power down the pyramid, unsanctioned power originated with Indians, who transferred that power up. Again, like sanctioned power, witchcraft was available to those who knew the right people. Indeed, anyone — even a Spanish corregidor — could effectively use witchcraft if he had the appropriate contacts.

### THE DEVIL MADE THEM DO IT

In Latin America, as elsewhere, witchcraft was something of an idiom for cultural anxieties mapped onto women, who tend to "personify contradictions in troubled times and places."[12] Colonial Mexican witchcraft retained this focus on women, but as it did so it integrated discourse on gender relations typical of witchcraft in Spain[13] with the unfolding meanings of caste in New Spain. Thus, Indians, blacks, mulattoes, mestizos, and even Spaniards themselves became caught up in it, just as everyone was caught up in sanctioned power. A feminizing discourse mapped onto Indians, witchcraft drew women and Indians together in practice, and it blended femaleness and Indianness ideologically as the gendered dimensions of caste transformed the implications of Indian weakness.

As we have seen, many of the first friars to arrive in Mexico believed Indians were innocents. Yet many also feared that they were battling the devil for Indian souls. The Franciscan Toribio Motolinía believed that before Christians arrived, the devil ministered to Indians.[14] The friars' duty to save Indians therefore included extirpating the devil's influence and what Taussig calls the Indian "memory" of the past, which Spaniards read into Indian custom and friars saw revived in every ritual practice.[15] Even with the Inquisition's jurisdiction over Indians still in effect during the first decades of the colony, extirpation was no small task. In 1540, the Augustinian Antonio de Aguilar told the inquisitors that as he was preaching to the Indians in Oquila (southwest of Mexico City) he discovered that one Indian offered *copal* to the idols he had in his home, where Father Antonio also discovered "devil's skulls," painted cloaks, pulque, and other alleged offerings.[16] In its early years, the Inquisition repeatedly punished Indians accused of making sacrifices to and worshiping the devil, "talking many times with the devil at night," claiming to be devils, ingesting demonic "fungus" (*honguillos*), the "devil's body," and subsequently seeing demonic visions, sacrificing to idols with the devil's face, "having business" with demons, and being obligated to do things for them.[17]

Many of these texts reference established local practices, which of course were seriously misunderstood by Spaniards.[18] But the meanings ascribed to these practices also take on a colonial significance that, as Gruzinski points out, had consequences for the subsequent course of indigenous ritual.[19] Those meanings also reinforced the devil/Indian connection that, ironically — given the fervor with which Spanish friars and inquisitors went about extirpating what they understood to be idolatry — grew even stronger by the end of the sixteenth century, when Indians were no longer under the Inquisition's direct gaze. By then, as Fernando Cervantes concludes, as "genuine interest in the logic of Indian cultures" along with the optimistic beliefs of the first friars in the Indian capacity for conversion disappeared, Spaniards had become obsessed with Indian "diabolism."[20] For the seventeenth-century Franciscan Hernando Ruíz de Alarcón, the secret business of devil worship was hidden at the summit of every knoll and in the depths of every cave, the hidden geographical and spiritual centers of Indian life.[21]

In some respects, all Indians stood outside the sociospatial boundaries of the Hispanic colonial world, and in some respects all were therefore potential witches. But Spaniards and others attributed the most powerful forms of witchcraft to Chichimecs, who were at the greatest geographical and cultural distance from Spanish colonization and thus from Spanish control.[22] Whether or not it was the case that Chichimec leaders resisted colonialism by appropriating the devil for themselves, as Cervantes intriguingly argues, there are indicators that witchcraft was concentrated in these most "wild" of Indians.[23] This might be why, in 1618, the Indian wife of a Nahuatl-speaking mestizo told the inquisitors that before her husband had gone to the northern zone of the Chichimecas he had no understanding of witchcraft "or similar things."[24] Around the same time, two mulattoes who kept company with Indians and had been "in the Chichimecas" were accused of removing from a church sacred images that they then spit on and stepped on.[25] Late in the seventeenth century the Chichimec Antonio de la Cruz was actually put in an Inquisition cell in Querétaro because he was an "expert" in certain kinds of curing.[26] Questioned extensively about the source of the witchcraft with which several women were afflicted, he insisted to the inquisitors that "God revealed everything to him."[27] The devil appeared in many guises, but, in at least one instance, he "spoke Chichimecas."[28] The Chichimecs were strongly associated with peyote, which came from northern Mexico and was important to much of the witchcraft Indians performed for non-Indians,[29] and Ruíz de Alarcón insisted that much of the preconquest ritual Spaniards presented as devil worship predominated in areas far from Spanish settlement.[30]

According to what the inquisitors believed and recorded, the devil who found a home among Indians was the source of witchcraft. He helped people to know "only what God knows," and therefore to produce certain effects and predict the future.[31] One of his most prominent roles, and the one most examined by Mexicanist scholars, was to aid women with the "love magic" they used to control men.[32] Tales of love magic illuminate not only gender relations but also the unsanctioned affiliations women developed with Indians, the confessional nature of Inquisition proceedings, and, perhaps most importantly, a central and broader theme of witchcraft that connects it more concretely to the forms of control that characterized sanctioned practices. This theme was the acquisition of freedom and its deprivation, for witchcraft helped free people from their sanctioned places in the colonial social hierarchy while bringing others under their control.

Autonomy officially belonged to men and Spaniards. In the sanctioned domain, Spanish men routinely denied this right to women and to non-Spaniards by enclosing them, by resettling them, by forcing them to labor, by putting them in jail and in textile factories, and by turning homes into prisons. Women who turned on men through unsanctioned power were said to be robbing them of such autonomy, glossed as "free will" (*libre albedrio*).[33] This was a quintessentially male trait available only to those imbued with the reason that balanced or neutralized emotion. Women witches deprived men of their free will by coming to know "about the secrets of [their hearts]" and by "taming" (*amansar*) them.[34] This often involved the tying that Francesca Cerdan had allegedly inflicted on her Spanish lover. A man who found himself in such a state would surmise that the only woman with whom he could have intercourse was the witch who deprived him of his freedom. Witches thus neutralized men's potency, their control over the sexual act, and their access to women's bodies, thereby making men "weak." At the same time, witchy women gained agency as they imposed their own desires on those of the men they bewitched. Witchcraft therefore had dual consequences, for as one person lost his will another was exercising hers.[35]

Food was an important vehicle for female duplicity. Behar writes of the later colonial period that "typically women made men 'eat' their witchcraft, using their power over the domain of food preparation for subversive ends."[36] In this respect, witches produced comestibles—both ordinary (chocolate, milk) and odd (menstrual blood, pubic hair, and underarm sweat)—that they adulterated with powders, roots, and herbs acquired directly or indirectly from Indians, and then fed to men.[37] But, in keeping with the idea that witchcraft was a weapon used by lazy and unproductive women, those who failed to produce food could also be accused of witchcraft. Let us recall in this respect what happened to Francesca Cerdan, who was punished by the Spaniard Francisco because she did not have lunch waiting for him. We saw that as Francisco accused Francesca of starving him, he claimed to know more than the mulatto woman because he "was a man." But he also insisted that by tying him Francesca had made him, in his own words, "not a man." We thus have the ironic situation of a man understanding that he is "not a man" precisely because of his masculine knowledge.[38]

Francisco went on to make direct allegations about Francesca's sexuality. During the time he had known her, he complained, she had not only been "seduced" by the devil; she had literally copulated with him. She also had "access to many men" and had simulated sex with others that the Spaniard claimed "were not there." In his mind, then, the mulatto woman's failure to produce his lunch was tied to other forms of insubordination, the source of which was a devil who unleashed what the Spaniard deemed to be the mulatto woman's perverse and unfettered sexuality. While Indians, then, were the source of the wild food-stuffs meant to harm men and liberate women, the devil was the source of this Spaniard's emasculation and of the mulatto woman's emancipation from the drudgery of domestic work.

Although Indians and devils often appear separately, they were also juxtaposed in the colonial imagination. They seem to have met in the wilderness, to which downtrodden Indians fled as they escaped their labor obligations and the abuses heaped on them by settlers, servants, and slaves. There they mixed the herbs and concocted the powders which they sold to others, presumably including the black women hagglers who waylaid them on the way to market with their produce.

There they also lived indolently "without catechism and mass," and there they worshipped their strange gods.

If Indians distant from the colonial center were closely identified with supernaturalism, so too were "wild" women: those who were unmarried, widowed, or poor, and those like Francesca Cerdan who defied the rigorous control of men.[39] Poor and old women became witches, wrote the sixteenth-century Spanish Franciscan Martín de Castañega, because when men had no use for women, "women appealed to the devil, who fulfill[ed] their appetites."[40] Castañega's allusions to classical European associations between women for whom men had no "use," loose sexual mores ("appetites"), and witchcraft suggest that fallen women were not just witches. They were also whores possessed of a "voracious sexuality."[41] Women were "adulteresses [and] fornicatresses" wrote the fifteenth-century European Dominican inquisitors Kramer and Sprenger in the *Malleus Maleficarum*, their vitriolic and widely distributed treatise on witchcraft and female nature.[42] And the devil liberated their "insatiable" "carnal lust," which was otherwise suppressed by men.[43] Through their unbridled sexuality, women therefore undermined both the secular authority of the male state and the religious authority of the Spanish God, for they were "the concubines of the Great [Satan]."[44] Indeed, mild as the reference was, a priest described Adriana Ruíz de Cabrera, whom we met up with in the introduction, as "too much given to sensuality" before she found God.

As men linked together women's defiance of sexual and religious values, Spaniards linked together the sexual and religious immorality of Indians. Like the sexuality of women, that of Indians became a site of social control, for if Indians were left unsupervised the friars believed they would, like women, "fall into sexual sin" while they corrupted the socioreligious order through idolatry and witchcraft.[45] Therefore, conversion to Christianity entailed weaning Indians from illicit sexual *and* religious practices. The two were closely associated by the mendicants responsible for the initial conversion of Indian "pagans." For instance, Motolinía's account of what he identified as Indian witchcraft follows directly his account of Indian polygamy.[46] He linked the twin Spanish virtues of baptism and monogamy as he described Indian devotion to the departing friars: "Our fathers, why are you abandoning us now after baptizing us and marrying us? . . . If you leave us, to whom will we turn? The devils will try to deceive us again as they used to do, and return us to idolatry."[47]

Some Spaniards directed their gaze to voracious Indian sexual appetites, as did an Augustinian friar who, while claiming Indians were "very carnal" and "incapable of self restraint," reserved most of his condemnations for Indian women.[48] Sexual consumption was tied to other excesses of hunger, such as the belief that Indians ate human beings.[49] Spanish religious authorities were also concerned about "the enormous [Indian] vices of incest . . . and marrying two or three times"—as Archbishop Montúfar wrote to the Council of the Indies in Spain.[50]

### UNSPEAKABLE SINS

Montúfar's letter hints at another issue. According to him, Indians engaged in "unspeakable vices" (*bicios nefandos*) beyond incest and duplicate marriages. One of these he identified as "the unspeakable sin" (*el pecado nefando*). While we cannot be entirely sure of the kind of act the archbishop had in mind, pecado nefando described sexual contact between men in colonial Mexico.[51] It was likely a euphemism for sodomy, and "Sodom" is also a part of the Latin phrase the archbishop inserted into his letter: *hec fuit iniquitos sodome abundantia panis et ocium* (here were sinners in the excess of Sodom both in bread and kisses).[52]

In European discourse sodomy has meant "everything from ordinary heterosexual intercourse in an atypical position to oral sexual contact with animals," as Boswell writes.[53] Here it likely referred to anal intercourse between men. Pecados nefandos had long been harshly punished under Spanish law, and in Mexico offenders were persecuted by the Inquisition.[54] Thus, the effeminate "fag" (*efeminida, mariquita*) mulatto Juan de la Vega found himself called before the Inquisition after he was accused of "playing like a dog" with a mestizo man he mounted. The descriptions of Juan and his cohorts return again and again to their feminine dress, gestures, and activities. Juan de la Vega "cinched his waist," carried a woman's handkerchief, and wore a woman's necklace. He also "sat like a woman . . . and made tortillas and cleaned and cooked."[55] He and his friends were put to death in Mexico City in 1658.

Juan de la Vega and the others had adopted for themselves the names of notable Mexico City prostitutes, which symbolically connects the "homosexuality" of men to the slack mores of whores.[56] Indeed, the term *puto*, which might be loosely translated as "fag," seems to have referred not just to men who had sexual relations with each other but also to the kind of unfettered sexuality in which loose (emancipated?) women engaged. The Indian woman Juana who was rescued by her Spanish comadre Leonor was called an "old whore witch" (*una puta vieja hechicera*) by the Spaniards who were beating her. I have suggested that being a witch and a whore, and sometimes old, were closely associated states. Insults like puto and puta, often directed at Indians, spoke to what was perceived to be their degenerate and capricious sexuality, openness and penetrability, and mastery of witchcraft brought by the devil.[57] In his dictionary, Covarrubias defines a puta in Spanish as a "whore" (*ramera*) or "base woman" (*ruín muger*) with an "evil odor," but he silences puto with a Latin definition—*notae significationes et nefandae*—which might be translated as "marks of their shame and unspeakable sin."[58] A puto, then, was something quite a bit more unnatural than a puta: whereas the latter was a woman acting out her natural inclinations, the former was a man acting like a woman.

Although I would not want to overinterpret this point from a single case, it is nevertheless instructive to consider an incident that came before the Inquisition in the late seventeenth century. The documentation feminizes an Indian man by depicting him as exceptionally morally weak and sexually degenerate in the context of a pecado nefando, an act that was itself a perversion of what was considered appropriate male behavior.

An Indian sacristan brought the case to the attention of the inquisitors after he caught another Indian with a mulatto in the corridor of a Mérida church. The two were committing what is described in the text as *un acto diabólico* (a diabolical act), a *crimen somético* (a crime of submission), and a *pecado contra naturum* (a sin against nature), as well as a pecado nefando. The sacristan claimed that he had earlier seen the mulatto making advances to an Indian boy, at which point he had confronted the mulatto and called him a "woman." A female friend of the mulatto testified in his defense, but she probably did not help his case when she pointed out that he aided her with domestic tasks, and had performed similar chores, including cooking, bread and chocolate making, and washing and starching clothes, while working for another woman in Campeche.

Although the details of the mulatto's social affiliations and practices speak — like Juan de la Vega's — to his feminine qualities, with respect to the actual sexual act described in the narrative, the Indian is portrayed as the more effeminate of the two. For in addition to turning the Indian and mulatto in, the sacristan also wanted the inquisitors to know that the Indian was the *paciente* (the passive partner), with the mulatto "on top" of him. While both the mulatto and the Indian were therefore engaged in a same-sex act, the Indian was the one "opened up" like a woman.[59]

As this text clearly feminizes the Indian, it also opens a window on the concept of seduction, which, in its sexual and more general sense, is key to understanding the intertwined qualities of femaleness and Indianness, and the ways in which women and Indians engaged the devil — or rather the ways the devil engaged them. Indeed, in an interesting and telling defense, the Indian claimed that he was the victim of aggressive enticements, for the mulatto had seduced him by pinching him, teasing him, touching his "privates," and promising to take him to Campeche.[60]

## SEDUCTION AND A MORAL TRAP:
### ALL THE GOOD AND THE BAD IN THE WORLD

Seduction is a rather ambivalent concept, for it simultaneously captures willingness and resistance as it points to a certain lack of self-control in the one being seduced. In colonial discourse it links the sexuality of women and Indians to sacrilege through the quality of weakness. Indeed, because of this weakness the inquisitors' hands were sometimes tied: they rarely accused women of actively courting the devil. Instead, women were usually accused of implicit pacts with the devil, who seduced them into committing superstitious and sexual acts. In contrast, men had explicit pacts with the devil, a difference that points to the deliberateness characteristic of their free will and self-control.

As noted, self-control was central to Spanish notions of reason and to the achievement of honor.[61] We saw Sepúlveda link women to Indians because he believed that, like children, both lacked the full capacity to reason and therefore to master their impulses. We also saw women and Indians subject to forms of enclosure meant to regulate those impulses and turn them into productive workers. The moral flaccidity of women and Indians presented a challenge to the authority of men and Spaniards, for without the guidance of Christian men, women were as de-

fenseless before the devil's seductions as Indians were without the guidance of Christian Spaniards. "When a woman thinks alone she thinks
evil," wrote Kramer and Sprenger, and women tried to protect themselves through a defense that understandably rested on the devil's trickery.[62] Thus, a Spanish woman taught to divine with fava beans by a
mulatto woman (and caught in the act by her husband who kicked her
and told her the beans were the "devil's inventions") confessed under
interrogation that she knew all along what she was doing was wrong,
but since she was "weak" and "sinful" the devil was able to trick her.[63] A
mulatto woman accused of witchcraft echoed this excuse in a related
case as she told the inquisitors, while she cried and begged them to
take pity on her, that the devil had also tricked her.[64] Ana María, the
woman who accused Adriana, also claimed the devil had "tricked" and
"blinded" her as she begged forgiveness for lying.[65]

Although Indians — who had little fear of punishment — rarely spoke
in such terms to the inquisitors, their suspicious actions were sometimes also described as tricks of the devil. We have, for instance, the
comments of a friar who, in 1623, came to the Inquisition to recount a
tale told him by another friar regarding the confession of an Indian
under the auspices of his Guadalajara convent. "Take care with the
Indian Augustín," the other friar had warned him, "whip him a lot and
take his votive offerings and rosaries away from him . . . and make him
scratch out all of the devils he has painted in the house because the
Indian talks to the devil at every moment and *the devil has him blinded
and tricked*."[66]

Because the text lacks more description, we do not know what, exactly, the Indian Augustín was painting. Mexica architecture was covered with sculpture and pictures, and Indian pictographic expression
survived on monumental Christian architecture. Serge Gruzinski writes
that Spaniards understood it as ornamental motifs lacking "symbolic
content."[67] But the friar's warning suggests that in fact they read veiled
expressions of Indian diabolism into pictographs. That warning also
alludes to the complications of the Indian/devil relationship, the success of which depended on the instability of the Indian character: this
Indian actively talked to the devil and painted his likeness on walls, but
he was also a victim of the devil who had him "blinded" and "tricked."
The Indian, then, might have acquiesced but only because, like a
woman and like the Indian puto from Mérida, he was too weak to resist.

It is perhaps again through the idea of the child that we can best
grasp the position of colonial authorities with respect to the appropri-

ate punishment for women and Indians who were in league with the devil. We might recall that for Sepúlveda, children were "ward[s] in need of a guardian." And even for Mendieta, who had a much more generous view, Indians were "children" "in need of a father."[68] Both kinds of children had to be supervised if they were to behave in a civilized manner, not because they were inherently evil but because they were unstable.

This trait was also characteristic of women and Indians. As Adriana's attorney told the inquisitors, all women were "fragile" and "fickle," a position with which even the Dominican authors of the *Malleus Maleficarum* might have concurred, for according to them: "[women] reach the greatest heights and the lowest depths of goodness and vice. When they are governed by a good spirit, they are most excellent in virtue; but when they are governed by an evil spirit, they indulge the worst possible vices." Women without "moderation in goodness or vice" were just as likely to embrace the devil as they were God.[69] They were thus capable of "all the good and [all] the bad in this world," as the early-sixteenth-century Spanish educator and humanist Luis Víves wrote.[70]

I noted that the earliest friars associated Indians' preconquest practices with the devil, and many of those practices were thought to have survived in the caves, hills, and even homes of Indians. But some of those friars also believed that Indians had rapidly and happily taken to Christianity following the conquest. Thus, Mendieta wrote that the Indians "instinctively practiced those virtues which Christ in his Sermon on the Mount said belonged to all those children who inherited the kingdom of God."[71] And Motolinía insisted that "the Spaniards marveled at seeing the fervor with which they recited [Christian doctrine] and their eagerness to learn it."[72]

Some mendicants, however, pointedly acknowledged the dangerous uncertainties of Indianness. Diego de Landa, an early Franciscan missionary to Yucatán, wrote that "while the Indians seem a simple people . . . they are up to any mischief," for they engaged in the "rites and ceremonies of their forefathers."[73] Motolinía himself believed that even after the friars destroyed the temples and baptized their eager charges the Indians continued to "meet and call upon and celebrate the devil." This, he added, they did at night.[74] His ambivalent description of Indians who were Christian by day and devilish by night recalls the well-known witches' Sabbat of European women who might have been ordinary by day but who consorted with the devil at night.[75]

Of course any individual Christian could sin, but the sins of Indians and women were essential and collective sensibilities. As Sepúlveda had written, sin was a part of Indians' "customs and public institutions."[76] One seventeenth-century inquisitor insisted that "almost always these superstitious Indians cure by invoking the devil." It is "[their] tradition," he went on to claim, "derived from their heathendom of which traces are found, and they normally do it in silence . . . or by moving their lips."[77] Thus, even after years of colonization and efforts at conversion, Indians were still seen as flawed, for they appeared to fold traces of anti-Christian beliefs and practices into a scary silence.

The parallels in this respect between colonial women and Indians is striking. And some evidence comes straight from the mouths of women themselves, as in the case of a Spanish one from Mexico City who related to the inquisitors that she had overheard another woman say, "a woman without witchcraft [is] like a door without hinges."[78] This claim, which playfully rhymes in Spanish (*la mujer sin hechizo [es] como la puerta sin quicio*), locates witchcraft in the very essence of femaleness: just as a door without hinges could not function as a door, a woman without witchcraft was not really a woman; and just as a door leads to the outside, so did witchcraft enable women to escape their confinement by men as they opened themselves up to the devil, often — not surprisingly — through alliances with Indians.

By definition, witches lacked "good sense" because people became witches by escaping the control of their superiors and acquiring a freedom they were not adult enough to handle.[79] Women who fled the shelter of upstanding men and Indians who fled from the priests meant to husband them were both easily misguided. And their naivete placed inquisitors in something of a conundrum, for punishments clearly had to be tempered. Women were "intellectually like children," Kramer and Sprenger wrote, and "children," even metaphorical ones, could not be disciplined with the same rigor as adults.[80] Thus, as time went on, the Inquisition "trivialized" women's witchcraft through paternalistic forms of punishment like public humiliation, attendance at mass, or enclosure in a home that would be "like a jail."[81] Such punishments reinforced the idea that witches were ignorant and weak, that there was a metaphorical relationship between the not fully capable woman and the child.

The contradictions reach their extremes, of course, when we return to the fact that although Indians had clearly not yet internalized proper Christian beliefs and behavior, they were nevertheless pardoned from the Inquisition's jurisdiction after 1571 because its methods were considered too harsh for them. We might want to keep in mind the contrast between this treatment and that meted out to blacks, many of whom were newly converted themselves. Could it be that while blacks were believed to be more willful and aggressive than Indians, they were also seen as more fully Christian? If we look at the issue in this way, subjecting blacks to the Inquisition was an acknowledgment of their Hispanization, as well as of their penchant for explicitly choosing witchcraft. It might be counterintuitive, but it was precisely because of their seemingly muddled heads that Indians were more vulnerable to the devil's "tricks," occupied more powerful positions in witchcraft, *and* escaped the Inquisition's punishing arm.

The question of whether Indians and women were good or bad was of course never officially resolved, and this perhaps explains why they could be both seduced by the devil and lightly punished, or not punished at all, by the Inquisition. But in the end one is left with the impression that Indians and women retained a difference that was not easily erased, for despite the best efforts of the colonial state, they were never fully "converted." Indians would never be self-governing Spaniards, and women would never be self-governing men.

### SPANISH WOMEN AND INDIANS: PARTNERS IN CRIME?

It is not surprising that women and Indians often joined forces through witchcraft, tales of which were something of a constant throughout the late sixteenth and seventeenth centuries in the accusations and confessions of moral wrongdoing brought before the Inquisition.[82] Indians have a pervasive, if often shadowy, presence in these tales, and they sold their knowledge to accomplices or supplicants for money. Typical cases depict "out of control" women — including Spanish ones — entering into contracts with mysterious Indians, who in turn sometimes appeared out of nowhere. Because Indians were beyond the Inquisition's jurisdiction and women were seduced by devils with whom they had only implicit pacts, it is no wonder that the inquisitors seem more like confessors than castigators.

Let us begin with Juana de Escaredo, a married, twenty-six-year-old Spaniard from Mexico City, who came voluntarily to the Inquisition because she "heard it said that an Indian midwife was a witch . . . and believing that a witch could give her a remedy" she went to her hoping to get something to "tame" (*amansar*) her lover and separate him from his best (male) friend, of whom she was jealous. Juana paid the Indian woman for brown powders. The Indian, for her part, did not tell Juana what the powders were, but did give her instructions on how to prepare them in chocolate while directing her to "keep it a secret." Over three days, Juana fed the powders to her lover three times, as instructed, but with no success. Instead, she reported, her lover's relation with his friend grew even stronger, and she became even more "irritated," "hateful," and "jealous."

Despite this setback, Juana's belief in the efficacy of Indian witchcraft did not waver, for she simply tried a different tack by approaching an unmarried Spanish woman named Cathalina de Naxera, who lived in "a house with Indian women" (*una casa de indias*). When Juana asked Cathalina if she knew of someone who could give her something to accomplish her goals, Cathalina responded that she would "go to the plaza and see the *pusteca* Indians who normally carry powders for that."[83] "I will look around and buy something," she assured Juana. The next day Cathalina asked Juana for money and a carafe of water. Apparently, she had found an Indian woman who would sell her powders to dissolve. She and Juana were to mix in chocolate and feed the resulting concoction to Juana's lover. Juana gave Cathalina the money, and Cathalina soon returned with some white powders wrapped up in paper. The Indian who had sold them to her had described the powders as "very nice," and reassured Cathalina that she would "soon see what they could do." Cathalina gave Juana a carafe one-quarter full of colored water together with the powders. But Juana told the inquisitors that she did not know what this liquid was, nor did Cathalina tell her.

The following day Juana fed the powders to her lover in chocolate as instructed. (She volunteered to the inquisitors that this was easy, since her lover lived in the same house as she and her husband, and all of them ate together.) The powders had no effect, however, and Cathalina subsequently told her that she would return to the same Indian woman. This time she acquired green powders as well as more white ones, along with three pieces of a white stick. At this point the testimony ends with Juana declaring that because she was married and pregnant, she wanted to be absolved.[84]

Interestingly, we see that while the married woman Juana freely admitted to having a lover, she also lacked control over him. She attempted to subvert his will by taming him and imposing her own, but to do this she had to gain entry to the Indian world of witchcraft. Failing once on her own, Juana sought out the unmarried (and therefore ungoverned) Cathalina, who not only lived with Indians but knew where to purchase Indian remedies, which she acquired for Juana not once but twice.

Juana was not the only Spanish woman to go to Indians (and to great lengths) looking for a way to tame a wayward man. Doña María Jacinto de Bargas, also from Mexico City, reported that Doña Mariana de Bargas, perhaps a relative, had told her to "give an Indian servant of hers a *peso*, and she would buy a root to make powders that she could put in chocolate and give to a man."[85] A Spanish woman from Zacatecas allegedly asked a Spanish man to contact an Indian woman known as "Catalina la Droguera" (Catalina the druggist), also called "La Tizil," because she needed "herbs with which to make men want her."[86] She apparently told the man that another Indian had offered her different herbs "for the same crude ends."[87] Then we have a Spanish woman from Guadalajara who confessed that she had approached "many Indian men and women" looking for herbs or other remedies that would permit her to impose her will on her mulatto lover. She encountered a Spanish-speaking Indian woman (who was married to a mestizo), and asked her for a remedy. The Indian told her she would give her a root, and instructed her to grind it into powder and give it to her lover in his food or drink. The Spanish woman subsequently fed the root to the mulatto, and also to another man she was involved with, "so that he would love her well and not make fun of her." Later on, she ground more of the root for yet another Spanish woman's use, while informing her that in the river was a "very good" herb the same Indian had told her about, and she had also used that. She retrieved the herb for the woman, who subsequently used it on her own lover. When "a mulatto woman of hers" (presumably a servant or a slave) later became "demented," and rumor had it that she was bewitched, the Spanish woman went to an Indian man to ask him to cure the mulatto woman because she had been told that this man knew how to cure witchcraft.[88] She had also been told that the Indian gave "remedies" and she paid him three reales for a piece of a root.[89] A cleric told the inquisitors of still another Spanish woman from Mexico City, who had sent an "orphan girl" she employed to an Indian woman for some thistles. The girl told the cleric that her mistress put powders an Indian woman had given her into the food she sent to a man, with whom she was "illicitly communicating."[90]

Indian diviners and healers fulfilled other kinds of needs for Spanish women. Together with her husband, one of these women, from a village to the southwest of Pátzcuaro, called in an Indian man to cure her son of an illness.[91] A Spanish woman from Guadalajara offered an Indian woman a silver plate and a dozen pesos to look for a specific herb. The Indian woman refused the plate and the money, but told the Spaniard that she knew an Indian man who had knowledge of the herb. Subsequently, the Spaniard dispatched one of her mulatto servant girls to find that Indian.[92] The same document indicates that a pregnant Spanish woman, whose husband had "absented himself" from the house, had asked an Indian woman to divine his whereabouts, and that another Spanish woman sent for an Indian woman to find a lost silver plate; it also indicates that a Spanish family repeatedly called on another Indian woman to tell them what was wrong with an ill daughter.[93] After reciting ten masses to the Virgin Mary, to Saint Anthony, and to "other saints," asking them to bring back a lost daughter, a Spanish woman from Mexico City decided that this Christian remedy had failed and so asked an Indian woman (or perhaps man, she could not remember!) to take ololiuque and divine for her. The daughter subsequently reappeared.[94]

In 1622, a Spanish woman confessed to the inquisitors that eight years previously a niece of hers had disappeared from her house in Mexico City. She, too, first tried a Christian remedy that failed to work. Shortly thereafter, an Indian man entered the house unbidden. Seeing her "so sad," he asked what was wrong, and she told him. He responded by asking for three pesos, two for a candle and another to buy the peyote that he would take to find the niece. He asked that she not say anything to anyone because there had been official announcements (in 1621) not to take peyote. Hearing this, the woman did not want to give the Indian money, but one of her daughters insisted and she gave in. The next day the Indian came to her saying that he had taken the peyote, but "his heart had not spoken well." He left, and she never saw him again.[95]

In 1650, the Spaniard Doña Maria de Solis seems to have approached an Indian woman clairvoyant (*zahori*) near San Miguel who could read the stars, and asked her when the ships (*naos*) would come.[96] That same year, a Spanish woman from Tlalpuxagua stated in her confession to the inquisitors that her husband had been missing some spurs and had fought with her over their whereabouts. She had then argued with a young mulatto whom she suspected of having stolen them. Shortly thereafter, an Indian woman appeared "out of nowhere" and told the Spaniard that she could find the spurs. The Spaniard told the inquisitors that she had refused the Indian's offer, but the woman had nevertheless asked for some water, taken out a piece of white copal she was carrying, broken it into pieces, and put it into the water. She looked at the water and turned to the Spanish woman, who was watching what she did, to ask her about other people who had been hanging around her house. The Spanish woman mentioned some muleteers and the Indian declared, "well, they are the ones that took the spurs, which are in [your husband's] room underneath some boards. Go and get them. If I hadn't come just now, you would not have found them." The Spaniard followed the instructions, found the spurs, and paid the Indian two reales. The Indian then departed.[97]

### MARKETING INDIAN KNOWLEDGE

These stories expose characteristic patterns in the social affiliations, actors, and themes of the unsanctioned domain. In the process, and not unimportantly, they also show that Indians were consistently paid for their knowledge and expertise. One receives the impression that Indians actively participated in the market for their products, which were bought and consumed by Spaniards as well as by non-Spaniards. An intriguing point with respect to this issue is that the "pusteca," or *pochteca*, Indians the Spanish woman Cathalina went to see in the plaza were in the preconquest period long-distance traders and specialists in high-value goods, such as cotton and cacao. Lockhart has found little in the way of evidence for the activities of the postconquest pochteca, and he speculates that Spaniards took over much of this trade, thereby rendering the pochteca's functions obsolete.[98] But perhaps the pochteca became specialized suppliers of magical remedies brought from rural areas. Although by the middle of the seventeenth century the term might simply have been a generic word for Indian traders, Cathalina's contention that pusteca merchants "normally" carried remedies used in witchcraft suggests that certain kinds of traders were associated with special wares and that this was—if not a well-known fact—at least a known one.

These finer distinctions aside, Indians were clearly selling supernatural remedies even as they failed to produce sanctioned goods and services, lost their land, fled haciendas, and were waylaid by con artists and thieves on their way to market (con artists and thieves who seem to have sometimes used Indian remedies to increase their own luck). In answering the demand for illicit substances — some of which, like peyote, were banned by law — Indians seem to have found a niche and a way to survive in an increasingly cash-oriented economy. The above tales demonstrate that transactions occurred in markets where other commercial items were traded; that clients sought Indians out in their villages and neighborhoods; and that Indians sometimes brought their goods and services directly to their clients' homes. Gruzinski points out that the growth of a market for Indian supernaturalism breathed new life into so-called idolatry while simultaneously transforming its "meaning, impact and substance."[99] It also, apparently, gave Indians significant roles in and inroads into an expanding market economy. In the process, unwittingly or not, Indians themselves might have fed the Spanish obsession with their diabolism as they circulated that diabolism with the coinage of the colonial regime.

## THE DEVIL IN THE INDIAN

Inquisitorial punishments aside, the tales told above are rather benign in their consequences for the Spanish women caught up in the adventures they depict. Clearly these women did not feel threatened by Indian witchcraft. Instead, they freely used it to gain control of their own lives. The innocuous nature of these Indian/Spanish encounters is rather striking, and it is probably not coincidental that in virtually none of them does the devil actually make an appearance. When Indians dragged the devil with them, Spaniards' forays into the unsanctioned domain seem to have taken on more pernicious overtones. For while blacks, mulattoes, and mestizos considered the devil more of a helpmate than a threat, to Spaniards the devil embodied all the caste dangers the colonial world could muster.

We can begin to explore these dangers with an incident from Cuacomán, Michoacán, which plunges us into yet another series of complicated entanglements between Indians and a priest. Here, however, when the priest whipped an Indian for an illicit sexual relationship, the Indian repaid the priest with a supernatural assault, an indication of just how deeply the sanctioned and unsanctioned domains were entwined.

The priest in question, one Hernán Sánchez de Ordiales, initially described the situation to the local Inquisition in a letter sent from Cuacomán, far to the southwest of Pátzcuaro, in 1624.[100] In the letter, he maintained that an Indian had bewitched him, and the inquisitors soon brought the priest before them to elaborate. His testimony made it clear how hard he had tried to free himself from the Indian's power, and his initial letter read as follows:

> An Indian named Miguel Lázaro, who lives in the parish of Cuacomán, is a well-known witch. All the natives of the village know it because of the superstitions they have seen him [do]. He has bewitched many Indians and he bewitched me for punishing him after he had a sexual liaison (*amancebamiento*) with one of his own daughters. An Indian woman said I was bewitched, and the authorities verified it after I gave them news of it so that [Miguel Lázaro] would be punished. But having been given the information, [the authorities] did not sentence him; they did not punish him, as [would have been] just. So I grabbed him and whipped him and he confessed in front of me, and in front of the whole village, that he was a witch and that apart from me he had bewitched four Indian men who had complained of him, and that he had killed out of jealousy four Indian women to whom he was married, and [he had killed] six Indian men of whom he was suspicious, and he had taught witchcraft to one of his sons so that he would be a good witch like him. I sent this confession to the secular justices . . . and now several Indian men and women have cured me with beverages and balms of herbs and incense, and by touching me with their hands and the lower part of their mouths.

When the inquisitors followed up, Sánchez told them that five years previously one of his legs had begun to feel very painful above the ankle. Several years later, his other leg began to bother him as well. Although he had tried various cures, including visits to doctors, nothing seemed to help. About a year and a half before the hearing, Indians from his village had begun to intimate that he was bewitched, and persuaded him to let himself be cured "their way." It was well known, he continued, that Miguel Lázaro (who, at the time of Sánchez's hearing, was governor of Cuacomán)—the witch who had presumably bewitched him—had killed many people.[101]

Over the years, Sánchez had suffered very much, with the "life going out of him." No longer able to even say mass, he was determined to find a cure. With that goal in mind, he went to the nearby Indian village of Maquili, where he told local people of his illness and about what the Indians of Cuacomán said of Miguel Lázaro. They told him that an Indian woman named Marichi cured witchcraft, and he sent for her. Miguel Lázaro was present when Marichi arrived. (Sánchez told the inquisitors that his presence was necessary because the witchcraft had really taken root and in order for a cure to be effective, Miguel Lázaro's permission and approval were required.)<sup>102</sup> In front of everyone, Marichi said to Miguel Lázaro (in *mexicano* [Nahuatl] which was understood by all), "Why have you bewitched the priest? Cure him." "I didn't bewitch him," Miguel Lázaro replied. But Marichi insisted that he had. As proof she placed a jar of water on the ground, extinguished the candle that was lighting up the room, and held a lit torch in her hand. As she gazed at the water in the jar she called Miguel Lázaro over and asked him, "What do you see?" To which he responded, rather sarcastically one supposes, "I see myself."[103]

Marichi then asked him: "Don't you see that you have bewitched the priest and many other people? Don't you see yourself covered with the blood of the people you have killed?" Standing there naked, Miguel Lázaro assured her that he only saw her and himself in the water. This enraged Marichi, who then fought openly with him. "Why did you bewitch the priest?" she demanded. "Cure him and take away the witchcraft." According to the priest, the Indian was so "disturbed" at this point that he did not speak or move. But after a while he did tell Marichi that he did not know how to cure. She should cure the priest, he told her, and he would pay her, or he would look for another Indian woman to cure the priest. She then asked him whether he gave his "consent" for the priest to be cured and for the witchcraft to be removed, and Miguel Lázaro affirmed that he did. Sánchez added for the inquisitors' benefit another bit of information about witches: he told them that Lázaro had to approve of the cure, because witches can do evil with witchcraft and if they do not agree to cure it, it is difficult to undo.

With Miguel Lázaro's consent, Marichi cured Sánchez by sucking his bare leg at the point where he felt pain. Soon she pulled out with her teeth a long white bone, "without any decay," which she set in the jar of water. She showed Miguel Lázaro the bone, admonished him to look at what he had done, and ordered him to "take out the rest." Sánchez seconded Marichi's demands, and Miguel Lázaro — almost by force, shaking, and "troubled" — approached the bed where the priest lay. The priest, however, quickly concluded that Miguel Lázaro really "did not have the skills" to remove the bones; indeed, Miguel Lázaro did not even attempt to do so. Instead, he took two or three pesos from his bag and gave them to Marichi so that she would continue with the cure. She, in turn, again asked for Miguel Lázaro's consent "without any kind of fraud," so she could finish her task ("given to understand," the priest reported, "that in Miguel Lázaro's consent lay the ability to do it or not"). The Indian woman then sucked out of the same part of the priest's leg two other small bones, about an inch long, smooth and without any "stench." She then threw the bones into the jar so that everyone would see them.

Miguel Lázaro was taken prisoner, and Sánchez began to improve. He slept through the night, and the next day walked to the *casa real,* the headquarters for local magistrates, to see the alcalde mayor, who kicked his leg and saw the effects of the cure. Sánchez ate, slept, and gained weight but, as he had said in his letter, local justices failed to punish the Indian. In fact, the alcalde mayor apparently jailed those who had brought Miguel Lázaro to prison. So Sánchez decided to punish Miguel Lázaro himself with the whipping he had also mentioned in his letter.

Fifteen days after whipping the Indian, Sánchez began to feel badly again, suffering from the same pains as before. This time, Indians told him that Miguel Lázaro had bewitched him in retaliation for the whipping. Yet another Indian temporarily cured the priest, whose condition soon worsened again, and four and a half months before that, another Indian, Lorenzo Francisco, who Sánchez was told had successfully cured many Spaniards and Indians, had also temporarily cured him by invoking the names of Jesus and Joseph and making the sign of the cross. But according to what the Indians said, Miguel Lázaro had announced that Sánchez would not get better unless he himself cured him, and when all of the cures proved unsuccessful, Sánchez became convinced that Indians in general were full of "tricks," that they were "barbarians," and, in "common opinion," witches.

Sánchez seems to have never forgotten that he was a priest and that he was talking to the inquisitors, for he made a point of distancing the Indians, and therefore himself, from the devil. For instance, he told the inquisitors rather intentionally that while he did understand that the cures were Indian tricks, he never suspected the Indians of having tacit or even explicit pacts with the devil. If he had seen signs of such pacts, he added, he would have stopped the curing process even though he was not yet well. Sánchez's denial of the devil might have affirmed his own orthodoxy, for in seeking a cure from the same Indian trickster barbarians who produced such a witch as Miguel Lázaro, he was verging on blasphemy himself. Desperate Spaniards, even orthodox ones, often had no other recourse. But in incidents where Indians brought them too close to the devil, Spaniards also typically went to the inquisitors to denounce the Indians and to confess their fear.

This is what the Spanish woman Ana Baptista did after an Indian from Xalapa, María López, "tricked" her along with two of her daughters and another Spanish woman. The Indian woman had asked them to accompany her to pick berries. When they agreed to go on what they must have thought would be a brief jaunt, she led them from the domestic safety of their homes and the town, and took them "quickly" to the countryside (monte). The Indian then proceeded to "disappear," leaving the four Spanish women to fend for themselves.[104]

As night fell, they failed to find a road or a trace of the Indian who had led them to the spot. So they huddled together in the rain and thunder. As they listened to the "great noise" "above and below" them, it seemed to them that "demons" or something from "the other life" was out there. In the morning light, they discovered smudges on each other's faces and bodies that they were unable to remove. (Such spots, of course, suggest the "mark" that in classical European witchcraft sealed the devil's pact with the witch.) Not until three that afternoon did the women finally find their way home. And they failed to understand how it could have taken them so long to return, because their initial journey to that spot where the Indian had left them had not taken nearly as much time.

Escorted by an Indian from one life to "the other," from the safety of their town to the dangerous wilds of the monte, they connected the spots on their faces and bodies that they could not remove, the noises they heard during the night, and the fact that they were lost to the Indian, who must have tricked them into their befuddlement and helplessness. Ana Baptista added, in the manner of a well-behaved Spanish wife, that she had never told her husband, who happened to be out of town at the time. He later died, however, and she decided to report what had happened to another male authority, the alcalde mayor, who brought the case to the inquisitors' attention. Although the Indian could not be tried for witchcraft, the alcalde had apparently been looking for another pretext to have her confined, for she had had an "illicit" relationship with a mulatto. But she had already fled the area.

THE DEVIL'S FAMILY

We learn a lot more about devils—including their caste and their kinship—from a Spanish woman near Mexico City who told a friar, who then told the Inquisition, what had happened to her when an old

Indian woman literally introduced a demon to her.[105] Her ordeal began when she asked an Indian woman named Catalina for a stick to kill a dog that was eating the food she had around. Catalina responded to her request with the rather enigmatic question, "Why do you want a stick?" And then she announced "it's better to kill it with something else." She gave the Spanish woman a potion (*bebedizo*), presumably for the dog. But maybe the Spanish woman drank it (the text does not say) because when she went to lie down, she sensed a "change in herself." Suddenly, she had a vision of the Indian woman as a hen, and the hen spoke to her, asking, "How are you? How are you? Let's go call on our companions."

For a whole year, reported the friar, the two women would go to a place where people danced and "sinned" together. Some of these people, whom the Spanish woman described as "half-black" (*medio prieto*) men and women, looked like ragamuffins (*avechucos*) and others looked like goats. Some of the men had horns and dark faces and were dressed like demons. They had servants who had tails as well as horns, and who brought the chairs on which the devils sat. With "great happiness" people and devils danced together to a huge kettledrum (*atabal*) made of leather.

During one of their visits, the Indian Catalina ordered the Spanish woman to kneel before one of the demons. "How lucky that you have come," the demon told her. "I'm glad to see you. Otherwise I would be very much alone . . . and poor . . . look at all my children and my disciples." The "detested" demon continued to speak to her, telling her that he had to be her father and her master, that he would give her whatever she asked of him, whatever she needed, and that he would take away her "troubles." The Spanish woman described the demon as a tall man with faces on his knees, a penis as big as a club, eyes "like those of black Indians," a dark beard, and hands and feet like turkey buzzard nails, very long and dark. He hugged the "poor" Spanish woman as he put his left hand on her and said prayers. "I have my heaven," he then said to the old Indian woman, whom he referred to as his "daughter."

During this particular visit, the demon called to another demon, his horned servant, who was beardless "like a young black." Taking the "poor" Spanish woman by the hand, the servant said to her, "I am a demon. You must be obedient and humble before me, and you must take pride in your service (to me) . . . entrust yourself to me; I have to help you . . . always carry me in your memory, eating or drinking or sleeping . . . do not forget me." Later he reminded her, "you understand what I have said to you and you must do it, because if you do not, I must punish you before you leave." The Spanish woman responded that she understood. An old woman with horns and a great tail was also there, she recalled. This "ugly black woman" was dressed in a skirt that looked like black velvet. The first demon referred to her as his mother, and the old woman told the "poor little" Spanish woman that she had to do what her son and servant had ordered her to do.

At the end of this visit, the demon announced that it was time to say goodbye. Everyone kneeled before him and kissed his hand; then they kneeled before his mother and kissed her hand. As the demons and witches said goodbye to each other, the principal demon took them "as far as his house." This all happened, the Spanish woman told the priest, in the night hours "before the rooster crows."

Following this incident, Catalina was always calling to the "poor little" Spanish woman who, for six months, resisted visiting the place where the witches gathered. She did not see anything untoward until one day she was at her godfather's farm when the Indian called out angrily to her. Soon the demon servant of the one that "served the sins of the witches" appeared as a black man dressed in a dark suit, and approached her as she was sitting on a box "between the chapel and the kitchen," which were, of course, two sites of female confinement. "I have been looking for you for days," the demon told her. "My master cries for you . . . Give me a bit of blood from your arm, I have to take it and give it [to him]." And he then warned her, "be careful that you do not go back on your promises. My master will kill you. He is very strong."

What can we conclude from the preceding three "devil" cases? First, each draws a connection between Indians and the devil, beginning with vague references and ending with a full-blown encounter in which a devil claims a kinship connection to an Indian woman. Second, the Indians most heavily involved in bewitching were also said to have engaged in perverse kinds of sexual behavior (having sexual relations with their own daughters and trysts with a devil with a club-sized penis). Third, the Indians brought near-death experiences for the Spaniards involved: Sánchez was wasting away from his bewitchment; Ana Baptista, her daughters, and friend spent a terrifying night in the wilderness; and in the last case the devil actually threatened to kill the Spanish woman as he made clear his lineage connection to the Indian: he called her his "daughter." He also referred to the black woman as his mother and, as perhaps is fitting, he himself had eyes like "black Indians." The Spanish woman, of course, did not want to give him a bit of her "blood," for that would have meant joining his family.

Clearly, encounters with the devil had frightening consequences for Spaniards, who were walking a tightrope between the demon and the Indians who provided them with herbs and powders, and even taught them how to bewitch. Again, we see one hand slapping the other in endless ambivalent mini-replays of the whole colonial situation: Do we use Indians and risk the consequences? Do we run to officials, friars, and inquisitors to report on the blasphemy that we ourselves have set in motion? Do we ask for protection when we create the situations that undermine our own authority? Do we fear Indians or do we need them?

### THE DOUBLE KNOT

One way to grasp how Spaniards could both rely on Indians and dread being dragged by them to the devil's lair is to regard unsanctioned power as fundamentally like the sanctioned kind. The latter had Spaniards exploiting Indians but also "curing" them in court and through other modes of intervention. In the former, the Indian and Spanish roles are reversed: Indians can back Spaniards in their supernatural endeavors (sometimes with a figurative hand, as with the pulquería owner Juan Ortíz), but they can also use their power to harm Spaniards, which harm appears to be most acute when the devil becomes deeply involved.

Again, it might be useful to view Indian litigiousness in the sanctioned domain as an indication of the way Indians understood Spanish power. It might also be worth thinking about how Spaniards understood power in a domain not theirs to control: as the contexts reversed, Indians came to play the roles for Spaniards that Spaniards otherwise played for Indians. Sánchez's statement that his tormentor Miguel Lázaro had to be forced to cure or to give permission to cure has interesting implications when seen in this light, for it indicates that healing and witchery both came from the same general Indian source and that, just as Spanish justices might withhold their support, Indian witches (and maybe other kinds as well) could withhold theirs. The evidence suggests then that Indian power, like its Spanish counterpart, was integral to the politics of caste.

But it is important to remember as well that by endangering Spaniards, Indian power compelled the kinds of sanctioned violence that the colonial judiciary had its hands full prosecuting. In this respect we should remember that witchcraft was not a peripheralized world hidden from the center and carried out in secret but rather a set of beliefs and practices with consequences for basic colonial social dynamics. As Taussig has remarked, "the magic of the Indian [was] intrinsic . . . to [Indian] oppression."[106] That sanctioned punishments—including beatings—could be and were visited on Indian witches identifies Spaniards as the final masters of the colonial world, a position reinforced in disputes between Indian witches and their frustrated victims, who might quickly run to authorities that included inquisitorial confidants and priests.

The inquisitors themselves were not legally permitted to punish Indians. But clearly there were other well-established means for doing so. Thus we have the priest Sánchez dragging the witch Miguel Lázaro to the secular authorities, and the alcalde mayor to whom Ana Baptista complained using another "crime" as a pretext for capturing the Indian woman María. Moreover, the Inquisition did sometimes get involved: the Chichimec Indian Antonio de la Cruz was imprisoned in Querétaro by the Inquisition at the end of the seventeenth century. The Indian Ixcach, mentioned by the Spanish witch Doña Leonor, whose case was cited at the beginning of this chapter, had also been imprisoned by a judicial body, as was another Indian woman, "jailed for being a witch" in mid-seventeenth-century San Miguel.[107]

Indian witches might also have been punished through popular vengeance. For instance, the priest Sánchez not only dragged Miguel Lázaro to the authorities. He also took it upon himself to whip the Indian. We have also seen that the Indian Domingo de la Cruz from Tulancingo, who claimed that he was the king's vassal and was owed protection, was beaten by the two mulattoes who were trying to force him to cure an Indian woman he had allegedly bewitched. Clearly some of what we understand as sanctioned violence was provoked by fears of Indian supernaturalism. Similar fears provoked violence against women, as the Spanish woman whose husband kicked her when he caught her divining with fava beans must have known, and as the mulatto Francesca discovered when she was knocked to the ground by the Spanish man who accused her of sabotaging his own intentions while she consorted with her demon lover.

# 6

## Mapping

## Unsanctioned Power

Non-Spanish clients for Indian magic were as plentiful as Spanish ones. They included people like a mulatto woman who acquired powders from an Indian in Mexico City;[1] a black woman, one of many "blacks and mulatto women said to be witches" in Guadalajara, who learned what she knew from "a great Indian witch";[2] a black slave who confessed under pressure in Querétero that he had appealed to an Indian for "something to attract women";[3] another black slave from Celaya who confessed voluntarily that she had received from an Indian woman powders made of worms, which she then fed to her husband;[4] a mestizo couple from the Nueva Galicia region for whom an Indian woman drank peyote to recover a lost box full of money and jewels;[5] a mulatto from near Cuernavaca who reportedly asked an Indian to take ololiuqui to divine who had bewitched him;[6] a black slave woman near Puebla who confessed to obtaining from Indians an herb she could give to a man so he would "want her";[7] a young black slave from Mexico City who reported to his master that an "old black man" had given powders he received from an Indian herbalist to a group of black women to enhance their commercial skills,[8] and also to the young man himself, so that his master would not beat him;[9] a mulatto woman who was accused by another mulatto woman in San Miguel de Allende of having traded a shirt (*huipil*) to an Indian woman for something to "subdue" her mulatto husband;[10] a mestizo woman from San Miguel accused of approaching an Indian for something "to be well liked by men";[11] a black slave woman, also from San Miguel, who boasted that she learned her potent witchcraft from an Indian;[12] a mulatto from Mérida who claimed he had escaped jail by flying, a talent he had acquired from some Indians, who "taught him to be a witch";[13] another mulatto who confessed in Zacatecas that an Indian woman had brought her cotton, silk, powders, and roots to take revenge on a lover who had left her;[14] and a mulatto who himself drank ololiuqui on the advice of an Indian from Pátzcuaro, who accompanied him to divine what had become of some of his cattle.[15]

We can credit part of the fame of Indian witches to their extensive knowledge of native flora and fauna. In the wilderness they readied that knowledge for purchase and consumption by individuals like the mulatto woman who, around 1570, was bringing people out to the countryside (*campo*) around Durango to see "how the herbs were stirred."[16] Indians were guarding their secrets from non-Indians into the seventeenth century: in 1611 a mulatto woman had to ask an Indian what *puyomate* was, and in 1650 an Indian had to explain to a mestizo woman the uses of a small dried bird (probably a hummingbird).[17] But the notoriety of Indian witches was also a product of their intimacy with the devil, and he was a Spanish nightmare. While Spaniards typically ran from the devil, however, non-Spaniards turned him into something of an ally.

### THE "AMBIVALENT AND SHIFTING MESTIZO": THE POLITICS OF WITCHCRAFT

We can begin to map unsanctioned caste affiliations and to explain the role and presence of the devil by turning to mestizos, who are really not all that common in the Inquisition cases documenting witchcraft. Alberro believes that their absence can be explained by the fact that they masqueraded as Indians in order to escape the Inquisition.[18] Yet it is not at all evident to me that mestizos could fabricate Indian identities. As we saw with Juana Isabel in chapter 5, the inquisitors would go to great lengths to determine genealogies—especially if a person's Indian ancestry was in question. We have also seen genealogies debated among witnesses before the Inquisition and other courts. It would therefore be difficult for a mestizo to feign being wholly Indian in a strict genealogical sense.

In the sanctioned domain, mestizos occupied particularly sensitive public offices and therefore became important to the ways that Spaniards controlled Indian villages. Perhaps, therefore, instead of passing themselves off as Indians to the inquisitors, they played the "innocent" to Indian supernaturalism and/or are buried in witchcraft accounts that otherwise involve only Spanish witches (documents which I passed over). This would be a sensible explanation if mestizos in fact did identify as more "Spanish" in the sanctioned domain, where they tended to have a higher status than mulattoes and blacks. But, perhaps more than any other group, mestizos had split identities. If upper-status ones distanced themselves from Indians, lower-status ones (such as those brought up by their Indian mothers in Indian villages, and probably poorer mestizos in general, including the mestizo woman who petitioned to dress like an Indian because she was too poor to dress like an "ordinary" Spaniard[19]) might have identified more with Indians. If this is the case, greater attention to class issues may shed light on many of the mestizo patterns we see.

The evidence is not all that conclusive, but it is still worth exploring. We can start by turning again to mestizos and governors. We have seen how caste and class entwined in Indian discourse about governors who, like other officials, did not look after "the people." Extending historians' observations that elite Indians often scaled the social pyramid by identifying with mestizos and Spaniards instead of with Indian commoners, it would make sense that the Hispanization of the Indian elite would be paralleled by the "Indianization" of Indian commoners, and therefore their identification with witchcraft. Did witchcraft then figure in the local politics of Indian communities? Miguel Lázaro's entanglement with the priest Sánchez intimated as much, for the Indian was governor, and, although the politics of that fact were not elaborated in the documentation, it is likely that his position was contested within the village. Additional evidence comes not from the Inquisition but from the criminal courts, where witchcraft accusations are buried in what on the surface are sanctioned disputes.

In the late seventeenth century, a governor from the Toluca region brought charges against an Indian named Franciso. The governor—whose caste status is unclear but who was either Indian or mestizo—complained that he had been suffering for six months from witchcraft inflicted by Francisco. An Indian witness told the justices that the governor had called Francisco to the governor's own house in order to ask the Indian why he had bewitched him. Without admitting that he had, Francisco nevertheless promised to call a female healer to cure the governor and make him as he was "before." The governor took this offer of help as Francisco's confession and confronted him. Francisco claimed to be a Christian and not a witch at all, but the governor had him thrown in jail.[20]

Earlier in the century, a mestizo governor from the Tezcuco region accused another Indian, also named Francisco, of bewitching him and threatening him with the words: "So, Don Miguel Geronimo is governor. Well, I will arrange it so that he does not [have] three months." Shortly after this threat, the governor began "wasting away so that his life [was] ending." The Indian Francisco had "incited riots," insisted the governor to the inquisitors, and had "used" the post of governor without an order. He was "scandalous, malicious, poorly spoken and lived badly"; he had violated cultural norms by marrying his own comadre and his own sister-in-law; he also "knew how to punish friars and corregidores." Francisco was an "upstart" (*adbenediço*), one Spanish witness claimed, "the worst and most scandalous Indian in New Spain."[21]

The language of this narrative is remarkably similar to that used by the Indian nobility to describe Indian commoners in the dispute involving the mulatto governor Alonso Martín, as described in chapter 3. Those commoners were said to be "persons whose lives, reputations and customs were evil," who aimed to "destroy the governors by making the other natives rebel." The principal Indian plaintiff, insisted the Indian nobles, was "an Indian macegual . . . rebellious . . . an instigator of riots throughout the republic," "vile and low."[22]

The language of the second Francisco's case is similar as well to the accusations made against the Indian commoner Lucas Martín, also introduced in chapter 3. Recall that the Indian village officials in that incident said Martín had named himself governor, led a band of Indians that constantly disturbed the village's "peace and calm," and generally caused such dissent and confusion that villagers were unable to live up to their labor and religious obligations.

The accusations against the second Francisco were more or less in the same genre: they grew out of a conflict with a governor, the Indian was accused of being an unruly and defiant "upstart," and he occupied the governership illegally. The difference pivoted on the witchcraft accusations—coupled as they often were with references to sexual transgressions—that were clearly part of the narrative of Francisco's condemnation. We might guess that witchcraft entered into village disputes more often than not, but that its presence is rarely detailed in court because it did not pay to accuse Indians of witchcraft. If this is accurate, it might be that Indian witchcraft was even more widespread than the Inquisition documentation suggests, as Indians were beaten in private or dragged for some other offense before judicial bodies other than the Inquisition.

## THE MATTER OF TWO DIEGOS

As a counterpart to the mestizo governor who suffered from the witchcraft of a commoner Indian upstart, there is the interesting story of two Diegos, which situates a mestizo between a Spaniard and an Indian in the context of an elaborate caste hierarchy that culminates in witchcraft acquired from the devil. One of the Diegos was a Spaniard from Puebla in search of witchcraft to help him recover lost cattle, the other Diego was the mestizo he approached for help and then denounced.[23] The Spanish Diego came to the Inquisition to tell the authorities that he had mentioned to the mestizo Diego that the Indians from his father's ranch who used to bring him remedies for finding lost cattle were no longer around. The mestizo Diego replied that he knew of "something to make them appear," and said he would find the animals for the Spaniard. He even promised to put it in writing.

At first the Spaniard declined the mestizo's help. But eight days later, missing seven oxen "through his own fault," and worried about his father's reaction to the loss, the Spaniard approached the mestizo once again. This time, the mestizo suggested to him that he take advantage of what a Tarascan Indian had once told him when the mestizo had himself lost several mares in the Chichimecas.[24] After spending three fruitless days searching for the mares, he encountered the Indian, who instructed him to say "certain words" in a "certain place" (which words, said the Spaniard, the mestizo did not recount during their conversation). The Indian told the mestizo that as he said the words, a well-dressed man would appear. The mestizo followed the Indian's instructions and, just as predicted, "a well-dressed man with a pleasant face" appeared and reassured him not to be upset, that his mares would return. The man then asked if the mestizo wanted to "note it down in my book" with the mestizo's own blood. The mestizo declined but, he told the Spaniard, what occurred was exactly what the Indian had predicted would occur. Later, the well-dressed man told the mestizo where to find the mares.

Drawing on his experience with the Tarascan Indian, Diego the mestizo then found all but one of Diego the Spaniard's oxen. As he handed the animals over, he told the Spaniard he had seen the same well-dressed man, who had spoken "Chichimeca." The man had scolded, "You want me only when you need me, [then] you look for me, and when you don't [need me], you don't remember me," to which reproach the mestizo replied, "don't worry, I'll remember you." The Spaniard explained to the inquisitors that he was certain the man who "spoke Chichimeca" was the devil, because how else would the mestizo have known where to find the oxen?

This story has a mestizo affording a Spaniard entry into the supernatural world, a world controlled by an Indian with privileged access to the devil (who, like the "wildest" and possibly witchiest of Indians, spoke Chichimeca). It thus presents a chain of unsanctioned social affiliations that moves from the devil through an Indian and then through a mestizo to a Spaniard who turned on his unsanctioned accomplices and to his sanctioned counterparts as he reasserted his own legitimacy.

Clearly the mestizo in this story was more involved with the supernaturalism of Indians than with the rationalism of Spaniards, at least from the Spaniard's point of view. And this might point to contrasting mestizo roles, for along with the mestizos who turned in Indian witches, we have instances of a mestizo described as "more Indian than mixed";[25] a mestizo witch said to have acquired witchcraft from a Chimec woman;[26] a mestizo said to have known a great deal about the "herbs and powders" that Indians use;[27] a mestizo who spoke "mexicana" with his Indian wife and was said to have learned his witchcraft when he went to the Chichimec region;[28] and a mestizo who had devils painted on his body and actually instructed an Indian woman how to grind peyote.[29]

What sorts of conclusions can we draw about "mestizoness" from these cases? Did mestizos play both sides of the fence? Could we say that this was because some were Indianized and some were Hispanized? Did Hispanized mestizos aspire to Spanishness and therefore distance themselves from witchcraft while Indianized ones found solutions to their problems precisely through witchcraft? Perhaps it is not coincidental that the mestizo Juan Luis, accused of consorting with the devil with the help of an Indian, was just a lowly cowhand.

Juan Luis was eighteen years old in 1595 when two fellow cowhands from Xochimilco denounced him to a priest.[30] He quickly found himself before the Inquisition, where he was accused of believing that "the devil was as powerful as God . . . and [that] the devil could know the hidden things [of the] heart, as God knows them." Having offered himself "body and soul" to the devil, the accusation alleged, Juan Luis had not confessed, taken communion, prayed, or heard mass. In short, he had rejected the Christian (Spanish) way of life fully embraced by his five brothers, two of whom he claimed were Franciscan friars and three Dominicans.[31]

Juan Luis was not a mestizo in a position of authority, and he had been jailed on numerous occasions. His adventures suggest that lower-status, vagabondish mestizos were more apt to cavort with Indians and devils than to endear themselves to Spaniards. Those adventures also allow a broadened approach to gender issues, for Juan Luis was accused — as men generally were — of a "pact with the devil." Although the themes and affiliations of women's witchcraft and men's pacts with the devil were similar, the former foregrounded Indians and made the devil something of an implied force while the latter foregrounded the devil and concealed his Indian facilitators. Gender codes deemed women "weak" and men "willful." Therefore, while women were unwittingly seduced in indirect ways into having implicit pacts with the devil, men's willfulness left them open to charges of deliberately invoking the devil, with whom they had explicit pacts.

Juan Luis had spent his adolescence in and out of prisons and obrajes that functioned as such. In fact, only eleven days before his interrogation, the local corregidor of Xochimilco had put him in an obraje after his two companions reported on his alleged conversations with the devil. Transferred soon after to a Holy Office secret prison, Juan Luis quickly volunteered to the inquisitors that he had two hearts, a figure of Jesus, and a night owl tattooed on his left arm.[32] When he was eight, he said, he had requested the tattoos from an old Indian named Clemente, who was now dead. The inquisitors asked him why he had requested them, and he offhandedly replied, "No reason."

The inquisitors then ordered Juan Luis to uncover his arm. The notary meticulously jotted down that Juan Luis's outer forearm contained a Jesus and two hearts pierced by arrows between the wrist and elbow. Near the inner part of his elbow was a sore "the size of the palm of a hand." Running down the inner forearm, nearly obliterated, was a figure with nails (*huñas*) that "appear[ed] to be evil," as one of the inquisitors commented and the notary dutifully recorded. Juan Luis insisted it was an owl. The inquisitor then asked him what had been tattooed where the sore now was, and why he had obliterated it. Juan Luis said that it had been a tree, and that right before the corregidor had caught him, he had erased it with the aid of an herb (the name of which he did not know) that an old Otomí Indian who lived next to the church had told him to use.[33] Urged by the inquisitors to tell them why he had erased just that one figure, Juan Luis admitted that the tattoo was not a tree, but a figure "like a man."

Juan Luis insisted that the tattoo did not mean anything. But as the inquisitors pursued their line of inquiry, they asked him why, if it had only been a meaningless figure of a man, he had tried to get rid of it and in so doing had created such a large sore that he risked the loss of his arm. Juan Luis repeated that the figure was a man, but this time he added that the figure had "nails like a bird on his hands and his feet." He continued, however, to profess ignorance about what the image meant.

But the following day he confessed, "kneeling and in tears," that the figure of a man was actually a demon named "Mantelillos," who was "Lucifer's page."[34] He further admitted that the Indian Clemente had painted it when Juan Luis was thirteen, not eight as he had previously stated. Juan Luis said that he had solicited it because the local corregidor punished him with prison for repeatedly consorting with an Indian girl. In prison he met Clemente, who told him that he would tattoo on his left arm a devil who would come to his aid.

Juan Luis then told the inquisitors how, when he was out of prison sometime later, he had again solicited Mantelillos. As he lay flat on his stomach in the grasslands where he was herding cattle he said the following words: "I pray you come to help me because I have parted from God and forsaken Him and his mother and the Archangel Michael and all the saints." He described how he fell asleep, only to be awakened two hours later by a well-dressed man alighting from a horse. Juan Luis asked the figure to prove who he was by gathering together all of the cattle wandering about. When the man took off his cape and mounted his horse to do as he was bid, Juan Luis realized that the man had two faces — one behind and the other in front. The one in front was of a dark-skinned man with a reddish beard, while the one behind looked "like fire," with bulging eyes, a huge nose and mouth, and horns "like a stag." The man departed, an hour later all the cattle returned, and when the man subsequently came back, Juan Luis promptly offered him his body and his soul. But Mantelillos responded that he only wanted his soul.

In the years following this initial encounter, Mantelillos was always there to help him. He would herd his cattle, protect him from the rain, help him tame fillies, and, most importantly it seems, find women for him ("more than 100," as Juan Luis said, all of them Indian and all but two unmarried). At some point, one of these women would not consent to his advances and Juan Luis renounced Mantelillos in frustration. But eight days later, when he again needed his help, he called upon him once again.

Juan Luis also told the inquisitors that Mantelillos had freed him from prison nine times. At one point, when he was in an obraje for a full year, Mantelillos also repeatedly helped him card wool.[35] When he was released from the obraje, he went back to live with his Indian wife but still had all of the women he wanted. The last time he was imprisoned, on his way to the Holy Office, Mantelillos came to him and told him that he could no longer help him because "God did not want it."[36] Besides, the demon added rather mischievously, or perhaps angrily, "look at the mountain of shoes I have ruined helping you and following behind you."[37] He promised, however, that if Juan Luis denied everything to the Holy Office, he would help him when he got out.

As the testimony concluded, the inquisitors began to ask Juan Luis detailed questions about Lucifer's pages and the meaning of the tattoos on his arm. Juan Luis responded that the Indian Clemente told him there were three pages apart from Mantelillos, and that they all wandered the earth looking for the bodies and souls of people like him. Clemente had also tattooed the pictures. The Jesus meant that he was forsaken; the hearts represented Juan Luis's own and the devil's, with the arrow signifying the linkage between them. The owl was not an owl, he said. It was actually Mantelillos's paw (*pata*), which he did not erase so as not to make the sore any worse. He also explained that his left arm was tattooed because it was usually covered, while his right shirt sleeve was always turned up. This admission of course indicated that he had willingly entered into a pact with the devil.

The inquisitors then asked Juan Luis an extremely revealing question: they wondered how he had "dared" to greet the devil on his own out in the grasslands without the Indian Clemente's help. Juan Luis declared that Clemente had already spoken with Mantelillos, and that therefore he, Juan Luis, "had nothing to fear." At any rate, said Juan

Luis, "his heart was so distressed" because he had been jailed so often that he had no choice but to approach the devil. Clemente had assured him, moreover, that when he renounced God he would not go to hell but would instead be with Mantelillos "without a care."

INDIAN SILENCE

Juan Luis spent several months in prison before confessing that Clemente was not dead, but alive and residing in an obraje in Tezcuco, and that his real name was Gabriel Sánchez Matheo. Several weeks later the inquisitors called Gabriel before them. They noted that he was "very closed" and, as he did not speak Spanish, they provided him with an interpreter. At first the Indian denied everything, but soon he conceded that Juan Luis did come to him asking for advice and that he had indeed told him to put himself in the devil's care and to renounce God and the saints. Shortly after that, Gabriel told the inquisitors, Juan Luis's parents removed him from the obraje. Yet Gabriel still denied having tattooed the devil or invoking him by the name "Mantelillos." Instead, he said that he had simply implored, "Demon, help whoever is in your care, help me, I am in your care." Because the devil "flees from God and the saints," he added, he had deliberately renounced these Christian figures so that the devil would come to him.

When the inquisitors asked him who had taught him to renounce God and to invoke the devil by whatever name, Gabriel insisted that no one had taught him. He just knew — it was "born from his heart" — that the devil would help him and take away "the sorrow," for he remembered the ancient Indians invoked the devil to help them. With this remarkable claim, Gabriel seems to have infused colonial content into his historical memory and the "Indian past" that he was prompted to recall. His vision therefore seemingly coincided with the Spanish one that located the devil in the very heart of the Indian.

Cervantes suggests that "the devil in many cases . . . constitut[ed] a useful tool in the process of [Indian] resistance."[38] Undoubtedly, this is one way to consider the issue. But we saw in the previous chapter that the Chichimec Antonio de la Cruz claimed to have received his supernatural knowledge from God.[39] It might therefore be worthwhile here to stress that the texts are a reflection: they mirror the confusion in colonial thought and practice over the forces — good or evil — with which Indians should be identified. In the present case, this confusion is quite acute: here is an Indian who has a name, but we are not sure of what it is, and he cannot be persecuted by the Inquisition even though his mysterious "silence" and subsequent confession confirm the inquisitors' assumption that Indians are indeed the devil's conduits. Regardless of whether Gabriel/Clemente believed it of himself, or even presented himself to the inquisitors in such a way, this bedeviled Indian represented both a counter-force to Spanish authority and an acquiescence to that authority, which turned Indians to devils and even into devils in the first place. Because Indian resistance grew out of the context of the caste hierarchies created by Spaniards to oversee Indians, it points to the hegemonic origins and even functions of witchcraft itself: the devil/Indian association confirmed the Spanish need to oversee Indians.

### "OUT OF THE CREVICE OF THE EARTH": INDIANS EXPOSED

Other cases of pacts with the devil reinforce the sense that Indians and their magic were enmeshed in the caste networks and meanings that gave definition to the whole colonial project. The mulatto Francisco Ruíz de Castrejon, who was also brought before the inquisitors in Pátzcuaro for a pact with the devil, allegedly had two small books in his possession on different occasions.[40] In one, the devil named "To (or Yo) Sanchito" illustrated every page.[41] In the other, "My master Lucifer I offer myself to you so that you might help me in my endeavors" was written in Tarascan.[42] In noting that among the Indian shamans of the Andes, "*magia* required a pact with the devil *and* the use of magic books," Taussig links the buying of these books—which standardized magical knowledge—to the anonymity of market transactions and ultimately to colonial domination and "all that is civilized."[43] It is curious, of course, that non-literate peoples—as most non-Spaniards were— would carry around books with the devil's words. But God spoke to these same people through "the Book," the Bible, which was probably equally incomprehensible to many of them. As Taussig further points out, judicial authorities also used "magical words." Therefore, the book motif suggests another and quite interesting dimension to subordinated peoples' understandings of Spanishness and its attendant powers.

The first witness in Francisco's case was a Spaniard who claimed that—according to what a black slave had told him—Francisco had given the second of the two books to the Indian Juan Aguera. The Spaniard also told the inquisitors that the Indians called Francisco "Mahoma," a variation of Mohammed Indians likely picked up in the course of their religious reeducation. Francisco's anti-Christian name highlighted his unsanctioned authority while insinuating that he had more such authority than the Indians who gave him the name. Indeed, the Indian Juan Aguera, who was brought in for questioning, even denied culpability, telling the inquisitors that he had taken the book from the mulatto, but also that he had not really wanted it as he was Christian and, at any rate, did not know how to read. This testimony removed the Indian altogether from the social affiliations of this developing hierarchy of effective action.[44]

Then the mestizo Pedro Navarrete testified to knowing Francisco, who had once told him in front of the black slave Pedro Garrote not to be "pained," that he would give him "something" to quell his fear of colonial officials. Navarrete, who also could not read, later told the inquisitors that he had found the book in a small basket in the Indian Juan's house, and had turned it in to his boss's wife. Garrote corroborated what the others had said, as did the boss's wife herself.

Francisco then "confessed," telling the inquisitors that eight years previously he had seen the free mulatto Gabriel de Tapia handling a horse well. Gabriel told him that he had a "familiar" (*familiar*).[45] Francisco begged him for it. Because Gabriel had two, he consented to give one to Francisco on the condition that he not let anyone discover it. Francisco promised that he would not, and from his boot Gabriel retrieved a small black taffeta pouch containing the first of the books, the one with "the devil on every page." When he was riding, Francisco told the inquisitors, he was to whip the horse with his hat and say "To (or Yo) Sanchito," which meant "come here Sanchito" (Sanchito being the proper name of the devil, according to the mulatto Gabriel). Francisco transferred the book to his own boot, and began to handle horses just as Gabriel did, until he arrived at a ravine and his filly, prancing around, threw him to the other side. Disenchanted, Francisco decided to confess, and he gave the pouch to a priest who burned it.

Francisco then recounted the successes he had in his life with the books in his possession. For instance, another black slave, Manuel, told him about an Indian girl "whose body no one had been able to 'get.'" Francisco vowed to get her, and he did. When the town's Indians chased after him, he prayed to the book and they were unable to catch him. Later, he "got" many other women this way and even instructed the mestizo Pedro Navarrete, Manuel, and two Indians, Dieguillo and Petruche, in the use of the book. Francisco also pointed out that while the book was in his possession he was more arrogant and daring than usual. These are interesting admissions because they tell us that just as the devil made women and Indians "wild," he could also set loose a passion in the men with whom he entered into pacts by relaxing their self-control.

Francisco spent several months in prison while the inquisitors waited for more information, for clearly what he had told them did not entirely make sense to them. Sure enough, Francisco declared that he had lied, that the first book was given to him not by the mulatto Gabriel, but by an Indian named Anton Churi. This was not the same book as the one in Tarascan that Francisco had supposedly given to the Indian Juan Aguera. That one Francisco originally claimed to have found in a river. But he eventually conceded that two years previously, while he was in Pátzcuaro (Michoacán), an Indian (presumably Tarascan) had come up to him and offered him that book for a payment of two reales, which Francisco paid. Finally, then, Indians are linked to both books, and therefore to Francisco's communion with the devil.

Indians and devils are almost completely juxtaposed in Juan de Morga's story. He was a mulatto slave who threw himself at the mercy of the inquisitors for a pact with the devil after having complained to the authorities for years that his mestizo master treated him with extreme cruelty. Although it had taken several attempts before his case was heard, in the end the inquisitors fulfilled their obligation to protect slaves when they determined that he should not be returned to his master.[46]

Juan's story began with a rare genealogy as he told the inquisitors that his father was a Spaniard from Antequera, and his mother a black slave from the same city. Because his mother was a slave, Juan was too. Instead of freeing him, his father sold him when he was rather young to a public accountant in Mexico City. At some point he ran away, but after several months on the lam he was caught through a chance encounter with an acquaintance of his master. He was returned to the master, who told him that instead of flogging Juan he would send him to Zacatecas to be sold. In Zacatecas he encountered a mestizo "while walking down the street." The mestizo remarked to Juan that he was "handsome," and asked Juan if he wanted him for a master. Juan responded with derision that "there [were] enough Spaniards" for him to serve, implying, of course, that the mestizo was of too low a status to serve as a mulatto's master. This is a reminder of the thin line between freedom and captivity — between owning and being owned — for both the mestizo master and the mulatto slave had Spanish fathers. Out of spite, it seems, the mestizo promptly bought Juan, thus initiating a hellish life that routinely included imprisonment, beatings, arduous labor, and twice involved extensive brandings. Impervious to Juan's pleas, the mestizo refused to sell him "even for a thousand pesos."

Juan escaped again to Mexico City. But he was again caught and this time sent to work in an obraje as the authorities pondered his case. During this period, friends betrothed Juan to a black slave named Micaela. But the mestizo master sent his agents after Juan, and they scared Micaela away by threatening to buy her and take her to Zacatecas too. As Juan journeyed back to Zacatecas with his tormentors, he renounced God by declaring that "neither His justice, His prayers nor His excommunication were worth anything" since "there was no God in heaven and . . . no reason to believe in the saints." When the party stopped one night, Juan was tied to a sack of goods to prevent his escape. At midnight he "earnestly" called to the devil, telling him that he would exchange his soul for his freedom. Almost at once the bag burst and Juan escaped. He grabbed the rope with which he had been tied, and contemplated suicide by hanging.[47] But his master's cronies awoke and severely beat him. When the group arrived back in Zacatecas, Juan's mestizo master told him that if Juan ran off to Mexico City again he would get him back, even if cost him everything he had.

One day Juan dawdled on his way to work. His master came after him and dragged him off to the mines, running him over with his horse and knocking him into some cactus spines. Juan worked a full day, but when it was over he stood next to a wall and implored of no one in particular, "Isn't there a demon that can help me get away from this man?" As he cried, an Indian approached him and asked what was wrong. Juan told him and showed him his face, which was covered with scratches from the cactus spines. Certainly, the Indian advised Juan, he would gain more from serving the devil than not. "Promise me this," the Indian said, "and I will give you an herb to make your master fond of you and never do you wrong." Juan agreed as the Indian told him that he could never again go to mass or worship any saint or God, gave him an herb, and instructed him to ask the devil for help. His master subsequently treated him well, said Juan, but when the Lenten season approached Juan felt the need to reconcile himself to God, so he threw away the herb the Indian had given him. He never got the chance to reconcile himself, however, for his master did not allow the slaves to go to mass that season.[48] Several months later, following a fight that two young women had over him, and perhaps fearing the consequences, Juan mounted a mule at midnight, determined to reach the Holy Office.

The Inquisition's main task was not to oversee slaveholders' treatment of their slaves but to police unorthodox religious beliefs and behaviors. Although in the end they did offer Juan protection, they were less interested in the (probably) not unusual story of his master's brutality than they were in Juan's association with the devil, and they focused on this aspect of the story as they questioned Juan. In particular, they grilled him about the Indian, for they wanted to know if Juan believed this Indian to be the devil, or if he thought the man was "truly" an Indian. Juan's reply was just as muddled as the question: he said that at first he truly thought the man was an Indian, but when the remedy turned out to work, he decided he was the devil.

Although details of the stories told by Juan de Morga, Juan Luis, and Francisco change to accommodate individual experiences, the tales have similar structures. First, in all of them the devil appears outside and in the wilderness. (In fact, the devil never simply wanders the streets looking for victims. He is mostly outside in "male" spaces welcoming men or inside homes in "female" spaces having intercourse with women.) Second, in all three instances, Indians are the link to the devil. In Juan Luis's case, as well as Juan de Morga's, an Indian introduced the men to the devil; in Francisco's case two Indians were the source of his devilish books. Third, two of the defendants reported that they had first tried to elicit the devil's help without the aid of an Indian, once through a mulatto's "familiar" and once through a mulatto's own direct appeal.[49] Both attempts quickly ended in failure: Juan Luis was thrown from his horse and concluded that the familiar his mulatto friend gave him was a sham; Juan de Morga escaped from his bindings only to have his captors awaken. The inquisitors themselves wondered at Juan Luis's bravery or stupidity, as they initially believed he had invoked the devil without the Indian's mediation. In Juan de Morga's case, moreover, they were particularly interested in whether the figure who helped him was "truly" an Indian or the devil himself. The inquisitors' and Juan's own confusion over whether the Indian actually was the devil speaks to the interpenetration of the two figures in the colonial imagination.

Devilish Indians of course did not fall under the Inquisition's jurisdiction, even if they were sometimes brought in for questioning, and the full extent of their roles sometimes surfaces only after much prodding by the inquisitors. It is almost as if the Indian/devil connection was so taken for granted that it was submerged in the back of the transgressor's mind. As Carlo Ginzburg so eloquently describes the testimony of the miller Menocchio in another Inquisition context, "We see emerging, as if out of the crevice of the earth, a deep-rooted cultural stratum."[50] The fact that in the present case the Indian/devil combination was frequently acknowledged at the end of a confession that meandered here and there might also tell us something about the inquisitors, who perhaps believed that a case was not resolved nor a confession complete until an Indian appeared. For instance, they seem not to have been satisfied with the mulatto Francisco's confession until he named the Indians he had encountered; and we saw how they grilled Juan de Morga. We might conclude, then, that an Indian was utterly necessary to any successful dealings with the devil, at least as far as the inquisitors were concerned. The narratives also suggest, however, that popular belief gave Indians over to the devil as well.[51]

REGARDING HYBRIDITY:
BLACKS, DEVILS, AND INDIANS

That the mulatto Francisco described the devil as a black man (as well as as a horned dog and a cow) and the mestizo Juan Luis described him as dark might lead us to conclude that the colonial Mexican devil was black. By extension, we might then conclude that blackness prevailed over Indianness in the unsanctioned domain. It is true that in the European imagination, and especially in the Spanish one, the devil was male and his image was often black, and we have already seen how Spaniards associated blackness with a host of negative qualities.[52] In this respect, although the documentation refers only occasionally to the skin color of Indians, and then only for purposes of caste identification, skin color and other features of blacks' physiognomy figure prominently in it.[53] Such physiognomy is invariably disparaged and often coupled with reports of sacrilege. Thus we have one Inquisition text describing a mulatto burned at the stake in 1605 for impersonating a priest, "stealing" a black woman, and breaking out of jail as "a tall dark man with wide shoulders, a very ugly (*feyissimo*) face, a wide, blunt nose, and thick lips like a black."[54] Another text has the devil possessing "a large colored face, ugly and dark."[55] Another contains the claim of a Jesuit friar that two "ugly" blacks with "small, sunken eyes" were wandering around the northern zone of Nueva Vizcaya, "preaching the devil's words to the Indians."[56] In yet another, a mulatto woman suspected of witchcraft is described as "fat with an ugly face."[57]

According to Jean Devisse and Michel Mollat, for Europeans black has historically been "the color of affliction, of bereavement and of penance, the expression of darkness — in a word, the evocation of evil and unhappiness . . . socially . . . unacceptable — the color of ugliness, of bodily uncleanliness, of poverty, the color of lepers and old people."[58] And we saw how Covarrubias defined "black" as a "sad and unlucky color." But the roots in Christian tradition of these negative perceptions are unclear.[59]

St. Clair Drake argues for the coexistence of negative and positive images of blacks in medieval Christianity; some of the early Christian fathers envisioned devils as black, he writes, but this imagery was not consistent until later on. Moreover, while dark skin was the mark of the infidel, consciousness of it was not highly diffused. According to him, black Madonnas and saints were venerated by white Europeans even as the devil was often depicted as black. Only after the middle of the fifteenth century and the growth of the Atlantic slave trade did negative ideas about blackness replace neutral and favorable ones. These negative ideas then helped justify the subordination of blacks to whites, as did the idea that blacks were bellicose, which also grew out of slavery.[60] The European association between blacks and the devil may also have been reinforced in the New World by the colonists' contrasting perceptions of Indians who, in the eighteenth century, would become the first of the fully developed "Noble Savages."[61]

Yet while blackness had certain connotations and consequences in European / Spanish thought, in the colonial context the devil actually appeared in many guises. While he almost always had a caste and a color, he was not always black. Instead, his appearance seems to have depended on who was seeing him. It is therefore not surprising that he was sometimes a Spanish man, which is how, for instance, an Indian woman saw him in one case and a mulatto woman in another.[62] Several black women even described him as a Spanish priest.[63] One of these women, a slave, said that a certain "man" who "they swore was master of the world" was the devil "in the figure of a cleric," and that when the host was raised, he hid.[64] A black male slave, in turn, once saw the devil as an Indian woman and once as a mestizo woman.[65] A free mulatto, however, described the devil as a man with a "huge and ugly colored face, something like a half-breed black."[66] And as we have just seen, the mulatto Francisco described the devil as a black man (as well as as a horned dog and a cow) and the mestizo Juan Luis described him as dark-complexioned. But it was the Spanish woman we met in the previous chapter, who was taken to the witches' Sabbat by the old Indian woman, who gave us the most detail. While she seemed unable to decide whether the devils she met were black, half-black, or black Indians, she insisted that the principal devil in this case had a black devil mother and had called an Indian his daughter.[67]

It is highly suggestive that the devil was as heterogeneous as the social world he inhabited. But that he was often described as dark, half-breed, a black Indian, or half-black, and, in our most detailed description, as black-Indian with a black mother and an Indian daughter, intimates something rather more than a close "friendship" between blacks, Indians, and the devil. That "something more" clearly plays out through the lineage idiom that connects blacks, Indians, and devils not just socially but also by the blood that is sometimes solicited to seal a pact. In the end, devil imagery in important ways condenses and concentrates the major themes of this study: interstitiality, hybridity, social and genealogical affiliations, and power.

### BLACK-INDIAN WITCHES

Slippage between blackness and Indianness occurred in instances of witchcraft that did not directly implicate the devil. This slippage is not surprising for several reasons. First, Indians and some black slaves occupied the lowest strata of the colonial pyramid, with *bozales* directly from Africa more likely than others to be unskilled workers and therefore to have more intimate contact with Indians.[68] Second, African slaves might also have brought with them their own supernatural skills and knowledge. While the documentary evidence is more sparse than we would like, one slave professed to know how to cure, having "learned it in his land."[69] It is telling, however, that he was unable to cure a Spanish woman because, as he told her, she had been bewitched by an Indian. This implies that even blacks skilled in the supernatural arts could not undo Indian witchcraft.

The intimacy of blackness and Indianness, as well as the final triumph of Indianness, comes through in the thwarted claims of Juana de

Chaide, a black slave denounced to the Inquisition by a *morisca* (Spanish mulatto woman). Juana apparently told the morisca that she was planning a robbery and would share the stolen goods with her. By her own account, the morisca replied to Juana, "Why would you want to do this? Don't you see that it will be discovered, that the Indians will take peyote to 'see' and 'know' who committed the robbery?" Juana then responded that one could get around Indian magic by tossing behind one's back a bit of coal ground by a virgin. "With this [the Indians] will not see anything," she insisted.[70]

Although Juana was confident in her own abilities, we again see a breakdown in conventional caste hierarchies when people attempt to reverse the normal order of things, for the robbery failed and Juana therefore missed the opportunity to try her hand at duping Indians. Rather extraordinary, moreover, are the morisca's offhanded remarks to the effect that Indians enjoyed privileged access to the supernatural. Juana's claim that she knew how to bypass Indian witchcraft becomes even more significant in this light. For, like the slave who learned how to cure "in his land," Juana had been born in Guinea. Although we know nothing about her history, it seems meaningful that an African rather than a Mexican-born (creole) black claimed to be able to circumvent Indian power. In contrast to Spaniards and people who approached their status, such as mestizo governors and the morisca in the present case, who would technically have been three-quarters Spanish and had "warned" the black woman about Indian witches, those toward the lower end of the sanctioned pyramid, like Juana de Chaide, were often willing to meet Indians head on in the unsanctioned domain.

Consider, in this light, the case of Lucas Olola, an African slave who seems to have gained a reputation as a mighty witch by combining Indian with African ritual.[71] Before introducing this story, it is important to point out that it is notoriously difficult to sort African supernatural practices from indigenous and even from Spanish ones, for the different traditions merged as the meanings of the practices changed to accommodate the new social context. Aguirre Beltrán adds to this that language difficulties and the relative youth of bozal slaves hampered the retention of African cultural traits.[72] But Lucas Olola's activities as described by a friar in a letter sent to the Inquisition in 1624 are nevertheless intriguing, for they suggest that even if from our contemporary perspective different practices mesh, colonial people might have been able to untangle and even rank them.

The friar's letter speaks of the Huasteca Indians in the province of

Pánuco, who had among their gods a most powerful one—a *cantarillo* (a type of bird effigy) made of different colored feathers—out of whose mouth came flowers of different colors. The smallest Indians carried the effigy around, he noted, while they danced to the sound of a stick instrument called ("in the Mexican language") a *teponastle,* and to a drum that they also used. In addition, they carried a wooden musical instrument (*sonajas*) in their hands and used long hair pieces (*caballera*) on their heads.[73] Even as he wrote, said the friar, this dance was taking place throughout the province in several villages that "still had the same superstitious and heathenish rites as before." With this dance "the natives" celebrated their god "Paya," together eating and drinking what was offered to the cantarillo. In some villages the natives danced "only to stay happy," but in others they made offerings to the cantarillo to cure their illnesses.[74]

Although the dance and the "superstitions" (as the friar called them) were Indian, some blacks, mulattoes, and mestizos participated as well. Lucas Olola became uniquely involved: he would dress himself in the costume the Indians used for the dance, go into a state of rapture, faint, and let himself fall. He would be senseless for a time, but suddenly he would foam at the mouth and right himself "with a great deal of fury" announcing that his spirit had now come to him, that it was "seven gods," and that as a "glorious body or spirit" he could penetrate walls.[75]

Everything came to a stop, wrote the friar, since the Indians took Olola to be divine and powerful. Male Indians (fathers, brothers, husbands, and other relatives) would give him the Indian woman of his choice so that he could "take advantage" of her, and not even the woman would resist. "Selling himself" to the Indians as a divine being, and dressing in Indian costume, Olola also cured illnesses by lighting a torch and "sucking" Indians in a ceremony that they did themselves, when they "pretended to have," or when they "truly did have," a pact with the devil. And Olola made them believe that he "saw" who had done something evil to them and that he "knew" who it was.

The priest then described the abuses Indians suffered. "Everyone," he said (referring to mestizos, mulattoes, and blacks, including Lucas Olola) took the Indians from the local haciendas, where presumably they were meant to be working. Out of fear that they would be killed if they resisted, the Indian women let themselves be taken advantage of. Lucas Olola "made sick Indians die hating other Indians" whom they were convinced had bewitched them. Abandoning God, the Indians would go to similar "swindlers" to be cured. Furthermore, Olola had killed through whippings and torture Indian men and women who were taken for witches, in this way displaying his divinity and power.

The inquisitor saw Olola as just another black "swindler," out to take advantage of gullible Indians. But what is interesting for our purposes is that while the African overpowered Indians, the strength of his persona and his control over them were enhanced by his appropriation of elements of Indian magic: Olola might have introduced "Africanisms"—such as possession—into the supernatural repetoire, but he also wore Indian clothing and engaged in Indian rituals.

We have seen such Indiancentric behavior and symbolism in other witchcraft tales, such as that of the pulqueria owner Juan Ortíz and the other powerful Spanish witches we met in the previous chapter, all of whom were alleged to have beaten Indians at their own game, but who did so only by appropriating Indian magic. In general, however, blacks and mulattos seem to have been more tightly caught up in Indian witchcraft than were Spaniards or even mestizos. We thus have a free mulatto woman who denounced another for having said that she would "chase the witches away." The accused had apparently cured two Indian women of witchcraft, one in a cave with copal and one with cotton—both indigenous treatments—with which she drew sand out of the woman's body.[76] One of the Indian women—who testified in Nahuatl—corroborated the plaintiff's testimony.[77] In another incident, a mulatto or mestizo gave an Indian an "idol" to "help" him. The Indian was called before the inquisitors, but then sent to a secular judge as the Inquisition had no jurisdiction in the matter.[78]

One of the most intriguing points of black/Indian convergence is around Indian *naguales*.[79] The only non-Indians that I have seen make reference to Indian naguales are black and mulatto women. This is intriguing as it marks the predilection these women seem to have had for one of the most powerful tools in the Indian magical repertoire. One of these women, a mulatto from Mérida, claimed to have a nagual in the form of a bird and to "know the things that go on in the corners and in secret."[80] Another, from a village to the northeast of Ometepec, told the inquisitors that she was not a witch, but a nagual.[81] This is an interesting distinction because it implies that the mulatto woman not only knew that Spaniards confused naguales with witches; she also knew a lot about nagualismo itself. In fact, she claimed to have transformed herself into a tiger, the fiercest and most harmful of the nagual's many identities.[82]

Finally, near Cuernavaca, the black woman "Ana the pythonness" combined nagualismo with what we might call "ventriloquism," an uncommon practice that I have seen associated only with blacks.[83] Ana apparently responded to questions by hissing "through her chest," through a wooden cross, or through an "evil spirit" in the form of a bird she carried with her. When she divined, she would see "many naguales," one of which she described as possessing "a long tail." Despite the powerful symbolism of her claims, the questions her clients—including an Indian woman—put to her were mundane ones about everyday objects, animals and spouses: Where was that lost cup? That shawl? Those rolls? That husband? That horse? That mule? That spoon? One woman asked the pythonness to "guess" if she and her husband, who was not present, were "Spanish or mestizo." What a comment on both the muddle and the routine nature of caste.[84]

### CYCLES OF UNSANCTIONED POWER: INDIANS, BLACKS, MULATTOES, AND SPANIARDS

We can begin to give more depth and nuance to the caste hierarchies that developed as mulattoes and blacks appropriated Indian witchcraft by turning to the 1621 case of a mulatto slave couple from Tasco, who approached their master on bended knee to beg forgiveness.[85] The woman, it seems, had taken peyote "without knowing what it was . . . as if it were the holy sacrament" in an attempt to cure an illness. Under its influence she had seen "a thousand visions of Indian women and bulls dancing."[86]

The mulattoes had obtained this peyote with its images of Indians from a black slave named Matheo and his Indian wife, María. Matheo came before the inquisitors along with the mulattoes. He conceded that he had indeed given the mulatto woman peyote because "he had taken pity on her for her illness." He had also provided her with grains of ololiuqui and with the seed of an herb that, in Matheo's words, "is called '*cuexpaltzi*' in the Mexican language."[87] As he described Indian medicinal remedies in great detail and in the "Mexican language," Matheo candidly admitted that he had taken such remedies himself. He also explained that his Indian wife had ground the herbs Matheo had given to the mulattoes.[88]

That Matheo's Indian wife rather than Matheo himself prepared the treatment points once more to the transferral of Indian/female power to others through food preparation. Moreover, taken as a whole, the case portrays a rather elaborate caste hierarchy grounded in unsanctioned social and kin affiliations. Here power rooted in an Indian woman wended its way through her husband, a black man knowledgeable in the Indian arts, and from him into the lives of two desperate mulattoes, connected to him by their blackness. They, in turn, confessed to a Spanish master, who then reported everyone to the highest Spanish authority of the Inquisition.

Spaniards were not just confessors in the witchcraft of blacks, mulattoes, and Indians. They also sent their black and mulatto slaves and servants to purchase witchcraft from Indians, or used those slaves and servants to prepare Indian remedies for them. Thus, one Spanish woman from Guadalajara dispatched her mulatto servant girl to find an Indian who had knowledge of an herb the Spaniard wanted; another from the same denunciation told a black slave girl to grind roots an Indian "from Tonala" had brought to the Spaniard for witchcraft.[89]

Involving blacks and mulattoes in their witchcraft intrigues with Indians could prove dangerous to Spaniards, however, because, unlike Indians — who might not have wanted to sabotage the spending power of their clientele — blacks and mulattoes turned Spaniards over to the Inquisition. This might have been what the "black Mandinga woman" Catalina sought to do when she voluntarily confessed her own witchcraft to the inquisitors in Celaya and in the course of that confession denounced her Spanish mistress, who had sent Catalina to an Indian for some yellow powders the mistress could use to "tame men."[90] Another story tells of a free black woman from Guadalajara whose "master and mistress" had sent her to an Indian "famous for being a witch" in order to save themselves from exile by the justices (their transgression is not stated).[91] In Mexico City, a Spanish man reported to the Inquisition that a black slave woman had told him that her mistress had ordered her to put some powders she had gotten from an Indian healer (*curandera*) under the woman's husband's pillow, to make him "stupid and foolish."[92]

Many of the blacks and mulattoes who acted as mediators between Spaniards and Indians in the unsanctioned domain were adhering to the requisites of their legal status. They had to do what their masters and mistresses ordered them to do, and in this sense going to Indians for remedies was probably much like any other shopping excursion their masters and mistresses sent them on. Spaniards might have engaged in this practice, however, not only because black and mulatto servants and slaves had to do their bidding but also because blacks and mulattoes were more intimately involved with Indians, whose superstitious knowledge and tendencies they shared.

This might explain the actions of a man described as "Portuguese," who was denounced by a free black woman to the inquisitors in San Miguel.[93] She told the authorities that the man had several times "begged" her to talk with an Indian. In a twist on the typical love magic women inflicted on men to thwart their free will, this man wanted the powders he needed to get a woman back who "did not love him anymore." The black woman had done as he asked, paying the Indian with money the Portuguese had given her. The Indian had then brought the powders directly to the man and provided instructions for their use. The man took the powders, but asked yet another black woman to actually sprinkle them on his lover. When he realized that they did not have the desired effect, he took a close look at them and concluded that he had been given what "appeared to be tobacco."

Tobacco was a preconquest magical substance but clearly the Portuguese did not recognize it as having any special properties. Instead, he confronted the Indian and asked for his money back. The Indian responded, however, that he owed nothing to the Portuguese, who could "go to the devil." The Portuguese replied in typical fashion that the Indian was a "dog," and threatened to kill him. But still the Indian refused to return the man's money.

Again the Portuguese begged the first black woman to help him. This time he asked her to speak to yet another Indian man who "knew well the art of giving powders." She complied, but warned the second Indian "although you know about and have [the powders], do not give them to him because he is very angry." The Indian subsequently told the Portuguese that he had nothing to give.

The lengths to which this man apparently went to get the most appropriate remedy for his problem, and his steadfast reliance on two black women—who were not his slaves or even his servants and therefore not legally under his control—attests to the unsanctioned authority of Indians as well as to the intimacy between blacks and Indians in this domain. The first black woman even told the second Indian of the Portuguese man's state of mind, and she did it out of the man's earshot (perhaps in an indigenous language, although this is not clear from the text).

Once again we also see Indians charge money for their knowledge of witchcraft. Yet as we expand the analysis to include Spaniards, Indians, and intermediaries, we also see that such currency is not simply ex-changed; it is more complexly *circulated* through the caste affiliations that made the unsanctioned hierarchy operational. Ultimately, in another ironic twist on markets and modernity, money was the medium that transformed Spanish power into Indian power (whether or not the commodity it bought had the desired outcome). The commodi-tization of the world controlled by Indians, coupled with the apparent savvy of Indian marketeers, points us once again to empowerment directly related to a developing market economy into which Indians were drawn, perhaps unwillingly but not, it seems, unwittingly.

### AVENGING SLAVES

Given the close affiliations between blacks/mulattoes and Indians, it would make sense that Spaniards sometimes turned for witchcraft di-rectly to blacks and mulattoes, who had likely been in contact with Indians themselves. These blacks and mulattoes, like the ones who brought Spaniards into contact with Indians, also turned around and denounced to the Inquisition the Spaniards who asked for their ser-vices. One black slave woman did just that less than twenty years after the conquest. Apparently, her Spanish mistress had asked her to do some witchcraft, promising her a velvet skirt and an Indian slave if she carried it out. In her account of the events to the inquisitors, the slave reported that the woman had begged her not to say anything, and that she had replied to her mistress's request with the rather ironic remark, "Ma'am, I have no need for an Indian; I am a slave." She also accused the woman of not going to mass and of working on Sundays and holidays, in short, of what might have been veiled accusations of Judaizing.[94] This is but one example of how black and mulatto slaves could take advan-tage of the uncertainties of "white" identities by turning their masters and mistresses in for "whipping figures of Christ" and effecting rituals on Friday evenings and Saturdays, the Jewish Sabbath.[95]

Slaves and servants also used witchcraft to repay their Spanish mas-ters. But Spaniards' greater access to colonial courts also meant that—while they could not denounce Indians—they could denounce blacks and mulattoes. We have seen that slaves also denounced their masters for sending them to Indian witches or for asking the slaves to do witch-craft for them, so one would suppose that had blacks and mulattoes been threatened by Spanish witches they would not have hesitated to turn those Spaniards in to the Inquisition. The fact that they did not do this might mean that non-Spaniards had little to fear from relatively mild Spanish witches. One mulatto woman from near Celaya did denounce a Spaniard (who was in cahoots with a very active Indian witch, it should be noted), reporting that the Spaniard had given her powdered worms in chocolate but that she had poured the drink out, which act highlights that reversals of the conventional caste hierarchies generally were inconclusive.[96]

The Spaniard Juan Gutiérrez made a rather typical—and amusing—denunciation of a black slave.[97] He had had to abandon his house in Mexico City when its furnishings began to mysteriously move about. At first he thought that "a woman who lived in the house" was at fault, but when it also happened in his new home, he began to suspect his slave Catalina. He sold her, and she was taken to Zacatecas (which once again appears as a place of exile for slaves), but she was then resold and brought back to Mexico City. Her new owner had the same experiences as Gutiérrez; he also abandoned his house and moved to another one. As Gutiérrez came to believe that the same slave, Catalina, was the source of both his and her new master's troubles, he denounced her to the Holy Office.

Another Spanish man, also in Mexico City, was bedeviled by a sixty-year-old mulatto, Polonia, a freed slave who was "assisting" him in his home.[98] The man kept a box containing a small bag with seventy pesos in his room. One day he went to count his money only to discover that it was missing. No one had come into the room except the mulatto woman, and he therefore suspected that she had taken the money. When she next came to fix lunch for him and to make the bed, he closed the door to the street and beat her for what he suspected she had done. She confessed that she had taken the money, but refused to tell him where it was. The Spaniard then took her to her "master's" house.[99] But in front of her master, she retracted her confession, insisting only that she had occasionally stolen one or two coins. The two Spaniards talked it over, and the master paid the other Spanish man his seventy pesos. From then on, the man carried a key to the room with him, and as far as he knew, no one had entered it.

Nevertheless, as he went to lie down one Tuesday night he found the small bag at the foot of his bed. When he took a look inside he saw several coins of reales instead of the pesos he had originally had. This "terrified him," he told the inquisitors. Without counting the money, he put it back in the box. The following morning, he found forty-eight pesos total, only half of those in reales. The pesos, he declared, were "the same coins of the seventy that had been missing." He again went to the house of the mulatto's master and accused her of having accomplished her tricks "by the devil's artistry," for how else would she have been able to enter his locked room? This time, however, the master defended the mulatto. The other Spaniard had no doubt, however, and warned both of them to stay away from his house.

Then there was the Spanish man, also from Mexico City, who denounced the black slave woman who told him that a mulatto woman had given her powders to smear on the door of the room where her master kept his money.[100] This way, she could get the keys to the room and the box with the money, and take out whatever she wanted, which she subsequently did. She told the Spaniard that the mulatto woman was a curandera and that another black woman, who also lived in her master's house, knew a great deal about such powders. The Spaniard said that he had also witnessed the black woman putting powders and animal hairs in chocolate, presumably to feed to men. In yet another incident, this one from San Luis Potosí, a priest claimed that a mulatto woman he was attempting to prevent from running off with a young Spanish man, and had called an "old whore witch" in the process, turned into a dog and attacked the priest.[101]

In a social context in which Spanish men often took mulatto and black women (who were sometimes their slaves) as lovers, and in which erotic magic was a prevalent means of exercising control over men, it is not at all surprising that many of the complaints lodged by Spanish men were against the mulatto and black women with whom they were involved.[102] This is why the Spaniard Bernava de Andia told the Mexico City inquisitors about his brief relationship with a mulatto slave woman, Catalina St. Joseph.[103] He left her to take up with a Spanish woman, but like the Spaniard who knocked the mulatto Francesca to the ground and claimed that he knew more because "he was a man," Bernava found that he had "some impediment" and was unable to have intercourse with the Spanish woman. He of course suspected Catalina, and his suspicions were confirmed when he went back to her, for then the "impediment" left him. But when he returned to the Spanish woman, the problem returned. Clearly the mulatto woman wanted to sully his lineage. And he subsequently threatened her with the Holy Office if she did not remove the impediment (which she declined to do).

In both general and specific senses, unsanctioned knowledge came from Indians, and sometimes the Indian sources of rather elaborate caste hierarchies are clearly delineated. When blacks and mulattoes, as well as the few mestizos we have seen, used Indian witchcraft to switch places with Spaniards, they were of course still acting as intermediaries. But this time they were making Spaniards submit to Indian power rather than making Indians submit to the Spanish kind. And just as blacks and mulattoes, especially, often bore the brunt of punishment for their Spanish masters' and bosses' treatment of Indians, they also bore the brunt of punishment for what was, in the broadest sense, Indian authority over Spaniards. Intermediaries who found themselves before the Inquisition included a mulatto slave woman who fed her abusive master herbs she received from Indians;[104] the young black slave mentioned above who reported to his master that an "old black man" had given him powders that he received from an Indian herbalist in the hopes that these would tame the master;[105] a free mulatto woman who claimed to have her own Indian herb-seller in the plaza of Mexico City and was accused of almost blinding a Spaniard;[106] and a mulatto slave woman who was denounced by a Spanish woman through the woman's husband for having, at different times and with the help of Indians, fed her mistress "bat powders" and "ass brains" in an effort to tame her (presumably the slave wished to moderate the woman's temper), and half of the head of a turkey buzzard to make her "crazy."[107] Here we have blacks and mulattoes attempting to domesticate Spaniards with witchcraft obtained from Indians. But it is not the Indians who end up exposed to the Inquisition; it is instead the blacks and mulattoes they supplied.

In another twist, Indians might have provided blacks and mulattoes with witchcraft, but Spaniards bewitched by blacks and mulattoes also solicited cures from Indians. This was the other side of Indian power, and it parallels in an interesting way the Spanish dispensation of justice to Indians for the crimes wrought by blacks, mulattoes, and mestizos in Spaniards' names. Indeed, my impression is that the dangers posed especially by blacks and mulattoes, who might seek revenge on their masters and mistresses by reporting them to the Inquisition, were enhanced by the fact that although they seemed to be able to bewitch, they were not very accomplished healers. This was the case with the mulatto woman mentioned above who claimed to be a witch rather than a nagual. She said her aunt had taught her to bewitch but not to cure.[108] We also have the case of a black male slave from Mexico City who was unable to cure a young slave after he gave him powders received from Indians and the youngster fell ill;[109] and then there was the mulato Pedro de Castellanos, who was unable to cure an Indian;[110] and the mulatto slave woman Catalina de St. Joseph just mentioned, who could not or would not cure a Spanish man she had "tied."[111] Again there are evident parallels with the sanctioned domain, where blacks, mulattoes, and mestizos were a source of Indian exploitation but also impotent "healers" since they did not "own" the power there.

The parallels between Spanish and Indian power were thus doubly paradoxical as Indians dispensed justice by healing Spaniards bewitched by blacks, mulattoes, and mestizos who, in the final analysis, received their knowledge of witchcraft, and consequently their authority, either directly or indirectly from Indians in the first place. The fact that witchcraft and healing came from the same Indian source did not escape Spaniards who, like the priest Sánchez, in the end could obviously not trust the trickster Indians who might be in cahoots with other vile persons.

Just as the protection Spaniards offered Indians through the judicial system was inconsistent, so was what Indians with their healing skills offered to Spaniards. One Indian woman, for instance, was at first able to cure the son of a Spanish man from Guadalajara, who was bewitched by a black woman. Despite other interventions, the boy had not recovered. He later died after his mother saw a bird called a *papalote* (butterfly) perched over the mattress where the boy slept. Live birds, as we have seen, were one medium through which blacks seemed to practice their witchcraft.[112]

Nevertheless, just as Indians kept on going to Spanish justices even as their situation deteriorated in the face of the continuing onslaught from Spaniards, blacks, mulattoes, and mestizos, we also see that Spaniards continued to have faith not only in the witchcraft they used to tame their lovers, but also in the Indian healers who were ultimately the very source of their bedevilment. Several incidents speak to the ability of these healers to correct the injustices perpetrated by mulattoes, who seemed to be able to bewitch, at least in the minds of their Spanish victims, but seem to have also been singled out for their inability or unwillingness to cure.[113]

One Spanish victim was Doña Sebastiana Martinez de Castrejona, a resident of Mexico City, who came before the inquisitors to complain of the mulatto Dorothea, a former slave of hers.[114] According to Doña Sebastiana, about five years previously she had fought with the mulatto woman and subsequently beaten her with a firebrand. As she finished the beating, an ant fastened itself to her hand between her index finger and her thumb. She flicked it off, but a great burning sensation (*ardor*) coursed through her body, which was soon covered with welts. She was also afflicted "from her stomach to her throat" with a drowning sensation. From eight that night until four the next morning, when she vomited phlegm, she suffered. She called on two mulatto women to cure her, and they came and greased her with fat, from which treatment she gained some relief. Finally able to rest, the maladies left her for a time, until one evening three months later, when she again beat Dorothea. When Doña Sebastiana was ready to go to sleep that night, she went out to the patio where Dorothea was sitting and urinated in front of her. Immediately she felt a pinch in her genitals. Without saying anything, she started back to her room, but before she'd even reached the door her legs and vagina had swelled up. Again she felt a great burning sensation throughout her body.

As well as she was able, she undressed herself, lay down in bed and summoned her son to call on a mulatto named Miguel, a son of one of the mulatto women who had cured her the first time. Miguel came to her aid and greased her with fat, just as his mother had done. Again Sebastiana suffered until four in the morning, when the attacks ended. The next day she recounted this tale to the mulattoes who had cured her the first time, and to one of her sisters-in-law. They suspected that Dorothea had bewitched her and advised her to go to the Inquisition and denounce the slave. Overhearing the conversation, Dorothea confronted her mistress. "I did nothing wrong to you, ma'am," she said, "nor do I understand these things." Doña Sebastiana scornfully replied, "Do not pretend that it wasn't you, because you are great friends with Felipa the mestiza" to the extent, Doña Sebastiana pointed out, that Felipa and Dorothea lent each other clothes.

Some days later Doña Sebastiana's sister-in-law recounted the story to Felipa, who laughed and said it was nothing, that if Doña Sebastiana had gone out to the street or patio and shaken her clothing or cleaned it with a broom, she would have been fine. Disregarding Felipa's sensible explanation, Doña Sebastiana continued to claim that the mestiza was a famed witch and that she therefore suspected Dorothea was as well. She was convinced Dorothea had caused her pain through "tricks of the devil."

The previous year, Doña Sebastiana continued to tell the court, her husband had also beaten Dorothea. He was afflicted with such eye pain the following day that they had to call a doctor. The doctor cured the pain but several days later her husband lost his sight in one eye and began to lose vision in the other. He then became almost totally blind. Two months earlier, she continued, her husband went to an Indian who treated his affliction by rubbing and cleansing him with *estafiate* and drawing sand from his eyes.[115] Doña Sebastiana claimed to have watched the whole process and she noted explicitly to the inquisitors that what she had seen was not "trickery." Indeed, she believed so strongly in the efficacy of Indian cures that she later sought out another Indian, a woman named Maria, who treated her husband in the same manner. By the time Doña Sebastiana testified, he was able to see a bit out of one eye.[116]

The caste hierarchy for curing was bounded on the one hand by ineffective Spanish victims (and even ineffective "doctors") and, on the other, by masterful Indian curanderos who could heal the witchcraft of mulattoes unwilling or unable to effect their own cures.[117] As the next tale suggests, the power of Indians to both bewitch and cure was sometimes embodied in the same person. This duality was explained to the inquisitors in a rather matter-of-fact way by the priest Sánchez. And we should not forget that the two mulattoes who beat Domingo de la Cruz were trying to get him to cure an Indian woman they accused him of bewitching.

We can elaborate the gender and further caste dimensions to the issue of double-sided Indian power by examining an incident in which an Indian woman was approached to undo the witchcraft a mulatto woman had inflicted on a Spanish man, who then came to believe that the Indian was actually the source of the witchcraft bedeviling him. Toward the end of the seventeenth century, the Spaniard, a man named Joseph Baptista de Sosa, accused a "light-skinned mulatto" slave woman named Juana of bewitching him, and came before the Mexico City inquisitors to tell his story.[118] According to Joseph, he and Juana had been lovers for ten months, and sometimes he would tell her that he would give her money to buy her freedom. As he further explained, Juana had been under the erroneous impression that he was going to marry her, although he had never said that he would. One night, the Spaniard suffered from insomnia, and Juana, apparently unsolicited, sent him a milk drink to help him sleep. He consumed it and subsequently became anxious and nauseous. By morning he was incapacitated. Suspecting that the mulatto woman had bewitched him, Joseph's friends advised him to go see an Indian woman named María Theresa, who, they said, "understood things like this."[119] María Theresa, they told him, would undo the damage and could also tell him if it was indeed due to witch-craft and if Juana was the cause. He went to see the Indian and told her about the drink and about how Juana had sent it to him. The Indian probed his stomach and heart, and told him that the mulatto woman had, in fact, done something evil with the drink. He should go and tell her to take away the evil she had caused, the Indian said, and when he returned the Indian would cure him.[120] The implication, of course, is that a witch has to give permission for a cure, but also that an Indian can undo the supernatural damage caused by a mulatto.

That night, Joseph went to see the mulatto Juana. He told her what the Indian had said, but she insisted that the accusation was false, for she had not put anything wicked in the drink. At this point, Jo-seph decided to part company with her. He then remained healthy for six months but when he began to feel poorly again he suspected, once more, that Juana was again the cause. This time, however, Joseph claimed that she was reaching him through another woman—his own mulatto cook who, of course, controlled his food. He returned to the Indian woman with his suspicions, and she confirmed them, again verifying her authority in these matters. Suddenly, however, Joseph found himself conflicted about the Indian woman's role, and he began to suspect that she was actually aiding Juana. The Indian, then, was harming instead of helping him. Forswearing his reliance on deceitful women, he went to see a Spanish doctor who treated him over the course of two months but failed to make him well.

The gendered themes of this story rest on the conspiratorial nature of women and their ability to subvert men's intentions through the prac-tice of witchcraft. The story also shows that, like the "male" powers of Spaniards, the "female" powers of Indians were contradictory. Joseph thus repeatedly approached the Indian María Teresa to heal him as he attempted to counteract the effects of the mulatto woman's witchcraft, but in the end he became convinced that she was harming him by acting out her trickery in cahoots with the mulatto. Either way, he was subor-dinate to the Indian woman's knowledge and abilities. In this unsanc-tioned domain, then, the Spaniard continued to play a male role, but here he was a passive rather than an active male—or "not a man" at all, as the mulatto Francesca's Spanish lover had lamented—as he was subject to the contradictory power of the agentive feminized Indian. She might have been able to cure him, but she could also further harm him.

Joseph became so desperate about his situation that he asked Juana's master to confine her to a convent. Enclosing her, of course, would cut her off from the devil and Indians while presumably protecting men, including Joseph, from the witchcraft that undermined his gender and caste status. Luckily, the master accommodated his request. Because if the mulatto woman had not been so confined, said Joseph as he concluded his testimony, he himself would have had to kill her in order to be "free of her." His belief that only an act of extreme violence—an end to the mulatto woman—could right the inverted social order and restore his effectiveness and free will brings into stark relief the tensions between distinct but altogether similar systems of colonial power. While Spaniards threatened to kill insubordinate mulatto witches who conspired with Indians, the devil, who channeled his power through the selfsame Indians, threatened to kill Spaniards who did not heed his will.

THE DEVIL AS REBEL:
THE INFECTIOUS INDIAN ANA TIZIL

In 1627, an out-of-control situation in Zacatecas was brought to the attention of the Inquisition. We have already seen that mid-seventeenth-century Zacatecas was a rather hellish place for slaves like Juan de Morga. At that time, it was an established silver mining and trading center with a strong Spanish presence and flavor. Here upwards of 1,500 immigrant Indian laborers from the south mixed with hundreds of black and mulatto slaves and also with Chichimec Indians displaced by Spanish incursions to the north.[121] Given the economic and sociological characteristics of the town, it is perhaps not surprising that local Spaniards feared unrest. And because the northern zones were home to Chichimec Indians with their powerful forms of witchcraft, Zacatecas might also have been a hub of witchcraft activity. Indeed, references to a "cave in Zacatecas where the demons are" came from a mestizo accused of a pact with the devil as well as from a mulatto mineworker who linked the devil to such a cave.[122] A letter to the inquisitors from a late-sixteenth-century friar mentions the "women witches" of

Zacatecas, and, in 1627, another letter tells of the activities of the Indian woman Ana Tizil.[123]

The Ana Tizil story is a fascinating and pertinent way to wind down our discussion of the cultural politics of caste because it links the Indian woman directly to the devil as well as to what is presented as popular rebellion against Spanish governance. Tizil was initially brought to the attention of the local Zacatecan inquisitor by a Spanish man, who had "jokingly" approached this alleged witch to find a horse he had lost. Although she told him that his horse had run away, she also assured him that it would be at his house upon his return. As he arrived home, the Spaniard did indeed find his horse, but it was in the hands of several muleteers who claimed to have found it out on a plain and asked to be paid for its recovery. It is not clear whether the Spaniard was alarmed by the Indian's successful divination or enraged by the muleteers' demand for money, but he decided to punish Tizil by denouncing her, for he was "a Christian," he said, "the son of noble parents," and she was "a witch who gives powders so that men love [women] well."

The local inquisitor gave context to the case by telling his Mexico City counterparts that the "common people" (*gente vil*) of Zacatecas were in turmoil. "Each day," he wrote, "the influence of the devil spreads more among people such as mulatto and mestizo women, who not only use amatory herbs and powders . . . [but] peyote . . . More and more blacks and slaves, whipped and oppressed by the grave punishments that are common in the mines, blaspheme by cursing God." The inquisitor then linked the presence of the devil to Ana Tizil, whom he held responsible for the dissension. This "healer," he insisted, had "infected" the city with the herbs and powders that then fomented blasphemy and discord among the mestizas, mulatas, negros, and "slaves," categories that embraced men and women alike, and included almost all of the gente vil. The discourse of the text thus makes this Indian woman someone who at once "cured" some people's problems and inflicted the devil on others. It should come as no surprise at this point that the people who found the Indian helpful were not the same ones who found her dangerous. When all was said and done, one person's love magic was definitely someone else's hell.

Of course we have seen the Indian/devil phenomenon elsewhere, but here the meaning of devilish behavior shifts somewhat, for the Indian/devil in this story is not just threatening the health and well-being of individuals like the poor Spanish woman who was asked for her blood. She is generating a wider and collective uprising against

Spanish governance. By linking Tizil to the devil *and* to the source of the turmoil breaking out among laborers oppressed in the Zacatecan mines, the inquisitor makes the Indian the conduit for a metaphorical illness that jeopardizes the entire colonial project. The Indian/devil affiliations contracted by blacks, mulattos, and mestizos thus in the end did create a counter-system of power. This was understandably symbolized by an afflicted rather than a healthy social body. And the afflicted body was one that shifted the relative positions of Indian and Spanish authority, with blacks, mulattoes, and mestizos reoriented but still betwixt and between the two poles of the colonial world.

# 7

## Hall of Mirrors

A startling tale from the geographical and chronological fringes of this study—far northern Parral, at the end of the seventeenth century—turns a woman into a man rather than feminizing a man through witchcraft. In doing so, this story elucidates and draws together many of the cultural processes examined here.

The central protagonist of the story is the mulatto slave woman Antonia de Soto, who—as should not be surprising at this point—confessed to the inquisitors she had obtained "herbs and flowers" from an Indian man in a successful bid to escape her master's house.[1] Antonia fled that house in the company of the Indian, and shortly thereafter dressed herself in a man's clothing, which she continued to wear until her adventure ended. Her clothing functioned as something of a magical disguise, for with it she was able to engage undiscovered in activities that included fighting bulls and taming horses as she "served different masters as a cowboy (*vaquero*)."

Antonia maintained her male identity with the Indian's flowers and herbs, which she periodically rubbed all over her body while "calling and invoking the devil to help her." The devil would do everything she commanded, she said, and when he appeared to her he would tell her not to be afraid. He certainly gave her courage, for she claimed to have killed the Indian in the course of her adventures, and to have put a cross on the spot where she left him for dead. She then joined up with the brother of one of her employers, along with three other companions. Together they killed three muleteers—one of whom was a Spaniard—

and stole the silver the muleteers had been carrying. When one of Antonia's accomplices subsequently stole her portion of the take, he too was found dead. Antonia also confessed to having killed yet another man in a scuffle, a mulatto servant of another of her employers. She could do these things, she told the inquisitors, because of the herbs and flowers that the Indian had given her and because of her own ability to invoke the devil.

In the inquisitors' response to her confession they referred to her explicit pact with the devil — a charge, as I have noted, generally leveled against male practitioners of witchcraft. But the inquisitors also expressed skepticism about Antonia's fantastic story, and advised that she be reexamined, which she subsequently was. For the second set of inquisitors she retracted the claim that she had killed the Indian, but she otherwise embellished her tale in several ways. She told them, for instance, that in the Indian's company she would drink a half jar of peyote every Sunday, exactly at midday, become intoxicated and see a variety of visions, including a dark bull and "a beautiful woman" with a guitar in hand who taught her and the Indian how to dance. Other times she saw vipers and snakes, and twice she saw a man who told her that if she went with him she would be free.

These inquisitors asked her what words the Indian gave her to invoke the devil, and she told them that she was to say "*yuman*" and "*achula*."[2] When she uttered those words, she would see the devil on Sundays, in the figure of a white man. He would give her the strength and the bravery to do what she wanted. Once she saw this devil's spirit (*la sombra*) as it was talking with the Indian, and she heard that spirit bellow like a bear, which was perhaps a veiled reference to Indian naguales. She never had "illicit friendships" with her male companions, she said, and they never discovered that she was a woman.

One night she awoke to find herself flying through the air toward a mountain. This was the beginning of the end, for as it became light she saw a figure dressed in dark clothes with a palm frond in his hand and a hair cut "like a priest's." She followed the figure down the mountain, and he disappeared as she went to confess. It was San Antonio, she said, and she knew it was he, because the previous day she had intentionally asked for his help.

The cultural processes and themes central to this book are clearly refracted through the imagery of Antonia's story. Most obviously, the main character, a mulatto slave woman, was subordinated in the sanctioned domain through a form of labor control (slavery) that restricted her movements and enclosed her in her "master's house." Drawing on the affiliations or broadly conceived lineage connections that I have argued are central to how we understand the enactment—and hence the meanings—of caste, the mulatto allied with another subordinated subject: an Indian. With the aid of the Indian's herbs and flowers she manipulated the surface signs of gender through a costume that transformed her inner self even as it theatricalized her outer one.

Of interest is Antonia's initial insistence that she had killed the Indian in the course of her adventure, for this means that in her female incarnation she allied with the Indian but as she internalized maleness she turned on her helper, and even sanctified his murder with a cross. That Antonia ultimately hedged about whether or not the Indian was dead speaks to the ambivalence that runs throughout the tale: Was Antonia of the sanctioned world or was she of the unsanctioned? Was she captive or free? Was she female or male? Was she mulatto or something else? Was she resisting or acquiescing? For rather than dispensing with her master, she embarked on a journey that really did not go anywhere. Indeed, it eventually led back to exactly where it had begun.

The herbs and flowers provided by the Indian launched Antonia initially into freedom. They gave her mobility, which was central to a journey also punctuated by the accumulation of wealth. Antonia escaped her master's house, she rode horses, and she even flew through the air but she also sold her labor—which of course her master received from this slave woman for free—and she stole significant amounts of silver. These themes converge around what I believe was at the core of colonial witchcraft: it fostered physical mobilities symbolically enmeshed with status ones.

In the sanctioned context, such mobilities, of course, belonged mostly to Spanish men with the free will that enabled them to reasonably move about without fear that the state would force them back into limited spaces and places. In that context, such mobilities could be achieved by non-Spaniards, but only through genealogical or social lineage connections to Spaniards, especially to Spanish men. Women and non-Spaniards who attempted to assert their independence in this domain without linking themselves to Spanish men — as did Adriana's accuser the "vagabond" Ana María from the introduction, or the Spanish woman from Mexico City who was accused of a "disorderly way of life" after she donned a man's clothing "in order to go out on the street at night" — were denounced for various transgressions and punished accordingly.[3] But sanctioned affiliations with Spaniards "magically" helped people to overcome their marginality, to gain mobility without engaging the authorities' wrath.

When we compare Adriana's position to that of Antonia, the interesting parallel that wends its ways through this book is brought sharply into focus: Adriana accomplished sanctioned mobility through affiliations with Spaniards, while Antonia accomplished unsanctioned mobility through an affiliation with an Indian. This "magical" Indian affiliation, like Adriana's Spanish one, allowed Antonia — like Adriana — to overcome gender, caste, and class limitations, but in unsanctioned rather than sanctioned ways, for Antonia, like other "witches," by definition did not go through the proper channels. Witchcraft might thus best be viewed as what Jean and John Comaroff describe as a "refashioned" way of "producing immense wealth and power — against all odds, at supernatural speed, and with striking ingenuity."[4]

Neither Adriana nor Antonia transformed the system at hand. They simply worked within it in two different ways that both spoke to the politics of caste. Adriana legitimated herself legitimately, by drawing on Spanishness and aligning herself with Spaniards. Antonia legitimated herself illegitimately by drawing on Indianness and aligning herself with Indians. But in freeing herself from servitude to one Spanish master, Antonia simply went to work for others, including a white devil. Her story, in fact, clarifies the ways in which the power of witchcraft supplied by Indians and carried by a mulatto acted as something of a bridge between the unsanctioned and sanctioned domains. On the one hand, the story tells us that femaleness, Indianness, and captivity (witchcraft) were possible paths to attaining the transforming privileges of maleness, Spanishness, and freedom (not witchcraft). On the other hand, it clarifies the limitations of feminized and Indianized power. This is because witchcraft did not empower women *as* women or slaves *as* slaves; instead, it allowed women, slaves, and others to function as free men would function in the world controlled by Spaniards. The extraordinary ambivalence of Antonia's story thus tells us that witchcraft provided a way for people restricted by state control to take by unsanctioned stealth what others had by sanctioned right — to claim through means of subterfuge what others received "naturally," by virtue of their blood and their sex. Witchcraft, then, was something of an Indianized short cut through the social thicket.

As witchcraft gave subordinated people control, it simultaneously marginalized the sanctioned elite. But in the end that elite reasserted itself through the rule of the courts, for the consequences for breaches of social protocol—witchcraft and other kinds—consisted of punishment through judicial institutions like the Inquisition—the same one that freed Adriana because it determined that she had followed the proper paths. Such institutions brought the power of the state to bear on people who misstepped, only to be stuffed back into the niches they were fated to occupy.

We cannot ignore that Antonia herself reaffirmed that rule by casting off her masculinity and her liberty—in effect de-emancipating herself—and giving up to the rationality of a saint, priests, inquisitors, Spaniards, and, ultimately, to masters, all of whom held the power to "heal" her transgressions. She reverses positions as soon as she is ready to confess, which she does after she is set back on the right path by the mirror image of the white devil, an apparition of San Antonio, who turns her in to the other Spanish men. The themes of her case and the fact that she found her way back on her own suggest that she had internalized the disiplinary apparatus the state/church was attempting to inculcate in its quasi-citizens, even in its slave ones.

## ANTONIO/ANTONIA/ANTONIO: WORLDS WITHIN WORLDS

Was witchcraft, then, a form of resistance? A space of "autonomy," a "female cultural construct" and "a distinctively female sensibility," as some scholars have argued?[5] Did it challenge state control? Or was its source found in the very imposition of such control? The more closely and systematically we tie witchcraft to what witchcraft was not, the more difficult it is to consider it an alternative to power or a form of resistance.

We can revisit these questions by acknowledging that women and non-Spaniards were indeed the focus of the state's witch-punishing activities. But the fact that they were "witches"—that they were *not* "doors without hinges"—cannot be attributed to their intrinsic affinity for some forms of action, or to female or Indian sensibilities, any more than sanctioned practices can be accounted for with reference to the presumed innate aggression of blacks or natural superiority of Spaniards. The fact that the colonial state *did* constitute women and non-Spaniards as likely witches, and men and Spaniards as not, does not reflect Spanish rationality or the essential differences of women and non-Spaniards, but rather colonial ideologies that entwined with colonial political economic processes designating some people as "rulers" and others as "ruled." The forms of agency that accompanied these designations and were effectuated in both the sanctioned and the unsanctioned domains were therefore culturally specific assumptions about natural capacities and innate differences. To merge this point with Foucalt's "thematics of power," people act upon other persons, who are also potential actors in their own right, deploying the strategies that their social world assigns them as fitting for who that world says they are.[6] In colonial Mexico cultural assumptions about who people were and what they were like produced genealogical and social lineages that mirrored each other as they culminated in Indian magic on the one hand, and Spanish magic on the other.

Antonia's case clarifies how deeply entwined and internalized the two domains outlined in these pages were, for her actions were adjudicated both institutionally and through her own consciousness of her transgressions, which indicated her vulnerability to a competing discourse of unbecoming conduct. The symbolism of the two interpenetrating worlds straddled by a single person is superbly evoked by the proper names of several of the principal actors: when the inquisitors asked Antonia what she had done with the Indian's herbs and flowers that aided her transcendent journey, she told them that she had given them — along with advice about fighting bulls and the other feats she accomplished in her flower-induced disguise — to another Indian, an Apache named Antonio, who therefore shared both her name and that of the Catholic saint.[7]

One Antonio in the story is thus a "sacred" (masculinized) Spaniard and the other is a "sacreligious" (feminized) Indian, while Antonia, the betwixt-and-between mulatto female turned to male, vascillated between the two. Antonio/Spaniard-Antonia/mulata-Antonio/Indian — this sequence of similar names connecting this woman to sanctioned power and to its unsanctioned counterpart evokes the tension between the sanctioned and the unsanctioned, the Spanish and Indian worlds, which were mediated by mestizos, mulattoes, and blacks.

Was it a coincidence that Indians were both ubiquitous witches and extremely litigious? Did magic have something in common with going to court? Was one a system of justice dispensed by Indians while Spaniards dispensed theirs through the "words" that Taussig finds indexical of "white" magic?[8] Did each have its traps and dungeons? We can attend to these intertwined processes of magic/justice, unsanctioned/sanctioned by returning to the paradoxes of Spanish colonialism, which themselves set the stage for the strategies Indians, Spaniards, and others engaged in search of justice.

The colonial state emphasized both the exploitation and the protection of Indians, thereby granting Indians roles as both exploited and protected subjects. At the same time, Spanish ideology imbued Indians with a supernaturalism commensurate with their feminine weakness and need for protection, a weakness that subsequently opened Indians up to the Spanish nemesis, the devil himself. This figure precipitated all kinds of morally unsound behaviors and his machinations were of supreme interest to an Inquisition convinced that Indians were his helpmates. Why? Because the devil transformed Spanish power into a weakness that, in the unsanctioned domain, bowed before Indian brilliance. As Indians were drawn into the world of things European and things Christian, then, Spaniards were simultaneously drawn into the world of things *not* Christian and not European, which things Indians were marketing to Spaniards even as they fled the labor obligations Spaniards tried to impose on them. In the end, then, Spanish hegemony spoke both to power and to the subversion of that power. Like a Möbius strip, it inevitably folded back on itself to colonize Spaniards themselves, as the Indian weakness Spaniards conjured up allowed the devil to infiltrate the social body.

The consequences for Spaniards drawn into the Indian-centered world were of course not as dire as those for Indians drawn into the Spanish-centered world, for in the end Spaniards ruled through the power of the state and the privilege that came with their status. That is why Indians spent as much time litigating in Spanish courts as Spaniards spent seeking out Indian witches, and why women like Antonia burst their restraints asunder and then went to confess their wrongdoing. But the consequences of witchcraft for Spaniards nevertheless had their scary and destructive side, and Spaniards mirrored the bases for their own sanctioned authority when they sought out Indians to cure them, just as Indians mirrored their own unsanctioned authority through their litigiousness. Thus, both Indians and Spaniards meted out justice just as surely as they meted out destruction. The result was that Spaniards dispensed equity through the legal system in an attempt to repair the havoc they had wrought while Indians repaid the debt by sometimes healing the same Spaniards they had bewitched. In the end, just as Spaniards were deemed superior healers in the arena in which they were responsible for most of the abuse, that is, in the domain in which their social power was most efficacious, Indians were the most powerful healers of the witchcraft they controlled. We can therefore recognize in colonial Mexico a hegemonic space — Roseberry's "meaningful framework" for living through (performing, in Sayer's words) social orders characterized by domination. This was framed on the one hand not simply by the Indian (female) but by her doubleness as witch and healer in one domain; and, on the other, not simply by the Spaniard (male), but by his doubleness as exploiter and bearer of justice in the other domain.

If Spaniards and Indians had remained two extreme poles of colonization we might have had to tell a different story, though a no less complicated one. Yet the Spanish/Indian relationship has not been my only consideration. For as Spaniards colonized Indians and constructed them as weak and witchy subjects, they also found that if they were to efficiently manage them they were compelled to engage blacks, mulattoes, and mestizos as intermediaries. These intermediaries were crucial to the consolidation of Spanish control, and Spaniards disciplined them by sending them to discipline Indians. But Spaniards disciplined intermediaries in the ways of colonial hegemony, not simply in the ways of colonial power. In sending out these minions to control Indians, then, Spaniards inevitably created the circumstances whereby they would bring back to Spaniards the very supernaturalism of Indians — the counterpoint to their moral system embodied in both the judiciary and the church — that Spaniards feared.

Blacks, mulattoes, and mestizos therefore forged with Indians in the unsanctioned domain *and* with Spaniards in the sanctioned one an interdependence in practice and belief that moved with them back and forth as they developed social affiliations to both Spaniards and Indians. Through reciprocal processes, then, these intermediaries "contaminated" or "cross-pollinated" the Spanish and Indian worlds, the sanctioned and unsanctioned lineages of this study.

In some sense, then, everyone was colonized because colonialism itself created new ways of thinking about, acting in, and being limited by a world that affected Spaniards, Indians, blacks, mulattoes, and mestizos alike. In light of that assertion, and as a way of moving beyond the nature of this colonialism and to a conclusion, it might be useful to take up J. Jorge Klor de Alva's argument that during the colonial period all non-Indians came to identify with the dominant Spanish class, and that the tendency to valorize Europeannness has since that time characterized Latin American (non-Indian) national identity formations. According to him, the only truly colonized Mexican subjects were the "tribute-paying non-noble indigenes [who] with minor exceptions, served primarily as unskilled laborers and providers of foodstuffs for the mines and for the *criollos* and *castas* in the cities."[9] He therefore takes the position that we cannot effectively consider pre-independence, non-Indian groups in Latin America in general and in Mexico in particular to have been colonized. Moreover, postcolonial nation-building processes and cultural practices have firmly oriented non-Indians toward the West so that today only the descendants of indigenous peoples are undergoing decolonization through social movements revitalizing indigenous languages, values, and political rights, often in direct challenges to what are now mestizo nation-states.

This position can be interrogated from several angles. First, scholars have argued that the revitalization movements Klor de Alva looks to for evidence of "decolonization," and therefore for colonization, are themselves modeled on European political culture and the tensions therein, including tensions over which groups are "authentically" Indian.[10] Moreover, these movements are often "mixed" Indian/peasant ones, sometimes led by outsiders.[11] In some parts of Latin America they have come to include people classified as "black."[12]

An interesting twist on specifically Mexican postcolonial identities is the black/Indian *moreno,* whom I have discussed at length elsewhere.[13] This hybrid raza is distinct from the dominant, though also hybrid, mestizo of Mexican national identity. Contemporary moreno identity speaks to some of the historical processes outlined in this book, which subjected blacks and Indians to various forms of cultural conditioning, discrimination, coercion, and force. Those processes in some ways assimilated blacks and mulattoes, and of course mestizos, to the "Spanish Republic," as Spaniards deliberately pitted them against Indians in order to form the hierarchies that I have described here. At the same time, such hierarchies created the possibilities for alliances through kinship and also through witchcraft, especially among blacks, mulattoes, and Indians. These alliances were often discouraged and punished even as new identities were generated.

Both results were signs of black, mulatto, mestizo, and even Spanish colonization, for colonialism was not a simple question of domination and subjugation. It rather created caste, gender, and class overlaps that made "commoner" Indians more "Indian" and feminized than noble ones, mestizos more "Spanish" than blacks and mulattoes, and it created cultural spaces in which the whole range of colonial subjects—including Indians and Spaniards—identified with "things Indian" as well as with "things Spanish." In the sanctioned domain we see the Hispanization that mestizos especially—but also blacks and mulattoes—engaged as lackeys of Spaniards when they turned Spanish power on Indians. But in the unsanctioned domain we see the "Indianization" through witchcraft of especially blacks and mulattoes, who turned Indian power on Spaniards. Thus, in the end, by colonizing Indians, Spaniards also colonized themselves.

These issues resonate today in identities like those of morenos. They take up Indianness because the people they call "whites"—who are really the heirs of mestizo ambivalence—reject blackness except as black aggression has aided them in subduing Indians;[14] because morenos deem themselves to have common historical, cultural, and genealogical ties to Indians; and because morenos—following contemporary and romantic Mexican national identity formations—view Indians as the "real" Mexicans who "broke the chains of slavery."[15] When they act out these formations, it becomes clear that morenos replace the mestizo as the national ideal with one of their own making.

In the end, all of this suggests that instead of distinguishing between the "colonized" and the "not colonized," we might want to complicate the whole idea of Spanish colonialism, the character and efficacy of which were tied to the cultural processes of incorporation I have described. Because those processes not only created certain ideas about "Spanishness" and others about "Indianness" but also forced blacks, mulattoes, and mestizos into contact with both Spaniards and Indians, it was inevitable that the ensuing identities—Indian, black/Indian, mestizo/white, or otherwise—would themselves be, and have continued to be, the products of colonialism's complexities.

It has been argued that colonial Spanish America stood "outside the quintessential colonial experience."[16] Although it is not possible or desirable to develop a single model of colonialism that works for all times and places, the colonial Mexican material nevertheless makes many aspects of later colonial and postcolonial formations look eerily familiar.[17] This invites us to think about the ways in which European colonialisms might be intelligently connected. Without doing a genealogy here, I nevertheless raise the question of the extent to which "quintessential" later colonialisms were influenced by the earlier experience of Spain. If nothing else, the multicentric character of law, and the later emergence of state-dominated forums, seem to have been commonalities. Moreover, legal regimes constituted an institutional framework that operated globally, and colonial authorities could read each other's legal orders.[18]

Certainly contemporary and later colonial powers were familiar with the general Spanish experience. One need only turn in this respect to Winthrop Jordan's discussion of Spanish influences on Anglo perspectives on slavery; or to Ann Stoler's evidence that nineteenth-century Dutch officials drew on (sketchy) "Spanish models" to solve their own "race" problems.[19] Of course, it is well known that Anglo identities and political processes in North America were constructed in large part against the "Black Legend" of Spain. And Stoler's evidence suggests that Dutch colonials on Sumatra's east coast also consciously rejected the perceived cruelties of Spanish colonialism.[20] But that evidence also contains intriguing hints that aspects of the Spanish model, which was after all contradictory, might have been embraced. For instance, while I could be wrong, I am struck by what might be covert references to Bartolomé de Las Casas in the Dutch official Frans Carl Valck's 1876 letter to his friend Henry Levyssohn Norman, in which he details the brutalities of Europeans, whom he calls the "so-called pioneers of civilization."[21] The imagery of inversion is so similar to that used by Las Casas in *The Devastation of the Indies* that one cannot help but wonder whether Valck read the Spanish Dominican's work.[22]

Certainly we have to accept that British, Dutch, and, of course, French colonials were aware of Spanish approaches to many of the same issues these other Europeans were facing as they took up their own "burdens," and that they might have incorporated some of those approaches into their own projects even as they were identifying themselves against Spain. Therefore, while Dirks's warning about denying colonialism's "fundamental historicity" and Rolena Adorno's claim that we have been too quick to homogenize all colonial formations and "lump together the symbolic practices of all variations of European domination over other peoples and places across five centuries" are well taken, it is clearly *not* the case that Spain was "irrelevant" to the later paradigms.[23] In this respect, we can and should challenge Adorno's insistence that the "battles" over "racial and cultural differences" that characterized mid-eighteenth-century and later colonial discourse did not emerge in sixteenth- and seventeenth-century Mexican writings, and also temper Steve Stern's position that gender was not a prominent discourse in Mexico until the eighteenth century. I have shown that struggles around caste and gender, and even around class, permeated at least one genre of colonial texts—court records. These are probably the closest we will ever come to knowing what colonial lives were really like, and they seem to point to lives framed by complex and in some ways quite modern notions of difference.

## CASTE AND COLONY / RACE AND NATION

But when all is said and done, the sixteenth and seventeenth centuries were not the late eighteenth and nineteenth ones. Perhaps one of the most salient distinctions rests on the notion of race itself, which is so central to the ways later colonial projects were organized and justified. Like the Western "science" of race at the foundation of those later projects, the colonial Mexican caste system was explicitly hierarchical and stressed "whiteness" (Spanishness) as an ideal. Also, the values and roles assigned to the different "lineage segments" or the castes that spawned one another, and were therefore broadly related genealogically, were intrinsically tied to the material project of colonialism, which assigned to the different castes certain roles in the political economy, ultimately to the benefit of the head of the "clan," which was Spanish.

But unlike modern race ideologies, caste conveyed a sense of inclusion made operational through what were seen as legitimate lineage claims through kinship and sanctioned social affiliations, and as illegitimate ones through the unsanctioned and feminized shortcut that was witchcraft. Caste also conveyed a sense of reciprocity—most notably here through the judicial system, Catholic conversion (which contrasts, of course, with later Anglo resistance to Protestant conversion for slaves in the British colonies), and through the idea that everyone had rights. The social body, then, was unified through lineage but at the same time hierarchized as the state inculcated certain kinds of behavior through regimens that both unified and differentiated its subjects.

During the first centuries of colonization, one could and was expected to move up both the sanctioned and the unsanctioned social scales through genealogical ties, marriage, fictive kin relations, friendships, labor relations, and other kinds of affiliations. This has been amply demonstrated throughout this book. However, let us shift our attention for the moment back to the later colonial period caste portraits discussed in chapter 3, because in some ways these seem to embody a tension between caste and race. We saw from the portraits, for instance, that the offspring of black and mulatto women appear to have been classified, at least sentimentally, "up" with their lighter-skinned fathers, as would have been normal for the earlier colonial period. But we also saw that the black and mulatto women depicted in the portraits were distinguished categorically from their non-black spouses and offspring. Could it be that in the ways the portraits — and slavery itself — excluded blackness, they foreshadow restrictive social rules more in keeping with race than with caste?

A brief look at the Pragmatic Sanction, or the Royal Pragmatic, which was implemented in 1778, gives us some sense of what might have been changing. The Pragmatic Sanction was a deliberate move by the crown to intervene in marriage choice, thereby nullifying what for centuries had been church-supported freedom in such matters. The new laws stipulated that parents had to consent to marriages between persons under the age of twenty-five if there were substantial social inequality between the partners, with disinheritance the punishment for a disobedient couple.[24] Patricia Seed notes that this was something of a change from the sixteenth and seventeenth centuries, when "threats of financial penalties . . . had been regarded as morally reprehensible and as prima facie evidence of malicious interference regarding the selection of marriage partner."[25] In her estimation, "changing attitudes toward the enterprise of making money" legitimized the new social stance favoring disinheritance. Moreover, the only criterion determining social inequality was "racial disparity," with "black ancestry . . . isolated as the fundamental determinant."[26] In effect, then, the Pragmatic Sanction kept family wealth out of the hands of blacks and mulattoes. We seem to therefore be seeing the full weight of the law brought to bear on mixed unions as both money and social distinctions based on race grew in importance. Black ancestry in particular was carved out for exclusion as the infamy of slavery — even as emancipation was looming — continued to deny blacks' lineage but also, now, claims to material wealth overtly tied to lineage.

Seed notes that most cases of social inequality did not revolve explicitly around racial questions. Rather, they were couched in the language of class as a marker of social difference.[27] Martínez-Alier's Cuban evidence, however, indicates that by the nineteenth century social difference was quite clearly about race, the " 'stain of different colours.' "[28] In addition, she points out that by that time, race and class had so converged in Cuba that "ultimately race relations [were] class relations."[29] Indeed, while the Pragmatic Sanction did not initially include "mulattoes, negroes, coyotes," the law was revised at the beginning of the nineteenth century to include "negroes, mulattoes and other castes."[30] As Martínez-Alier argues, this indicates that white hegemony was reaching deeply into the ranks of the non-white community, thereby intensifying the effect of race-as-distinction and enhancing the move toward "whitening" and the marginalization of blackness.

My own readings indicate that the words *casta* and *raza* were used almost interchangeably in the Pragmatic Sanction decrees issued by the crown.[31] This contrasts markedly with the documentation upon which this study is based. Here *raza* almost never appears, and when it does it is distinguished from *caste*. Though I would hesitate to place too much weight on the significance of this — principally because carefully documenting it would take much more sleuthing than I have been able to do — the clear overlap of *raza* and *casta* in the language of late-eighteenth-century officials raises interesting questions about new ways of identifying and emphasizing lineage differences. With respect to such differences, Verena Stolcke (also known as Martínez-Alier) argues elsewhere that the Pragmatic Sanction was a response to the blurring of caste boundaries as white elites attempted to maintain their position over an increasingly mixed population.[32]

Yet it is clear that caste boundaries were blurred from the very beginning and that Spaniards were also outnumbered from the beginning. I would therefore argue that it was not so much that "biological" boundaries changed as it was the ways in which lineage was understood. The elite shifted its focus from graded statuses modeled more on kinship concepts buttressed by religious ideologies and notions of reciprocity, to statuses that needed to work with expanding capital accumulation and the consolidation of new relations of production. Mechanisms like the Pragmatic Sanction developed to preserve wealth, as well as to reserve some people as labor. Indeed, in later decades as slaves were emancipated in many parts of Latin America, people of African descent could serve that purpose, especially in places like Cuba, where Indian populations were small and scattered.

It is not coincidental that the Spanish state implemented the Pragmatic Sanction as part of an attempt to assert royal privileges over ecclesiastical ones shortly before Spain was to lose much of the Americas to independence movements that left whites in power while removing whatever protections non-Spaniards had under colonial law.[33] It might be that the new guidelines were a way for the Spanish state to inculcate loyalty among whites rather than to explicitly exclude the wrong races, although exclusions of Jews and Moors were still in force. In this respect, we might recall that although Jews and Moors had different religious traditions than Spanish Christians, at base they posed an economic threat to Spanish monopolies on wealth and privilege, a threat transposed onto the language of raza, which included religion. We might therefore want to understand the new exclusions that arose as caste and race were interposed in the context of rising economic competition, expanding capitalist relations of production, new routes to wealth accumulation, and the presence and potential demands of newly freed peoples. This precipitated a shift in emphasis from people promoting their "majority" lineage affiliations (i.e., their ties to Spaniards), to the state promoting their "minority" ones (i.e., the "taint" of blackness) and their exclusion from white privilege. As this shift took place, descent principles did not so much disappear as change their rules from inclusion to exclusion, a social hierarchy of degree to one of kind, from casta to raza, from kinship to race, from (my neologism) "hyperdescent" to what we know as hypodescent, as it were.

All of this suggests, finally, that in contrast to arguments made by historians of colonial Mexico who tend to see class as undermining race as time went on, race and class both took on increasing importance. The result, as Lomnitz succinctly puts it, was that the Mexican national period saw the "complex racial dynamics of the colonial period . . . simplified . . . into a bipolar model (Indians/whites) with an intermediate class of 'mestizos.'"[34] At the same time, blacks and mulattoes in Mexico all but disappeared from official records and from popular consciousness as blackness itself came to be seen as an undesirable quality for new, and later for post-revolutionary renewed, Mexicans to have.[35]

As elsewhere, in Mexico nation-building processes were forged out of "the fabric of European conquest."[36] What Benedict Anderson refers to as the "social thinness" of this and other Latin American movements, led by a numerically inferior elite against a by-then weakened European power, compelled the redefinition of local, oppressed, and often non-Spanish speaking populations as "fellow nationals."[37] Yet these movements also left Spaniards, now tellingly called whites, in power while continuing the oppression of indigenous people, this time through modernization processes that constituted them as barriers to economic and cultural progress, again based on a western model.[38] This double move crystallizes in the figure of the mestizo, the putative biological and cultural mixture of Indian and Spaniard, who became the symbol of Mexican identity and the Mexican nation.

When we look closely at this mestizo, we would have to conclude that in the end caste did not altogether give way to race in Mexico. In fact, the distinguishing characteristic of Mexican national identity might well be the complicated ways in which blood manages to be *both* composite and separate, both caste and race, as the mestizo — the first of the illegitimate colonial castes, then the major caste closest to Spanishness, then the cornerstone of the national identity of mixing (mestizaje), and finally Mexico's post-revolutionary "cosmic race" (*raza cósmica*) — ideologically bridged the gulf between colony and nation, Europe and the New World, and whiteness and Indianness.

With the addition of Indianness, the mestizo distinguishes the Mexican white from his European counterpart. Yet at the same time, with the exception of the revolutionary rhetoric promoting *indigenismo* (indigenism), the figure of the mestizo retains whiteness as the ideal. In this figure we see evidence that the Mexican past — anchored in Indian heroism — became an important site of opposition to the racializing discourses emanating from Europe that made even elite Latin Americans "impure" and therefore inferior to white Europeans.[39] But the mestizo also provides the most conspicuous evidence of colonialism's ability to duplicate itself, as it recreates the Indian and the Spaniard as the cornerstones of social, political, and cultural identities.[40] Mexico's contemporary morenos recognize that Mexican mestizo national identities privilege qualities associated with Indians and whites. Indeed, perhaps they have inherited the strategies of colonial blacks and mulattoes like Adriana and Antonia, who had to take on oppositions and interpenetrations as they devised ways to invent themselves through and around the hall of mirrors fashioned out of Indian and Spanish magic.

# Notes

1 I refer to *hechicería* as "witchcraft" following Behar (1987a, 1987b) who translates *hechicera/o* variously as "witch," "shaman," or "sorcer/ess," yet calls the whole complex "witchcraft." In the New World the definition of witchcraft included classic European practices like devil-worship, orations, divination, causing male sexual impotence (*ligatura*), and also and especially the use of herbs and powders, and forms of divination associated with Indians. The Inquisition distinguished between "explicit" and "implicit" pacts with the devil, depending primarily on whether the perpetrator was male or female, as I discuss below.

2 AGN, Inq vol. 457, exp. 16, 1655.

3 Emphasis added. Defense attorneys (who were referred to as *letrados* or *abogados*, depending on their training) were routinely assigned to defendants, including to slaves (for example, AGN, Inq vol. 444, exp. 4, 1659).

4 As Van Young notes, such texts are where "private lives cross the public record" (1999: 238).

5 The term *casta* also sometimes referred to colonial Mexican blacks, mulattoes, and mestizos as a group.

6 On many levels my argument contrasts with that made by Cope in his study of the impact of colonial Mexican "racial" ideologies on "plebeians" (1994). For example, Cope interprets the evidence to suggest that the caste system was "not ritually woven into the fabric of daily life" (1992: 162) and that the fluidity of that system indexed the failure of colonial domination rather than its success, as I argue here. Cope also understands class as more meaningful to plebeians than race, whereas I

understand class and caste to be overlapping idioms about difference and hierarchy.

7 I expand on these issues in chapter 1 (pages 22–26), and note also my own earlier tendency to blend concepts that I now see as more distinct.

8 Foucault 1978: 96.

9 Foucault 1978: 92–94; 1982: 220–21; Dirks et al. 1994: 9. This is not to say that my framework is entirely Foucauldian. For instance, whereas Foucault seems to "look everywhere else but the state" for relations of power (Dirks et al. 1994: 7; Foucault 1980: 121–22) I was led to inevitably consider the colonial state as a kind of social actor. In part this is because early modern Spanish thinkers did not separate the state from society (McAlister 1963: 349), and indeed Foucault's work mostly concerns the modern state. But it is also because the material itself implicates the state in surprisingly direct ways.

10 Comaroff and Comaroff underscore this point particularly well when they draw connections between what ethnographers and cultural historians do. Both recover "dispersed fragments" of subaltern worlds, the one from the field and the other from texts. Understanding those fragments requires their contextualization in a wider world that is "home to other dramatic personae": the bourgeoisie, the missionaries, the colonizers, the elite (1992: 16–17). Their important observation that in many ways ethnographers are no more privileged than historians is a crucial counter to historians' often confused understanding of ethnographic interpretations as "verifiable" by informants who can serve as a "check on the anthropological imagination" (Mallon 1999: 334; Van Young 1999). To my way of thinking, a historian's "rehydration" of texts into rich cultural worlds is more easily checked because the texts remain in the archives, where anyone can read them. In contrast, the ethnographer's moments are lost as soon as they happen, and verification by the natives of an ethnographer's reading is shaped by the subject positions of the natives, who are as diverse as the inhabitants of the ethnographer's world.

11 McAlister 1963: 350.

12 The term *weakness* and variations thereof are repeatedly associated with women and Indians in colonial texts. Franco writes in this regard that "the 'natural' weakness of women was the ideological pin that rotated the axis of power" in New Spain (1989: xiii; Silverblatt 1987: 161). I extend the implications of this observation to Indians.

13 Munn 1986: 311.

14 Munn 1986: 215.

15 Munn 1986: 233.

16 Munn 1986: 215.

17 Raymond Williams 1977: 114. I find the most fruitful discussions on the nature of hegemony to be ones that, like Williams's, present it as process and conflict rather than as "end point" and consent (Comaroff and Comaroff 1991: 19–27; 1992; Mallon 1999; Roseberry 1994; Taussig 1987). For recent perspectives on the relationship between resistance and domi-

nation see Abu-Lughod 1990; Jean Comaroff 1985; John Comaroff 1989; Comaroff and Comaroff 1991: 26; Foucault 1978: 95; 1982: 21; Ortner 1993; Roseberry 1994; Sayer 1994; James Scott 1985, 1990; Taussig 1987.

18  Roseberry 1994: 358.

19  For Comaroff and Comaroff, hegemony's fissures are what permit the emergence of ideological contestation and social change (1991: 26–27). I mean to emphasize a slightly different take on hegemony, one that sees the fissures themselves as part of the hegemonic project.

20  Taussig 1987.

21  Taussig 1987: 220.

22  I have found the following works, which draw from Latin American and other contexts, especially helpful for thinking through class/race and gender/race coconstructions: Banet-Weiser 1999; Bourgois 1989; de la Cadena 1991; Friedlander 1975; Gilman 1991, 1985; Hendrickson 1991; Martínez-Alier 1989; Smedley 1999; Stepan 1990; Stoler 1989; and White 1985.

23  Unlike Stern, I think a "reliable picture of enduring gender patterns" can be culled from what he sees as the "experimental" and "fluid" quality of sixteenth-century colonial Mexican social relations (1995: 22). As shall become clear, my perspectives on gender issues in the sixteenth and seventeenth centuries have been shaped in part by the work of Alberro (1987), Behar (1987a, 1987b, 1989), and Franco (1989) on Mexico, Silverblatt (1987) on Peru, and Perry (1999, 1992, 1990) on Spain. Most of these authors deal either fully or in part with the politics of witchcraft, but generally with reference to women.

24  Dean 1999: 47.

25  For instance, Jean Comaroff 1985; John Comaroff 1989; Comaroff and Comaroff 1991; Cooper and Stoler 1989, 1997; Dirks 1992b; Stoler 1989, 1992a.

26  On the history of disciplinary boundaries, parallels, and shortcomings see Axel 2002.

27  See especially Mallon 1994 and Comaroff and Comaroff 1992.

28  Mallon 1994; Joseph and Nugent 1994; Spivak 1988: 197–221.

29  Axel 2002: 2–3.

30  Coroníl 1997: 16.

31  As Mallon writes in her discussion of the ways in which Latin Americanists have taken up subaltern studies, "most subalterns are both dominated and dominating subjects, depending on the circumstances and the location in which we encounter them" (1994: 1511). See also Ortner (1993) on the failure to grapple with the ethnographic messiness of subalternity, particularly in the Latin American scholarship.

32  See especially Mallon 1994; the essays in *HAHR* 1999 (especially Van Young 1999); and Knight 2002. Van Young argues that the move to put culture into history only dates back to 1990 or so (1999: 221), but certainly one of cultural history's main concerns — recovering the voices of members of marginalized groups — can probably be traced back to Gibson's pathbreaking work (1964) (as Van Young also acknowledges).

With its focus on Indian peoples, Gibson's book marked a transition from older Mexican historiography almost uniformly focused on Spanish institutions and perspectives (Leonard 1959; Ricard 1966; Simpson 1982; Chevalier 1963). More recent work has focused on subordinated peoples, probing in the main the intersection of Indian and Spanish visions and values (Behar 1987a; Burkhart 1989; Cline 1986; Gruzinski 1988, 1989, 1993; Farriss 1984; Hanks 1986; Haskett 1991b; Kellogg 1995; León-Portilla 1994; Lockhart 1991, 1992; Oueweneel 1995; Seed 1991; Taylor 1979). Scholars have also recently extended attention to the histories of women (Alberro 1987; Arrom 1985; Behar 1987b, 1989; Giraud 1987; Gonzalbo 1987; Franco 1989; Lavrin 1978, 1989; Stern 1995) and to the largely unexplored experiences of blacks (Aguirre Beltrán 1972; Alberro 1979; Carroll 1991a; Martínez Montiel 1994; Palmer 1976) and the urban lower classes (Hoberman and Socolow 1986; Cope 1994).

33  The issues outlined here are discussed by Knight (2002) and Van Young (1999).

34  Van Young 1999: 243–44; Knight 2002: 142.

35  Knight 2002: 142.

36  Ortner 1993: 186. See also Comaroff and Comaroff 1992.

37  See Note on Sources.

38  Knight 2002: 136.

39  Hoberman 1991: 6.

40  Although I did not use ethnographic evidence to guide my historical work — having done the latter long before the former — some of the patterns to which the present study speaks are still apparent in the historically black region of Mexico where I conduct ethnographic fieldwork today. See Lewis 2000, 2001; Flanet 1977.


1 FORGING A COLONIAL LANDSCAPE

1  Neighboring territories such as Nueva Galicia, Nueva Vizcaya, Nuevo León, and Nuevo México had their own judicial bodies, but they all also answered to Mexico City.

2  Hoberman 1991: 22. The Viceroyalty of New Spain eventually included territories in North America as well as Central America, the Caribbean, and the Philippines. The Viceroyalty of Peru, with the viceregal seat in Lima, included in its jurisdiction parts of Central America and South America.

3  Rama 1984. Late-eighteenth-century urban Mexican spaces were also organized along caste lines. For instance, Spaniards occupied the center of the city of Xalapa (Veracruz), mulattoes and mestizos the periphery of this core, and Indians the outlying villages (Carroll 1991a: 115, fig. 4).

4  This summary draws on Hoberman, who provides a detailed overview of production and trade during this period (1991: 1–32). Other sources on specific aspects of the colonial economy are cited where appropriate.

5  Over the three hundred year colonial period, about two hundred thousand slaves were brought to New Spain (Aguirre Beltrán 1972: 81–95; Rout 1977: 95, 279). New Spain's (and Peru's) slave importations slowed dramatically during the late seventeenth and eighteenth centuries, as the colonists' need for slave labor became less acute. By the end of the eighteenth century, slave importations were occurring mostly in sparsely inhabited districts of the Yucatán, and the Mexican population included only about nine thousand enslaved blacks and mulattoes (Aguirre Beltrán 1972: 15–95). When slavery was abolished with independence in the early nineteenth century, it had in fact nearly ended: in 1821 fewer than three thousand people were still enslaved in what would become the Mexican Republic. The Mexican trade needs to be understood in tandem with that of other New World colonies. The scholarship is massive and impossible to cite here but the broad contours of the trade (from Klein 1986) are as follows: by 1700 the trade to Spanish America had been eclipsed by Brazil and the West Indies, where sugar production was developing. As the plantation system took hold in the sugar-producing islands (Jamaica, Barbados, and Saint Domingue), where African slaves outnumbered Europeans, Brazil's output dropped to third place, and gold mining came to dominate the Brazilian economy. By the end of the eighteenth century, a new stage of Spanish American slavery centering on Cuba and Puerto Rico took shape as Saint Domingue experienced a slave rebellion that led to revolution, and dropped out of the sugar market. In the nineteenth century, Cuba came to dominate the sugar industry and Brazil rebounded as the second largest producer. At the same time, the United States became the largest slave society in the Americas.

6  Historical demographers have long debated the size of Mexico's preconquest population (see McAlister 1984: 83–85). Although some estimates are higher, a figure of twenty-five million, mostly concentrated in the central valley, is generally accepted. The population likely spiraled to a low of perhaps one million to one and a half million by the first decades of the seventeenth century and began to rebound in the 1650s (Cook and Borah 1979; Gerhard 1972: 22–23). It tends to be forgotten that diseases also felled great numbers of Africans on slave ships and once they were in the New World (Gerhard 1972: 25; Palmer 1976: 49), and that blacks as well as Indians died from malnutrition, overwork, and violence. Woodrow Borah (1951) has characterized the seventeenth century as one of economic depression brought on by the decline in the Indian population. Subsequent studies show, however, that trade and mining grew until the 1630s, contracted from the 1640s through the 1660s or 1670s, and experienced something of an erratic recovery until the end of the century. Market-oriented agriculture remained strong throughout this period, while textile enterprises expanded into new regions (Hoberman 1991: 16–17).

7  See Stern 1988.

8  Kellogg 1995: 48–49; Lockhart 1992: 166–70.

9 Semo 1973; Stern 1988; Zavala 1988.

10 On the New World encomienda see Gibson 1964: 58–97, 194–219; Liss 1975; Lockhart 1992: 28–29; Lockhart and Schwartz 1983: 68–71; Mac-Lachlan 1988; Robert Williams 1990; Zavala 1992. Some precedent for encomienda existed in Spain, where the Crown awarded "deserving persons or corporations" with temporary rights to dues and services from villagers (McAlister 1984: 157). The Mexica state had also collected tribute and draft labor from subjugated populations.

11 Robert Williams 1990: 86.

12 Ulloa 1977; Robert Williams 1990: 85–86; Zavala 1992: 20–36.

13 Robert Williams 1990: 86–88; Liss 1975: 18.

14 Zavala 1992: 40–73.

15 Liss 1975: 96.

16 By the beginning of the seventeenth century, in areas most closely connected to the Spanish economy, tribute in money began to be paid alongside tribute in kind (Lockhart 1992: 180), but money did not replace in-kind tribute for some time (Semo 1973: 87).

17 Indian enslavement continued in Central Mexico for at least a decade after the New Laws were implemented (Haskett 1991a: 453) and for an even longer period at the colony's peripheries. Forms of slavery had also existed in pre-Columbian times throughout the Americas (Clendinnen 1991: 101; Gibson 1964: 153). Following the conquest, Indian slave-holding of other Indians was forbidden under Spanish law as all Indians became subordinated to Spaniards. Indian nobles in Mexico nevertheless continued to hold Indian slaves until the middle of the sixteenth century (Gibson 1964: 154).

18 Cintrón Tiryakian 1979: 28; Liss 1975: 40; MacLachlan 1988: 58–65.

19 On the nature of Spanish kingship in this period see especially Cintrón Tiryakian 1979; Hoberman 1980; MacLachlan 1988; and Elliott 1989.

20 MacLachlan 1988: 1–12; Elliott 1989: 167.

21 McAlister 1963: 353; MacLachlan 1988: 13–19.

22 *Miserable* referred to Crown paternalism toward Indians, and to Indian "wretchedness" due to poverty and illness. Borah (1983) argues that the term emerged in tandem with the move away from Indian autonomy and toward the political and legal incorporation of Indians as a class in Spanish society.

23 McAlister 1963: 358; Borah 1983: 13, 80.

24 Zavala 1988: 217. Since the work of Chevalier (1963) and Borah (1951), a primary focus of Mexican agrarian history has been the development of the hacienda system and the prevalence of debt as a "controlling feature of labor" (Bauer 1979: 62). Chevalier's and Borah's analyses of the "feudal" Mexican countryside with its large, and underproductive, estates and labor forces held captive through debt-peonage (Van Young 1983: 10) was not contradicted until Gibson published his findings that debt-peonage was less prevalent than earlier studies had suggested (1964: 248–49). While I have nothing to add to the debate, I refer the reader to Van Young's excellent review of the scholarship on this issue (1983), and

to the work of Bauer (1979), who suggests that the practice prevailed only in Yucatán and southeast Mexico.

25 Gibson 1964: 149–50; MacLachlan 1974: 30–31; Cope 1994: 20–21.

26 Gibson 1964: 282–83; Lockhart 1992: 44–46. Although most congregaciones were formed during the seventeenth century, the earliest ones date to the middle of the sixteenth century (Gerhard 1975; Lockhart 1992: 45). Lockhart discusses the complex ways in which Spanish political organization affected, and was affected by, the central settlements of indigenous *altepetl* units, territorial entities headed by dynastic rulers (1992: 14–58).

27 Gibson 1964: 282–89; Lockhart 1992: 164–70.

28 Zavala 1988; Gerhard 1972: 17–22.

29 Gibson 1964: 84–85.

30 Even before Columbus's voyages, African slave labor was established in a limited way in Spain and on the Portuguese-controlled islands off the West African coast, where the sugar plantation model that would later dominate the Caribbean had already taken root.

31 Palmer 1976: 8.

32 Palmer 1976: 6–10. Ferdinand and Isabella attempted to control who entered the New World in order to exclude those—such as Jews and Moors—who might seriously undermine processes of conversion. As a result, Islamic "Wolof" slaves from Guinea were the most systematically kept out of the colonies (Palmer 1976: 7).

33 Between the initial conquest in 1519 and 1640, when the indigenous population was on the rebound and large numbers of mulattoes and mestizos had been added to the labor force, probably one hundred thousand African slaves arrived in New Spain (Palmer 1995: 226). In the sixteenth century, slaves came mostly from West Africa (Senegal, Guinea-Bissau, and Sierra Leone); in the seventeenth century they were drawn more from Central Africa, principally from Angola and the Congo (Palmer 1976: 20–23). Palmer attributes this shift to the Portuguese penetration of Angola (1976: 20–21; Aguirre Beltrán 1972: 240–41). The first black in the Americas was actually probably a free man who arrived with Columbus in 1493. At least one free black, a man named Juan Garrido, also accompanied the first conquistadors to Mexico, who also brought several black slaves. Garrido might have taken part in the conquest of Tenochtitlán. He was definitely involved in post-conquest expeditions to control outlying lands, and was the first person to farm wheat in Mexico (Gerhard 1978).

34 Israel 1975: 63–64; Palmer 1976: 6–35; Aguirre Beltrán 1972.

35 AGN, RCO vol. 6, exp. 232, 1619.

36 Partly due to sexual imbalances in the population, the replenishment of slaves depended more on the external trade than on internal reproduction (Palmer 1976: ch. 1; Aguirre Beltrán 1972: 240–41).

37 Konrad 1980: chap. 10.

38 Davidson 1979; Dusenberry 1948; Palmer 1976: chaps. 2 and 3.

39 I cannot do justice here to the arguments surrounding the nature of slave

societies in the Americas. Essentially, the liberal nature of Spanish laws prompted a generation of comparativists to argue that the traditional (Catholic) customs and institutions of Spanish America tempered the harsh realities of the Protestant/capitalist slaveholding societies of the north (Tannenbaum 1947; Elkins 1976; Klein 1967, 1969). The comparison seems a faulty exercise in ethnology, however, as it presents Protestant North America as the norm and Catholic Latin America as the romanticized other. The question is still unresolved (Smith 1992: 358). Part of the problem is that legislation and implementation are two different things. The Spanish and Portuguese were clearly "tainted by racial prejudice" (Davis 1969: 70; also Mörner 1969; Sweet 1978; Rout 1977), and Genovese maintains that in some respects the treatment of slaves in Latin America—especially in nineteenth-century Brazil—was much harsher than it was in North America. Keeping different time frames in perspective, he also points out that North America had its share of paternalism (1967; also Davis 1969: 75–76). Davis argues that although it is probably true that "slavery in Latin America, compared with that in North America, was less subject to the pressures of competitive capitalism and was closer to a system of patriarchal rights and semifeudalistic services," scholars also need to stop opposing "patriarchy" to "capitalism" (1969: 73). Slavery was not radically different in the two contexts, he contends, but rather different manifestations of the same general construct. I would add that we should also contextualize slavery in developing racial ideologies, which were themselves linked in important ways to capitalism. As I discuss in chapter 7, the Latin American evidence suggests that in the eighteenth century race began shifting from a lineage-based ideology that allowed for mobility (caste) to one that emphasized exclusion (race). We therefore need to understand different forms of slavery in concert with changing racial ideas, as race became a more difficult line to cross in the nineteenth and twentieth centuries when scientific theories promoted competitive models that supported sharp racial distinctions as well as free market economics.

40  Cope finds high rates of endogamy in a late-seventeenth-century Mexico City parish for all social groups (1994: 80), but he also points out that because most black women in seventeenth-century Mexico were slaves (1994: 81), they were not favored as marriage partners by free persons, or even by male slaves, who were more likely to marry free persons themselves (1994: 81; see also Love 1971; Palmer 1976: 56; 1995: 219–20).

41  The state did not actively intervene in marriage choice until the latter part of the eighteenth century. This issue is taken up in chapter 7.

42  AGN, Inq vol. 29, exp. 4, 1572.

43  Palmer 1976: 173–79; Davidson 1979: 88; but see AGN, Inq vol. 418, exp. 4, 1643; AGN, Criminal vol. 685, exp. 4, 1622 for exceptions.

44  Palmer 1976: 176–78; Rout 1977: 90. Most free women and children were in fact mulatto. Palmer believes that this reflects slaveholders' favorable treatment of persons of Spanish/black ancestry over "pure" blacks

(1976: 179). However, as "mulatto" also referred to people of Indian/black ancestry, it is equally likely that the high numbers of free mulattoes can be accounted for by the fact that many of them were free because of the status held by their Indian mothers.

45  Palmer 1976: 43; Karasch 1986: 253; Cope 1994: 88, table 5.1. Although free blacks and mulattoes were restricted from participation in particular craft guilds, an area in which Indians were encouraged to develop their skills (Gibson 1964: 398–99; Cope 1994: 88–90), these guilds nevertheless appear to have been the main avenues for freedmen's economic advancement because labor shortages created opportunities for them (Bowser 1972: 50; Johnson 1986: 238–39). This, however, was the only Spanish profession into which free blacks, especially, made inroads.

46  Black and mulatto women, for instance, were forbidden from wearing silks and adorning themselves with gold, silver, and pearls, because doing so meant that they were "trying to put themselves ahead of Spanish women" (AGN, Ord vol. 2, exp. 169, f. 158v, 1604; also AGN, RCD vol. 3, exp. 182bis, f. 157, 1598, which also refers to the appropriate dress for mulatto men, and Gage 1958: 68) A later decree allowed free black and mulatto women who paid tribute to adorn themselves with gold and silver, and to wear silk capes and dresses (AGN, RCD vol. 48, exp. 247, f. 160v–161r, 1644).

47  AGN, Ord vol. 3, exp. 56, 77v, 1618; and vol. 4, exp. 40, f. 40v, 1622; AGN, RCD vol. 48, exp. 440, fs. 320r–321r, 1644; also Cope 1994: 18.

48  Pitt-Rivers 1971; Corominas and Pascual 1980, vol. 1: 913–16.

49  In earlier versions of this work (Lewis 1996a, 1996b, 1995, 1993) I did not make this distinction either.

50  AGN, Inq vol. 206, exp. 5, 1593.

51  Corominas and Pascual 1980, vol. 4: 800.

52  Covarrubias implicitly tied blood to "biological" inheritance by noting that "blood . . . sometimes signifies kinship (*parentesco*)" ([1611] 1984: 925). (Smith also notes the links between concepts of race in modern Euro-America and kinship through the concept of "a common substance symbolized by blood" [1992: 265].)

53  Covarrubias [1611] 1984: 896–97; Root 1988. The derogatory aspects of raza might also be related to a similar Spanish word, *raça*, which signified "defect or blemish in a piece of cloth" (Delacampagne 1983: 33; Stolcke 1991: 24; Corominas and Pascual 1980, vol. 4: 800). Covarrubias defines this blemish as "the thread unlike the rest of the threads in the weft" ([1611] 1984: 896).

54  Unconverted Jews did not fall under the Inquisition's jurisdiction in the fourteen years leading up to their 1492 expulsion, but suspected conversos were persecuted in Spain until the end of the eighteenth century. Moors were forced to convert beginning in the early sixteenth century, but moriscos were not expelled for another hundred years.

55  Root 1988: 132; Perry 1999.

56  Covarrubias [1611] 1984: 316.

57  Corominas and Pascual 1980, vol. 1: 914–15. They add that "it is much

easier to move from the general idea of 'class or kind' to a 'kind apart,' [or] 'pure lineage,' than the reverse" (ibid.).

58 Covarrubias [1611] 1984: 824. Although he states that "nature" derived from "caste *or* nation" (emphasis added), which might suggest that caste and nation were interchangeable, it rather seems that he means to distinguish them, for he does not include "nation" in his definition of caste.

59 Lomnitz 1993: 263–64; Silverblatt 2002.

60 Silverblatt 2002: 106.

61 Lyle McAlister's well-known and often-cited definition of New World caste includes adherence to religious orthodoxy (1963: 355). Yet one reason why this does not make sense is that blacks were in fact legally inferior to Indians, who were on the whole less orthodox than blacks.

62 Lomnitz 1993: 273–74.

63 Katzew also addresses this issue (1996: 10–11) but with reference to the later colonial context that I return to in chapter 7.

64 Lomnitz 1993: 269–70.

65 Pagden 1982: 71; Solano 1990: 18.

66 Only Tenochtitlán and the Inca center of Cuzco were completely destroyed and replaced with new cities. Dean discusses how the colonizers actually used fragments of indigenous architectural structures to construct their own buildings in Cuzco (1999: 25–26). Colonial urban settlements were built to enclose and protect Spaniards. As Solano writes, they "were evidence of permanent possession, of dominion, of the constant presence of sovereignty" (1990: 20).

67 In Mexico *indio* was sometimes followed by further descriptive qualifiers describing the exact ethnic group, such as *otomí* or *tarasco*. Indians were less frequently referred to as *naturales* (natives). According to Lockhart, while other ethnic terms brought by the Spanish became Nahuatl loanwords, *indio* was an exception. By 1600, away from Spaniards, so-called indios, regardless of rank, referred to themselves as *macehualli* which, at the time of the conquest, was the Nahuatl term for "commoner" (1992: 114–15). According to Kellogg, however, Indian elites used *macegual* in a derogatory way (1995: 71).

68 Haskett 1991b.

69 Following the conquest, the Indian nobility convinced Spaniards that it had not paid tribute, even though it had (Lockhart 1992: 106; 132). Lockhart (1992: 130–31) argues that the nobility survived for a much longer period than that suggested by Gibson (1964: 163–64). Although its members continued to marry among themselves, many became "Hispanicized in their material culture" (Gibson 1964: 154), which commoners also adopted in complex ways (Lockhart 1991: 3–4). Some commoners also began to accumulate wealth and to be recognized as nobles, thereby turning what had principally been a hereditary rank into an achieved one (Gibson 1964: 156).

70 Archivo General de la Nación 1938: 16, 12. Non-Indians, in turn, could not dress like Indian commoners. One mestizo woman who dressed in

Indian attire claimed to be too poor to dress like an "ordinary" Spaniard (AGN, GP vol. 4, exps. 502 and 505, fs. 142–43, 1591).

71 AGN, Ind vol. 32, exp. 73, 1692.

72 This point is elaborated in chapter 2, n. 8. It should also be noted here that many missionaries thought Indians had been seduced by the devil, and many were not sure of which force—God or the devil—inspired Indians. This point is taken up in chapter 5.

73 Trexler 1984.

74 The meaning of the word *chichimec* is unknown, but it was used by the indigenous peoples of Central Mexico to refer in a generic way to nomadic northern groups (Behar 1987b: 132–35). Particularly in the territory of Nueva Galicia, with important silver deposits around Zacatecas, Chichimec nomads gained a reputation for fierceness that contrasted sharply with sedentary Central Mexican agriculturalists and their neighbors. See Powell (1975) for a history of early Spanish colonization of the northern zones of Mexico.

75 Trexler 1984: 199.

76 Pagden 1982: 77.

77 AGN, Criminal vol. 369, exp. 2, 1661. Covarrubias defines *duendes* as house spirits that in ancient times accompanied people in their daily lives ([1611] 1984: 752). In the European Middle Ages elves or fairies were "part of the great army of good and bad spirits with which the world was thought to be infested" and were frequently considered "highly malevolent" (Thomas 1971: 606–7).

78 AGN, RCD vol. 47, exp. 423, f. 262, 1567; AGN, RCD vol. 4, exp. 17, 1651. On the northern frontier churches and priests represented institutional authority in an area where other institutions were sparse. They played an important role in pacifying Indians and implementing Spanish political authority. Gutiérrez's account of the Franciscan missions that "civilized" New Mexico is indispensable to an understanding of this process (1991). Here, too, Indians targeted religious *sacra*.

79 Moriscos in sixteenth-century Spain were portrayed in similar ways. "The association of Moriscos with disease," writes Root, "resurfaces in references to infection and vermin, and the need to 'cleanse' Spain and make it 'pure and clean from this people'" (1988: 131; Boase 1990).

80 AGN, RCD vol. 30, exps. 8, 9, and 45, 1672. In places far from the centers of Spanish settlement, such as New Mexico and presumably other areas to the north of New Spain, Indian enslavement was also tolerated as a form of compensation for settlers (Gutiérrez 1991: 150). In New Spain, black slaves were always favored over Chichimec ones, and were much more expensive. As a Spaniard noted somewhat redundantly when he did not want to pay more than five pesos for the recovery of a runaway Chichimec, "one must be charged less for a chichimec than for a black because of the black's higher value" (AGN, GP vol. 1, exp. 74, f. 14–14v, 1575).

81 Pagden 1982: 33.

82 Davis 1984: 65; Martínez-Alier 1989: 6; Jordan 1977.

83 Cited in Friede 1971: 165.

84 Scholars have debated Las Casas's position on African slavery. For instance, Friede notes that Las Casas began to have doubts about it. He did not consider the institution itself to be inhuman. Instead, he seems to have become aware of the unjust nature of the capture of black slaves by Portuguese slavers (1971: 165–66). Also Bataillon 1971: 415–16. Montúfar wrote to the king that "we do not know what reason exists that blacks be captives more than Indians, because they willingly receive the holy spirit and do not wage war against Christians" (BNAH Archivo Histórico, Colección Francisco de Paso y Troncoso, Legajo 115, June 1560); Friede (1971: 166).

85 Davis 1966: 63–64, n. 2. Medieval Arab writers also invoked this biblical curse (Davis 1984: 42–43). Rout observes that for the mid-fifteenth-century Portuguese chronicler Eanes de Zurana, "Canaan's descendants had [already] become a race" (1977: 12).

86 Sweet 1978: 110.

87 Sweet 1978: 105–6.

88 Fairchild 1934: 9–10. This perspective might point to the beginnings of modern exclusionary racism. I will show later that as the colonial period went on, blacks, like Jews and Moors in earlier periods, seemed to be carved out for exclusion. This is evident in the late eighteenth- and nineteenth-century caste paintings that I discuss in chapter 3, and in the Crown's intervention in marriage choice toward the end of the eighteenth century, which I discuss in chapter 7.

89 Covarrubias [1611] 1984: 826.

90 *Zambo* and *zambaigo* were also terms for black/Indian mixtures, but they are rarely used in this documentation.

91 In New Mexico, where there were few blacks, *mestizo* and *mulato* were both used to refer to someone of mixed Spanish/Indian ancestry (Gutiérrez 1991: 197). I would speculate that this was because, like the northern Chichimecs, Indians in New Mexico were considered more barbarous than their Central Mexican counterparts and were therefore classified somewhat the way blacks were in New Spain, where most Indians were sedentary and closer to what Spaniards considered civilized. As the terminologies developed in New Spain were increasingly elaborated during the later colonial period, they displayed a marked propensity to identify non-Spaniards, especially blacks and mulattoes, with color or animal terms (Aguirre Beltrán 1972: 163–79; van den Berghe 1978: 52; Palmer 1976: 41–42). Indeed, *mulato* and *negro* are themselves animal and color terms.

92 AGN, Inq vol. 559, exp. 1, 1652.

93 AGN, Civil vol. 862, exp. 2, 1579; Zapata 1989: 73; Aguirre Beltrán 1972: 186–87. Whether or not Africans identified with people from their own land has been little explored. Palmer has published an interesting study suggesting that African-born blacks in Mexico preferred marriage partners of similar linguistic and cultural backgrounds. He did not find the

same preferences among creole blacks (1995). Although I have not systematically investigated the question, I have found intriguing evidence that cultural ties were indeed significant to African-born blacks. For instance, one black slave, reporting on the Judaizing practices of a Spanish captain as told to him by another black slave, who had heard it from an Indian, who had heard it from one of the Spaniard's mulatto slaves, testified that he had told the other black slave that he would have to confirm the story by asking yet another black, who was from "the same land and would tell him the truth" (AGN, Inq vol. 435 [1], f. 78, 1650).

94  Palmer 1995: 225.

95  Cited in Bataillon 1971: 417.

96  AGN, Inq vol. 284, exp. 77, 1609.

97  *Cimarrón* also meant "untamed," "wild," "savage," and "uncultivated." The word probably derived from the word *cima* (summit) because of the mountains and woods to which runaways often fled (Corominas and Pascual 1980, vol. 2). Most cimarrón communities were overrun. This one seems to have been a satellite of San Lorenzo de los Negros, which survived, but only by accommodating the realities of colonial domination through developing economic relationships with surrounding communities and by agreeing to return runaway slaves in exchange for its community's independence (Carroll 1977). San Lorenzo (also called San Lorenzo de Cerralvo) was headed by an African named Yanga and granted a charter as a free settlement in 1612. Over a century later in the same general vicinity of Veracruz, slave uprisings in sugar mills produced new cimarrón activity. Through negotiations with colonial authorities, these cimarrones came to aid Spaniards in their mid-eighteenth-century war against Great Britain, and were granted autonomy at the war's conclusion. Historians have also speculated that on the Pacific Coast during the same period slaves escaped the ports of Acapulco and Huatulco, setting up communities in the present-day states of Guerrero and Oaxaca (Rout 1977: 106–7; Carroll 1977; Davidson 1979; Palmer 1976: 119–24). While freedom for blacks was generally restricted by legislation that persecuted any hint of independence, it is possible that in relatively autonomous cimarrón communities aspects of ancestral cultures could successfully be maintained (Palmer 1976: 52–53). The fact that an emissary from the head town came to complain about the friar's presence in the San Lorenzo satellite also points to a conscious, politicized rejection of Spanish religion and custom, and suggests that cimarrón communities could be highly organized. Challenges to Spanish authority were probably also brewing among groups of sedentary Indians, who hid in the hills when the daily abuses of encomenderos and priests overwhelmed them. Because these groups had experienced the colonial order, they might also have had the consciousness and the strength of a "communal identity" to reject it (Comaroff and Comaroff 1991: 24).

98  AGN, RCD vol. 49, exp. 10, fs. 14–15v, 1643.

99  AGN, RCD vol. 5, exp. 803, 1607. In the cited text a distinction seems to be made between cimarrones and *negros huídos* (runaway blacks). This

distinction may have differentiated blacks who had already established their own communities (cimarrones) from those who had only recently fled captivity.

100 AGN, GP vol. 4, exp. 328, f. 94, 1591.

101 AGN, GP vol. 5, exp. 284, f. 65, 1599. ; AGN, RCD vol. 5, exp. 803, f. 197, 1607; AGN, Criminal vol. 643, exp. 2, 1619; AGN, RCD vol. 49, exp. 10, fs. 14–15v, 1643.

102 For instance, AGN, RCD vol. 3, exp. 130, 1590.

103 "Social death" is the phrase Patterson (1982) coins to describe the slave's "liminal" state between enslavement and manumission. It refers to both the slave's natal alienation and to his or her incomplete assimilation to the new social context of enslavement. Davis states that in this respect slaves were the first "modern" people. Typically foreigners and outsiders torn from their families, their modernity lay in their "incomplete and ambiguous bonding to a social group" (1984: 15). See also the discussion in Smedley (1999: 120–21).

104 Genovese discusses the significance of masters' and former masters' surnames among slaves and freedmen in nineteenth-century North America (1972: 443–50). He also ties the matter to the importance of kinship to African Americans. He notes, for instance, that "when [slaves] married in formal ceremonies they often wanted to see their names written down in the master's family Bible" (1972: 445); moreover, freed slaves often took their master's names or the names of other whites who had owned their relatives. Genovese believes that this was a way to "recapture, as best they could, their own history" and a "genuine identity" (1972: 446).

105 Lomnitz 1993: 266.

106 AGN, Inq vol. 559, exp. 1, 1652.

107 AGN, Inq vol. 494, exp. 2, 1655.

108 See with respect to this issue Palmer 1995, especially 230–31; Brathwaite 1971: 204; Genovese 1972: 450–58; Smith 1992: 275.

109 Alberro 1979: 133.

110 AGN, RCD vol. 3, exp. 185, f. 160, 1598.

111 AGN, RCD vol. 20, exp. 47, f. 36, 1654.

112 Chance and Taylor 1977: 460; McAlister 1963.

113 Mörner 1967: 61; McAlister 1963: 356.

114 This issue has been raised, though not attended to at length, in Carroll 1991a: 89; Israel 1975; Lomnitz 1993: 266; Palmer 1976: 60–63; Mörner 1967: 30–31, 60–61; and Wade 1997: 30.

115 Lomnitz 1993: 269–70.

116 Israel 1975: chap. 1; Palmer 1976.

117 Bozales ("brutes" or "savages" [Aguirre Beltrán 1972: 157]) were African-born blacks while *negros criollos* were slaves born in Mexico and *ladinos* were those born elsewhere in the Hispanic world.

118 Palmer 1976: 34–35.

119 Carroll 1991b: 10; Israel 1975: 73; Konrad 1980: 246; C. Martin 1985: 138–39; Palmer 1976: 65–83.

120 Not all Spaniards fell into the elite class and not all non-Spaniards were poor. Nevertheless, the upper end of the lower classes was Spanish while non-Spaniards who achieved the greatest economic success were mostly mestizo and *castizo*, a Spanish/mestizo mix (Cope 1994: 24, 19). Cope argues that class rather than race characterized colonial Mexican society in the late seventeenth and early eighteenth centuries, in part because mestizos were found among the elite and Spaniards among the poor. His evidence could also support the conclusion, however, that racial ideologies did form a barrier to black, mulatto, mestizo, and Indian advancement, making the elite class almost exclusively Spanish. Perhaps a closer examination of the caste attitudes of Spanish plebeians would have helped to resolve this question.

121 Population estimates are suspect due to the nature of the data — particularly the fluid ways in which people were classified and the ways in which we understand those classifications — but these indicate more or less equal numbers of blacks/mulattoes (slave and free), Spaniards, and mestizos by the middle of the seventeenth century, with each group comprising about 140,000 persons (Aguirre Beltrán 1972: 219; Israel 1975: 21–22, 27). As noted, the Indian population experienced a "demographic collapse" from probably 25 million people in the preconquest period to between 1 million and 1.5 million people by the middle of the seventeenth century.

122 Pagden 1987: 69, n. 65.

123 Arendt 1966: 98.

124 Arendt 1966: 99.

125 Arendt 1966: 98.

126 MacLachlan 1988: 8; Liss 1975: 8–9. Conversion of blacks, in particular, presents an interesting contrast to the situation in the later Anglo colonies, where slaves were deliberately kept unbaptized as a way of keeping them culturally separate from, and therefore subordinate and less menacing to, their masters (Jordan 1977: 184–85).

127 Benton 2002.

128 Benton 2002: 86, 84; Kellogg 1992, 1995; Borah 1982. Benton seems to argue that state-dominated law did not fully emerge until the nineteenth century in "high" colonial contexts (2002: chap. 4). Yet the Mexican evidence she presents suggests that such domination was already prominent there in the sixteenth and seventeenth centuries (2002: 81–86).

129 Perry 1999; Root 1988.

130 Corrigan and Sayer 1985: chap. 3.

131 For instance, focusing on the revolutionary period, Knight draws on Corrigan and Sayer's work to highlight the broad processes of cultural change that took place in Mexico beginning in 1760. He remarks that "over the long term, Mexican development seems to display some structural features that are strongly reminiscent of England's 'cultural revolution'" (1994: 59).

132 Here I refer the reader to Corrigan and Sayer's work (1985), and to

Cohn and Dirks's observation that "culture is implicated in state projects" but not in overly deterministic ways (1988).

133 Liss 1975: 10.

134 AGN, RCD vol. 15, exp. 178, f. 140, 1645.

135 Cope 1994: 18, 22, 91.

136 The overwhelming flow of new laws and regulations from various sources eventually caused legislative chaos and repeated attempts to consolidate legal authority throughout the seventeenth century. These reforms mostly failed (Lhöest 1992).

137 Corrigan and Sayer 1985: 68.

138 *Peyote* was perhaps the most prestigious and widely diffused of all indigenous medicinal and magical plants (Aguirre Beltrán 1963: 140–62). Considered a "god" and used in pre-Hispanic indigenous rituals, during the sixteenth century it was identified with aspects of the Christian pantheon (Quezada 1984: 89–90). It was the most consistently outlawed of all Indian medicines, for the inquisitors believed it was used to "uncover robberies and divine other hidden future events which is superstitious activity and against the purity and sincerity of our Holy Catholic Faith" (AGN, Inq vol. 333, exp. 35, 1619). Peyote came to have its place in the colonial pantheon as a divination tool used by Indians to find mundane lost objects and missing persons for non-Indians. *Pulque* was an indigenous fermented alcoholic beverage produced from the maguey cactus. It was periodically banned by colonial officials in an effort to curb what they perceived to be excessive Indian drunkenness.

139 Headed by an attorney general for Indians (*procurador general de indios*) and an assessor, the General Indian Court was established in 1592 to ease the judicial process and lower costs for Indians otherwise routinely forced to pay exorbitant fees to various Spanish personnel. The best sources on the General Indian Court continue to be those of Borah (1982, 1983).

140 District political officials (corregidores and alcaldes mayor) along with municipal magistrates and local judges were responsible for maintaining order in their jurisdictions (del Refugio González and Lozano 1985). As Borah discusses, the viceroy would not have been able to handle hearing all Indian cases. Therefore, suits involving small value continued to be heard in local courts (1983: 99).

141 The viceregal system was introduced in 1535 as the Crown consolidated its authority over settlers (MacLachlan 1974: 18; McAlister 1984: 192–93). The viceroy was always an "authentic noble" (Lockhart and Schwartz 1983: 104–5) and because of this either a native-born (*peninsular*) Spaniard or the son of one.

142 Borah 1983; del Refugio González et al. 1985. These cases are identified in the notes as *Indios*.

143 Cases from these two courts are identified in the notes as *Criminal* and *Civil*.

144 The audiencia reviewed decisions of local magistrates, was a court of the first instance in the capital and the surrounding area, and appointed

agents beyond. The audiencia also heard appeals, but this responsibility was not in force for most of the sixteenth and seventeenth centuries (MacLachlan 1974: 23).

145 Borah 1983: 96.

146 Cases from this court are identified in the notes with the abbreviation BN (Bienes Nacionales).

147 The viceroy intervened in disputes between inquisitors and other judges, and also controlled the funds the crown sent to support the various tribunals. Relations between viceroys and inquisitors were generally poor, as were relations among the inquisitors themselves.

148 Inquisition cases are identified with the abbreviation Inq (Inquisicíon). Initially, New Spain's Inquisition operated informally with friars and bishops acting as inquisitors. Because it suffered clerical abuses of power, internal bickering, and general disorganization, toward the end of the sixteenth century Philip II established two tribunals—one in New Spain and one in Peru—to be staffed with apolitical prosecutors. Excellent sources on institutional and social aspects of the Mexican Inquisition include Greenleaf 1962, 1965, 1969 and Alberro 1979, 1981a, 1987, 1988.

149 Cited in Klor de Alva 1991: 14; Alberro 1981a: 100. Klor de Alva (1991) argues that the shift away from inquisitorial punishment for Indians was due to the recognition that its selective methods were ineffective in eliminating the "minute illegalities" that were the stuff of Indian deviance from Spanish social norms. What was required was a system of indoctrination and retraining led by priests and secular officials. In Peru such a system produced large-scale and violent extirpation campaigns (Mills 1994: 26–27). In Mexico, perceived links between Indians and the devil actually strengthened during the seventeenth century. (Cervantes 1991, 1994: chap. 1).

150 In general, blacks avoided the most serious heretical charges but were subject to accusations of blasphemy, including witchcraft. In addition, punishment for them was sometimes more severe than that called for in official guidelines (Palmer 1976: 149; Alberro 1979).

151 Corrigan and Sayer 1985: 59.

152 Alberro 1981a: 86. In addition to hechicería, the less common term *brujeria* is typically also translated as "witchcraft." Henningsen maintains a distinction in early modern Spain between brujería (which he identifies as witchcraft in the form of demonology and the witch's Sabbat) and hechicería (wizardry). He equates the latter with African witch doctors, whose primary task was to provide anti-witchcraft remedies by using material things to counteract the supernatural power of *brujo/as* (1980: 10). The Spanish inquisitors, Henningsen adds, were typically more interested in punishing brujo/as than hechicero/as. Alberro also distinguishes between colonial Mexican brujos/as as the perpetrators of psychic acts that cannot be real and hechiceros/as who killed their victims with magic and used concrete things to do so (1974: 343–44). Like Henningsen's distinction, Alberro's rests on Evans-

Pritchard's classic separation of "sorcery" and "witchcraft" because, for the mid-twentieth-century Azande among whom Evans-Pritchard did fieldwork, witchcraft was an inherited, physical trait, a "substance" that enabled the witch to perform harmful, psychic acts, while sorcery, or black magic, was the performance of magical rites with "bad medicines" (Evans-Pritchard 1976: 176). Evans-Pritchard's witch/sorcerer distinction has informed subsequent studies, which have also engendered a certain distortion of Evans-Pritchard's original intentions (Turner 1967: 118–19). In the colonial Mexican context the distinction seems mostly irrelevant, as Alberro elsewhere writes, because the two systems were inextricably intertwined (Alberro 1987: 93). The hechicera was both innately predisposed to evil *and* used material things to achieve her ends, as, in fact, did the European witch herself (Mair 1969: 27, 230; Monter 1976: 17; Thomas 1971:chap. 14; R. Martin 1989: 3 for other contexts). Practices considered classically witch-like such as participation in the Sabbat, intercourse with the devil, and consuming people "from within" were classified as aspects of hechicería in New Spain, and often arose in the course of a trial alongside more typical acts of "sorcery" such as the use of herbs and powders to tame a lover. A series of Inquisition trials involving three Spanish women and a castiza (mestizo/Spanish woman) collectively accused of hechicerías, *embustes* (lies), superstitions, and "invoking the devil" demonstrate the colonial melding of different traditions and the variety of acts that fell under the hechicería rubric. The women confessed to, and accused each other of, taking peyote. They also conjured a black cat outside at night; recited a variety of chants; divined with fava beans, lime, maize, coal, and bread; and attracted men by bringing them "through the air" (AGN, Inq vol. 206, exps. 4, 5, 6, 7, 1593). Elements of this complex repertoire clearly had distinct origins: for instance, peyote consumption and divination with maize were Indian practices (Quezada 1984: 78–86) while conjuring the black cat—which might have been a "familiar" (a low-ranking demon), or the devil himself—and flying through the air are aspects of the classic (European) demonic Sabbat, which was not all that common in New Spain, nor prominent in Spain, Italy, or England. (See Henningsen 1980 and Kamen 1985 on Spain; R. Martin 1989 on Italy; Thomas 1971 and Macfarlane 1970 on England.)

In my view, the term *brujería* in New Spain seems to have referred to something quite precise: an amalgamation of flying, as in the classic Sabbat (one text refers to a mulatto brujo who flew out of jail, for instance), and indigenous *nagualismo*, in which a person's animal "double" performed supernatural acts. Hechicería seems to have referred to everything *except* this flying/nagualismo combination. It was therefore a much broader category. Examples of seventeenth-century brujería are found in AGN, Inq vol. 297, exp. 5, 1612; vol. 478, exp. 18, 1612; vol. 439, exp. 3, 1654,; vol. 316, exp. 35, 1617; vol. 342, exp. 12, 1622; vol. 459, exp. 6, 1658; vol. 619, exp. 3, 1672; vol. 516, exp. 556, 1673.

153   Corrigan and Sayer 1985: 64–65, citing Larner 1982; Perry 1999:43–44.

154 Alberro 1981a; Greenleaf 1969: 162–71; Peters 1988: 99. Trevor-Roper points out the similarities between persecutions of Jews and witches in Spain and in other European countries, but also notes that these persecutions seem to have alternated—that is, Jews and witches were not the same, although both categories rested on social noncomformity and the persecutions themselves were interchangeable (1967: 110–11). Elements of Judaizing are sometimes present in colonial Mexican witchcraft narratives. This does not mean that "witches" and "Jews" were interchangeable. Indeed, they were persecuted separately in Mexico as well as in Spain.

155 On witchcraft in early modern Spain see Sánchez-Ortega 1992; Caro Baroja 1964; Henningsen 1980; Kamen 1985; Perry 1990.

156 In Spain, sixteen tribunals oversaw a territory of little more than five hundred thousand square kilometers while the Mexican Inquisition, which was a single tribunal, covered almost 3 million square kilometers of Spanish territory in Central America, Mexico, New Mexico, Yucatán, and the Philippines (Alberro 1988: 23).

157 Alberro 1988: 30–68; MacLachlan 1988: 32.

158 Alberro 1981a: 86; 1987, 1988: 192–96; Behar 1987a: 42; Cervantes 1994: chap. 5.

159 For instance, Stern 1995: 109.

160 This point is made throughout this book and also by Cervantes 1994: 37–38; 1991: 27.

161 Bienes Nacionales includes several trial transcripts concerning Indian "idolatry" in the sixteenth and seventeenth centuries. Others are in the process of being located and recorded (Moreno de los Arcos 1991). My perusal of the documentation did not uncover Indian involvement with members of other castes. Therefore, I did not use it.

162 Greenleaf 1965; 1978; Borah 1982, 1983; Moreno de los Arcos 1991; also Kagan 1981: 250.

163 As Kagan notes for Spain, "the labyrinthine state of Castilian law had its institutional analogue: an array of law courts and legal tribunals so bewildering that lawsuits regularly became lost in a confused jurisdictional morass" (1981: 32). The Crown might also have deliberately established interdependent overseas political and administrative entities to provide an effective check on its officers' New World powers (Gutiérrez 1991: 96).

164 Borah 1982: 283.

165 Palmer 1976: 88–89; Sweet 1978: 97. Slaveholders were obliged to feed and clothe their slaves and were discouraged from engaging in excessive cruelty (AGN, RCD vol. 30, exp. 1378, f. 477, 1683). The judiciary's role was sometimes complicated by the fact that justices themselves were slaveholders, and thus were torn between protecting their bureaucratic turf and the vision of justice they were meant to uphold, and acknowledging the realities of the slave system (Alberro 1979).

166 For example, AGN, Criminal vol. 685, exp. 4, 1622.

167 The ubiquity of the documentation on witchcraft itself reflects the

state's interest in it. (The prominence of the Inquisition material in the AGN, and the scrutiny given it by contemporary researchers, also reflects recent concerns with culture and subalternity.) Although the history and organization of the AGN, today housed in Mexico City's old panoptical penitentiary, is beyond the scope of this book, Dirks reminds us that archives themselves require ethnographic analysis, for their history and organization—indeed, their very existence—reflect state categories and concerns (2002).

168 AGN, Inq vol. 517, exp. 13, 1674. In Spain, as in Mexico, the Inquisition often clashed with diocesan courts and with the king's magistrates (Kagan 1981: 250).

169 This was true as well in sixteenth- and seventeenth-century Spain (Kagan 1981). In both places, moreover, witchcraft was just as ubiquitous as litigation.

170 An Edict of Grace was typically declared to allow people to confess voluntarily, or to denounce others, within a period of thirty or forty days, on pain of excommunication if they did not. Several of the records cited here are actually collections of denunciations and confessions gathered following Edicts of Grace.

171 For instance, many people—such as the Spanish woman cited above who complained about slave marriages—felt the need to confess their blasphemy. Confessions sometimes came years after the initial crime was committed. One can only speculate as to why this might have been so, but it suggests that the decision to confess was deeply entwined with other, often unstated, aspects of people's lives. Some voluntary confessions might, of course, be read as attempts to forestall accusations from others. But many seem to have been confessions of conscience.

172 Benton 2002: 137, 149, 127–66. For New Spain this point is most explicitly made by Kellogg 1992: 40, n. 11; 1995; see also Haskett 1991a: 474.

173 On this point see Benton 2002: 148–49, 130–31.

174 See also Stern 1982; Kellogg 1992, 1995; Foucault 1980; Darien-Smith 1994: 131; and Merry 1990 on the hegemonic function of judicial systems.

175 Indian litigation was rampant throughout the Americas (Benton 2002: 99; Borah 1982, 1983; Kellogg 1992, 1995; MacLachlan 1988: 48; Stern 1982).

176 I did not systematically track these cases, but an early one can be found in AGN, Inq vol. 38, exp. 6, 1537. A much later volume is full of such denunciations (AGN, Inq vol. 435[1], fs. 76 and 78, f. 216; vol. 435[2], f. 337, 1650). Hoberman notes that many Portuguese conversos, whose ancestors had fled Spain and who were allowed to emigrate to the New World in the early seventeenth century, joined the trading community and became "a vulnerable and controversial group within colonial society" (1991: 17). Many of these conversos had fled first back to Spain before heading for the New World. As Silverblatt writes, "the flight to Spain fed a burgeoning Iberian stereotype, found both on the continent

and in the New World, that all Portuguese, like all New Christians, were Jews" (2002: 99).

177  For example, AGN, Inq vol. 356, exp. 25, f. 27, 1626, in which a "Mandinga" slave denounces another slave; and AGN, Inq vol. 612, exp. 8, 1669, in which a black slave denounces a mulatto servant.

178  Following Merry (1990), Lazarus-Black defines "legal consciousness" as "the way people understand and use law" (1994: 269, n. 4). Her study of black slaves and colonial courts in the British Caribbean is significant for its conclusion that blacks used courts to express their rights and to resolve internal disputes (1994: 259), and for its assertion that legal consciousness and practices became hegemonic (1994). Unlike Lazarus-Black, however, I do not see subaltern use of the judiciary as evidence of resistance (also Darien-Smith 1994).

179  Dedieu offers insight into how to evaluate texts from the Spanish Inquisition by emphasizing that scholars of these texts, and therefore of the societies that produced them, must distinguish between the different kinds of texts produced by the Inquisition and between different aspects of a single text (1980, 1986). Most important for our purposes are trial records. As Dedieu points out, each stage of a trial produced particular kinds of writing and attendant distortions. Genealogies and life histories, for instance, were solicited according to a standard questionnaire with open-ended questions regarding the defendant's upbringing, religious orthodoxy, family members, occupation, place of birth, and residence. This information was taken down with precision by a scribe, who acted "like a tape recorder." Similar care was taken with the testimony of the defendant, plaintiff, and witnesses, according to Dedieu, who considers such testimony to be the most elaborated and the "rawest" source of information for the modern scholar (1980: 907–8). This testimony was sometimes recorded in the third person and sometimes in the first, depending on whether it consisted of answers to inquisitors' questions (third person) or initial complaints by the actual individuals and their testimony regarding conversations that they were involved in or they overheard (first person).

180  Also R. Martin 1989: 222.

181  Her possessions included the boarding house, clothing, and jewelry, and the slaves who conferred prestige by performing the manual and domestic tasks typically relegated to women and non-Spaniards. One was worth a considerable sum, Adriana pointed out, because she was a "good washer and [knew] how to cook an ordinary meal." The notary listed which items she could have in prison, including 100 pesos for sustenance. Other things were given to her as she requested them, and these requests were also noted with comments like the following: "The Señor Inquisitor told Christobal Muñoz de Mancilla, the warden of the secret prisons, that Adriana Ruíz de Cabrera be able to choose two shirts from the clothing that he had in his power, and that it be noted in the book where her clothing is listed."

182 Appeals, however, could drag the process out (also R. Kagan 1981: 47–48).

183 An example can be found in AGN, Inq vol. 444, exp. 4, 1659.

184 The act of searching one's conscience was meant to cleanse one's thoughts. The link between purity of mind and purity of blood should not go unremarked.

185 Physical evidence ranged from Indian pictographic manuscripts (Borah 1983: 241; Gruzinski 1993: 28–29) to evaluations by justices and outside professionals, including doctors, of a plaintiff or defendant's condition. For instance, the inquisitors who examined the tatooed arm of a mestizo accused of consorting with the devil noted with precision the tatooed images as well as the sore the mestizo seemed to have created through his attempts to eradicate those images before the inquisitors had the chance to see them (chapter 6); and the doctor who examined the aforementioned Domingo de la Cruz testified to the alcalde mayor about the extensive injuries the Indian suffered at the hands of the two mulattoes, including raw flesh and swollen testicles.

186 In Mexico torture seems to have been employed only in the most serious cases of heresy. I have come across only one such case, and the crime in question, which concerned slaves running messages back and forth for their imprisoned masters, who might have been suspected Judaizers, was political rather than religious (AGN, Inq vol. 396, exp. 3, 1642). Torture was also uncommon in Spain, and confessions gained in this way were not considered valid (Kamen 1985: 174; Tedeschi 1987).

187 Textile workshops often functioned as prisons, as confinement to an obraje was standard punishment for a criminal offense. More generally obrajes were sites for the maintenance and reproduction of a range of hierarchical relationships: between the state and criminals, masters and slaves, parents and children, husbands and wives; in short, between those with authority and those without. Once confined, people sometimes could not escape. An official visit to an obraje in Coyoacán undertaken in 1660 by Andrés Sánchez de Ocampo, an audiencia official, documented the presence of four mestizos (including one condemned for a crime, one paying off a debt and now enslaved against his will, and one who entered voluntarily for a wage and was subsequently kept against his will); nine mulatto slaves (including three condemned for crimes); four free mulattoes (including one condemned for a crime, one unjustly enslaved, one whose free black father put him there, and one female married to a slave of the boss); eleven Indian males (including five condemned for crimes and three paying off debts); at least five Indian females (including several who claimed they were "treated like slaves," one married to a mulatto slave of the boss, and one once locked in by her husband but now free to come and go); one free black (put there by his black slave father); two male black slaves and one female; and a number of young apprentices, caste unspecified, sent by their fathers for disruptive behavior. Of all the groups, it seems that the

Indians had the most liberty and the fewest complaints (Archivo General de la Nación 1940).

188 In one capital punishment case a mulatto from San Juan, Puerto Rico, Fernando Rodriguez de Castro, was convicted of impersonating a priest, abducting a black woman, and escaping once from the Inquisition's custody. He was ordered garroted "until he dies naturally" and then burned "until he turns into ashes and is obliterated from memory" (AGN, Inq vol. 275, exp. 14, 1605). In another, the mulatto Juan de la Vega was put to death along with several cohorts for same-sex sexual practices in Mexico City in 1658 (Gruzinski 1986; AGI, México, Correspondencia Virreinal, Leg. 38, no. 57-B, 1658). And eleven Indians, two mestizos, one mulatto, and one Spaniard were ordered put to death for their participation in the Mexico City riot of 1692 (Cope 1994: 157).

189 Henningsen 1980: 22.

190 One early punishment consisted of "two hundred lashes" (AGN, Inq vol. 38, exp. 5, 1537). This was a common sentence for many offenses throughout the period under investigation here, but it was likely formulaic since such excess would certainly kill the offender. See also AGN, Inq vol. 206, exps. 4, 5, 6, 7, 1593; AGN, Inq vol. 523, exp. 3, 1686.

191 Also R. Martin 1989: 84; Dedieu 1986: 189 n. 89.

192 Also Dedieu 1986: 165; 1980: 902–5.

193 See for instance Le Roy Ladurie 1979; Ginzburg 1985, 1982; R. Martin 1989; Henningsen 1980.

194 Ginzburg 1989: 160; also R. Martin 1989: 80; Dedieu 1986: 161.

195 Le Roy Ladurie 1979: vii.

196 Such as Rosaldo 1986: 78–79.

197 Peters makes the important point that "inquisitions" never constituted a coherent category. There was no "single, all-powerful, horrific tribunal, whose agents worked everywhere to thwart religious truth, intellectual freedom and political liberty" (Peters 1988: 3). Instead, a variety of inquisitorial institutions operated to rout heresy from the thirteenth century on at different times and in different parts of Europe and its colonies, and they should not be confused with each other (Peters 1988). One therefore has to study inquisitions, as well as other judicial contexts, as forums in which the issue of power was worked out on many different levels depending on the social and cultural contexts in which they operated. Recent studies have tried to do just that for a variety of inquisitions in Europe and the New World (Alcalá 1987; Haliczer 1987; Henningsen and Tedeschi 1986; Kamen 1985; R. Martin 1989; Peters 1988; Perry and Cruz 1991).

198 Mallon 1994: 1506–7; also Adorno 1993.

199 Authorities also had to contend with this issue in Spain, where many people did not speak Spanish (Castilian) (Dedieu 1980, 1986).

200 Translators were also provided for German, Flemish, French, and English speakers (Alberro 1988: 60). Although such considerations were not extended to bozal slaves, Africans were separated from their native

linguistic communities and would have had to learn Spanish in order to communicate with Spaniards as well as with Africans of other cultural groups.

201 Borah 1982: 284. The general tendency to summarize was balanced by the fact that notaries were paid by the page for their work (which could nevertheless result in oversized, rather than in more, letters).

202 Borah 1983: 62; Heath 1974: 12; Lockhart 1992: 320.

203 Streamlining judicial processes for Indians initially meant allowing cases to proceed on oral testimony, but this was in practice all but impossible because written records were required for the various bureaucratic procedures (Borah 1983: 250).

204 With respect to this issue, scholars of the Spanish, Italian, and Mexican Inquisitions have directly contended that the claim that inquisitors fabricated accusations and trials has not withstood critical scrutiny (Tedeschi 1986; R. Martin 1989; Dedieu 1980: 906–8; Alberro 1988). For Mexico, Alberro has noted in addition that inquisitors often went to great lengths to expose testimony fabricated by plaintiffs, which was costly but, as we have seen with respect to Ana María de la Concepción, might only be punished with a fine (albeit a considerable one of 200 pesos) (1988: 145).

205 Gruzinski 1993: 4.

206 Hanks 1986.

207 Texts written in Nahuatl by Indian nobles included titles regarding community boundaries and histories, annals, local litigation, wills, and deeds of sale and purchase (Lockhart 1991, 1992). While Lockhart (1992) in many ways downplays the impact of colonization on indigenous peoples, he quite convincingly uses such texts to trace subtle changes in indigenous thought and expression over a several-hundred-year period as contact with Spaniards became increasingly unavoidable. Because Kellogg does the same thing with Spanish-language texts containing Indian testimony (1995), the evidence does not seem to support Lockhart's position that Nahuatl texts tell us about one world while Spanish texts tell us about another (1991, 1992).

208 Readers interested in the original Spanish texts have access both to the archives in Mexico City and to my dissertation, which includes Spanish transcriptions of many of the texts cited here (Lewis 1993).

209 Sayer 1994: 374–75.

210 Taussig 1987: 288.

## 2 THE ROADS ARE HARSH

1 AGN, Criminal vol. 234, exp. 3, 1643. Angelina is not mentioned in the course of the narrative.

2 The comadre relationship is between a child's godmother and his mother. It is part of a wider system of fictive kinship (*compadrazgo*) with roots in Catholic ritual. The system establishes relationships between

parents and godparents based on their mutual obligation to a child. Godparents, in turn, are to be accorded respect by both those children and their parents. In Mexico, compadrazgo has traditionally been bound up with religious and social honor. Although Ingham points out the risks of reducing the institution to a utilitarian function (1986: 89), it can also play a role in overcoming economic differences in that having fictive kin of a higher status than oneself is generally desirable, for godparents have financial obligations to their godchildren. Cope makes the excellent point that during the colonial period, Spaniards drew on their Indian fictive kin "to recruit a new generation of indigenous workers" (1994: 92–93, 95; also Nutini and Bell 1980).

3 Dirks 1992a: 5.

4 Pagden 1982; Todorov 1984; Robert Williams 1990.

5 The most visible mendicant order in Mexico, and the first to arrive (in 1524), was the Franciscan. Twelve Dominicans followed in 1526 and came to form the second most visible presence. Augustinians arrived in 1533 and the Jesuits in the 1570s. The classic work on the earliest missionaries is Ricard (1966). Recent works that accomplish more sensitive cultural analyses of the missionizing process include Burkhart 1989; Cervantes 1994; Klor de Alva 1988; Phelan 1970; Trexler 1984; and Clendinnen, who reminds us that missionaries are as much "subjects for wonder and analysis" as the "natives" on which ethnohistorians traditionally focus (1982: 27).

6 Gruzinski 1993: 3.

7 Klor de Alva interprets Sahagún's work in the context of the postmodern anthropological concern with the problem of representing the other. He designates Sahagún "the first modern anthropologist" who produced the "first modern ethnographic fieldwork and narrative" (1988: 35) as he systematically collected data on Nahua culture, society, and history. In addition, Klor de Alva's insightful observation that the invention of modern anthropology was "waiting to happen" (1988: 37) links the birth of the discipline to the rise of colonialism in the sixteenth century (1988: 42).

8 Phelan characterizes the Franciscans as empirical and eclectic (1970: 10). Inspired by More's *Utopia* and St. Augustine's *City of God,* and influenced (as was the Dominican Las Casas) by an Erasmian theology that stressed tolerance, skepticism, and liberalism, the Franciscans were concerned with "this-worldly" political reform that would restore the Primitive Church in its original and uncorrupted form (Maravall 1949: 207–8). For the Franciscans, a new era was dawning in New Spain: together the friars and the Indians would build the City of God (Phelan 1970: 91). Following the teachings of Thomas Aquinas, who called for a "total adhesion to God's love" in preparation for the apocalypse (Ulloa 1977: 150), the Dominicans were more other-worldly. For them, the perfection of religious life was achieved through the integration of theology and evangelization (Ulloa 1977: 21). Unlike the Franciscans, their intent was not to replace a corrupt religion with a renewed one. It was to find an

"uncorrupted natural substance" beneath outward manifestations of evil. This substance and substratum — pure Christianity — provided for them the necessary link between the New World and the Old. For the Dominicans, unlike for the Franciscans, then, New Spain did not present an opportunity for a new beginning. It was simply a New World extension of Old World Christian history. Todorov characterizes this contrast in the following way: "we might see Durán and Sahagún as two opposing forms of a relation, somewhat as one used to describe the opposition of our classic and romantic: interpenetration of contraries in the former, separation in the latter" (1984: 227). Durán, the Dominican, fused the Indians with the sacred past, as a lost tribe of Israel (Duran 1964: 3; 1971: 63, 389, 419, 422). He suggested that the Mexica god Quetzalcoatl had been the apostle St. Thomas, whose endeavors to educate the Indians in the ways of Christianity were discouraged by their "rude, inconsistent, rough [and] slow" characters (1971: 59). Due to this apostle's presence, however, the groundwork for Christianity's rebirth in the New World had already been done. The Conquest, then, was providential. Moctezuma could not deflect Cortés's invasion because divine will favored the conquistadors (Sandoval 1945: 66). The conversion of the Indians, like the Conquest itself, was necessary and unavoidable. Instead of connecting Indians to the Old World Christian past, Sahagún and other Franciscans likened the Indians to the Old World profane past typified by the Greeks and the Romans and stressed similarities between Indian peoples and the Greek and Roman "barbarians" of Europe (1969, 2: 53). According to Sahagún, the Mexica gods Huitzilopochtli and Quetzalcoatl were like Hercules (1969, 1: 43, 278); the fire god Xiuhtecutli was "another Vulcan" (1969, 1: 56). In the typical manner of Greeks, Romans, and other barbarians, Sahagún wrote, the Indians were religious innocents. They could not be held accountable for their practices, for they had never known God and therefore stood outside the Christian tradition. "I have always had the opinion that the Gospel was not preached [here]," Sahagún wrote, "because nothing has ever been found; everything contradicts it. There is so much idolatry that I cannot believe that they have ever had the Gospel preached to them" (1969, 3: 358). Indigenous New Spain was "sterile," he wrote, and it was difficult "to cultivate where the Catholic faith has thin roots and where hard work bears little fruit" (1969, 3: 355).

9  Sahagún 1969, 3: 149.
10  López-Austín 1974.
11  Cited in Phelan 1970: 61.
12  Cited in Maravall 1949: 205.
13  Borah 1983: 29–30; Maravall 1949; Phelan 1970.
14  Rama 1984; Solano 1990.
15  MacLachlan 1988: 29; Liss 1975: 6.
16  On the internal dynamics of colonial Indian communities see P. Carrasco 1961; Cline 1986; Gibson 1964; Gruzinski 1989, 1993; Haskett 1991b; Lockhart 1992; Ouweneel 1995.

17 MacLachlan 1988: 28; Mörner 1970a; Bonfil Batalla 1987: 121; Borah 1983: 86.
18 Liss 1975: 43.
19 Wade 1997: 30.
20 Borah 1983: 83.
21 Lockhart 1991: 15–16.
22 These are found in the Ordenanzas, Mercedes, General de Parte, Reales Cédulas Duplicadas, and Indios branches of the AGN. See also Mörner 1967: 45–48; 1970a; Mörner and Gibson 1962; Borah 1983: 31–32.
23 AGN, Indios vol. 4, exp. 742, 1590.
24 AGN, Indios vol. 3, exp. 51, 1590.
25 AGN, Indios vol. 6 (1), exp. 495, 1593.
26 AGN, Tierras vol. 48, exp. 6, 1593.
27 AGN, Indios vol. 9, exps. 277 and 279, 1620. Although Indian women were not legally required to labor in mines and on haciendas, they were vulnerable to involuntary servitude in public industries as well as to other forms of abuse (see Haskett 1991a: 451–52 on women in the Tasco mines). An Indian named Juliana, for instance, related how her daughter Maria was being held in the house of a Spaniard, where she had been put by a friar. She had fled, but the friar had caught up with her and confined her and her child to an obraje where she was "suffering" (AGN, Indios vol. 2, exp. 596, 1583). In the late seventeenth century, northern hacendados aided by their overseers and servants were said to be taking Indian women and children by force to Mexico City, where they sold them like slaves (AGN, Criminal vol. 22, exp. 104, 1689). Some violence against women, of course, was sexual. One proceeding describes how a Spanish corregidor, among other abuses, habitually forced "young and good-looking" Indian girls to sleep with him (AGN, Criminal vol. 12, exp. 6, 1646). Another tells of a mulatto who had "stolen" an Indian woman from her village, taking her by force from her husband (AGN, Inq vol. 368, f. 248, 1604). Yet another tells of an Indian woman abducted by a Spaniard, a mestizo, and a mulatto (AGN, Civil vol. 1776, exp. 66, 1648). But there was little justice for women — whether Indian or Spanish — and rape (violación or estupro) seems to have been a criminal offense only if the woman (or girl) was a virgin (see Castañeda 1989: 75–87). Rape in these texts is presented as an incidental event, alluded to or described in the context of other expressions of control.
28 AGN, Indios vol. 11, exp. 485, 1640.
29 AGI, México, Correspondencia Virreinal, Leg. 20, no. 9, 1578.
30 AGN, RCD vol. 2, exp. 459, f. 260, ca. 1585.
31 See, for example, AGN, RCO vol. 6, exp. 232, f. 529, 1619; vol. 25, exp. 68, f. 240, 1693. AGN, RCD vol. 26, exp. 146, f. 150, 1668; vol. 30 exp. 1261, f. 355, 1676.
32 AGN, RCO vol. 19, exp. 33, fs. 75–76, 1682; vol. 20, exp. 100, f. 5, 1685; AGI, México, Correspondencia Virreinal, Leg. 20, no. 9, 1578. Emphasis added.
33 This witness also calls repartimiento by its Nahuatl name, coatequil.

34   AGN, Criminal vol. 219, exp. 11, 1634; also Haskett 1991a.

35   AGN, Criminal vol. 219, exp. 11, 1634.

36   Lockhart 1992: 206; Cintrón Tiryakian 1979; Zavala 1988.

37   Israel 1975: 47–57. In the mid-seventeenth century there were about three thousand mendicants and six thousand ordained priests in New Spain (Israel 1975: 48, nn. 93, 95).

38   Israel 1975: 49–52.

39   AGN, RCD vol. 52, f. 22v, 1644.

40   Gage 1958: 45.

41   Gage 1958: 39.

42   AGN, RCD vol. 52, f. 22v, 1644.

43   Gibson reviews the official sixteenth-century instructions to priests regarding their conduct and duties (1964: 114–15).

44   Ololiuque, the seed of the coriander plant, was one of the most important medicines in the indigenous repertoire. Like peyote it could produce supernatural visions. Another name for it, signifying its more mystical character, was *cuexpaltzi* (Aguirre Beltrán 1963: 130–37; Quezada 1984: 92–93).

45   AGN, Inq vol. 510, exp. 133, 1625.

46   AGN, RCO vol. 2, exp. 43, f. 78, 1644.

47   In Nahuatl culture the seizing of the warrior lock, a single strip of hair on an otherwise shaven head, was a formal sign of submission, and warriors expelled for offenses had their heads shaved "into the tonsure of the *tamene*, or carrier, the lowliest of Mexica occupations" (Clendinnen 1991: 115–16, 118). Perhaps this priest was aware that hair held some significance to this Indian.

48   AGN, BN vol. 542, exp. 9, 1693.

49   AGN, BN vol. 596, exp. 13, 1682.

50   By the sixteenth century, reason had become the pursuit of rational knowledge as knowledge of God's goodness. This was not unconnected to Aristotelian ideas linking reason to the overcoming of passion, for all rested on perfection, however defined, as the pinnacle of creation (and Lovejoy links the Platonic Idea of the Good to the "God of Plato" as well as to the "God" of Aristotle [1936: 5, 42]). During the Enlightenment "reason" would come to counter rather than to reinforce Christian faith and a "rationalist" would become an unbeliever (Becker 1932: 8). Lloyd (1984) traces the ways in which reason — however construed — has been defined as male and valued, while "feminine traits" — principally identified with nature — have been understood as inferior.

51   Liss 1975: 39; Borah 1983: 30.

52   Burkhart 1989: 17; Clendinnen 1982: 43; Borah 1983: 30.

53   Sahagún 1969, 3: 161.

54   Gutiérrez 1991: 75–76.

55   The debate, during which Sepúlveda and Las Casas never actually met face to face, has been treated extensively in the English-language scholarship (Hanke 1959, 1974; Phelan 1969, 1970; Pagden 1982; Todorov 1984) and much has been written on Las Casas and his work (Friede and

Keen 1971: 603–16). Sepúlveda's work has been published in many Spanish editions but never fully translated into English (although long excerpts can be found in Phelan 1969).

56 In the Spanish view a "barbarian" was someone who spoke Spanish badly or not at all, was unable to write, did not obey Spanish law or behave according to Spanish custom, lacked reason and was "merciless and cruel" (Covarrubias [1611] 1984: 194).

57 Phelan 1970: 65.

58 Sepúlveda [1545] 1941: 109.

59 The view of indigenous technology as inferior often manifested itself in the physical symbols of conquest. As Valerie Fraser writes in reference to Andean colonial society, "Inca architecture [was] often described as having *primor* [skill] and *artificio* [workmanship], but never *arte* . . . Each individual [Spanish] church . . . exemplified the Art of Architecture and represented the triumph of civilization over the skillful but nevertheless essentially barbarous buildings of the Indians" (1986: 330–31; also Pagden 1982: 73).

60 Phelan 1970: 65.

61 Sepúlveda [1545] 1941: 85, 123–135. Covarrubias defines *inhumana* as "the cruel one; he who is not a man, but a wild beast" ([1611] 1984: 737).

62 Sepúlveda [1545] 1941: 1, editor's n. 1; Pagden 1982: 109–18.

63 For instance, Pagden 1982: 110, 145.

64 Phelan 1969: 63.

65 On this point see Pagden 1982: 119; Todorov 1984: 161; Zavala [1935] 1992: 32.

66 Las Casas [1552] 1992: 30, emphasis added. Despite his belief that Christianity should "receive all nations" and not reduce any to "servitude on the pretext that they are slaves 'by nature'" (cited in Martínez 1971: 309), Las Casas also made distinctions, and not only initially between Indians and blacks. For instance, apart from arguing that Indians were reasonable people whose hearts, if not their minds, were in the right place, he argued that Aristotle's "barbarian" was a misconstrued idea — Aristotle was himself a "pagan," he had insisted to Charles V. This was not because barbarians did not exist, but because the category failed to distinguish between those who had achieved the partially civilized cultural level of the Inca and the Aztec, and those who had not, such as the Caribbean tribes that Columbus encountered and the nomadic ones of northern Mexico.

67 Las Casas [1552] 1992.

68 On this point see Pagden 1982: 42. During the Enlightenment the concept of nature would take on characteristics similar to those associated with passion or animal instincts. Nature became both "pre-social" and good (as in Rousseau's "State of Nature") as well as an explanation for the inferiority of women, whose special relationship with nature (a relationship that can be traced all the way to the Greeks and beyond) also devalued nature (Bloch and Bloch 1980; Lloyd 1984).

69　Sepúlveda [1545] 1941: 83.

70　Sepúlveda [1545] 1941: 101. Sepúlveda further likened the differences between Indian "rudeness" and Spanish "civility" to differences between "monkeys" and "men" (ibid.: 101). In Spain animal metaphors were frequently employed as invectives condemning non-Christians (Root 1988: 30; Boase 1990: 18). In the New World similar invectives dehumanized non-Spanish populations such as "wild" nomadic Indians (Behar 1987b: 116) and runaway black slaves (cimarrones). As noted, animal types such as *mulato, coyote,* and *lobo* also surface in the *sistema de castas* nomenclature, applied, of course, to non-Spaniards.

71　Pagden further notes Sepúlveda's "acerbic" language and his use of "images of inversion, commonly reserved for witches and other deviants" (1982: 117). Colonial witchcraft was considered a practice of women and Indians, who, as discussed in chapter 5, were also linked through the metaphor of the witch.

72　Sepúlveda [1545] 1941: 85, 107.

73　Sepúlveda [1545] 1941: 107. Sepúlveda's belief in this female-like cowardice stemmed from what he had read about the conquest, in particular about the Mexica lack of resistance to the invaders. Moctezuma's alleged passivity when confronted with the conquerors seems to have contributed to Sepúlveda's disdain. "Having had news of Hernan Cortés's arrival and his victories, and of the wish he had to come to Mexico to meet with him," wrote Sepúlveda, "[Moctezuma] tried everything to avoid it, but not being able to, filled with terror he received in his city Cortés and a small number of Spaniards" (ibid.).

74　Pagden 1982: 44; also Silverblatt 1987: 176.

75　Adorno 1989: 225–26.

76　Stepan 1990: 55, n. 11.

77　For example, de la Cadena 1991; Hendrickson 1991; Stephen 1999.

78　Fernández 1994; Zamora 1993: 152–79; Montrose 1993.

79　As discussed in Fernández 1994: 977.

80　As Kagan notes for Spain (1981: 10).

81　Lavrin 1978: 40–41; Behar 1987a: 35; Liss 1975: 98–99.

82　As Seed (1988: 7) notes. It is perhaps not a coincidence that the Pragmatic Sanction, a late-eighteenth-century Crown directive, tried to enforce race/caste distinctions by legislating parental rights over the marriage choices of their children (Seed 1988; Martínez-Alier 1989; Stolcke 1991; chapter 7 below).

83　Kellogg 1992, 1995.

84　Cascardi 1992: 237; Franco 1989: xiv; Perry 1992: 7.

85　Lavrin 1989: 10.

86　Sánchez-Ortega 1992: 197; Perry 1992.

87　Seed 1988: 63; Perry 1990: 58–59; Martínez-Alier 1989: chap. 1.

88　Lavrin 1978: 26; Gonzalbo Aizpuru 1987: 117; Behar 1987a: 39.

89　Lavrin 1978: 40. Religious enclosure could also be liberating insofar as it freed women from the burdens of "womanhood," and some women "preferred to become nuns rather than wives" (Perry 1990: 89). Nuns learned to read and to write, and the intensity of their religious experiences also produced potentially subversive "visions" (Perry 1990: 82–84; Franco 1989).

90  Cited in Perry 1990: 47. In seventeenth-century Spain other kinds of enclosed spaces in the form of Magdalen or "halfway" houses were available for those wanting to leave prostitution, and jail, yet another form of enclosure, awaited "incorrigibles" who insisted on practicing outside the confines of a brothel (Perry 1990: 135).

91  Gonzalbo Aizpuru 1987: 114.

92  Gonzalbo Aizpuru 1987: chap. 6; Lavrin 1978: 30.

93  Hanke observes that in the New World all Spaniards became *caballeros* (gentlemen), and when native labor was in short supply, they complained to the king (1959: 14). Cope reminds us, however, that by the late sixteenth century a class of impoverished Spaniards who had to labor for a living had already come into existence (1994: 22–24).

94  BNAH, Archivo Histórico, Colección Francisco de Paso y Troncoso, Leg. 113, no. 418, 1554.

95  AGI, México, Correspondencia Virreinal, Leg. 25, no. 26-A, 1603. Indians, wrote the seventeenth-century Spanish jurist Juan de Solórzano y Pereyra, have to be "made to work, because they have always been notably lazy." Cited in de la Peña 1984: 188.

96  MacLachlan 1988: 48.

97  Boyer 1989: 252–53. Most later colonial Mexican violence against women, including homicides, came from primary male relatives, especially husbands (Stern 1995: 60–69).

98  Zavala (1988: 209) notes that in Mexico overseers would often go to considerable lengths to catch runaway Indian workers. Taussig's analysis of the political economy of extreme "terror" and Indian responses to it concerns a much later Latin American context (1987: chaps. 1–3).

99  AGN, Indios vol. 6 (1), exp. 262, 1591.

100  AGN, Inq vol. 619, exp. 1, 1672.

101  As discussed in chapter 5, men who were "tied" were unable to have intercourse with women at will. Typically, they were able to perform with only one woman, who would then be identified as the witch.

102  Lavrin 1978: 27.

103  Franco 1989: xiv.


3  *LA MALA YERBA*

1  AGI, México, Correspondencia Vierreinal, Leg. 27, no. 52, 1608. An Aragonese priest used the same nature metaphor to describe another class of infectious undesirables: sixteenth-century moriscos (Root 1988: 130–31).

2  Israel 1975; Cope 1994: 6, 20; Mörner 1967: 30–31; Bonfil Batalla 1987: 125. Pagden contends that blacks had "no place on the social map at all" (Pagden 1987: 69), while others reduce them to the Spanish or Indian

orbit, the world of the "colonizers or the colonized" (Bonfil Batalla 1987: 125; Cope 1994: 14–15).

3 Wade 1997.

4 Foucault 1980: 15–16.

5 Díaz del Castillo [1632] 1956: 293–94.

6 AGI, México Correspondencia Vierreinal, Leg. 20, no. 9, 1578; and Leg. 19, no. 125, 1574; AGN, Ord vol. 2, exp. 38, f. 36v, 1623; Cope 1994: 17; Israel 1975: 73; Palmer 1976: 42.

7 AGI, México Correspondencia Vierreinal, Leg. 20, no. 29, 1579.

8 AGI, México Correspondencia Vierreinal, Leg. 25, no. 26-A 1603.

9 Cited in Israel 1975: 74.

10 AGN, Mercedes vol. 2, exp. 728, 1544.

11 AGN, Mercedes vol. 5–6, exp. 288, 1560.

12 AGN, Indios vol. 6 (1), exp. 177, 1592.

13 AGN, BN vol. 732, exp. 2, 1605.

14 AGN, Criminal vol. 265, exp. 26, 1647.

15 Again Indians are referred to as "dogs." According to Taylor, *perro* (dog) and *borracho* (drunkard) were "stock Spanish insults." In the southern part of the country they appeared "only on the lips of non-Indians." But in central Mexico there is little distinction between Indian and non-Indian usage (1979: 82). The documents under consideration here suggest that the epithet "dog" was reserved mostly for Indians.

16 This was an incessant problem because under Spanish law livestock were permitted to graze on any land once one crop was harvested and before the next was planted. Nearly wild, and with ravenous appetites, cattle tended to wander onto Indian cornfields (*milpas*), which they destroyed before the corn could be harvested (Borah 1982: 275; Gibson 1964: 280–81; Baretta, Duncan, and Markhoff 1978).

17 *Principales* were members of the Indian nobility; *caciques* (fem. *cacica*) were also nobles, but more specifically local leaders.

18 Although Indians were to be taught Spanish, priests were also required to learn native languages. They were also forbidden from engaging in business (Gibson 1964: 115).

19 AGN, Indios vol. 21, exp. 2, 1656.

20 AGN, GP vol. 2, exp. 342, f. 71v, 1579.

21 AGN, Indios vol. 4, exp. 626, 1590.

22 AGN, Criminal vol. 235, exp. 28, 1618.

23 AGN, Criminal vol. 34, exp. 13, 1639.

24 AGN, Criminal vol. 57, exp. 5, 1650.

25 AGN, Indios vol. 23, exp. 350, 1659; also Kagen 1977: 211.

26 This punishment was sometimes inflicted on black slaves. Here it clearly signaled the mulatto's domination of the Indian.

27 AGN, Indios vol. 20, exp. 136, 1656.

28 I remark on paired Indian/black slave assaults on Indians at the end of chapter 4.

29 AGN, Criminal vol. 645, exp. 29, 1578. Chapter 5 contains a discussion of the term *puto* (fag) and the feminine *puta* (whore).

30 AGN, Criminal vol. 34, exp. 13, 1639.

31 AGN, Criminal vol. 235, exp. 33, 1655.

32 Charles V had forbidden trade and commerce between Indians and blacks as early as 1541 because such contact could be detrimental to Indians (Palmer 1976: 62). Subsequent ordinances prohibited Spaniards, mestizos, mulattoes, and blacks from selling goods that might have been extorted from Indians (for instance, AGN, RCD vol. 3, exp. 24, f. 12, 1587). The commercial practices of black women in Spanish America have not, to my knowledge, been closely examined. Karasch (1986) mentions them in the context of colonial Latin American society, especially Brazil, but Mintz and Price express surprise at the emergence of black women marketers in post-emancipation Jamaica and post-revolutionary Haiti (1992: 77–78). The Mexican evidence clearly suggests that such marketers were active early in the colonial period, at least in Spanish America.

33 AGN, Civil vol. 75, exp. 9, 1599.

34 There are thought to be about fifty series of these paintings, and they are an enigma to art historians and colonial Mexicanists alike. They seem to have been painted for Spaniards who wanted "exotic" and naturalistic scenes of life in the New World to place on their walls in the Old World (Sullivan 1990), but they do not seem to have followed any entrenched artistic tradition. For an excellent analysis of the paintings see Katzew 1996.

35 *Coyote* sometimes refers to a mestizo/Indian mix; other times its use seems to have been arbitrary (Moreno Navarro 1973: 142).

36 Although an issue of *Artes de México* (1990) devoted to the caste paintings conspicuously excludes the portraits mentioned here, the plates are reproduced in Isidoro Moreno Navarro (1973), Laminas III, XVII, XLVIII, and LI. See also the compilation in María Concepción García Saíz (1980), and Ilona Katzew's discussion (1996: 23–24) in a volume that also reproduces some of the plates. Katzew focuses on the relationships between the primary (parental) pairs without attending to the children who, in my view, offer important clues to the workings of lineage.

37 Davis 1966: 275, n. 24.

38 Martínez-Alier 1989: 17.

39 Martínez-Alier 1989: 117. It seems to me that this would mean that "hypodescent" could be overruled if the mother were white.

40 AGN, RCD vol. 15, exp. 178, 1645.

41 AGN, RCD vol. 16, exp. 249, f. 128, 1620.

42 AGN, RCD vol. 20, exp. 47, f. 36, 1654.

43 AGN, GP vol. 6, exp. 155, f. 158, 1602; vol. 6, exp. 643, f. 333, 1603. AGN, RCD vol. 5, exp. 511, f. 123, 1607; vol. 5, exp. 815, f. 200, 1607; vol. 16, exp. 267, f. 136, 1620; vol. 48, exp. 408, f. 296–296v, 1644; vol. 20, exp. 46, f. 35, 1654; vol. 20, exp. 127, f. 81, 1660; vol. 67, f. 7, 1688.

44 AGN, Indios vol. 2, exp. 998, 1583; and vol. 2, exp. 994, 1583.

45 AGI, México, Correspondencia Vierreinal, Leg. 20, no. 29, 1579.

46 Chance and Taylor 1979: 438; also R. Anderson 1988; Seed and Rust 1983; Hoberman 1986; Cope 1994.

47 Carroll 1991a: chap. 7; McCaa et al. 1979.

48 AGN, Mercedes vol. 2, exp. 241, 1543; vol. 2, exp. 674, 1544; Baretta, Duncan, and Markhoff 1978: 595.

49 AGI, México, Correspondencia Vierreinal, Leg. 19, no. 142-A, 1573.

50 AGN, RCD vol. 3, exp. 7, f. 5, 1587.

51 AGN, GP vol. 11, exp. 367, f. 333, 1663; AGN, RCD vol. 3, exp. 7, f. 4, 1587.

52 Cope 1994: 21; also Borah 1983: 255.

53 AGN, Ord vol. 4, exp. 51, f. 51v, 1622.

54 AGN, Criminal vol. 46, exp. 11, 1648.

55 Baretta, Duncan, and Markoff 1978: 592.

56 Taussig 1987: 37–50, 122–23.

57 AGN, Indios vol. 12, exp. 55, 1632.

58 AGN, Indios vol. 11, exp. 456, 1640.

59 AGN, Indios vol. 10 (2), exp. 190, 1632.

60 AGN, Criminal vol. 105, exp. 18, 1644.

61 Haskett 1991b: 47–48, 138–41; Lockhart 1992: 384; C. Martin 1985; Ouweneel 1995.

62 AGN, Criminal vol. 230, exp. 14, 1643. By the last decades of the colonial period Indian leaders in Morelos were often allying themselves with hacendados and other Spaniards for a variety of reasons, some of them personal and self-serving (C. Martin 1985: 156; Haskett 1991a). These leaders in effect also served as intermediaries between Indian villages and non-Indian neighbors.

63 Lockhart 1992: 384–85.

64 AGN, BN vol. 875, exp. 10, 1692.

65 AGN, Criminal vol. 580, exp. 4, 1644. As Kellogg notes, *macegual* could be derogatory (1995: 71).

66 Haskett (1991b) and Lockhart (1992: 384–85) note the same tendency in indigenous language texts. Again this suggests that Spanish-language texts can be just as nuanced as indigenous-language ones in depicting Indian perspectives.

67 Israel 1975: 64; Cope 1994: 18–20.

68 AGN, Mercedes vol. 2, exp. 241, 1543; vol. 2, exp. 674, 1544.

69 Baretta, Duncan, and Markhoff 1978: 595. Formal marriages between Spaniards and Indians were probably less frequent than has been supposed, even when Spanish women were in short supply in the first decades after the conquest (Israel 1975: 61).

70 Israel 1975: 66; Dusenberry 1948; Cope 1994: 19.

71 AGN, RCD vol. 5, exp. 355, f. 89, 1606; vol. 5, exp. 416, f. 101, 1606.

72 AGN, Criminal vol. 643, exp. 4, 1643. There is some debate in the course of the testimony regarding whether the defendant is actually Spanish, and therefore not even included in the arms-bearing bans.

73 AGN, RCD vol. 15, exp. 211, 1648.

74 AGN, RCD vol. 20, exp. 118, f. 74, 1659.

75  AGN, RCD vol. 25, exp. 564, f. 299, 1663.

76  Because I do not know whether the arms petitions represent a complete sample, it is difficult to say for certain whether the numbers of mestizo petitions drop off. But because the number of mulatto ones remained fairly constant, it is probably a safe guess.

77  Cited in Israel 1975: 65.

78  AGN, Inq vol. 491, exp. 16, 1616.

79  Cited in Lockhart 1992: 384–85.

80  AGN, Civil vol. 270, exp. 1, 1680–81.

81  AGN, Criminal vol. 139, exps. 19 and 22, 1647.

82  New Spain's encomienda, parish, and municipality divisions were organized around pre-existing indigenous sociopolitical divisions known as *altepetl*, which were headed by dynastic rulers (*tlatoani*) and contained the main temple and central market. Spaniards understood altepetl units, which Lockhart calls "ethnic states," as "peoples" or "villages" (*pueblos*) but they were basically confederations of strongly endogamous subunits (*calpolli* or *tlaxilacalli*), each with a ruler, a god and a portion of altepetl land. These subunits contributed to the altepetl tribute, military units in times of war and labor, sometimes on a rotational basis. This necessarily abbreviated discussion of indigenous sociopolitical units and social divisions is taken from Lockhart 1992: 14–15, 84–85, 206.

83  Gibson 1964: 154–55; Lockhart 1992: 111–12.

84  AGN, Mercedes vol. 4, exp. 136, 1555.

85  Israel 1975: 63.

86  Gibson 1964: 168–69, 196–97, 217–18. Gobernadores were still being jailed as late as 1809 (ibid.: 219).

87  AGN, Indios vol. 10(2), exp. 109, 1631.

88  AGN, Indios vol. 13, exp. 71, 1640.

89  AGN, RCD vol. 15, exp. 171, 1644.

90  AGN, Criminal vol. 57, exp. 5, 1650.

91  AGN, Indios vol. 20, exp. 277, 1656.

92  AGN, Criminal vol. 218, exp. 8, 1674.

93  AGN, Criminal vol. 41, exps. 38 and 48, 1640; AGN, RCD vol. 15, exp. 179, f. 141, 1645.

94  Mulattoes seem to have been preferred as jail wardens. One was the *alcaide* (warden) of a Cuernavaca prison, and allegedly used his post to extort money, goods, and labor from Indians. "With the backing from [his post] he aggravates the natives, making them give him an Indian to serve him food and [he takes] hens and mules that he needs and Indians. If they are late in doing what he orders, he catches them and mistreats them and the Indians caught [and put in jail], even if it is for very trifling reasons, and although they are prisoners in jail . . . he does not want to let them go until they have given him four *reales*" (AGN, Indios vol. 17, exp. 76, 1654; also AGN, Criminal vol. 590, exp. 3, 1692; AGN, RCD vol. 49, exp. 8, fs. 12v–13v, 1643).

95  AGN, GP vol. 12, exp. 7, f. 5, 1664.

96  Taussig 1987: 109.

97 AGN, Indios vol. 11, exp. 485, 1640.
98 AGN, Inq vol. 517, exp. 13, 1674.
99 AGN, Civil vol. 428, exp. 5, 1544.
100 AGN, Criminal vol. 12, exp. 6, 1646.
101 AGN, Criminal vol. 109, exp. 20, 1683.

## 4 FROM ANIMOSITIES TO ALLIANCES

1 Bonfíl Battala 1987: 125.
2 Palmer 1976: 55; Davidson 1979: 243; Israel 1975: 70; Gibson 1954–55: 600; P. Carrasco 1961.
3 In both cases a king and a queen were elected. That rebellious blacks seem to have frequently named "kings" and "queens" — and sometimes whole royal courts — to lead them indicates internal hierarchies in the slave system based sometimes on indigenous African rankings and sometimes on slaves' affiliations to prominent Spanish masters (Palmer 1976: 136). One might imagine that the former type of recognition would give way to the latter as African-born slaves and their de-scendents were assimilated to the colonial social hierarchy.
4 Palmer 1976: 139.
5 Palmer 1976: 133–39.
6 AGI, México, Correspondencia Vierreinal, Leg. 45, no. 57-A, 1671.
7 Cope 1994: 18.
8 Cope makes a similar argument for urban riots, interpreting them as responses to the failure of patrons to uphold their duties to plebeians rather than as wholesale attempts to overthrow the system (1994: 42, 48).
9 Taylor 1979: 113, 119–20, 134–35. The paucity of Indian revolts in rural areas has been attributed to the fact that both church and state consciously tried to protect the rights of Indian communities (Katz 1988b: 79), and to the extreme decimation of the population through disease, which diminished not only the "will to resist" but also the need to do so as conflicts over land, for example, were lessened (Katz 1988a: 6). Indeed, as the Indian population increased in the eighteenth century so did the number of rural revolts (Katz 1988b: 93).
10 AGI, México, Correspondencia Vierreinal, Leg. 41, no. 44, 1666 and no. 44a, 1665; AGN, RCO vol. 8, exp. 69, f. 4, 1665; and vol. 10, exp. 74, f. 251, 1668.
11 Farriss 1984: 14, 70. She considers only one Yucatecan uprising, the eighteenth-century Canek rebellion, to be "genuine" as it took place long after the colonial regime was in place and so cannot be considered part of the process of conquest (1984: 68).
12 Davidson 1979; Cope 1994: 17.
13 AGN, Mercedes vol. 5, exp. 201, 1561.
14 AGN, Criminal vol. 643, exp. 2, 1619; vol. 132, exp. 2, 1647.
15 Together these elements managed to bring down the Marqués de

Gelves, the thirteenth viceroy of New Spain, in less than a day. This outcome was ironic, for Gelves, although unpopular, was "genuinely anxious to relieve the sufferings of the poor" and not "afraid to alienate powerful elements of the bureaucracy and the Creole haute bourgeousie" (Israel 1975: 138, 140). But he was an enemy of the archbishop of Mexico and had been feuding with him over the use of churches as sanctuaries for criminals. The archbishop summarily declared Gelves excommunicated, and Gelves in turn had the archbishop expelled from Mexico City. This act precipitated his downfall, for the archibishop was beloved by the urban "riff-raff." (See Israel 1975: chap. 5 and Guthrie 1945 for a full discussion of the riot.)

16  Gibson 1964: 384; Cope 1994: chap. 7, 157, table 7.2; Israel 1975: 58–59.

17  The decrees, which are too numerous to list here, are almost all found in AGN, Ord, Mercedes, and RCD; also Mörner 1970b.

18  Mörner and Gibson 1962, who discuss only this aspect of the decree. AGN, RCO vol. 6, exp. 292, f. 597, 1578, emphasis added; also AGN, GP vol. 7, exp. 122, f. 84, 1632.

19  AGN, Inq vol. 510, exp. 30, 1625.

20  AGN, Criminal vol. 187, f. 276–87, 1645.

21  AGN, Inq vol. 303, exp. 38, 1624.

22  AGI, México, Correspondencia Virreinal, Leg. 19, no. 82, 1572.

23  AGN, Criminal vol. 4, exp. 5, 1591.

24  Behar 1989: 197.


5  AUTHORITY REVERSED

1  AGN, Inq vol. 486, exp. 85, 1621.

2  Again, *dog* was a common epithet directed at Indians. Its significance is unclear to me. It was probably connected to the perceived lowliness of dogs, still reviled in rural parts of Mexico, and perhaps to the ways in which they slink in and out of human spaces.

3  This and other cases suggest that the authorities sometimes went to great lengths to determine a person's genealogy. Cope cites an incident in which a person was judged to be Indian by the inquisitors not on the basis of lineage but rather on the basis of phenotype (1994: 54). He does not provide a date for the case, which might have helped to determine whether the official criteria for classifying persons were changing as caste distinctions further blurred (as discussed in McAlister 1963: 368–69).

4  AGN, Inq vol. 520, exp. 4, 1678.

5  The word was probably *semomatzin* which would translate as "one of your (honorific) hands" (Jonathan Amith, personal communication) Ruíz de Alarcón describes indigenous "sorcery of the hands" as a form of divination used in conjunction with "spells" ([1629] 1982: 202).

6  AGN, Inq vol. 520, exp. 79, 1684; emphasis added.

7  Comaroff and Comaroff 1993, 1999; Thomas 1971; Schneider 1989.

8  AGN, Inq vol. 342, exp. 3, 1622.

9 Like peyote, *ololiuqui* (morning glory seeds) provoked visions and was identified with indigenous gods. It was utilized mostly in erotic magic (Quezada 1984: 92–93). *Puyomate* was an indigenous root thought to have properties of sexual attraction and also to be effective in the colonial practice of tying an individual and therefore subverting his will (Quezada 1984: 95–96).

10  AGN, Inq vol. 316, exp. 17, 1616.

11  A quescomate or, more accurately, a *cuezcomatl*, was a type of indigenous grain bin.

12  Comaroff and Comaroff 1993: xxvii; also Thomas 1971; Silverblatt 1987; Behar 1987a, 1987b, 1989; Karlsen 1987.

13  Sánchez-Ortega 1992.

14  Motolinía [1541] 1914.

15  Taussig 1987: 142–43.

16  AGN, Inq vol. 1, exp. 6, 1540. *Copal* was a resin thought to have protective properties and used as incense by Indians. Gruzinski notes that postconquest "idolatry" was first and foremost preserved in the domestic sphere which, for a variety of reasons, was more closed to Christianity than the public one (1993: 152–53). Yet households were also an important focal point for saint worship, which was often accompanied by the paraphenalia of preconquest ritual (Lockhart 1992: 237, 258–59).

17  Archivo General de la Nación 1912.

18  See Gruzinski (1989, 1993) for analyses of Indian "idolatry" from indigenous perspectives grounded in the political and social realities of conquest and acculturation during the sixteenth and seventeenth centuries, and Lockhart (1992: chap. 6) for the religious mixture of things Christian and things Indian in the postconquest era.

19  Gruzinski 1993.

20  Cervantes 1991: 27, n. 107.

21  Ruíz de Alarcón [1629] 1982: 77.

22  Cervantes 1994: 91–93; also Taussig 1987.

23  Cervantes 1994: 92–94.

24  AGN, Inq vol. 317, exp. 2, 1618.

25  AGN, Inq vol. 283, exp. 16, 1608.

26  AGN, Inq vol. 527, exp. 9, 1691.

27  Gruzinski traces the ironic twists that had occurred by the middle of the seventeenth century as Indian "shamans" began seeing Christian "visions," and non-Indian consumers of peyote began seeing "*what the Indians saw*" (1993: 217). While Antonio de la Cruz claimed to have acquired his knowledge "from God," chapter 6 includes the testimony of an Indian who claimed to have received his knowledge from "the devil." As noted there, it seems that Indian claims to have links to both the devil and to God reflected Spaniards' own confusions about what spirit forces they should identify with Indians.

28  AGN, Inq vol. 328, fs. 360–62, 1620.

29  Aguirre Beltrán 1963: 140–62.

30  Ruíz de Alarcón [1629] 1982: 70; Lockhart 1992: 258.

31  AGN, Inq vol. 206, exp. 4, 1593.
32  Behar 1987a, 1989; Alberro 1987; Quezada 1984.
33  AGN, Inq vol. 209, exp. 1B, 1597.
34  AGN, Inq vol. 206, exp. 3, 1592.
35  Rather exceptional in this regard are cases involving a Spanish woman who fed menstrual blood to her own sister (AGN, Inq vol. 457, exp. 24, 1655), two men who rubbed their "shameful parts" with animal brains and fat, using the resulting concoction to attract women (AGN, Inq vol. 301, exp. 22, 1614), and a Spanish widow "tied" by a free mulatto woman, who caused the Spaniard to suffer from a *"flux de sangre"* (perhaps a sudden blood flow) during which her "lower parts" became obstructed. Although the Spanish woman subsequently recovered and her "parts" returned to their ordinary form, she complained that she had no desire for intercourse with her lover (AGN, Inq vol. 520, exp. 233, 1694).
36  Behar 1989: 180.
37  Just as a variety of practices were classified under the category hechicería, a single act could combine natural and supernatural elements (R. Martin 1989: 196). Taking menstrual blood as an example, we see that a medium of transmission normally thought to be innocuous could actually kill someone if it was used, as one Spanish doctor testified, "against nature as poison to kill . . . or . . . superstitiously with an implicit or explicit pact with the devil" (AGN, Inq vol. 442, exp. 33, 1652), that is, if it was adulterated in either a material (poison) or in an immaterial (superstition, pact with the devil) way. One woman seems to have confused the menstrual blood issue by attaching leeches to her "lower parts." When the leeches filled with blood, she would squeeze the blood out and use it to attract men (AGN, Inq vol. 435[1], f. 217B, 1650).
38  AGN, Inq vol. 619, exp. 1, 1672.
39  Alberro 1987: 89.
40  Castañega [1529] 1946: 39. Cervantes (1991) argues that the work of such theologians as Castañega marks a reorientation of beliefs about witchcraft. In earlier works, such as the *Malleus Maleficarum*, the focus was on *maleficium*. Later works, such as Castañega's, emphasized devil-worship and idolatry. Their dissemination coincided with an increasingly prominent belief in Indian diabolism (which in some respects was clearly evident from the very beginning of colonization).
41  Silverblatt 1987: 166.
42  Kramer and Sprenger [1484] 1971: 47. The "'science' of demonology" (Silverblatt 1987: 161) was most notoriously codified in the *Malleus Maleficarum*, thirty editions of which had been published by 1669. Julio Caro Baroja situates this work at the center of intellectual thought about witchcraft during this period (1964: 94–98), for it connected maleficia (popular sorcery or "black magic") with demonology, and it relentlessly identified the "diabolical sorcerers" who practiced witchcraft as women (Monter 1976: 24–25).
43  Kramer and Sprenger [1484] 1971: 47.
44  Kramer and Sprenger [1484] 1971: 47.

45  Burkhart 1989: 158.

46  Motolinía [1541] 1914: 125.

47  Motolinía [1541] 1914: 135.

48  Ortega Noriega 1986: 38–39.

49  Pagden 1982: 86.

50  BNAH Archivo Histórico, Colección Francisco de Paso y Troncoso, Leg. 113, 418, 1554.

51  Gruzinski 1986: 260–61.

52  I thank both Nicholas Ruddall and Rachel Sternberg (personal communication) for assistance with the Latin translation.

53  Boswell 1980: 93, n. 2; also Greenberg 1990: 276.

54  Greenberg 1990: 168; Boswell 1980: 174, 288–89; Perry 1990: 123–24; Greenleaf 1962: 108.

55  Gruzinski 1986: 272; also AGI, México, Correspondencia Virreinal, Leg. 38, no. 57-B, 1658.

56  Gruzinski 1986: 272–73. Such men were not termed "homosexuals" until the nineteenth century (Gruzinski 1986: 256). For lack of a better word, I use it here, keeping in mind that it fails to address the social relationships embedded in culturally specific sexual systems (Lancaster 1993: 270; also Gruzinski 1986: 274).

57  These cases include two Indian messengers for the Holy Office called putos, among other things, by several men described as mestizo and mulatto who had robbed them (AGN, Inq vol. 316, exp. 40, 1617), and an Indian called a puto by a Spaniard who assaulted him (AGN, Criminal vol. 645, exp. 29, 1578). In another case, an Indian woman from Mexico City was called a puta by a Spaniard who came to her house looking for "black thieves and runaways" (AGN, Criminal vol. 132, exp. 2, 1647). In another, an Indian woman also from Mexico City was called a puta by an unidentified man who grabbed her by the hair and punched her (AGN, BN vol. 753, exp. 25, 1604). Taylor identifies a variety of insults, including *joto* (homosexual) and *cornudo* (cuckold) as part of the stock of sexual epithets employed as "fighting words" by Indian peasants in the late colonial period (1979: 81). Although puta is among the terms he references, puto is not.

58  Covarrubias [1611] 1984: 889. I again thank both Nicholas Ruddall and Rachel Sternberg (personal communication) for assistance with the Latin translation.

59  Lancaster writes about the gendering of sex roles in contemporary Nicaragua and elsewhere in Latin America with respect to male-male sexual relations. "Whoever is acted upon, dominated, or entered," he writes, "is feminine" (1993: 242; also Paz 1961: 39–40). According to Laqueur, for the ancient Greeks "it was the weak, womanly male partner who was deeply flawed, medically and morally. His very countenance proclaimed his nature: *pathicus,* the one being penetrated; *cinaedus,* the one who engages in unnatural lust; *mollis,* the passive, effeminate one" (1990: 53); Boswell writes that Aristotle considered passivity the least "normal" aspect of male homosexual behavior (1980: 50).

60  AGN, Inq vol. 498, exp. 16, 1691.

61  Cascardi 1992.

62  Kramer and Sprenger [1484] 1971: 43.

63  AGN, Inq vol. 209, exp. 7, 1597.

64  AGN, Inq vol. 209, exp. 1B, 1597.

65  AGN, Inq vol. 457, exp. 16, 1655.

66  AGN, Inq vol. 346, exp. 12, 1623; emphasis added.

67  Gruzinski 1993: 38–39; Lockhart 1992: 418–19.

68  Phelan 1970: 67–68.

69  Kramer and Sprenger [1484] 1971: 42.

70  Cited in Lavrin 1978: 26.

71  Phelan 1970: 59–60.

72  Motolinía [1541] 1914: 28.

73  Cited in Clendinnen 1982: 46; Gruzinski 1993: 178.

74  Motolinía [1541] 1914: 28–29.

75  A description of the first witches' Sabbat appeared between 1330 and 1340 in the Inquisition trials of Toulouse. "From the beginning," Caro Baroja writes, "the 'Sabbath' always took the same form," and it was attended on Friday nights which, of course, was also the Jewish Sabbath (1964: 84).

76  Sepúlveda [1545] 1941: 123–25.

77  AGN, Inq vol. 317, exp. 19, 1618/19.

78  AGN, Inq vol. 206, exp. 4, 1593.

79  Alberro 1981a: 86.

80  Alberro 1987: 91.

81  Behar 1989: 200.

82  Alberro (1981a) has compiled a useful statistical profile of Inquisition cases. Her analysis of witchcraft and related offenses is in pages 73–86.

83  This intriguing reference was probably to the *pochteca*, a Nahuatl term for professional merchants. See p. 122.

84  AGN, Inq vol. 609, exp. 11, 1668.

85  AGN, Inq vol. 317, exp. 23, 1617.

86  *Tizitl* means "healer" in Nahuatl. It again surfaces as an Indian woman's name in another Zacatecan case discussed at the end of the following chapter. Ruíz de Alarcón states that "the name should be taken as suspicious" since sorcerers and diviners are almost always "the same thing as curers" ([1629] 1982: 202).

87  AGN, Inq vol. 600, exp. 22, 1655.

88  Blacks and mulattoes were frequently cured by Indians because presumably Spanish witchcraft was not powerful enough to accomplish the task. It seems that black and mulatto witchcraft could also be undone by Indians (See chapter 6).

89  AGN, Inq vol. 631, exp. 10, 1686.

90  AGN, Inq vol. 685, exp. 6, 1692.

91  AGN, Inq vol. 317, exp. 19, 1618/19.

92  The roles of mulatto and black intermediaries in witchcraft are treated at length in the following chapter.

93 AGN, Inq vol. 339, exp. 84/89, 1621.

94 AGN, Inq vol. 342, exp. 15, 1622.

95 AGN, Inq vol. 335, exp. 96, 1622.

96 AGN, Inq vol. 435 (1), f. 145, 1650. Women whose husbands were away at sea often asked this question of clairvoyants.

97 AGN, Inq vol. 435(1), f. 256, 1650.

98 Lockhart 1992: 191–97.

99 Gruzinski 1993: 177, 220; also Silverblatt 1987.

100 AGN, Inq vol. 348, exp. 4, 1624.

101 That Miguel Lázaro managed to become governor, and that Spanish officials refused to punish him for his witchery, suggests that there was an unstated political context to the case.

102 This necessity is sometimes spoken of directly in these cases, but because witches were often uncooperative or, especially in the case of mulattoes, unable to cure what they had wrought, other *curanderos* might be called in. When the Indian Domingo de la Cruz was accused by two mulattoes of bewitching an Indian comadre of one, he denied the charges. The mulattoes tried to force him to cure the woman, but to no avail. In the end, another Indian curandero was brought in.

103 The use of water as a mirror, as opposed to floating objects for divinatory purposes, is akin to the use of "crystal balls" and the like, and therefore a practice that is Spanish in origin (Quezada 1984: 84).

104 AGN, Inq vol. 442, exp. 34, 1652.

105 This is one of the few reports of a classic Sabbat that I have found. AGN, Inq vol. 218, exp. 4, 1598.

106 Taussig 1987: 171.

107 AGN, Inq 435(1), f. 71, 1650; also AGN, BN vol. 596, exp. 29, 1699.

## 6 MAPPING UNSANCTIONED POWER

1 AGN, Inq vol. 317, exp. 22, 1618.

2 AGN, Inq vol. 339, exp. 84/89, 1621.

3 AGN, Inq vol. 486, exp. 70, 1621.

4 AGN, Inq vol. 486, exp. 76, 1621.

5 AGN, Inq vol. 510, exp. 112, 1624.

6 AGN, Inq vol. 303, exp. 19, 1624.

7 AGN, Inq vol. 356, exp. 25, f. 47, 1626.

8 Again there are evident links between black women and commerce. It is most interesting to note that "hagglers" said to swindle Indians might have honed their expertise with magical remedies purchased from the selfsame Indians.

9 AGN, Inq vol. 376, exp. 17, 1632.

10 AGN, Inq vol. 435(1), f. 71, 1650.

11 AGN, Inq vol. 435(1), f. 24, 1650.

12 AGN, Inq vol. 435, f. 148, 1650.

13 AGN, Inq vol. 516, exp. 556, 1673. This text refers to a brujo rather than to a hechicero. See note 152 in chapter 1.

14 AGN, Inq vol. 600, exp. 21, 1665.

15 AGN, Inq vol. 674, exp. 19, 1689.

16 AGN, Inq vol. 39, exp. 4, 1570.

17 AGN, Inq vol. 292, exp. 28, 1611; AGN, Inq vol. 435(2), f. 432, 1650. Even today, Mexicans of African descent consider Indians to be the most knowledgeable and powerful witches and healers (Lewis 2000).

18 Alberro 1981a: 104.

19 AGN, GP vol. 4, exp. 502, f. 5, 1591.

20 AGN, Criminal vol. 630, exp. 2, 1698.

21 AGN, Criminal vol. 260, exp. 22, 1619.

22 AGN, Criminal vol. 580, exp. 4, 1644.

23 AGN, Inq vol. 328, fs. 360–362, 1620.

24 This is reminiscent of the case of Francisco Ruíz de Castrejon, a mulatto in possession of a "devil's book" allegedly given to him by a Tarascan Indian.

25 AGN, Inq vol. 523, exp. 3, 1686.

26 AGN, Inq vol. 520, exp. 160, 1689.

27 AGN, Inq vol. 562, exp. 6, 1692.

28 AGN, Inq vol. 317, exp. 2, 1618.

29 AGN, Inq vol. 388, exp. 12, 1639.

30 AGN, Inq vol. 147, exp. 6, 1595.

31 Juan Luis was identified as mestizo but he was actually the son of a Spaniard and a mestizo woman and thus technically a castizo, one step up from a mestizo. His "brothers" were probably his half-brothers. He did not know their names, and if they all belonged to religious orders, as he said they did, they most likely had a Spanish mother, though this was never made explicit. Juan Luis himself was married to an Indian woman at the time of his trial and had one living daughter, an infant. The marriage must have reinforced the perception that Juan Luis had abandoned Christianity, for even before he found himself facing the inquisitors he had taken a step backward: although he was nearly Spanish, he had married an Indian woman and produced offspring who were correspondingly further removed from Spanishness. Several of the more euphemistic eighteenth- and nineteenth-century terms for complicated caste mixtures, such as *throwback* (*salta atrás* or *torno atrás*), signify a turn away from whiteness and a "regression" toward "darkness" (Aguirre Beltrán 1972: 177).

32 The indigenous man-owl (*hombre-buho* or *tlacatecótotl*) was a particularly malevolent character (López-Austin 1966: 97–98).

33 The Otomí were a cultural and linguistic minority in preconquest central Mexico, where they were subjected to Mexica political control and held the lowest status among the cultural groups occupying the Valley of Mexico. Cortés described them as "mountain people" and Mexica slaves. The three grades of pulque recognized in the colonial era were known as fine, ordinary, and Otomí (Gibson 1964: 10, 21; Lockhart 1992: 27).

34 The name of the devil, Mantelillos, has no obvious significance to me other than the association made between a cape or shawl (*manta*) and this particular devil. Perhaps it was a diminutive form of *mantel* or "altar cloth," in which case it would have had interesting religious connotations.

35 Again we see parallels with European spinning tales.

36 The notion that "God did not want it" suggests that once the Holy Office had caught a blasphemer the devil had lost his battle with God.

37 Mantelillos resurfaces several years later again making reference to worn-out shoes in the testimony of the mulatto Pedro Hernández. It is not clear from that text whether Mantelillos was the devil, but Hernández told the inquisitors a "Mantelillos" had said that a "familiar" had helped him get out of jail. When Hernández asked this Mantelillos for help in getting him out of an Inquisition prison, however, Mantelillos responded that he did not have the power. He then showed him a lot of shoes, which he said he had worn out in Hernández's service (AGN, Inq vol. 276, exp. 2, 1605). A demon is also named Mantelillos in an Inquisition case from 1620 in New Granada, Colombia (Ceballos Gómez 2000).

38 Cervantes 1994: 93.

39 AGN, Inq vol. 527, exp. 9, 1691; for other examples see Gruzinski 1993: 217, chap. 6.

40 AGN, Inq vol. 209, exp. 9, 1597. Cervantes identifies him as a Spaniard (1994: 49) but the text clearly states that he was mulatto, and there seem to be three books mentioned at the beginning of the case but only two are described in the course of it.

41 The orthography is unreadable but the mulatto's translation of this phrase for the inquisitors indicates that the language was something other than Spanish.

42 Tarascans were the dominant linguistic/ethnic group in the Pátzcuaro area.

43 Taussig 1987: 259, 264.

44 We can note that reversals of what is understood to be the hierarchy of authority — here a mulatto passes unsanctioned knowledge to an Indian — terminate without the action being realized. Other unrealized reversals are noted below. They can perhaps be likened to reversals in the sanctioned domain when Indians, for instance, are put in charge of blacks and mulattoes whom they then cannot control.

45 Covarrubias identified "familiars" as "demons that had dealings with a person." Their origins were in the house spirits (*duendes*) that in ancient times accompanied people in their daily lives ([1611] 1984: 584, 752; also Thomas 1971: 606–7). It is ironic that the word also refers to the Inquisition police.

46 AGN, Inq vol. 454, exp. 14, 1650. Solange Alberro also tells Juan de Morga's story, but she transcribes and emphasizes quite different aspects than I do here without mentioning the Indian/devil link (1981: 165–76)

47 Alberro cites several other cases of suicide or attempted suicide by black slaves (1979: 140).

48 This reveals another contradiction of the slave system, for the church was often in conflict with slaveholders over their unwillingness to attend to their slaves' religious training.

49 Although this turned out to have been a lie, it nevertheless reinforces the idea that a relationship with the devil that is not mediated by an Indian will ultimately fail.

50 Ginzburg 1982: 58.

51 Cervantes 1991: 27.

52 Devisse and Mollat 1979, 2: 58, 64–65.

53 A good example would be the case of Juana Isabel discussed in chapter 3. I have encountered only one reference to color with respect to Spaniards. This was in the testimony of a slave woman, who refers to a group of jailed Spaniards as "the whites" (*las blancas*) (AGN, Inq vol. 491, exp. 16, 1616).

54 AGN, Inq vol. 275, exp. 14, 1605.

55 AGN, Inq vol. 515, exp. 17, 1670.

56 AGN, Historia vol. 19, exp. 14, 1598.

57 AGN, Inq vol. 296, exp. 3, 1612.

58 Devisse and Mollat 1979, 2: 73.

59 Nor is it clear how negative perceptions emerged in Islamic tradition (Drake 1990, 2: 200).

60 Drake 1990, 2: 192–93. To my knowledge, Drake's treatment of the symbolism of blackness is the most extensive to date (1990, 2). See also Rout 1977: chap. 1. For treatments of color symbolism in Islamic culture, the imagery of which suggested later Christian imagery, see Davis 1984: chap. 4; Drake 1990, 2: chap. 6). Drake and Rout also discuss Portuguese attitudes toward blackness and blacks.

61 Fairchild 1934.

62 AGN, Inq vol. 303, exp. 15, 1624; vol. 525, exp. 48, 1691.

63 AGN, Inq vol. 341, exp. 4, 1622; vol. 439, exp. 14, 1656.

64 AGN, Inq vol. 439, exp. 14, 1656.

65 AGN, Inq vol. 530, exp. 23, 1695.

66 AGN, Inq vol. 515, exp. 17, 1670.

67 AGN, Inq vol. 218, exp. 4, 1598.

68 Palmer 1976: 34–35.

69 AGN, Inq vol. 302, exp. 9, 1614.

70 AGN, Inq vol. 559, exp. 1, 1652.

71 Unfortunately, the text contains little information on Olola's background. Aguirre Beltrán, who also discusses this incident (1963: 65–72), speculates that given his name he was probably a Biafran from Portuguese Guinea (1963: 67). However, I am also told that Olola is a Yoruba name meaning the owner of wealth or a person of high estate (Andrew Apter, personal communication).

72 Aguirre Beltrán 1994: 112–13. Both Aguirre Beltrán (1963) and Palmer

(1976: 52–53, chap. 6) speculate about African cultural survivals, particularly in cimarrón communities.

73 Alan Sandstrom notes that in the present-day Huasteca, Nahuatl-speaking Indians perform elaborate religious "flower" rituals wearing ornate headresses and shaking gourd rattles (1991: 279–80).

74 AGN, Inq vol. 303, exp. 38, 1624.

75 Again one might speculate about the African origins of the possession ritual and of the "seven gods" which, I am told, later emerged as part of a syncretic paradigm in Afrolatino religious practices linking seven African powers (*orisha*) with seven Catholic saints (Andrew Apter, personal communication).

76 Quezada details the use of both copal and cotton in a water divination associated with erotic magic carried out by an Indian woman for a Spaniard in the same year (1984: 84–85).

77 AGN, Inq vol. 301, exp. 51, 1614.

78 AGN, Inq vol. 372, exp. 14, 1631.

79 A nagual was technically an indigenous category of human with supernatural powers who could transform him or herself into an animal in order to cause harm to another. In prehispanic times it was a characteristic possessed by a priestly class known as *nahualli,* but during the colonial period it came to be associated with non-priestly individual Indians and also with the Spanish idea of a "witch" (Dehouve 1994: 147–48; Aguirre Beltrán 1963: chap. 5). I believe that the Spanish term brujería, which some have likened to Evans-Pritchard's "witch" category, was most often employed with reference to supernatural acts that combined flying and nagualismo.

80 AGN, Inq vol. 297, exp. 5, 1612.

81 AGN, Inq vol. 439, exp. 14, 1656.

82 Aguirre Beltrán 1963: 101; also AGN, Mercedes vol. 3, exp. 67, 1550.

83 See Palmer 1976: 164.

84 AGN, Inq vol. 458, exp. 34, 1658.

85 AGN, Inq vol. 339, exps. 33/34, 1621.

86 Although I do not know what the bulls might have signified, the reference to Indian women presumably invokes supernatural potency.

87 *Cuexpaltzi* was another name for ololiuqui (Aguirre Beltrán 1963: 130–37).

88 As in the Juana de Chaide case discussed above, the question of who grinds the herbs and powders seems to have had supernatural importance.

89 AGN, Inq vol. 339, exps. 84/89, 1621.

90 AGN, Inq vol. 486, exp. 76, 1621.

91 AGN, Inq vol. 376, exp. 22, 1636.

92 AGN, Inq vol. 520, exp. 18, 1679.

93 AGN, Inq vol. 435(1), f. 86, 1650. Whether or not the man was actually Portuguese is unclear, but just as Indians denounced unpopular villagers as "mestizo" or "mulatto," black and mulatto slaves, as mentioned above, sometimes conflated the allegedly "Portuguese" identities of their mas-

ters and mistresses with their allegedly "Jewish" ones as a way of enhancing charges of heresy.

94 AGN, Inq vol. 38, exp. 6, 1537.

95 For example, AGN, Inq vol. 296, exp. 3, 1612; vol. 316, exp. 26, 1617; vol. 510, exp. 128, 1625; vol. 435(1), fs. 78, 254, 1650; vol. 435(2), f. 410, 1650; vol. 458, exp. 34, 1658; vol. 520, exp. 101, 1685.

96 AGN, Inq vol. 510, exp. 28, 1625.

97 AGN, Inq vol. 317, exp. 18, 1618.

98 AGN, Inq vol. 522, fs. 505–507, 1684.

99 It may well be that she was a slave hired out by her master for a daily wage (*jornal*), or that she lived in another house as a servant and worked for others in her spare time.

100 AGN, Inq vol. 520, exp. 2, 1678.

101 AGN, Inq vol. 283, exp. 34, 1608. Again we see Spanish authorities attempting to thwart inter-caste alliances. The reference to the mulatto woman turning into a dog evokes Indian practices. If we recall, at the beginning of chapter 5 we met the young "Indian" woman Juana Isabel, who was able to turn into a dog and walk through walls, and the Indian Mariana, who turned into a dog and attacked a Spanish woman.

102 This relation was not only about men's power over women—as is blatantly obvious, for instance, in the case of a master entering into a sexual relation with his slave, who not only had an "ambiguous status as a human being," but was also his property (Alberro 1991: 162)—it was also often used as a means of advancement for women of color (Alberro 1991: 164; also Martínez-Alier 1989).

103 AGN, Inq vol. 520, exp. 60, 1682.

104 AGN, Inq vol. 356, f. 46, 1626.

105 AGN, Inq vol. 376, exp. 17, 1632.

106 AGN, Inq vol. 599, exp. 15, 1644.

107 AGN, Inq vol. 561, exp. 1, 1652.

108 AGN, Inq vol. 439, exp. 14, 1656. Adriana Ruiz de Cabrera also alluded to woman-to-woman transmission of witchcraft when she told the inquisitors that had she been brought up by some "suspicious" woman she might well have become a witch. Several cases document mother-to-daughter transmission (for example, AGN, Inq vol. 297, exp. 5, 1612; vol. 439, exp. 3, 1654), but Miguel Lázaro had allegedly taught his son witchcraft. So perhaps transmission of witchcraft, like lineage itself, was bilateral.

109 AGN, Inq vol. 376, exp. 17, 1632.

110 AGN, Inq vol. 301, exp. 47, 1614.

111 AGN, Inq vol. 520, exp. 60, 1682.

112 AGN, Inq vol. 339, exps. 84/89, 1621. Indians, of course, used hummingbird amulets in their erotic magic (Quezada 1984: 97–106), but these were dead birds treated with herbs and powders and carried against the body, not live ones used as "familiars." One might imagine that these live birds were parrots or parakeets.

113 It might be that Indians were more adept at curing the witchcraft of

mulattoes than of blacks because blacks were almost as strong as Indians in the unsanctioned domain.

114 AGN, Inq vol. 530, exp. 16, 1695.

115 This would be wormwood, a plant indigenous to Mexico and endowed with magical and medicinal properties. Its versatility and effectiveness caused even Spaniards in the colonial period to consider it a "sacred herb capable of alleviating the most diverse maladies" (Aguirre Beltran 1963: 126, my translation).

116 The failure of Spanish doctors to accomplish what an Indian curandero can accomplish is a theme in other Inquisition texts. (AGN, Inq vol. 536, exp. 2, 1697.)

117 Remedies Indians acquired from non-Indians usually seem to have failed to have the desired effect. For instance, an Indian from southwest of Toluca testified that although a mulatto set out to cure him through an elaborate ritual, he "stayed as ill and as paralyzed" as he was before the mulatto tried to cure him. For his part, the mulatto apparently told the Indian's wife that the Indian had not paid him his ten pesos, and that was why he had not cured him (AGN, Inq vol. 31, exp. 47, 1614). In another case a black woman from Guadalajara gave a magical remedy to an Indian, but the Indian, who again came before the inquisitors to testify, claimed not to have used it. The black then told the Indian that what she had given her would not have worked anyway (AGN, Inq vol. 339, exps. 84/89, 1621).

118 AGN, Inq vol. 530, exp. 6, 1695. Alberro briefly recounts the same story (1979) but, as in the case of Juan de Morga, she does not attend to the issue of the Indian presence, which I see as central to understanding the importance of the case for the enactment of caste.

119 Also AGN, Inq vol. 316, exp. 17, 1616; vol. 429, exp. 2, 1647.

120 As in the case of the priest Sánchez, we see the witch has to "grant permission" in order for a cure to take hold.

121 Bakewell 1976: 201–4, 217; Palmer 1976: 78, 80–81.

122 AGN, Inq vol. 284, exp. 9, 1609; vol. 276, exp. 2, 1605.

123 AGN, Inq vol. 133, exp. 4, 1583; vol. 360, f. 31, 1627. In the previous chapter, I noted with reference to another Zacatecan witch that *tizitl* means "healer" in Nahuatl.

7 HALL OF MIRRORS

1 AGN, Inq vol. 525, exp. 48, 1691.

2 I do not know what *achula* means, but *yuman* is the name of an indigenous Baja California people.

3 AGN, BN vol. 596, 1684.

4 Comaroff and Comaroff 1999: 284.

5 Stern 1995: 109. At certain points Behar refers to colonial Mexican witchcraft as an "alternative consciousness" of "resistance" (1989: 184, 186); Silverblatt views colonial Andean witchcraft as a "response to

colonialism" and a "means of resistance" (1987: 195); and Cárdenas argues that for "afromestizo" women in seventeenth-century Acapulco, witchcraft constituted "resistance" and a "resource" for the powerless (1997: 117). To my way of thinking, these kinds of arguments risk replicating colonial ideologies making women and the non-Spanish castes essentially different from men and Spaniards. They tend to present witchcraft as a kind of idiom and belief system exclusive to women and the powerless by opposing witchcraft to colonial power rather than examining how witchcraft grew out of colonial power, and by depicting women, especially non-Spanish ones, as taking "naturally" to witchcraft practices.

6   Foucault 1978: 92–96; 1982: 220–21; Dirks et al. 1994: 9.
7   Enslaved Apache Indians were routinely sold by New Mexican Spaniards to miners in northern New Spain (Gutiérrez 1991: 112, 147). During the eighteenth and early nineteenth centuries, Apache "prisoners of war," including women and children, were also distributed throughout New Spain (Alonso 1995: 37–38).
8   Taussig 1987: 262.
9   Klor de Alva 1992: 9.
10  B. Anderson 1993; Urban and Sherzer 1991; Díaz Polanco 1992; Hale 1994.
11  Such as the indigenous/peasant Zapatista movement in Chiapas, Mexico; also Royce 1991.
12  Wade 1995.
13  Lewis 2000, 2001.
14  Flanet 1977.
15  Lewis 2000.
16  Klor de Alva 1992; Adorno 1993.
17  Dirks 1992a: 7.
18  Benton 2002: 13.
19  Jordan 1977: 56–63; Stoler 2002: 167; 1992b.
20  Stoler 1992b: 160.
21  Stoler 1992b: 154.
22  The *Devastation* was translated into every major European language shortly after it was written, and served as a basis for the Black Legend (Donovan 1992: 2).
23  Dirks 1992a: 7; Adorno 1993: 142.
24  See the discussion in Seed 1988: 200–225.
25  Seed 1988: 204.
26  Seed 1988: 206.
27  Seed 1988: 208.
28  Martínez-Alier 1989: 84.
29  Martínez-Alier 1989: 124.
30  Martínez-Alier 1989: 92.
31  Konetzke 1958 III (1): 285, 438–39; (2): 476–77, 625, 686–87.
32  Stolcke 1991. Katzew argues along the same lines that at least the later series of caste paintings "respond to the elite's increasing concern over

the impossibility of discerning the different social groups in the colony" (1996: 20) in part because of dress but also because of "the increasing blurring of social boundaries as the necessary consequence of racial mixing" (1996: 12).

33 Seed 1988: 201. Slavery disappeared with independence at the beginning of the nineteenth century but so did the General Indian Court, which offered protections to Indians.

34 Lomnitz 1993: 276.

35 Stepan 1991; Aguirre Beltrán 1976; Vasconcelos 192?.

36 Basch, Schiller, and Szanton Blanc 1994: 38; B. Anderson 1993.

37 B. Anderson 1993: 47–50.

38 B. Anderson 1993; Lomnitz 1993; Rout 1977; Carroll 1991a; Knight 1990.

39 Graham 1990.

40 Dirks 1992a: 15.

# Works Cited

ARCHIVAL SOURCES

*Archivo General de la Nación* (AGN)

Bienes Nacionales (BN)
Civil (Civil)
Criminal (Criminal)
General de Parte (GP)
Historia (Historia)
Indios (Indios)
Inquisición (Inq)
Mercedes (Mercedes)
Ordenanzas (Ord)
Reales Cédulas Duplicadas (RCD)
Reales Cédulas Originales (RCO)
Tierras (Tierras)

*Biblioteca Nacional de Antropología e Historia (BNAH)*

Histórico, Colección Francisco de Paso y Troncoso

*BNAH Microfilm collection from Archivo General de Indias (AGI), Sevilla, Spain*

México, Correspondencia Virreinal

PUBLISHED SOURCES

Abu-Lughod, Lila. 1990. "The Romance of Resistance: Tracing Transformations of Power Through Bedouin Women." *American Ethnologist* 17 (1): 41–55.
Adorno, Rolena. 1993. "Reconsidering Colonial Discourse for Sixteenth- and Seventeenth-Century Latin America." *Latin American Research Review* 28 (3): 135–45.

Aguirre Beltrán, Gonzalo. 1963. *Medicina y magia: el proceso de aculturación en la estructura colonial*. Mexico City: Instituto Nacional Indigenista.

———. [1948] 1972. *La población negra de México*. Mexico City: Fondo de Cultura Económica.

———. 1976. "Introducción." In *Francisco Xavier Clavijero, Antología*, edited by Gonzalo Aguirre Beltrán. Mexico City: Secretaría de Educación Pública.

———. 1994. *El negro esclavo en Nueva España*. Mexico City: Fondo de Cultura Económica.

Alberro, Solange. 1974. "Inquisición y proceso de cambio social: delitos de hechicería en Celaya, 1614." *Revista de dialectologia y tradiciones populares* 30 (3/4): 327–85.

———. 1979. "Negros y mulatos en los documentos inquisitoriales: rechazo e integración." In *El trabajo y los trabajadores en la historia de México*, edited by Elsa Frost et al. Mexico City: El Colegio de México.

———. 1981a. *La actividad del Santo Oficio de la Inquisición en Nueva España, 1571–1700*. Mexico City: Instituto Nacional de Antropología e Historia.

———. 1981b. "Juan de Morga and Gertrudis de Escobar: Rebellious Slaves." In *Struggle and Survival in Colonial America*, edited by David G. Sweet and Gary B. Nash. Berkeley: University of California Press.

———. 1987. "Herejes, brujas y beatas: Mujeres ante el tribunal del Santo Oficio de la Inquisición en la Nueva España." In *Presencia y transparencia: la mujer en la historia de México*. Mexico City: El Colegio de México.

———. 1988. *Inquisición y sociedad en México, 1571–1700*. Mexico City: Fondo de Cultura Económica.

———. 1991. "El amancebamiento en los siglos XVI y XVII: un medio eventual de medrar." In *Familia y poder en Nueva España: memoria del tercer simposio de historia de las mentalidades*. Mexico City: Instituto Nacional de Antropología e Historia.

Alcalá, Angel, ed. 1987. *The Spanish Inquisition and the Inquisitorial Mind*. Boulder, Colo.: Social Science Monographs.

Alonso, Ana María. 1995. *Thread of Blood: Colonialism, Revolution and Gender on Mexico's Northern Frontier*. Tucson: University of Arizona Press.

Anderson, Benedict. 1993. *Imagined Communities: Reflections on the Origin and Spread of Nationalism*. New York: Verso.

Anderson, Rodney. 1988. "Race and Social Stratification: A Comparison of Working-Class Spaniards, Indians and Castas in Guadalajara, Mexico, in 1821." *Hispanic American Historical Review* 68 (2): 209–43.

Archivo General de la Nación. 1912. "Proceso del Santo Oficio contra Tacatetl y Tanixtetl, indios, por idolatras"; "Proceso del Santo Oficio contra Martin Ucelo, indio, por idolatra y hechicero"; "Proceso del Santo Oficio contra Mixcoatl y Papalotl, indios, por hechiceros"; "Proceso del Santo Oficio contra Miguel, indio, vecino de Mexico, por idolatra." In *Publicaciones del Archivo General de la Nacion* III. Mexico: Secretaria de Relaciones Exteriores, 1–78, 115–40.

———. 1938. "Sobre los inconvenientes de vivir los indios en el centro de la ciudad." In *Boletín del Archivo General de la Nación* IX (1): 1–34.

———. 1940. "Mandamientos sobre indios en los obrajes 1579–1633." In *Boletín del Archivo General de la Nación* II: 15–116.

Arendt, Hannah. 1966. *Between Past and Future: Six Exercises in Political Thought*. Cleveland: Meridian.

Arrom, Silvia. 1985. *The Women of Mexico City, 1790–1857*. Stanford, Calif.: Stanford University Press.

*Artes de México*. 1990. "La Pintura de Casta." 8 (verano).

Axel, Brian Keith. 2002. "Introduction: Historical Anthropology and Its Vicissitudes." In *From the Margins: Historical Anthropology and Its Futures*, edited by Brian Keith Axel. Durham, N.C.: Duke University Press.

Bakewell, Peter. 1976. "Zacatecas: An Economic and Social Outline of a Silver Mining District, 1547–1700." In *Provinces of Early Mexico*, edited by Ida Altman and James Lockhart. Los Angeles: UCLA Latin American Center.

Banet-Weiser, Sarah. 1999. *The Most Beautiful Girl in the World: Beauty Pageants and National Identity*. Berkeley: University of California Press.

Baretta, Silvio, R. Duncan, and John Markoff. 1978. "Civilization and Barbarism: Cattle Frontiers in Latin America." *Comparative Studies in Society and History* 20 (4): 587–620.

Basch, Linda, Nina Glick Schiller, and Cristina Szanton Blanc, eds. 1994. *Nations Unbound: Transnational Projects, Postcolonial Predicaments and Deterritorialized Nation-States*. Amsterdam: Gordon and Breach.

Bataillon, Marcel. 1971. "The *Clérigo* Casas, Colonist and Colonial Reformer." In *Bartolomé de las Casas in History*, edited by Juan Friede and Benjamin Keen. DeKalb: Northern Illinois University Press.

Bauer, Arnold. 1979. "Rural Workers in Spanish America: Problems of Peonage and Oppression." *Hispanic American Historical Review* 59 (1): 34–63.

Becker, Carl. 1932. *The Heavenly City of the Eighteenth-Century Philosophers*. New Haven, Conn.: Yale University Press.

Behar, Ruth. 1987a. "Sex and Sin, Witchcraft and the Devil in Late-Colonial Mexico." *American Ethnologist* 14 (1): 34–54

———. 1987b. "The Visions of a Guachichil Witch in 1599: A Window on the Subjugation of Mexico's Hunter-Gatherers." *Ethnohistory* 34 (2): 115–38.

———. 1989. "Sexual Witchcraft, Colonialism and Women's Powers: Views from the Mexican Inquisition." In *Sexuality and Marriage in Colonial Latin America*, edited by Asunción Lavrin. Lincoln: University of Nebraska Press.

Benton, Lauren. 2002. *Law and Colonial Cultures: Legal Regimes in World History, 1400–1800*. Cambridge: Cambridge University Press.

Bloch, Maurice, and Jean H. Bloch. 1980. "Women and the Dialectics of Nature in Eighteenth Century French Thought." In *Nature, Culture and Gender*, edited by Carol P. MacCormack and Marilyn Strathern. Cambridge: Cambridge University Press.

Boase, Roger. 1990. "The Morisco Expulsion and Diaspora: An Example of Racial and Religious Intolerance." In *Cultures in Contact in Medieval Spain*, edited by David Hook and Barry Taylor. London: King's College London Medieval Studies.

Bonfil Batalla, Guillermo. 1987. *México profundo.* Mexico: Grijalbo.

Borah, Woodrow. 1951. *New Spain's Century of Depression.* Berkeley: University of California Press.

——. 1982. "The Spanish and Indian Law: New Spain." In *The Inca and Aztec States, 1400–1800,* edited by George A. Collier, Renato I. Rosaldo, and John D. Wirth. New York: Academic Press.

——. 1983. *Justice by Insurance.* Berkeley: University of California Press.

Boswell, John. 1980. *Christianity, Social Tolerance and Homosexuality.* Chicago: University of Chicago Press.

Bourgois, Philippe. 1989. "Conjugated Oppression: Class and Ethnicity Among Guaymi and Kuna Banana Workers." *American Ethnologist* 15 (2): 328–48.

Bowser, Frederick. 1972. "Colonial Spanish America." In *Neither Slave Nor Free: The Freedmen of African Descent in the Slave Societies of the New World,* edited by David Cohen and Jack P. Greene. Baltimore, Md.: Johns Hopkins University Press.

Boyer, Richard. 1989. "Women, La Mala Vida, and the Politics of Marriage." In *Sexuality and Marriage in Colonial Latin America,* edited by Asunción Lavrin. Lincoln: University of Nebraska Press.

Brathwaite, Edward. 1971. *The Development of Creole Society in Jamaica.* Oxford: Clarendon Press.

Burkhart, Louise. 1989. *The Slippery Earth: Nahua-Christian Moral Dialogue in Sixteenth-Century Mexico.* Tucson: University of Arizona Press.

Cárdenas, Alejandra. 1997. *Hechicería, saber y transgresión: Afromestizas en Acapulco: 1621.* N.p.

Caro Baroja, Julio. 1964. *The World of the Witches.* Chicago: University of Chicago Press.

Carrasco, Pedro. 1961. "The Civil-Religious Hierarchy in Mesoamerican Communities: Pre-Spanish Background and Colonial Development." *American Anthropologist* 63.

Carroll, Patrick. 1977. "Mandinga: The Evolution of a Mexican Runaway Slave Community, 1735–1827." *Comparative Studies in Society and History* 19 (4): 488–505.

——. 1991a. *Blacks in Colonial Veracruz: Race, Ethnicity and Regional Development.* Austin: University of Texas Press.

——. 1991b "Afro-Americans and Colonial Social Development in Central Veracruz." Paper presented at the 106th Annual Meeting of the American Historical Society, December, Chicago.

Cascardi, Anthony J. 1992. "The Subject of Control." In *Culture and Control in Counter-Reformation Spain,* edited by Anne J. Cruz and Mary Elizabeth Perry. Minneapolis: University of Minnesota Press.

Castañeda, Carmen. 1989. *Violación, estupro y sexualidad: Nueva Galicia, 1790–1821.* Guadalajara: Editorial Hexágono.

Castañega, Fray Martín de. [1529] 1946. *Tratado de las supersticiones y hechicerías.* Madrid: N.p.

Ceballos Gómez, Diana Luz. 2000. "Sociedad y prácticas mágicas en el Nuevo

Reino de Granada." Paper presented at XI Congreso de Historia de Colombia, August, Bógota.

Cervantes, Fernando. 1991. *The Idea of the Devil and the Problem of the Indian: The Case of Mexico in the Sixteenth Century*. London: University of London Institute of Latin American Studies Research Papers, 24.

———. 1994. *The Devil in the New World*. New Haven, Conn.: Yale University Press.

Chance, John K., and William B. Taylor. 1977. "Estate and Class in a Colonial City: Oaxaca in 1792." *Comparative Studies in Society and History* 19: 454–87.

———. 1979. "Estate and Class: A Reply." *Comparative Studies in Society and History* 21: 434–42.

Chevalier, François. [1952] 1963. *Land and Society in Colonial Mexico: The Great Hacienda*. Translated by Alvin Eustis and edited by Lesley Byrd Simpson. Berkeley: University of California Press.

Cintrón Tiryakian, Josefina. 1979. "The Indian Labor Policy of Charles V." In *El trabajo y los trabajadores en la historia de México*, edited by Elsa Frost et al. Mexico City: El Colegio de Mexico.

Clendinnen, Inga. 1982. "Disciplining the Indians: Franciscan Ideology and Missionary Violence in Sixteenth-Century Yucatán." *Past and Present* 94 (February): 27–48.

———. 1991. *Aztecs*. Cambridge: Cambridge University Press.

Cline, S. L. 1986. *Colonial Culhuacan, 1580–1600: A Social History of an Aztec Town*. Albuquerque: University of New Mexico Press.

Cohn, Bernard S., and Nicholas B. Dirks. 1988. "Beyond the Fringe: the Nation State, Colonialism and the Technologies of Power." *Journal of Historical Sociology* 1 (2): 224–29.

Comaroff, Jean. 1985. *Body of Power, Spirit of Resistance: The Culture and History of a South African People*. Chicago: University of Chicago Press.

Comaroff, Jean, and John Comaroff. 1989. "Images of Empire, Contests of Conscience: Models of Colonial Domination in South Africa." *American Ethnologist* 16 (4): 661–85.

———. 1991. *Of Revelation and Revolution: Christianity, Colonialism and Consciousness in South Africa*. Vol. 1. Chicago: University of Chicago Press.

———. 1992. *Ethnography and the Historical Imagination*. Boulder, Colo.: Westview Press.

———. 1993. "Introduction." In *Modernity and Its Malcontents*, edited by Jean and John Comaroff. Chicago: University of Chicago Press.

———. 1999. "Occult Economies and the Violence of Abstraction: Notes from the South African Postcolony." *American Ethnologist* 26 (2): 279–303.

Contreras, Jaime. 1992. "Aldermen and Judaizers: Cryptojudaism, Counter-Reformation and Local Power." In *Culture and Control in Counter-Reformation Spain*, edited by Anne J. Cruz and Mary Elizabeth Perry. Minneapolis: University of Minnesota Press.

Cook, Sherburne F., and Woodrow Borah. 1979. *Essays in Population History: Mexico and California*. Berkeley: University of California Press.

Cooper, Frederick, and Ann Laura Stoler. 1989. "Introduction: Tensions of

Empire, Colonial Control and Visions of Rule." *American Ethnologist* 16 (4): 609–21.

Cooper, Frederick, and Ann Laura Stoler, eds. 1997. *Tensions of Empire: Colonial Cultures in a Bourgeois World*. Berkeley: University of California Press.

Cope, R. Douglas. 1994. *The Limits of Racial Domination: Plebeian Society in Colonial Mexico City, 1660–1720*. Madison: University of Wisconsin Press.

Corominas, Joan, and José A. Pascual. 1980. *Diccionario crítico etimológico Castellano e Hispánico*. Madrid: Editorial Gredor.

Coroníl, Fernando. 1997. *The Magical State: Nature, Money and Modernity in Venezuela*. Chicago: University of Chicago Press.

Corrigan, Philip, and Derek Sayer. 1985. *The Great Arch: English State Formation as Cultural Revolution*. Oxford: Blackwell.

Covarrubias Orozco, Sebastian de. [1611] 1984. *Tesoro de la lengua castellana o española*. 6 vols. Madrid: Ediciones Turner.

Darien-Smith, Eve. 1994. Review of *Legitimate Acts and Illegal Encounters: Law and Society in Antigua and Barbuda*, by Mindie Lazarus-Black. *PoLAR: Political and Legal Anthropology Review* 17 (2): 125–34.

Davidson, David. 1979. "Negro Slave Control and Resistance in Colonial Mexico, 1519–1650." In *Maroon Societies*, edited by Richard Price. Baltimore, Md.: Johns Hopkins University Press.

Davis, David Brion. 1966. *The Problem of Slavery in Western Culture*. Ithaca, N.Y.: Cornell University Press.

———. 1969. "A Comparison of British America and Latin America." In *Slavery in the New World*, edited by Laura Foner and Eugene D. Genovese. Englewood Cliffs, N.J.: Prentice-Hall.

———. 1984. *Slavery and Human Progress*. New York: Oxford University Press.

Dean, Carolyn. 1999. *Inka Bodies and the Body of Christ: Corpus Christi in Colonial Cuzco, Peru*. Durham, N.C.: Duke University Press.

Dedieu, Jean Pierre. 1980. "Les archives de l'inquisition, source pour une etude anthropologique des vieux-chretiens. Un exemple et quelques reflexions." In *La Inquisición española: Nueva visión, nuevos horizontes*, edited by Joaquin Perez Villanueva. Madrid: Siglo Veintiuno Editores.

———. 1986. "The Archives of the Holy Office of Toledo as a Source for Historical Anthropology." In *The Inquisition in Early Modern Europe: Studies in Sources and Methods*, edited by Gustav Henningsen and John Tedeschi. DeKalb: Northern Illinois University Press.

Dehouve, Danielle. 1994. *Entre el caimán y el jaguar: los pueblos indios de Guerrero*. Mexico City: Centro de Investigaciones y Estudios Superiores en Antropología Social.

de la Cadena, Marisol. 1991. "'Las mujeres son más indias': etnicidad y género en una comunidad del Cusco." *Revista Andina* 9 (1): 7–47.

del Refugio González, María, and Teresa Lozano. 1985. "La administración de la justicia." In *El gobierno provincial en la Nueva España, 1570–1787*, edited by Woodrow Borah. Mexico City: Universidad Nacional Autónoma de México.

Delacampagne, Christian. 1983. *Racismo y occidente*. Barcelona: Argos Vergara.

Devisse, Jean, and Michel Mollat. 1979. *From The Early Christian Era to the*

"*Age of Discovery.*" Parts 1/2. Vol. 2 of *The Image of the Black in Western Art*, series edited by Ladislas Bugner and translated by William Granger Ryan. Cambridge, Mass.: Menil Foundation.

Díaz del Castillo, Bernal. [1632] 1956. *The Discovery and Conquest of Mexico*, edited by Génaro Garcia. New York: Farrar, Straus and Cudahy.

Díaz-Polanco, Héctor. 1992. "Indian Communities and the Quincentenary." *Latin American Perspectives* 74 (19/3): 6–24.

Dirks, Nicholas B. 1992a. "Introduction." In *Colonialism and Culture*, edited by Nicholas B. Dirks. Ann Arbor: University of Michigan Press.

———, ed. 1992b. *Colonialism and Culture*. Ann Arbor: University of Michigan Press.

———. 2002. "Annals of the Archive: Ethnographic Notes on the Sources of History." In *From the Margins: Historical Anthropology and Its Futures*, edited by Brian Keith Axel. Durham, N.C.: Duke University Press.

Dirks, Nicholas B., Geoff Eley, and Sherry B. Ortner. 1994. "Introduction." In *Culture, Power, History*, edited by Nicholas B. Dirks et al. Princeton, N.J.: Princeton University Press.

Donovan, Bill M. 1992. "Introduction." In *The Devastation of the Indies: A Brief Account*, by Bartolomé de Las Casas, translated by Herma Briffault. Baltimore, Md.: Johns Hopkins University Press.

Drake, St. Clair. 1990. *Black Folk Here and There: An Essay in History and Anthropology*. Vol. 2. Los Angeles: University of California Center for Afro-American Studies.

Durán, Diego. 1964. *The Aztecs: The History of the Indians of New Spain*. Translated by Doris Heyden and Fernando Horcasitas. Introduction by Ignacio Bernal. New York: Orion Press.

———. 1971. *Book of the Gods and Rites and the Ancient Calendar*. Translated and edited by Fernando Horcasitas and Doris Heyden. Norman: University of Oklahoma Press.

Dusenberry, William H. 1948. "Discriminatory Aspects of Legislation in Colonial Mexico." In *Journal of Negro History* 33 (July): 284–302.

Elkins, Stanley. 1976. *Slavery*. 3d ed. Chicago: University of Chicago Press.

Elliott, John. 1989. *Spain and Its World, 1500–1700*. New Haven, Conn.: Yale University Press.

Evans-Pritchard, E. E. 1976. *Witchcraft, Oracles and Magic Among the Azande*. Oxford: Oxford University Press.

Fairchild, Hoxie. 1934. *The Noble Savage*. New York: Russell & Russell.

Farriss, Nancy. 1984. *Maya Society Under Colonial Rule*. Princeton, N.J.: Princeton University Press.

Fernández, James D. 1994. "The Bonds of Patrimony: Cervantes and the New World." *PMLA* 109 (5): 969–81.

Flanet, Veronique. 1977. *Viveré si dios quiere: an estudio de la violencia en la Mixteca de la Costa*. Mexico City: Instituto Nacional Indigenista.

Foucault, Michel. 1978. *The History of Sexuality*. Vol. I. New York: Random House.

———. 1980. *Power/Knowledge: Selected Interviews and Other Writings, 1972–1977*. Edited by Colin Gordon. New York: Pantheon.

———. 1982. "The Subject and Power." In *Michel Foucault, Beyond Structuralism and Hermeneutics*, 2d ed., edited by Hubert L. Dreyfus and Paul Rabinow. Chicago: University of Chicago Press.

Franco, Jean. 1989. *Plotting Women: Gender and Representation in Mexico*. New York: Columbia University Press.

Fraser, Valerie. 1986. "Architecture and Imperialism in Sixteenth-Century Spanish America." *Art History* 9 (3): 325–35.

Friede, Juan. 1971. "Las Casas and Indigenism in the Sixteenth Century." In *Bartolomé de Las Casas in History*, edited by Juan Friede and Benjamin Keen. DeKalb: Northern Illinois University Press.

Friede, Juan, and Benjamin Keen, eds. 1971. *Bartolomé de Las Casas in History*. DeKalb: Northern Illinois University Press.

Friedlander, Judith. 1975. *Being Indian in Hueyapan: A Study of Forced Identity in Contemporary Mexico*. New York: St. Martin's Press.

Gage, Thomas. 1958. *Travels in the New World*. Edited by J. Eric S. Thompson. Norman: University of Oklahoma Press.

García Sáiz, María Concepción. 1980. *La pintura colonial en el museo de América*. Madrid: Museo de América.

Genovese, Eugene. 1967. "The Treatment of Slaves in Different Countries: Problems in the Applications of the Comparative Method." In *Slavery in the New World*, edited by Laura Foner and Eugene Genovese. Englewood Cliffs, N.J.: Prentice-Hall.

———. 1972. *Roll, Jordan, Roll: The World the Slaves Made*. New York: Random House.

Gerhard, Peter. 1972. *Guide to the Historical Geography of New Spain*. Cambridge: Cambridge University Press.

———. 1975. "La evolución del pueblo rural mexicano: 1519–1975." *Historia mexicana* 24 (4): 566–78.

———. 1978. "A Black Conquistador in Mexico." *Hispanic American Historical Review* 58 (3): 451–59.

Gibson, Charles. 1954–1955. "The Transformation of the Indian Community in New Spain, 1500–1810." *Journal of World History* 2: 581–603.

———. 1964. *The Aztecs Under Spanish Rule*. Stanford, Calif.: Stanford University Press.

Gilman, Sander. 1985. *Difference and Pathology: Stereotypes of Sexuality, Race and Madness*. Ithaca, N.Y.: Cornell University Press.

———. 1991. *The Jew's Body*. New York: Routledge.

Ginzburg, Carlo. 1982. *The Cheese and the Worms*. New York: Penguin.

———. 1985. *Night Battles: Witchcraft and Agrarian Cults in the Sixteenth and Seventeenth Centuries*. New York: Penguin.

———. 1989. *Clues, Myths and the Historical Method*. Baltimore, Md.: Johns Hopkins University Press.

Giraud, François. 1987. "Mujeres y familia en Nueva España." In *Presencia y transparencia: la mujer en la historia de México*, edited by Carmen Ramos-Escandón. Mexico: El Colegio de México.

Gonzalbo Aizpuru, Pilar. 1987. *Las mujeres en la Nueva España: Educación y vida cotidiana*. Mexico: El Colegio de México.

Greenberg, David E. 1990. *The Construction of Homosexuality*. Chicago: University of Chicago Press.

Greenleaf, Richard. 1962. *Zumárraga and the Mexican Inquisition: 1536–1543*. Washington, D.C.: Academy of American Franciscan History.

———. 1965. "The Inquisition and the Indians of New Spain: A Study in Jurisdictional Confusion." *The Americas* 22 (2): 138–66.

———. 1969. *The Mexican Inquisition in the Sixteenth Century*. Albuquerque: University of New Mexico Press.

———. 1978. "The Mexican Inquisition and the Indians: Sources for the Ethnohistorian." *The Americas* 34 (3): 315–44.

Gruzinski, Serge. 1986. "Las cenizas del deseo. Homosexuales novohispanos a mediados del siglo XVII." In *De la santidad a la perversión: o de porqué no se cumplía la ley de Dios en la sociedad novohispana*, edited by Sergio Ortega. Mexico: Grijalbo.

———. 1988. "The Net Torn Apart: Ethnic Identities and Westernization in Colonial Mexico, Sixteenth–Nineteenth Centuries." In *Ethnicities and Nations: Processes of Interethnic Relations in Latin America, Southeast Asia and the Pacific*, edited by Remo Guidieri, F. Pellizzi, and Stanley Tambiah. Austin: University of Texas Press.

———. 1989. *Man-Gods in the Mexican Highlands: Indian Power and Colonial Society, 1520–1800*. Stanford, Calif.: Stanford University Press.

———. 1993. *The Conquest of Mexico*. Cambridge, England: Polity Press.

Guthrie, Chester Lyle. 1945. "Riots in Seventeenth Century Mexico City: A Study of Social and Economic Conditions." In *Greater America: Essays in Honor of Herbert Eugene Bolton*, edited by Adele Ogden and Engel Sluiter. Berkeley: University of California Press.

Gutiérrez, Ramón A. 1991. *When Jesus Came, the Corn Mothers Went Away: Marriage, Sexuality and Power in New Mexico, 1500–1846*. Stanford, Calif.: Stanford University Press.

Hale, Charles. 1994. "Between Che Guevara and the Pachamama: Mestizos, Indians and Identity Politics in the Anti-Quincentenary Campaign." *Critique of Anthropology* 14 (1): 9–39.

Haliczer, Steven, ed. and trans. 1987. *Inquisition and Society in Early Modern Europe*. Totowa, N.J.: Barnes and Noble Books.

Hanke, Lewis. 1959. *Aristotle and the American Indians*. Chicago: Henry Regnery Company.

———. 1974. *All Mankind Is One*. DeKalb: Northern Illinois University Press.

Hanks, William. 1986. "Authenticity and Ambivalence in the Text: A Colonial Maya Case." *American Ethnologist* 13 (4): 721–44.

Haskett, Robert. 1991a. "'Our Suffering with the Taxco Tribute': Involuntary Mine Labor and Indigenous Society in Central New Spain." *Hispanic American Historical Review* 71 (3): 447–75.

———. 1991b. *Indigenous Rulers: An Ethnohistory of Town Government in Colonial Cuernavaca*. Albuquerque: University of New Mexico Press.

Heath, Shirley Brice. 1974. *Telling Tongues: Language Policy in Mexico, Colony to Nation*. New York: Teachers College Press.

Hendrickson, Carol. 1991. "Images of the Indian in Guatemala: The Role of

Indigenous Dress in Indian and Ladino Constructions." In *Nation-States and Indians in Latin America*, edited by Greg Urban and Joel Sherzer. Austin: University of Texas Press.

Henningsen, Gustav. 1980. *The Witches' Advocate: Basque Witchcraft and the Spanish Inquisition (1609–1614)*. Reno: University of Nevada Press.

Henningsen, Gustav, and John Tedeschi, eds. 1986. *The Inquisition in Early Modern Europe: Studies in Sources and Methods*. DeKalb: Northern Illinois University Press.

*Hispanic American Historical Review.* 1999. "Mexico's New Cultural History: Una Lucha Libre?" Special issue 79 (2).

Hoberman, Louisa. 1980. "Hispanic American Political Theory as a Distinct Tradition." *Journal of the History of Ideas* 49 (2): 199–218.

——. 1986. "Conclusion." In *Cities and Society in Colonial Latin America*, edited by Louisa Schell Hoberman and Susan Migden Socolow. Albuquerque: University of New Mexico Press.

——. 1991. *Mexico's Merchant Elite, 1590–1660*. Durham, N.C.: Duke University Press.

Hoberman, Louisa Schell, and Susan Migden Socolow, eds. 1986. *Cities and Society in Colonial Latin America*. Albuquerque: University of New Mexico Press.

Ingham, John M. 1986. *Mary, Michael and Lucifer: Folk Catholicism in Central Mexico*. Austin: University of Texas Press.

Israel, Jonathan. 1975. *Race, Class and Politics in Colonial Mexico, 1610–1670*. Oxford: Oxford University Press.

Johnson, Lyman. 1986. "Artisans." In *Cities and Society in Colonial Latin America*, edited by Louisa Schell Hoberman and Susan Migden Socolow. Albuquerque: University of New Mexico Press.

Jordan, Winthrop. 1977. *White Over Black: American Attitudes Towards the Negro, 1550–1812*. New York: W.W. Norton & Co.

Joseph, Gilbert M., and Daniel Nugent. 1994. "Popular Culture and State Reformation in Revolutionary Mexico." In *Everyday Forms of State Formation*, edited by Gilbert M. Joseph and Daniel Nugent. Durham, N.C.: Duke University Press.

Kagan, Richard. 1981. *Lawsuits and Litigation in Castile*. Chapel Hill: University of North Carolina Press.

Kagen, Samuel. 1977. "The Labor of Prisoners in the Obrajes of Coyoacán: 1660–1673." In *El trabajo y los trabajadores en la historia de México*, edited by Elsa Frost et al. Mexico: El Colegio de México.

Kamen, Henry. 1985. *Inquisition and Society in Spain*. Bloomington: Indiana University Press.

Karasch, Mary. 1986. "Suppliers, Sellers, Servants and Slaves." In *Cities and Society in Colonial Latin America*, edited by Louisa Schell Hoberman and Susan Migden Socolow. Albuquerque: University of New Mexico Press.

Karlsen, Carol F. 1987. *The Devil in the Shape of a Woman: Witchcraft in Colonial New England*. New York: Norton.

Katz, Friedrich. 1988a. "Introduction: Rural Revolts in Mexico." In *Riot, Rebellion and Revolution: Rural Social Conflict in Mexico*, edited by Friedrich Katz. Princeton, N.J.: Princeton University Press.

———. 1988b. "Rural Uprisings in Preconquest and Colonial Mexico." In *Riot, Rebellion and Revolution: Rural Social Conflict in Mexico*, edited by Friedrich Katz. Princeton, N.J.: Princeton University Press.

Katzew, Ilona. 1996. "Casta Painting: Identity and Social Stratification in Colonial Mexico." In *New World Orders: Casta Painting and Colonial Latin America*, edited by Ilona Katzew. New York: Americas Society Art Gallery.

Kellogg, Susan. 1992. "Hegemony Out of Conquest: The First Two Centuries of Spanish Rule." *Radical History Review* 53 (spring): 27–46.

———. 1995. *Law and the Transformation of Aztec Culture, 1500–1700*. Norman: University of Oklahoma Press.

Klein, Herbert S. 1967. *Slavery in the Americas: A Comparative Study of Cuba and Virginia*. Chicago: University of Chicago Press.

———. 1969. "Anglicanism, Catholicism and the Negro Slave." In *Slavery in the New World*, edited by Laura Foner and Eugene D. Genovese. Englewood Cliffs, N.J.: Prentice-Hall.

———. 1986. *African Slavery in Latin America and the Caribbean*. New York: Oxford University Press.

Klor de Alva, J. Jorge. 1988. "Sahagún and the Birth of Modern Ethnography: Representing, Confessing, and Inscribing the Native Other." In *The Work of Bernardino de Sahagún: Pioneer Ethnographer of Sixteenth-Century Mexico*, vol. 2, edited by J. Klor de Alva, H. B. Nicholson, and Eloise Quiñones Keber. Albany: SUNY Albany Institute for Mesoamerican Studies.

———. 1991. "Colonizing Souls: The Failure of the Indian Inquisition and the Rise of Penitential Discipline." In *Cultural Encounters: The Impact of the Inquisition in Spain and the New World*, edited by Mary Elizabeth Perry and Anne J. Cruz. Berkeley: University of California Press.

———. 1992. "Colonialism and Postcolonialism as (Latin) American Mirages." *Colonial Latin American Review* 1 (1/2): 3–23.

Knight, Alan. 1990. "Racism, Revolution and Indigenismo: Mexico, 1910–1940." In *The Idea of Race in Latin America, 1870–1940*, edited by Richard Graham. Austin: University of Texas Press.

———. 1994. "Weapons and Arches in the Mexican Revolutionary Landscape." In *Everyday Forms of State Formation*, edited by Gilbert M. Joseph and Daniel Nugent. Durham, N.C.: Duke University Press.

———. 2002. "Subalterns, Signifiers, and Statistics: Perspectives on Mexican Historiography." *Latin American Research Review* 37 (2): 136–58.

Konetzke, Richard, ed. 1958. *Colección de documentos para la historia de la formación social de hispanoamérica, 1493–1810*. 3 vols. Madrid: Consejo Superior de Investigaciones Científicas.

Konrad, Herman. 1980. *A Jesuit Hacienda in Colonial Mexico: Santa Lucia*. Stanford, Calif.: Stanford University Press.

Kramer, Heinrich, and James Sprenger. [1484] 1971. *The Malleus Maleficarum*. Translated and annotated by Montague Summers. New York: Dover Publications.

LaFaye, Jacques. 1990. "La sociedad de castas en Nueva España." *Artes de México* 8 (summer).

Lancaster, Roger. 1993. *Life Is Hard: Machismo, Danger and the Intimacy of Power in Nicaragua*. Berkeley: University of California Press.

Laqueur, Thomas. 1990. *Making Sex: Body and Gender from the Greeks to Freud*. Cambridge, Mass.: Harvard University Press.

Larner, Christine. 1982. *The Thinking Peasant: Popular and Educated Belief in Pre-Industrial Culture*. Glasgow: Pressgang.

Las Casas, Bartolomé de. [1552] 1992. *The Devastation of the Indies*. Translated by Herma Briffault. Baltimore, Md.: Johns Hopkins University Press.

Lavrin, Asunción. 1978. "In Search of the Colonial Woman in Mexico: The Seventeenth and Eighteenth Centuries." In *Latin American Women: Historical Perspectives*, edited by Asunción Lavrin. Westport, Conn.: Greenwood Press.

———. 1989. "Introduction: The Scenarios, The Actors and the Issues." In *Sexuality and Marriage in Colonial Latin America*, edited by Asunción Lavrin. Lincoln: University of Nebraska Press.

Lazarus-Black, Mindie. 1994. "Slaves, Masters and Magistrates: Law and the Politics of Resistance in the British Caribbean, 1736–1834." In *Contested States: Law, Hegemony and Resistance*, edited by Mindie Lazarus-Black and Susan F. Hirsch. New York: Routledge.

Le Roy Ladurie, Emmanuel. 1979. *Montaillou*. New York: Vintage.

León-Portilla, Miguel. 1994. "Sociedad y cultura indígena en el México colonial: la perspectiva de los testimonios en náhuatl." *Estudios Mexicanos* 10 (1): 227–45.

Leonard, Irving B. 1959. *Baroque Times in Old Mexico*. Ann Arbor: University of Michigan Press.

Lewis, Laura A. 1993. *Race, Witchcraft and Power in Colonial Mexico*. Ph.D. diss., University of Chicago.

———. 1995. "'Blackness,' 'Femaleness' and Self-Representation: Constructing Persons in a Colonial Mexican Court." *PoLAR: Political and Legal Anthropology Review* 18 (2): 1–9.

———. 1996a. "Colonialism and Its Contradictions: Indians, Blacks and Social Power in Sixteenth and Seventeenth Century Mexico." *Journal of Historical Sociology* 9 (4): 408–29.

———. 1996b. "The 'Weakness' of Women and the Feminization of the Indian in Early Colonial Mexico." *Colonial Latin American Review* (NY) 5 (1): 73–94.

———. 2000. "Blacks, Black Indians, Afromexicans: The Dynamics of Race, Nation and Identity in a Mexican *Moreno* Community (Guerrero)." *American Ethnologist* 27 (4): 898–926.

———. 2001. "Of Ships and Saints: History, Memory and Place in the Making of *Moreno* Mexican Identity." *Cultural Anthropology* 16 (1): 62–82.

Lewis, Tom, and Francisco J. Sánchez, eds. 1999. *Culture and the State in Spain, 1550–1850*. New York: Garland.

Lhöest, Brigitte F. P. 1992. "Spanish American Law: A Product of Conflicting Interests?" *Itinerario* XVI (1): 21–34.

Liss, Peggy. 1975. *Mexico Under Spain, 1521–1556: Society and the Origins of Nationality*. Chicago: University of Chicago Press.

Lloyd, Genevieve. 1984. *The Man of Reason: "Male" and "Female" in Western Philosophy*. Minneapolis: University of Minnesota Press.

Lockhart, James. 1991. *Nahuas and Spaniards*. Stanford, Calif.: Stanford University Press.

———. 1992. *The Nahuas After the Conquest*. Stanford, Calif.: Stanford University Press.

Lockhart, James, and Stuart B. Schwartz. 1983. *Early Latin America: A History of Colonial Spanish America and Brazil*. Cambridge: Cambridge University Press.

Lomnitz, Claudio. 1993. *Exits from the Labyrinth*. Berkeley: University of California Press.

López-Austín, Alfredo. 1966. "Los temacpalitoitique: brujos, profanadores, ladonres y violadores." *Estudios de Cultura Nahuatl* 6.

———. 1974. "The Research Method of Fray Bernardino de Sahagún: The Questionnaires." In *Sixteenth Century Mexico: The Work of Sahagún*, edited by Monro S. Edmonson. Albuquerque: University of New Mexico Press.

Love, Edgar. 1971. "Marriage Patterns of Persons of African Descent in a Colonial Mexico City Parish." *Hispanic American Historical Review* 51 (4).

Lovejoy, Arthur O. 1936. *The Great Chain of Being*. Cambridge, Mass.: Harvard University Press.

Macfarlane, Alan. 1970. *Witchcraft in Tudor and Stuart England: A Comparative Study*. New York: Harper and Row.

MacLachlan, Colin. 1974. *Criminal Justice in Eighteenth Century Mexico*. Berkeley: University of California Press.

———. 1988. *Spain's Empire in the New World: The Role of Ideas in Institutional and Social Change*. Berkeley: University of California Press.

Mair, Lucy. 1969. *Witchcraft*. New York: McGraw-Hill.

Mallon, Florencia. 1994. "The Promise and Dilemma of Subaltern Studies: Perspectives from Latin American History." *American Historical Review* 99 (5): 1491–1515.

———. 1999. "Time on the Wheel: Cycles of Revisionism and the 'New Cultural History.'" *Hispanic American Historical Review* 79 (2) 331–51.

Maravall, Jose Antonio. 1949. "La utopia político-religiosa de los franciscanos en Nueva España." *Estudios Americanos* I (January).

Martin, Cheryl. 1985. *Rural Society in Colonial Morelos*. Albuquerque: University of New Mexico Press.

Martin, Ruth. 1989. *The Inquisition in Venice, 1550–1650*. New York: Basil Blackwell.

Martínez, Manuel M. 1971. "Las Casas on the Conquest of America." In *Bartolomé de Las Casas in History*, edited by Juan Friede and Benjamin Keen. DeKalb: Northern Illinois University Press.

Martínez-Alier, Verena. [Verena Stolcke] 1989. *Marriage, Class and Colour in Nineteenth Century Cuba*. 2d ed. Ann Arbor: University of Michigan Press.

Martínez Montiel, Luz María, ed. 1994. *Presencia africana en México*. Mexico City: Dirección General de Culturas Populares.

McAlister, L. N. 1963. "Social Structure and Social Change in New Spain." *Hispanic American Historical Review* 43 (3): 349–70.

———. 1984. *Spain and Portugal in the New World: 1492–1700*. Minneapolis: University of Minnesota Press.

McCaa, Robert, Stuart Schwartz, and Arturo Grubessich. 1979. "Race and Class in Colonial Latin America: A Critique." *Comparative Studies in Society and History* 21 (3).

Merry, Sally. 1990. *Getting Justice and Getting Even*. Chicago: University of Chicago Press.

Mills, Kenneth. 1994. *An Evil Lost to View? An Investigation of Post-Evangelisation Andean Religion in mid-Colonial Peru*. Monograph Series, no. 18. Liverpool: University of Liverpool Institute of Latin American Studies.

Mintz, Sidney, and Richard Price. [1976] 1992. *The Birth of African-American Culture: An Anthropological Perspective*. Boston: Beacon Press.

Monter, E. William. 1976. *Witchcraft in France and Switzerland: The Borderlands During the Reformation*. Ithaca, N.Y.: Cornell University Press.

Montrose, Louis. 1993. "The Work of Gender in the Discourse of Discovery." In *New World Encounters*, edited by Stephen Greenblatt. Berkeley: University of California Press.

Moreno de los Arcos, Roberto. 1991. "New Spain's Inquisition for Indians from the Sixteenth to the Nineteenth Century." In *Cultural Encounters: The Impact of the Inquisition in Spain and the New World*, edited by Mary Elizabeth Perry and Anne J. Cruz. Berkeley: University of California Press.

Moreno Navarro, Isidoro. 1973. *Los cuadros del mestizaje americano: estudio antropológico del mestizaje*. Madrid: José Porrúa Turanzas.

Mörner, Magnus. 1967. *Race Mixture in the History of Latin America*. Boston: Little, Brown & Co.

———. 1969. "The History of Race Relations in Latin America: Some Comments on the State of Research." In *Slavery in the New World*, edited by Laura Foner and Eugene D. Genovese. Englewood Cliffs, N.J.: Prentice-Hall.

———. 1970. *La corona española y los foraneos en los pueblos de indios de América*. Stockholm: Almquist and Wiksell.

Mörner, Magnus, and Charles Gibson. 1962. "Diego Muñoz Camargo and the Segregation Policy of the Spanish Crown." *Hispanic American Historical Review* 42: 558–68.

Motolinía, Fray Toribio. [1541] 1914. *Historia de los indios de la Nueva España escrita a mediados del siglo XVI*. Barcelona: Herederos de Juan Gili.

Munn, Nancy. 1986. *The Fame of Gawa*. Cambridge: Cambridge University Press.

Nutini, Hugo, and Betty Bell. 1980. *Ritual Kinship: The Structure and Historical Development of the Compadrazgo System in Rural Tlaxcala*. Princeton, N.J.: Princeton University Press.

Ortega Noriega, Sergio. 1986 "Teología novohispana sobre el matrimonio y comportamientos sexuales, 1519–1570." In *De la santidad a la perversión: o de porqué no se cumplía la ley de Dios en la sociedad novohispana*, edited by Sergio Ortega. Mexico: Grijalbo.

Ortner, Sherry B. 1993. "Resistance and the Problem of Ethnographic Refusal." *Comparative Studies in Society and History* 37 (1): 173–93.

Ouweneel, Arij. 1995. "From Tlahtocayotl to Gobernadoryotl: A Critical Examination of Indigenous Rule in 18th-Century Central Mexico." *American Ethnologist* 22 (4): 756–85.

Pagden, Anthony. 1982. *The Fall of Natural Man: The American Indian and the Origins of Comparative Ethnology*. Cambridge: Cambridge University Press.

———. 1987. "Identity Formation in Spanish America." In *Colonial Identity in the Atlantic World: 1500–1800*, edited by Nicholas Canny and Anthony Pagden. Princeton, N.J.: Princeton University Press.

Palmer, Colin. 1976. *Slaves of the White God: Blacks in Mexico, 1570–1650*. Cambridge, Mass.: Harvard University Press.

———. 1995. "From Africa to the Americas: Ethnicity in the Early Black Communities of the Americas." *Journal of World History* 6 (2): 223–36.

Patterson, Orlando. 1982. *Slavery and Social Death*. Cambridge, Mass.: Harvard University Press.

Paz, Octavio. 1961. *The Labyrinth of Solitude*. New York: Grove Press.

de la Peña, Guillermo. 1984. "Apuntes de un antropólogo a propósito de la Política Indiana de Juan de Solórzano y Pereyra." In *Humanismo y ciencia en la formación de México*, edited by Carlos Herrejón Peredo. Zamora: El Colegio de Michoacán/CONACYT.

Perry, Mary Elizabeth. 1990. *Gender and Disorder in Early Modern Seville*. Princeton, N.J.: Princeton University Press.

———. 1992. "Magdalens and Jezebels in Counter-Reformation Spain." In *Culture and Control in Counter-Reformation Spain*, edited by Anne J. Cruz and Mary Elizabeth Perry. Minneapolis: University of Minnesota Press.

———. 1999. "The Politics of Race, Ethnicity and Gender in the Making of the Spanish State." In *Culture and the State in Spain: 1550–1850*, edited by Tom Lewis and Francisco J. Sánchez. New York: Garland.

Perry, Mary Elizabeth, and Anne J. Cruz, eds. 1991. *Cultural Encounters: The Impact of the Inquisition in Spain and the New World*. Berkeley: University of California Press.

Peters, Edward. 1988. *Inquisition*. New York: The Free Press.

Phelan, John Leddy. 1960. "Authority and Flexibility in the Spanish Imperial Bureaucracy." *Administrative Science Quarterly* 5 (1960): 47–65.

———. 1969. "The Problem of Conflicting Spanish Imperial Ideologies in the Sixteenth Century." In *Latin American History: Select Problems*, edited by Frederick B. Pike. New York: Harcourt, Brace and World.

———. 1970. *The Millennial Kingdom of the Franciscans in the New World*. 2d ed. Berkeley: University of California Press.

Pitt-Rivers, Julian. 1971. "On the Word 'Caste.'" In *The Translation of Culture*, edited by T. O. Beidelman. London: Tavistock.

Powell, Philip W. 1975. *Soldiers, Indians and Silver: The Northward Advance of New Spain, 1550–1600*. Berkeley: University of California Press.

Quezada, Noemí. [1975] 1984. *Amor y magia amorosa entre los aztecas*. Mexico: Universidad Nacional Autónoma de México.

Rama, Angel. 1984. *La ciudad letrada*. Hanover, N.H.: Ediciones del Norte.

Ricard, Robert. [1933] 1966. *The Spiritual Conquest of Mexico*. Translated by Lesley Bird Simpson. Berkeley: University of California Press.

Root, Deborah. 1988. "Speaking Christian: Orthodoxy and Difference in Sixteenth Century Spain." *Representations* 23 (summer): 118–34.

Rosaldo, Renato. 1986. "From the Door of His Tent: The Fieldworker and the Inquisitor." In *Writing Culture: The Poetics and Politics of Ethnography*, edited by James Clifford and George E. Marcus. Berkeley: University of California Press.

Roseberry, William. 1994. "Hegemony and the Language of Contention." In *Everyday Forms of State Formation: Revolution and the Negotiation of Rule in Modern Mexico*, edited by Gilbert M. Joseph and Daniel Nugent. Durham, N.C.: Duke University Press.

Rout, Leslie B., Jr. 1977. *The African Experience in Spanish America*. Cambridge: Cambridge University Press.

Royce, Anya. 1991. "Ethnicity, Nationalism and the Role of the Intellectual." In *Ethnicity and the State*, edited by Judith D. Toland. Boulder, Colo.: Westview Press.

Ruíz de Alarcón, Hernando. [1629] 1982. *Aztec Sorcerers in Seventeenth Century Mexico: The Treatise on Superstitions by Hernando Ruíz de Alarcón*. Translated and edited by Michael D. Coe and Gordon Whittaker. Albany: SUNY Albany Institute for Mesoamerican Studies.

Sahagún, Bernardino de. [1956] 1969. *Historia general de las cosas de Nueva España*, 4 vols. Edited by Angel María Garibay K. Mexico City: Editorial Porrua.

Sánchez-Ortega, María Helena. 1992. "Women as a Source of 'Evil' in Counter-Reformation Spain." In *Culture and Control in Counter-Reformation Spain*, edited by Anne J. Cruz and Mary Elizabeth Perry. Minneapolis: University of Minnesota Press.

Sandoval, Fernando B. 1945. "La relación de la conquista de México en la *Historia* de Fray Diego Durán." In *Estudios de historiografía de la Nueva España*, edited by Ramón Iglesia. Mexico: El Colegio de México.

Sandstrom, Alan R. 1991. *Corn Is Our Blood*. Norman: University of Oklahoma Press.

Sayer, Derek. 1994. "Everyday Forms of State Formation: Some Dissident Remarks on 'Hegemony,'" In *Everyday Forms of State Formation: Revolution and the Negotiation of Rule in Modern Mexico*, edited by Gilbert M. Joseph and Daniel Nugent. Durham, N.C.: Duke University Press.

Schneider, Jane. 1989. "Rumpelstiltskin's Bargain: Folklore and the Merchant Capitalist Intensification of Linen Manufacture in Early Modern Europe." In *Cloth and Human Experience*, edited by Annette B. Weiner and Jane Schneider. Washington, D.C.: Smithsonian Institution Press.

Scott, James. 1985. *Weapons of the Weak: Everyday Forms of Peasant Resistance*. New Haven, Conn.: Yale University Press.

———. 1990. *Domination and the Arts of Resistance: Hidden Transcripts*. New Haven, Conn.: Yale University Press.

Seed, Patricia. 1988. *To Love, Honor and Obey in Colonial Mexico*. Stanford, Calif.: Stanford University Press.

———. 1991. "Colonial and Postcolonial Discourse." *Latin American Research Review* 26 (3): 181–200.

Seed, Patricia, and Philip F. Rust. 1983. "Estate and Class in Colonial Oaxaca Revisited." *Comparative Studies in Society and History* 25 (4).

Semo, Enrique. 1973. *Historia del capitalismo en México. Los orígenes, 1521/1763.* Mexico: Ediciones Era.

Sepúlveda, Juan Gínes. [1545] 1941. *Tratado sobre las justas causas de la guerra contra los indios*. Mexico: Fondo de Cultura Económica.

———. 1951. *Democrates segundo o De las justas causas de la guerra contra los indios*. Edited by Angel Losada. Madrid: Consejo Superior de Investigaciones Científicas. Instituto Francisco de Vitoria.

Silverblatt, Irene. 1987. *Moon, Sun and Witches: Gender Ideologies and Class in Inca and Colonial Peru*. Princeton, N.J.: Princeton University Press.

———. 2002. "New Christians and New World Fears in Seventeenth-Century Peru." In *From the Margins: Historical Anthropology and Its Futures*, edited by Brian Keith Axel. Durham, N.C.: Duke University Press.

Simpson, Lesley Bird. [1950] 1982. *The Encomienda in New Spain*. Berkeley: University of California Press.

Smedley, Audrey. 1999. *Race in North America: Origin and Evolution of a World View*. 2d ed. Boulder, Colo.: Westview Press.

Smith, Raymond T. 1992. "Race, Class and Gender in the Transition to Freedom." In *The Meaning of Freedom*, edited by Frank McGlynn and Seymour Drescher. Pittsburgh, Penn.: University of Pittsburgh Press.

Solano, Francisco de. 1990. *Ciudades hispanoamericanas y pueblos de indios*. Madrid: Consejo Superior de Investigaciones Científicas.

Spivak, Gayatri Chakravorty. 1988. *In Other Worlds: Essays in Cultural Politics*. New York: Routledge.

Stepan, Nancy Leys. 1990 "Race and Gender: The Role of Analogy in Science." In *Anatomy of Racism*, edited by David Theo Goldberg. Minneapolis: University of Minnesota Press.

———. 1991. *"The Hour of Eugenics": Race, Gender and Nation in Latin America*. Ithaca, N.Y.: Cornell University Press.

Stephen, Lynn. 1999. "The Construction of Indigenous Subjects: Militarization and the Gendered and Ethnic Dynamics of Human Rights Abuses in Southern Mexico." *American Ethnologist* 26 (4): 822–42.

Stern, Steve J. 1982. "The Social Significance of Judicial Institutions in an Exploitative Society: Huamanga, Peru, 1570–1640." In *The Inca and Aztec States, 1400–1800*, edited by George A. Collier, Renato I. Rosaldo, and John D. Wirth. New York: Academic Press.

———. 1988. "Feudalism, Capitalism and the World-System in the Perspective of Latin America and the Caribbean." *American Historical Review* 93 (4): 829–72.

———. 1995. *The Secret History of Gender: Women, Men and Power in Late Colonial Mexico*. Chapel Hill: University of North Carolina Press.

Stolcke, Verena. 1991. "Conquered Women." In *Inventing America: 1492–1992*. North American Congress on Latin America Report on the Americas XXIV (5): 23–28.

Stoler, Ann Laura. 1989. "Making Empire Respectable: The Politics of Race and Sexual Morality in 20th Century Colonial Cultures." *American Ethnologist* 16 (4): 634–60.

———. 1992a. "Rethinking Colonial Categories: European Communities and the Boundaries of Rule." In *Colonialism and Culture*, edited by Nicholas B. Dirks. Ann Arbor: University of Michigan Press.

———. 1992b. "'In Cold Blood': Hierarchies of Credibility and the Politics of Colonial Narratives." *Representations* 37 (winter): 151–89.

———. 2002. "Developing Historical Negatives: Race and the (Modernist) Visions of a Colonial State." In *From the Margins: Historical Anthropology and Its Futures*, edited by Brian Keith Axel. Durham, N.C.: Duke University Press.

Sullivan, Edward J. 1990. "Un fenómeno visual de América." *Artes de México* 8 (summer): 60–72.

Sweet, David G. 1978. "Black Robes and 'Black Destiny': Jesuit Views of African Slavery in 17th-Century Latin America." *Revista de historia de America* 86 (July–December): 87–133.

Tannenbaum, Frank. 1947. *Slave and Citizen: The Negro in the Americas*. New York: A. A. Knopf.

Taussig, Michael. 1987. *Shamanism, Colonialism and the Wild Man: A Study in Terror and Healing*. Chicago: University of Chicago Press.

Taylor, William B. 1979. *Drinking, Homicide and Rebellions in Colonial Mexican Villages*. Stanford, Calif.: Stanford University Press.

Tedeschi, John. 1987. "The Organization and Procedures of the Roman Inquisition: A Sketch." In *The Spanish Inquisition and the Inquisitorial Mind*, edited by Angel Alcalá. Boulder, Colo.: Social Science Monographs.

Thomas, Keith. 1971. *Religion and the Decline of Magic*. New York: Charles Scribner's Sons.

Todorov, Tzvetan. 1984. *The Conquest of America*. New York: Harper & Row.

Trevor-Roper, Hugh. 1967. *The European Witch Craze of the Sixteenth and Seventeenth Century and Other Essays*. New York: Harper & Row.

Trexler, Richard C. 1984. "We Think, They Act: Clerical Readings of Missionary Theatre in 16th Century New Spain." In *Understanding Popular Culture: Europe from the Middle Ages to the Nineteenth Century*, edited by Steve L. Kaplan. Berlin: Mouton Publishers.

Turner, Victor. 1967. *The Forest of Symbols*. Ithaca, N.Y.: Cornell University Press.

Ulloa, Daniel. 1977. *Los predicadores divididos*. Mexico: El Colegio de México.

Urban, Greg, and Joel Sherzer, eds. 1991. *Nation-States and Indians in Latin America*. Austin: University of Texas Press.

van den Berghe, Pierre L. 1978. *Race and Racism: A Comparative Perspective*. 2d ed. New York: John Wiley and Sons.

Van Young, Eric. 1983. "Mexican Rural History Since Chevalier: The Historiography of the Colonial Hacienda." *Latin American Research Review* 18 (2): 5–61.

———. 1999. "The New Cultural History Comes to Old Mexico." *Hispanic American Historical Review* 79 (2): 211–48.

Vasconcelos, José. 192?. *La raza cósmica*. Paris: Agencia mundial de librería.

Wade, Peter. 1995. "The Cultural Politics of Blackness in Colombia." *American Ethnologist* 22 (2): 341–57.

———. 1997. *Race and Ethnicity in Latin America*. London: Pluto Press.

White, Deborah. 1985. *Aren't I a Woman? Female Slaves in the Plantation South*. New York: Norton.

Williams, Raymond. 1977. *Marxism and Literature*. Oxford: Oxford University Press.

Williams, Robert A., Jr. 1990. *The American Indian in Western Legal Thought*. New York: Oxford University Press.

Zamora, Margarita. 1993. *Reading Columbus*. Berkeley: University of California Press.

Zapata Olivella, Manuel. 1989. *Las claves mágicas de América*. Bogotá: Plaza y Janés.

Zavala, Silvio. [1954] 1988. "La libertad de movimiento de los indios de Nueva España." In *Estudios acerca de la historia del trabajo en México*. Mexico City: El Colegio de México.

———. [1935] 1992. *La encomienda indiana*. 3d ed. Mexico City: Porrua.

# Index

Administration, colonial, 200 n.140
Adorno, Rolena, 178
Africans, 20, 220 n.3; as bozales, 149, 198 n.117; origins and identities of, 196–97 n.93, 229 n.71; and witchcraft, 150–52, 230 n.75. *See also* Blacks; Slavery; Slaves; Slave trade
Agency, 7, 10
Aguirre Beltrán, Gonzalo, 150
Alberro, Solange, 133, 201–2 n.152, 208 n.204, 228 n.46
Altepetl (Indian territorial) units, 54, 88, 191 n.26, 219 n.82
Amith, Jonathan D., 221 n.5
Anderson, Benedict, 182
Apaches, 233 n.7
Apter, Andrew, 229 n.71, 230 n.75
Archivo General de la Nación (AGN), 203–4 n.167
Arendt, Hannah, 34–35
Aristotle, 58–59, 213 n.66
Audiencia (Royal High Court). *See* Courts
Axel, Brian Keith, 9

Barbarians, 213 n.56
Behar, Ruth, 110, 185 n.1, 232–33 n.5

Benton, Lauren, 35, 199 n.128
Birds, 231 n.112
Blacks (negros), 29–30, 196 n.91; alliances with Indians, 97, 98; as bellicose, 30, 68, 70, 72, 101; denouncing Spaniards, 154–55; as extensions of Spanish control, 70–73; free, 22, 30; genealogies of, 32; images of, 71, 82–83, 147–48; as pernicious influences on Indians, 98, 101–2; as procurers of witchcraft, 153–54; proximity to Indians in witchcraft, 147–53; Spanish attitudes toward, 2, 20–31, 68–70, 100–101; as threats to Indians, 68–74, 151–52; women, 73–75
Blood, 22–26; and caste, 24–26; and the devil, 128–29; and race, 22–23; and witchcraft, 223 nn.35, 37
Bonfil Batalla, Guillermo, 95
Books, magical, 136, 142–44, 227 n.24
Borah, Woodrow, 200 nn.139, 140
Boswell, John, 112, 224 n.59
Bozales. *See* Africans
Brujería: and hechicería, 201–2 n.152; and nagualismo, 230 n.79

Cárdenas, Alejandra, 232–33 n.5
Caribbean, 16–17; African slavery in, 20; encomienda in, 16–17; Indian slavery in, 16
Caro Baroja, Julio, 223 n.42
Castañega, Martín de, 111, 223 n.40
Caste (casta), 1–2, 4–5, 23–26, 178, 194 n.58; and character, 24; claims about, 4, 32–33, 75–78, 81–84, 90; classifications, 1, 4; definition of, 24; and kinship, 75–78; legislation around, 36; and lineage, 74–75; mixing, 74–76; origins of term, 22; and power, 4; and race, 4–5, 22–24, 178; and religion, 194 n.61; and sanctioned and unsanctioned domains, 6–7; terminologies, 214 n.70, 217 n.35, 227 n.31; uses, 185 n.5. See also Caste paintings; Caste system; Kinship; Lineage; Race
Caste paintings (cuadernos de mestizaje), 74, 179, 217 nn.34, 36, 233–34 n.32
Caste system (sistema de castas), 4; as flexible, 5; and intermediaries, 8; modeled on lineage, 25–26; as system of inclusion, 24–25, 33–35; as system of power, 5, 33–35
Castizos, 86, 199 n.120
Central Mexico, 11
Cervantes, Fernando, 108, 141, 223 n.40
Chichimecs, 28, 57, 97, 195 n.74; as "barbarous" Indians, 28; enslavement of, 28; and peyote, 109; and witchcraft, 108–9, 164; and Zacatecas, 164
Children, as metaphor for women and Indians, 59, 65
Chimalpahin, 86
Christianity: blacks converted to, 199 n.126; Indians converted to, 49. See also Church, Catholic; Clergy; Conversion; Missionaries; Priests
Church, Catholic: and Spanish crown, 17. See also Christianity; Clergy; Conversion; Missionaries; Priests
Cimarrones. See Runaway slaves
Cities and civilization: in Peru, 194 n.66; in Spanish ideology, 26, 194 n.66
Class, 105, 215 n.93; and caste, 78–79, 83–84, 88; and race, 78, 181, 185 n.6
Clergy, 212 n.37; abuses by, 55–57; attitudes toward Indians, 49–50; conflicts among, 54; and crown policy, 54–55; duties of, 55, 212 n.43, 216 n.18; in northern territories, 195 n.78; and runaway slaves, 30–31. See also Christianity; Church, Catholic; Conversion; Missionaries; Priests
Cofradías. See Confraternities
Cohn, Bernard, 199–200 n.132. See also Dirks, Nicholas
Colonialism, Spanish, 12, 176; and contemporary Mexican identities, 175–76; contradictions of Spanish, 16–18, 48–51, 53–54, 67–69; ideologies of, 172; in general, 9, 177–78; Spanish influences on other Europeans, 177–78
Color: skin, 75–76, 103–4, 229 nn.53, 60; and caste terms, 29
Comaroff, Jean, and John Comaroff, 186 n.10, 187 n.19, 197 n.97
Commoners, Indian (maceguales), 27–28, 83–84, 194 n.67, 218 n.65; antipathy toward Indian nobles and mestizos, 88–91
Communities: autonomy of Indian, 50–51, 98; conflicts within Indian, 82–83, 134–35; Indian ones abandoned, 52–53, 63–64; protection of Indian, 98; of runaway slaves (cimarrones), 30–31, 197 n.97; witchcraft within Indian, 134–36
Concentrations (concentraciones), 19, 28, 191 n.26

Confessions, 204 n.171

Confraternities (cofradías), and slave rebellions, 95–96, 101

Conversion: of Africans, 20–21; and enslavement, 22; of Indians, 17, 28, 107–8, 111–12; as means of inclusion, 25

Conversos, 23, 154, 193 n.54; denounced by blacks, 40–41, 156; as "Portuguese," 40–41. *See also* Jews

Copal, 107, 222 n.16, 230 n.76

Cope, R. Douglas, 36, 97, 98, 185 n.6, 192 n.40, 199 n.120, 215 n.93, 220 n.8, 221 n.3

Corominas, Joan: and José Pascual, 24

Corregimiento. *See* Tribute

Corrigan, Philip: and Derek Sayer, 199 nn.131, 132

Cortés, Hernán, 15, 17–18, 59

Courts, 8, 35–43; General Indian, 36, 200 n.139, 234 n.33; Inquisition, Holy Office of the, 37–39, 201 n.148; overlapping responsibilities of, 39–40; proceedings of, 41–43; records of as sources, 3–4, 43–45; Royal High Court (audiencia), 36–37, 200–201 n.144; translation in, 44, 207–8 nn.199, 200

Covarrubias, Sebastián de, 193 nn.52, 53, 58, 213 n.61, 228 n.45

Criollos, 54, 198 n.117

Crown: authority of, 18–19; as benevolent, 18; and clergy, 54–55; Indian appeals to, 92–93; on marriage, 214 n.82; policies toward Indians, 50–53; as sacred, 18, 35

Cuadernos de mestizaje. *See* Caste portraits

Cuezcomatl, 222 n.11

Curing, 232 nn.117, 120

Davidson, David, 97

Davis, David Brion, 29, 198 nn.103, 104

Dean, Carolyn, 8

Debt-peonage, 190–91 n.24

Dedieu, Jean Pierre, 205 n.179

De Landa, Diego, 116

Denunciations, 156, 157, 158; among blacks, 205 n.177

*Devastation of the Indies*, 59, 233 n.22. *See also* Las Casas, Bartolomé de

Devil, 102; and caste, 127–30, 147–49; as helpmate, 123, 137–47; images of, 66, 128–30, 139, 147–49, 168; and Indians, 107–8, 110, 115, 127–30, 137–47; and mulattoes, mestizos, and blacks, 133; pacts with, 114; and seduction, 114; and sexuality, 66, 110–11; as source of witchcraft, 109; and Spaniards, 123–30; and women, 65–66, 109–11

Díaz del Castillo, Bernal, 68

Dirks, Nicholas, 48, 178, 199–200 n.132, 203–4 n.167

Drake, St. Clair, 148, 229 n.60

Dress codes, 193 n.46, 194–95 n.70; and gender, 167, 170

Duendes (elves), 195 n.77

Durán, Diego, 49

Economy, colonial, 16–20, 189 n.6; and blacks, 33–34, 73–74, 226 n.8; and encomienda, 16–19, 190 n.10; and Indian labor, 16–20, 33–34; and regulation of commerce, 217; and trade, 15–16, 73–74. *See also* Encomienda; Labor; Markets; Mining; Slavery; Tribute

Edicts of Grace, 204 n.170

Enclosure, 63, 65–66, 214–15 nn.89, 90

Encomienda, 16–19, 190 n.10

Enríquez, Martín, 53, 68, 77, 78, 101

Evans-Pritchard, E. E., 201–2 n.152

Farriss, Nancy, 97

Food preparation, and witchcraft, 64, 110, 153–54, 163

Foucault, Michel, 5, 67, 172, 186 n.9

Franco, Jean, 186 n.12

Free blacks and mulattoes, 22, 77–84

Gage, Thomas, 54–55

Gender, 8, 48–49, 57–60, 61–65, 70,

Gender (*cont.*)
109, 138, 163; and caste, 8; and economic production, 62–63, 64; and male qualities, 61, 65, 169; and race/caste analogies, 60, 63; and witchcraft, 168–69. *See also* Men; Women

Genealogy: of blacks and mulattoes, 31–32, 144; in court proceedings, 31–32; determinations of, 221 n.3; strategic claims about, 74–77, 100, 104; and witchcraft, 127–29

Gibson, Charles, 97–98

Ginzburg, Carlo, 147

Governors (gobernadores), 88–89; mestizo, in Indian villages, 88–91, 134–35; and witchcraft, 134–35

Gruzinski, Serge, 45, 108, 115, 123, 222 nn.16, 18, 27

Guilds, craft: blacks and mulattoes in, 193 n.45

Hands: and Indian witchcraft, 105, 221 n.5; and Spaniards (manos poderosas), 68

Hanks, William, 45

Harrieros (muleteers), 15–16, 51

Hegemony, 7, 186–87 nn.17, 19; judicial systems and, 204 nn.172, 174

Henningsen, Gustav, 201 n.152

Historical anthropology, 9–10

Hoberman, Louisa, 11

Homosexuality, 112–13, 224 nn.56, 59; and term *puto*, 113, 218 n.29, 224 n.57

Honor: and bearing arms, 75; Spanish conceptions of, 61, 75

Huasteca region, 230 n.73

Indigenism (indigenismo), postcolonial, 182

Indians (indios), 4, 6, 19, 26–28, 101, 194 n.67; and blacks, 33–34, 68–74, 97, 98, 101–2, 147–53; as children, 57–59, 65, 115–16; commoners, as witches, 134–35; confused with mestizos, 103; and crown policy, 19, 50–51; as

"dogs," 70, 72, 87, 103, 104, 105, 155, 158, 216 n.15, 221 n.2, 231 n.101; and the devil, 107–8, 110, 123, 141, 144, 146, 165–66; dualism as witches and healers, 162–63; as feminized, 6, 48, 57–60, 93–94, 102, 107, 113–15, 214 n.73; as fickle, 116; flight of, 52, 63–64, 215 n.98; as healers, 92, 124–26, 159–60, 162–63, 226 n.102; as innocents, 49, 59, 101, 210 n.8; and the Inquisition, 38–39; and the judicial system, 36–39; and labor, 16–19, 33–34, 62–63; as lazy, 48, 56, 63, 90, 215 n.95; and litigation, 40, 130; mestizos and, 86–87, 90; as miserables, 19, 105; as passive, 102; as a "people," 26–27; as quintessential witches, 3, 103; rebellions of, 96–97, 220 nn.9, 11; religion of, 28; and sexual sin, 111–12; Spanish treatment of, 51–57, 63–64, 82–83, 87, 90–91; weak, 6, 48–49, 101–2, 114–15; and witchcraft, 38–39, 105–7, 109–21, 132–66, 167–68. *See also* Commoners, Indian; Labor; Nobles, Indian; Witchcraft

Inquisition, Holy Office of the, 37–39, 201 nn.147, 148; and blacks, 37, 118, 201 n.150; and conversos, 23, 37; and Indians, 38–39, 104, 109, 117–18, 141, 201 n.149; and moriscos, 23; proceedings of, 41–43; records of, 43–45; in Spain, 23, 35, 37; and witchcraft, 37–38, 117; and women, 37–38, 66, 117

Intermediaries, 8, 34, 66, 67–94, 132–66, 174, 217 n.62; and class, 80; as conundrum for Spaniards, 8, 66, 67, 95

Jews, 23–25, 181, 193 n.54; and witchcraft, 203 n.154. *See also* Conversos

Jordan, Winthrop, 177

Jornal, 20, 231 n.99

Judaizers. *See* Conversos

Judicial system, 8, 35–43, 92–93, 131; compared to witchcraft, 8; contradictions of, 8; and Indians, 36–39, 208 nn.203, 204, 207; punishments, 216 n.26, 219 n.94. *See also* Courts

Justice: concepts and organization of, 35–41; Indian and Spanish forms of, 7, 159–60, 173–74; and Indian dualism, 92; and Spanish dualism, 91–94; witchcraft as a system of, 7, 173

Kagan, Richard, 203 n.163

Katzew, Ilona, 217 n.36, 233–34 n.32

Kellogg, Susan, 35, 61, 208 n.207

King. *See* Crown; *individual names*

Kinship: and blacks/mulattoes, 31–32; and caste, 25, 75–78, 127–28; in court proceedings, 31–32; and the devil, 127–28; fictive, 47, 208–9 n.2; and lineage, 75; and slaves, 21

Klor de Alva, J. Jorge, 175, 201 n.149, 209 n.7

Knight, Alan, 10, 11, 199 n.131

Kramer, Heinrich, 111

Labor: of blacks, 33–34; of Indians, 16–19, 33–34; of women, 62–63, 211 n.27

Ladinos, 198 n.117

Lancaster, Roger, 224 n.59

Laqueur, Thomas, 224 n.59

Las Casas, Bartolomé de, 18, 57, 58–60, 196 n.84, 213 n.66; and African slavery, 29; debate with Juan Gínes de Sepúlveda, 58–60, 212 n.55, 213 n.66; *Devastation of the Indies*, 59, 233 n.22

Laws of Burgos, 17

Lazarus-Black, Mindie, 205 n.178

Legal consciousness, 205 n.178

Legal pluralism, 35

Legislation, 200 n.136

Lineage, 25–26, 27; and blacks/mulattoes, 30, 31–33; in legal pro-

ceedings, 31–32; as model for caste, 25–26, 180–81; and women, 75. *See also* Caste; Genealogy; Kinship

Litigation: and blacks, 40; evidence in, 206 n.185; and Indians, 40, 204 n.175; and women, 46–48

Lockhart, James, 82, 122, 208 n.207, 219 n.82, 222 n.18

Lomnitz, Claudio, 24, 25, 26, 181

Maceguales. *See* Commoners, Indian

*Malleus Maleficarum*, 111, 116, 223 nn.40, 42

Mallon, Florencia, 187 n.31

Manos poderosas. *See* Hands

Manumission, 21

Markets, for Indian witchcraft, 64, 122, 132, 154–56

Marriage, 192 nn.40, 41; among African-born blacks, 196 n.93; intercaste, 99; and Pragmatic Sanction, 179–80; slave, 21; between Spaniards and Indians, 218 n.69; and status of women, 47

Martínez-Alier, Verena, 75, 180. *See also* Stolcke, Verena

McAlister, Lyle, 194 n.61

Men: bewitched by women, 109–10, 163–64; and free will, 109–10, 114, 138; and honor ideals, 61, 63; mestizo, witchcraft and, 138; Spanish ideas about, 60, 109–10; as witches, 105–6, 136–37. *See also* Gender; Women

Mendieta, Gerónimo de, 49, 116

Merchants, Indian, 122

Mestizos, 30, 84–91, 133–34, 196 n.91, 219 n.76; alliances with Indians, 98; ambiguity of, 85–91, 133–37; and caste claims, 90; as governors in Indian villages, 88–91, 134–35; and Indians, 87, 89–91, 98; kinship with Indians, 99; Spanish perceptions of, 86, 100; status of, 84–86; as symbols of

Mestizos (*cont.*)
Mexican nation, 86, 182; and
witchcraft, 133–34, 136–41
Mexico City, 15; riots in, 97–98, 220–
21 n.15; slave rebellions in, 96
Mining, 18, 20, 53, 54
Miserables, 105, 190 n.22
Missionaries, 28, 209 n.5, 209–10
n.8; attitudes toward Indians, 17,
48–49, 57; Dominicans, 17; Franciscans, 48. *See also* Church, Catholic; Clergy; Conversion
Moctezuma, 59
Monarchs. *See* Crown; *individual
names*
Monte. *See* Wilderness
Montúfar, Alonso de, 29, 63, 64, 112
Moors (moriscos), 23, 181, 193
n.54, 195 n.79
Morenos, in contemporary Mexico,
175–76
Motolinía, Fray Toribio de, 107,
111–12, 116
Mulattoes, 30, 196 n.91; alliances
with Indians, 98; and blacks in
witchcraft, 132–33, 142–46; as extensions of Spanish authority, 72;
free, 22, 77, 80–84, 192–93 n.44;
influences on Indians, 98; as jail
wardens, 219 n.94; kinship with
Indians, 98, 99–100; in New Mexico, 196 n.91; as officials, 81; perceptions of, 67–69, 77;
prohibitions regarding, 74–76,
77, 85; "white," 76–77
Munn, Nancy, 6–7

Naguales, 230, n.79; among blacks,
152–53
Nagualismo, 201–2 n.152; and brujería, 230 n.79
Nature, concept of, 212 n.50, 213
n.68, 215 n.1
New Laws, 18, 58
New Spain, Viceroyalty of, 188 n.2
Nobility, Indian, 27, 72, 87–88, 194
n.67; and clothing, 27; conflicts
with commoners, 82–83, 88; dis-

tinguished from commoners, 27;
exemptions from tribute, 87, 88;
as intermediaries, 218 n.62

Obrajes, 15, 137, 140, 206–7 n.187
Ololiuque, 55, 212 n.44, 222 n.9,
230 n.87
Ortner, Sherry, 7, 187 n.31
Otomí, 227 n.33

Pagden, Anthony, 29, 214 n.71,
215–16 n.2
Palmer, Colin, 95–96, 196–97 n.93
Pascual, José: and Joan Corominas,
24
Patterson, Orlando, 198 n.103
Peninsulares (Spaniards from
Spain), 54
Peru: architecture in, 213 n.59; extir-
pation campaigns in, 201 n.149;
Viceroyalty of, 188 n.2
Peters, Edward, 207 n.197
Peyote: banned, 36, 200 n.138;
among blacks and mulattoes, 153,
168; and Chichimecs, 109
Phelan, John Leddy, 58
Philip II, 37, 59, 68, 77
Philip III, 67, 69
Philip IV, 55
Pochteca (traders), 119, 122, 225 n.83
Population: density, 11; figures, 199
n.121; of Indians, 16, 189 n.6, 199
n.121; of non-Indians, 34
Postcolonial Mexico, 175; blackness
in, 181–82; indigenous movements
in, 175; mestizos and, 175–76,
182–83; morenos in, 175–76, 183
Powell, Philip W., 195 n.74
Portuguese: as Judaizers, 40, 204–5
n.176; uncertain identities of,
154–55, 230–31 n.93
Pragmatic Sanction, 179–80, 181,
214 n.82
Priests: and black slaves, 57, 71–72;
and Indians, 55–57, 87–88, 123–
26; and Indian witchcraft, 123–
26. *See also* Church, Catholic;
Clergy

Pulque, 36, 105, 108, 200 n.138
Punishment, 7, 117, 207 n.190; capital, 42, 96, 112, 207 n.188; by courts, 42–43; and popular vengeance, 131, 135–36
Puyomate, 222 n.9

Race (raza), 4–5, 22–24, 179–80, 193 n.53; and "blood," 193 n.52; and caste, 4–5, 22–24, 178–79; and class, 181, 185 n.6; and mala raza, 23–24
Rama, Angel, 50
Reason, 212 n.50; and Indians, 58; Spanish ideas regarding, 50, 57; and women, 61
Rebellions: Indian, 96–97; Mexico City, 97–98; slave, 95–96; and witchcraft, 164–66
Repartamiento (labor drafts), 19
Republics, Spanish and Indian, 49–51, 79, 88, 89, 99
Resistance, 171; witchcraft as, 7, 171, 232–33 n.5
Root, Deborah, 23, 195 n.79
Roseberry, William, 7, 174
Ruíz de Alarcón, Hernado, 109
Runaway slaves (cimarrones), 30–31, 97, 197 nn.97, 99; punishment of, 31; settlements, 197 n.97; Spanish attitudes toward, 30–31

Sabbat, witches', 225 n.75, 226 n.105
Sabbath, Jewish, 225 n.75
Sahagún, Bernardino de, 49, 209 n.7
Sanctioned and unsanctioned domains, 5–6, 11, 130; relations between, 130–31, 170–72
Sandstrom, Alan, 230 n.73
Sayer, Derek, 45, 174; and Philip Corrigan, 199 nn.131, 132
Seed, Patricia, 179–80
Sentences. See Punishments
Sepúlveda, Juan Gines de, 58–60, 116, 212–13 n.55, 214 nn.70, 71, 73; analogies between Indians and women, 59–60; and Bartolomé de Las Casas, 49, 58–60

Sexuality and sexual relations, 109–13, 231 n.101; dangers of, 61–62; as means of social control, 49, 61, 215 n.101; and notions of self-control, 61–62
Siete Partidas (Spanish legal code), 18, 21
Silverblatt, Irene, 24, 204–5 n.176, 232–33 n.5
Slaveholders, 20; obligations of, 21, 203 n.165, 229 n.48
Slavery: abolition of, 234 n.33; African, Caribbean, 20; African, Old World, 191 n.30; Indian, 18, 22, 29, 190 n.17; and Las Casas, 196 n.84; manumission, routes to, 21; and religious conversion, 22; religious justifications for, 29; in scholarly debates, 191–92 n.39, 196 n.85; "social death" and, 31, 198 n.103; urban, 20. See also New Laws; Slaves; Slave trade
Slaves: black, African origins of, 20, 191 n.33; bewitching Spaniards, 156–59, 161–62; bozales, 149; demographics, 20, 191 n.36; denouncing Spaniards, 154, 156; denunciations of, for witchcraft, 156–58; escaped, 145; and Indians, 57, 150; Indian, Chichimec, 195 n.80; and kinship, 21, 31; and marriage, 21; rebellions of, 95–96, 220 n.3; and Spaniards in witchcraft, 154; as unskilled workers, 149; and witchcraft, 150. See also Slavery; Slave trade
Slave trade, Atlantic, 16, 189 n.5, 191 nn.32, 33
Sodomy (pecados nefandos), 112–13
Spain: Inquisition in, 23, 35, 203 n.156, 204 n.168, 205 n.179; Jews in, 203 n.154; law and litigation in, 203 n.163, 204 n.169; legal institutions in, 35; as national state, 35–36; witchcraft in, 203 nn.154, 155, 204 n.169

Spaniards (españoles), 4, 27, 29;
class differences among, 79–80,
199 n.120, 215 n.93; as defenders
of Indians, 47–49; denunciations
of Indian witches, 123–30; Indian
complaints about, 51–57; as vagabonds, 79; as victims of witchcraft, 156–59; as witches, 105–7,
118–22
Sprenger, James, 111
Stern, Steve, 178
Stolcke, Verena, 180. *See also*
Martínez-Alier, Verena
Stoler, Ann Laura, 177
Subalterns, 9–10

Tarascans, 228 n.42
Tattoos, 138–39
Taussig, Michael, 7, 45, 80, 92, 107,
131, 142, 173
Taylor, William B., 224 n.57
Theologians, ideas about Indians,
49–50, 57–60. See also *individual
names*
Tizitl, 225 n.86, 232 n.122
Todorov, Tzvetan, 209–10 n.8
Torture, 42, 206 n.186
Trevor-Roper, Hugh, 203 n.154
Tribute, 18, 87, 88–89, 90, 190
nn.10, 16; in kind, 190 n.10; in
money, 190 n.10; paid by free
blacks and mulattoes, 193 n.46;
royal (corregimiento), 19
Tying (ligatura), 65

Vagabonds (vagamundos/vaga-
bundos), 78–80; as danger to
society, 79; laws regarding, 36,
78–79; Spanish and non-Spanish,
79
Van Young, Eric, 10, 187 n.32
Velasco, Luis de, 37, 67
Ventriloquism, 153
Vera Cruz, 1–3, 15
Viceregal system, 200 n.141. *See also*
Viceroys
Viceroys, 200 nn.141, 147

Wade, Peter, 51

Weakness: and Indians, 6, 48–49;
and witchcraft, 6; and women, 2,
186 n.12
Weapons: and caste claims, 75–76;
as privilege, 68, 75; punishments
for, 75
Whores (putas), 111, 113, 224 n.57
Williams, Raymond, 7, 186 n.17
Witchcraft (hechicería), 185 n.1; as
consequence of weakness, 6; and
food preparation, 64, 110; as hegemonic, 7–8, 170–71; and Indians, 38–39, 103–7, 132–66; and
the Inquisition, 37–39; marketed
by Indians, 110, 119, 123, 132–66;
as "negative," 6–7; as resistance,
171–72, 232–33 n.5; sexual aspects of, 65, 109; and Spaniards,
105–7; and subalterns, 7; transmission of, 231 n.108; and
women, 64–66, 107, 109, 111,
117, 118, 119–22
Wilderness (monte), 3, 31, 110,
127; and runaways, 3; and witchcraft, 64
Women: black and mulatto, 73–75;
as childlike, 117; and the devil,
114–15; as fickle, 116; and Indians, 111, 118, 119–22, 127–29;
and labor, 62–63, 211 n.27; legal
rights of, 60–61; and lineage, 74–
75; and litigation, 41, 46–48;
position in society, 46–48, 60–62,
64–65, 211 n.27, 214–15 n.89;
married, 47; and sexuality, 109–
11; Spanish, and witchcraft, 119–
22, 123, 127–29; in Spanish ideology, 2, 107; violence against, 64,
131, 164, 215 n.97; virginity of,
61; and witchcraft, 64–66, 107,
109, 111, 117, 118, 119–22
Wormwood (estafiate), 232 n.115

Yuman, 232 n.2

Zacatecas, 144–45, 157, 164–66
Zambo/Zambaigo, 196 n.90

LAURA A. LEWIS IS ASSOCIATE PROFESSOR

OF ANTHROPOLOGY AT JAMES MADISON

UNIVERSITY.

Library of Congress Cataloging-in-Publication Data

Lewis, Laura A.
Hall of mirrors: power, witchcraft, and caste in colonial Mexico / Laura
A. Lewis.
p. cm. — (Latin America otherwise)
Includes bibliographical references and index.
ISBN 0–8223–3111–X (cloth : alk. paper)
ISBN 0–8223–3147–0 (pbk. : alk. paper)
1. Mexico — Social conditions — To 1810. 2. Power (Social sciences) —
Mexico — History. 3. Caste — Mexico — History. 4. Witchcraft —
Mexico — History. I. Title. II. Series.
HN113.L48 2003
306'.0972 — dc21        2003005048